The New Chicken Breast Cookbook

The New Chicken Breast Cookbook

350 Easy & Delicious Recipes for Everybody's Favorite Food

• Diane Rozas •

M. Evans and Company, Inc.
New York

This book is dedicated to all those who helped along the way, from testing to tasting or simply enjoying the flavor combinations within. To Helen and Felix; Anita and Richard; to Kevin; Karen; Walley; Daphne; and to my editor, PJ Dempsey, for her vision.

Portions of this book were first published in *Chicken Breasts, More Chicken Breasts,* and *Low-Fat Chicken Breasts,* published by The Crown Publishing Group.

M. Evans and Company, Inc.
216 East 49th Street
New York, New York 10017

Library of Congress Cataloging-in-Publication Data

Rozas, Diane.
The new chicken breast cookbook : 350 easy & delicious ways to cook everybody's favorite food / Diane Rozas.
p. cm.
ISBN 159077017X
1. Cookery (Chicken) I. Title
TX 750.5.C45R6923 2003
641.6'65—dc21 2002192804

Printed in the United States of America

Contents

Introduction

Consider how much our tastes have changed in the decades of the 1980s and 1990s, and how the chicken breast has unquestionably become a staple in our kitchens. Due in part to its versatility and taste, the chicken breast now ranks supreme in the poultry department in almost any grocery or food emporium in almost every country in the western world. Just a decade or so ago the chicken breast was thought of as a luxury item, and could only be purchased separated from the wings and legs at the butcher's counter. Now chicken breasts can readily be found skin on and bone in, skin off and bone in, skin and bone off, halved or whole, and even in packages of tiny tender fillets available fresh or flash-frozen. Quality has always been part of the picture, especially when the breasts are from free-range chickens. Of course, the price usually reflects the degree of picking, patting, pounding, and customizing at the hands of the meat department professionals. Any way you weigh it, there's more versatility per ounce with chicken breasts than with any other meat in the market. There are so many delectable recipes requiring the tender and delectable white meat of chicken breasts (including the recipes herein), especially for light fare, finger food, and an array of full-flavored main dishes. If you've been stuck on one preparation for some time and are considering a change of flavors, here is where you'll begin your adventure—in the kitchen with the ever-delicious chicken breast.

Preparing Chicken Breasts

ADVICE FROM THE BUTCHER

The best way to buy, store, skin, bone, split, flatten, and freeze chicken breasts

If you have a trusted butcher who knows the origin of the chickens he sells, what they've been plumped with, and how to skin, split, and trim your chicken breasts, keep him around, by all means! Many of us, for the sake of convenience, simply buy a pack of chicken breasts from the meat section of the grocery store. These few simple suggestions may be worth some extra money in your pocket and the tenderest, tastiest chicken breast dishes for your cooking effort.

A CHICKEN BREAST ENCOUNTER IN THE POULTRY AISLE

Ideally, we should buy only the freshest chicken breast. Be sure to check out the date on the package, or use the old-fashioned, no-fail smell test. A less-than-fresh chicken breast cannot conceal its age! Look for plump, bruise-free meat. The color is meaningless; it varies depending on chicken feeds used throughout the country. Cook immediately, or clean and seal tightly in plastic wrap and freeze one day before the package expiration date.

CHICKEN BREASTS—THE POULTRY PART WITH A PALATABLE PRICE TAG

Prices range from less than one dollar per pound to six or seven dollars per pound, depending on whether you're taking home a value pack from Costco, a grocery store weekly special, or plump free-range organic-fed chicken breasts from a gourmet foods emporium like Whole Foods. Flash-frozen breasts and fillets can be even less expensive when bought in bulk. Undoubtedly, fresh is always best.

HANDLING THE DELICATE CHICKEN BREAST FILLETS

This tender, two-bite portion of the chicken breast has become a popular item on its own. The fillets or "tenders" as they are sometimes commercially called, is a part of the breast that is located on the underside. These pieces must be trimmed and the tendon removed before cooking.

STORING CHICKEN BREASTS FOR FLAVOR'S SAKE

It's best to use fresh chicken breasts within one day of bringing the meat home. However, if you are not cooking the breasts immediately, wrap in individual plastic sandwich bags or tightly in several layers of plastic wrap to prevent them from drying out in the refrigerator. Always freeze in individual portions.

DO-IT-YOURSELF SKINNING AND BONING

Time permitting, it ultimately helps the meat to remain moister, fresher and more succulent when the process takes place just before cooking. That's because the bone and skin act as a natural encasement, preventing the delicate meat from drying out—the greatest detriment to its final flavor and texture. It's a simple process and with a little practice, boning and skinning takes only a few minutes. Freezing the chicken breasts for half an hour before beginning makes the meat firmer and the process even easier. (Don't forget to save the bones for your stock (see pages 7–10 for a variety of flavorful and easy-to-make stock recipes).

Skinning:

1. Place the breast on a work surface, skin side up.
2. With your fingers, peel the skin back and off.
3. Trim away any remaining bits of skin and fat with a sharp knife.

Boning:

1. Using a very sharp boning knife with a flexible blade, insert the tip at one end of the breastbone between the rib cage and the meat, keep the knife as close as possible to the rib cage. Work the tip along the edge of

the breast from one end to the other, running the knife right along the ribs. Separate the meat from the bone to the depth of two inches. At this point, the breast meat will still be attached in the center to the breastbone on both sides.

2. With the knife and your fingers, scrape or push the meat toward the breastbone until it is completely loosened from the rib cage but still attached to the breastbone.
3. Scrape and push the meat away form the breastbone, being careful not to tear the meat. Remove the breast meat. (Save the bone for a quick stock.)

Splitting:

1. Use your sharp boning knife to slice the breast in half following the center indentation where it was attached to the bone.
2. Slice on either side of the cartilage and discard the hard white cartilage that separates the breasts.

Removing the Tendon:

Slip the point of the boning knife under one end of the white tendon running along the underside of the breast and lift the tendon away from the meat. Hold an end of the tendon with one hand while lifting and scraping the meat away carefully. Trim off any bits of fat or skin.

Flattening:

Use a flat-headed metal pounder, a wooden mallet, the heel of your palm, or the bottom of a heavy skillet to flatten chicken breasts to a uniform thickness. But be gentle, they flatten very easily.

1. On a work surface, place the breasts, skinned side up, between two sheets of plastic wrap.
2. Pound very gently to the desired thinness. The final thickness (or thinness) should be manageable for cooking and serving. Pounding the meat too thin results in a piece that will fall apart.

FREEZING & DEFROSTING

Chicken breasts freeze remarkably well without losing flavor or changing texture. After trimming, skinning, boning, or flattening the meat as desired, wrap each individual breast portion (either whole breasts or halves) in plastic wrap making sure the plastic is covering the meat and the ends are sealed by turning them back over the sealed seam. In a large freezer bag, place the individually wrapped breasts in a single layer and lock the bag, pushing out as much air as possible before freezing. To defrost one or more servings, remove from the freezer, place on a plate or flat dish, and put the breasts in the lowest part of the refrigerator to thaw for five to ten hours. Use immediately after thawing. Always thaw frozen poultry in the refrigerator, slowly, not at room temperature or in the microwave. DO NOT REFREEZE.

A NOTE ON HEALTH & SAFETY

Remember, chicken breasts are susceptible to salmonella bacteria. Raw chicken should not come in contact with other foods. Always wash the work surfaces, cutting boards, knives, and other utensils with hot soapy water after preparing raw chicken. Wash your hands as well. Never refreeze frozen-and-thawed chicken. If you are marinating raw chicken, discard any marinade that is not cooked along with the chicken. Never store it for reuse unless first cooked for five minutes over low heat.

A NOTE ON DONENESS

Chicken should never be served raw or cooked to only rare. The internal temperature of doneness for a boneless breast is 160 degrees F, or when the juices run clear or slightly yellow, but never pink. To make sure, cut one of the breasts open through the center before removing it from the heat.

CHICKEN BREAST SPECIFICS

The right size chicken breast is the perfect fit at meal time and for the sake of nutrition

PORTION SIZE

One whole chicken breast can be served whole or divided into two halves. Each half equals one average serving, and weighs six to eight ounces. Serving size, ultimately, depends on the appetites of those eating, as well as on the weight of the breast meat. The chicken breasts used to develop the recipes in this book were of above average size, weighing fourteen to sixteen ounces for a whole breast after skinning and boning, or about one pound each. However, depending on the size of the breasts and the appetite of those eating, one serving may be either a half or a whole breast. The number of servings from each recipe should be adjusted accordingly.

CALORIES

A 6.5-ounce skinless, boneless piece of chicken breast—an average half-breast serving—contains 197 calories and 6.5 grams of fat. That's all!

Note on Fat

Additional fat and calories are in the skin, so if you're watching calories, remove it before cooking. If you're broiling, grilling, or roasting, keeping the skin on adds to the moistness of the meat. Peel it off while the chicken is still hot and discard.

NUTRITION

The USDA recommendation of 30 percent maximum fat in the diet is an overall figure—not a per meal, per dish, or per item ration, rather a total figure of your entire intake, and the figures are calculated for a three-day period! Many of the recipes in this book are within the lower-fat guidelines of having 30 percent of their calories derived from fat. But the real skinny on fat grams is that in general, meals are meant to be integrated into an overall healthful and varied diet. So go ahead and eat something that is slightly higher in fat one day and another dish that is lower in fat on another; all you need to remember is that you should reach a reasonable nutritional balance in the end.

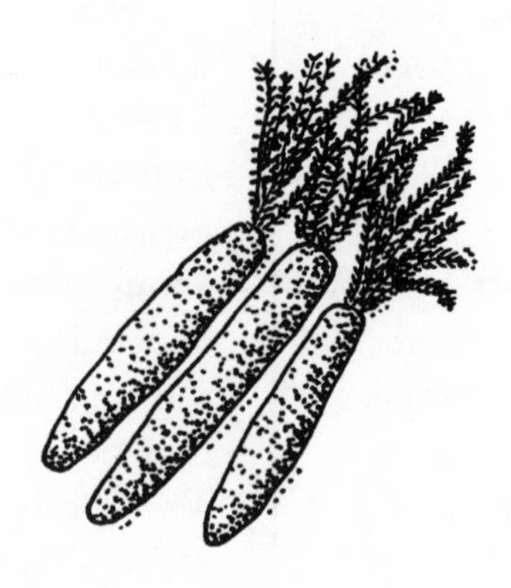

In the Kitchen with Chicken Breasts

RECIPE BASICS

The best ingredients and equipment to match up with chicken breasts and tips on how to make every recipe taste great

HOMEMADE STOCKS

Make It Now . . . Have Plenty for Later!

Stock is essential to many of the recipes on the following pages. It takes only a few minutes to assemble, then let the stock simmer slowly on its own for a couple of hours and strain. It is the ideal liquid in which to cook the flavor-absorbing chicken breast: to poach, to splash into a wok-cooked dish, to deglaze the sauté pan, to steam, or in any method where a liquid is called for. However, if in a pinch for time you decide to use canned stock, choose a low-sodium, defatted one to ensure that additional fat and salt is not added to the recipe.

STOCK TIPS

Skim the stock while cooking. A well-skimmed stock will be clear when chilled; a murky and cloudy broth will result if it hasn't been skimmed very well or if the stock is boiled. So, skim often and don't let the stock boil!

Don't salt the stock. Salt is added according to each individual recipe, not during cooking as the liquid reduces and intensifies any flavors within.

Pick the right stockpots. Do not use aluminum pots to cook stock. All others are non-reactive and are acceptable.

Storing. When a recipe calls for a small amount of stock, it's great to have a pure, fat-free ounce or two of your own homemade stock to toss into the mix of ingredients and enhance your cooking endeavors greatly. After the stock cooks, chills, and is strained, remove all the excess fat, if any, from its surface, divide the stock according to your typical uses in one- and two-cup containers, and freeze, or make stock cubes.

Making Stock Cubes. Reduce some of the stock to about one quarter of the original amount in a heavy non-aluminum pan. Pour it into ice cube trays and freeze. Transfer the frozen cubes to plastic Ziploc freezer bags.

Bouquet Garni. This classic French combination of fresh herbs, spices, and other highly flavored ingredients is used to infuse flavor into stocks. It usually contains bay leaf, parsley, thyme, leek, and black peppercorns. You can add garlic, fresh ginger, clove, lemon peel, celery leaf, or fennel bulb and tops instead of leek. Tie the ingredients in a bundle using cheesecloth and kitchen string. Leave it in the pot throughout the cooking process and discard when finished making stock or poaching liquid. See specific recipes for alternative bouquet garni blends, or see page 355 for other classic ethnic combinations.

SIMPLE CHICKEN STOCK

2 pounds chicken parts, including necks, backs, wings, bones
5 cups cold water, or more as needed
1 stalk celery, coarsely chopped, leaf included
1 carrot, peeled and quartered
1 halved onion (skin on), root end trimmed
1 leek, cleaned and coarsely chopped
Bouquet garni (see above) containing flat-leaf parsley, bay leaf, fresh thyme sprigs, peppercorns, and cloves (optional)

1. In a 4- to 6-quart non-reactive (non-aluminum) stockpot, combine the chicken parts and enough cold water to cover. Over medium heat, slowly bring just to a boil. Immediately reduce the heat and simmer for 45 minutes. Remember, do not boil stock! Frequently skim off the foam that collects on the surface until no more scum appears.

2. Add the celery, carrot, onion, leek, bouquet garni, and more water, if necessary, to cover the ingredients completely. Over low heat, simmer, partially covered, for 2 to 3 hours or until the stock is very flavorful.

3. Remove the stockpot from the heat. With a slotted spoon, remove and discard the vegetables. Pour the stock through a fine mesh strainer or a colander lined with a double layer of dampened cheese-cloth into a clean, non-reactive pot, pressing the bones and meat to extract all the liquid. Cool the stock to room temperature. Refrigerate, uncovered, for 12 hours.

4. When thoroughly chilled, remove the layer of yellow fat from the top with a spoon. Refrigerate, covered, for up to 4 days, or freeze in 1- to 2-cup individual containers, or make into stock cubes (see page 8).

RICH CHICKEN STOCK

Rich chicken stock is made simply by following the recipe above and reducing it by 50 percent or more. Start with 4 cups of stock and simmer, uncovered, until it is reduced to 2 cups or less. Use a non-reactive pan. Store rich stock in small containers or make into stock cubes. Use this stock in all recipes in this book where "rich chicken stock" is called for in the ingredient list and for deglazing the sauté pan for instant sauté sauces (see page 228).

DEFATTED CHICKEN STOCK

In most supermarkets and health food stores, cans of fat- and sodium-reduced stocks are available. However, you can make your own defatted chicken stock by the following method:

Using the above simple or rich chicken stock recipe, strain the stock through a fine mesh strainer to remove all the solids. To use the stock while it is still hot, measure out the amount you need right away. Line the strainer with several layers of cheese-cloth and pour the stock through again. Let it stand for a few minutes to allow the remaining fat to rise to the surface. Spoon the fat out carefully from the surface until no more remains on top. If stock is not needed right away, place the strained stock in the refrigerator overnight. The layer of fat that collects on top of the stock can be lifted up and removed. Check for fat particles on top of the stock and discard. Place in small containers for future use, or freeze in one cup containers or make into stock cubes.

HERB AND WINE STOCK

This French-style stock, *nage,* is a long-cooking, highly aromatic, fat-free vegetable, wine, and herb stock that can be strained and reduced further for richer flavor (follow instructions above for rich stock). It is used as a base for making highly flavored, low- and no-fat sauces, or as a poaching broth. It is very versatile and should be kept frozen for immediate availability. Once prepared, the flavorful *nage* can be thickened with vegetable purées (see page 12), and then drizzled over a poached chicken breast as a simple sauce or cooked with accompanying ingredients (such as beans, potatoes, pasta, or vegetable ragouts) to create the type of dish that is especially flavorful and fulfilling (see page 228).

1½ teaspoon canola or other vegetable oil
1 large onion, chopped
1 large leek, washed and chopped
12 stalks celery, chopped
1 whole head garlic, loose outside papery skin removed, cut in half crosswise
1 large fennel bulb, diced
12 branches fresh thyme
3 bay leaves
½ bunch flat-leaf parsley
1 bottle (750 ml) dry white wine (sauvignon blanc or chardonnay)

1. Heat the oil over medium heat in a large non-reactive saucepan. Add the onion, leek, celery, garlic, and fennel and cook just until the vegetables are translucent but not browned, or about 7 minutes.

2. Add the thyme, bay leaves, parsley, and wine. Bring to a boil, immediately reduce the heat and simmer for approximately 45 minutes. Add 2 cups of water and bring to a boil. Lower the heat and simmer for 20 minutes.

3. Being careful not to press down on the vegetables, pour the stock through a fine mesh strainer and discard the vegetables. Chill and reserve in the refrigerator for up to 2 days until ready to cook add to recipes, or freeze in smaller amounts for future use.

VEGETABLE STOCK

The quantities in this recipe depend on the size of your stockpot. Basically, a spa-style veggie stock consists of vegetables, fresh herbs, and bottled water. No fat. Use whatever vegetables you like that are available or in season, avoiding vegetables with very pungent flavors such as cabbage and green bell peppers. Make from 6 to 8 cups of stock. You'll use this stock with great results in many recipes, and it can be substituted for chicken stock. It is a perfect flavorful poaching liquid. Note: Do not boil vegetable stock during cooking. Do not reduce vegetable stock or it will become bitter.

Use the following vegetables in the proportions of your choice.

Zucchini
Sweet bell peppers (red and yellow, but not green)
Turnips
Onions
Celery (no tops)
Carrots
Garlic cloves

Bay leaf
Fresh herbs (such as parsley, lemon basil, thyme, rosemary)
Black peppercorns (10 or more)
Whole cloves (to taste)
Nutmeg (to taste)
Spring or filtered water to cover the vegetables

1. Place all the ingredients in a 6-quart non-reactive stockpot. Pour on 10 cups of filtered (or bottled) water. Bring to a boil, immediately lower the heat, and cook, partially covered, at a slow, low simmer for 1 hour. DO NOT BOIL.

2. Add more water as needed to keep the vegetables covered with water throughout the cooking process. Cool to room temperature.

3. Pour the stock through a fine mesh strainer lined with a double layer of dampened cheesecloth. Do not press on the vegetables, drain well and discard. Store the stock in the refrigerator for up to 1 week or freeze in small amounts.

TERMS AND TECHNIQUES

Here's how to get the most flavor and visual appeal out of your ingredients while creating delicious and healthy recipes at the same time

Chiffonade Cut. In an unorthodox twist, this technique for cutting leafy vegetables and herbs into ribbon-like strips can also be used for chicken breasts in recipes such as stir-fry and others that call for quick-cooking strips. Traditionally, chiffonade-cut herbs and leafy vegetables are used in sautés or sauces, as garnishes, or raw as a bed in many different types of salads. Chiffonade-cut ingredients can contribute to an attractive presentation on any dish. *How to:* Roll several leaves of lettuce, spinach, herbs, arugula, radicchio, chicory, or cabbage in a tight bundle of leaves together, slice to the required thickness, usually 1/8- to 1/4-inch. The result is a pile of curly, ribbon-like strips . . . ready to serve or cook with.

Deglaze. This technique is also a step in the sauté process. The bits of brown food and juices adhering to the sauté pan are remoistened and cooked with a flavorful liquid. The result is an instant pan sauce to drizzle or spoon over the chicken breasts that were cooked in the pan and set aside to keep warm. *How to:* First pour off any excess fat from the pan. Over medium-high heat, add either 1 cup of dry white wine, red wine, stock, poaching liquid, or juice to the pan, stirring and scraping to loosen the bits stuck to the bottom. Continue cooking over medium heat, stirring constantly until the liquid has almost completely reduced. Add spices, herbs, or other ingredients to the sauce, heat through and drizzle over the cooked chicken breasts. Serve immediately.

Julienne and Matchstick Cuts. This technique of making very thin strips of food such as vegetables and citrus rinds is best for quick-cooking recipes and for garnishes. *How to:* First cut the food into 1½-inch lengths, pile together, and cut into very thin strips (about ⅛th inch thick). For chicken, raw or cooked, or other bulkier ingredients, cut the strips individually and uniformly.

Reduce. This technique thickens a sauce or strengthens the flavor of liquids, such as juice or stock. *How to:* Cook the ingredients for a short time over high heat to decrease the amount of liquid (stock, water, wine, or cream). Season to taste after reducing.

Purée. With delicately flavored chicken breasts, concentrated herb and vegetable purées have that magical ability to enhance a recipe with intense flavors. If you're watching calories (and who isn't), these flavorful additions can also be made fat free. Needed only is a little extra time to create a puréed sauce. *What to purée?:* Roasted red, yellow, or orange peppers; oven-roasted garlic; roasted onions (red, yellow, especially sweet Maui or Vidalias); raw or steamed spinach; herb combinations (such as pestos); cooked potatoes (white or yams); and squash (starchier squashes work best). Keep herb purées on hand in the refrigerator or freezer—they can be used to enhance many different recipes and create new ones. A highly flavored wine and herb stock (see the recipes on pages 00–00) can be flavored and thickened with purées to make an elegant sauce to go with grilled breasts. Or simply use purées as thickeners to give body and interesting flavors to a deglazed pan sauce. By all means, experiment. Things could get very interesting in your kitchen! (Also see page 117—Sauces & Purées.)

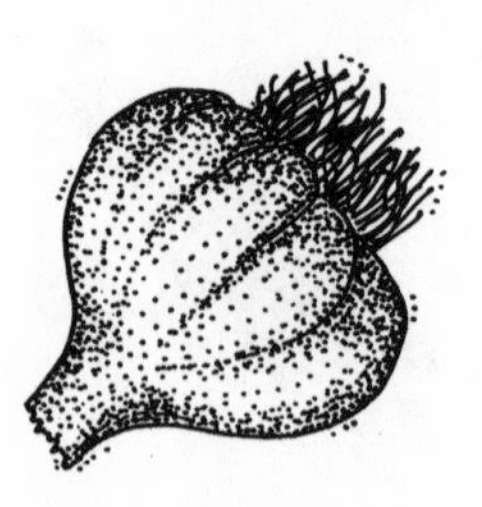

PANTRY PARTICULARS

Important things to have on hand in the pantry, freezer, and fridge for creating delicious recipes on the spot

THE BEST OF EVERYTHING WITH CHICKEN BREASTS

These following ingredients appear frequently throughout the pages of this book, especially in the lower-fat recipes where an intense concentration of flavors is used to make up for the reduction of fat flavor. Keep these in your pantry or refrigerator and a spontaneous meal—lunch, brunch, or dinner—will always be at your fingertips: a tin of anchovies; dried ancho chiles; a can of green chiles; a can of chipotle chiles in adobo sauce; oil-cured Niçoise and Kalamata olives; tree-ripened olives from California; canned or boxed cooked crushed tomatoes; sun-dried tomatoes (dry pack or moist in a jar); tamari (Japanese soy sauce) and soy sauce; Asian fish sauce; hoisin; vinegars (fruit essence flavored and wine—including balsamic, white wine, rice wine, sherry, herb—and fruit-infused vinegars); a selection of basic oils, including extra virgin olive oil, herb-infused olive oil, canola and light sesame oil.

BUTTER, OILS, & COOKING SPRAYS

Butter. Use only unsalted (sweet) butter to avoid adding extra salt where it is not required. Clarified butter, also called *ghee,* is a longer lasting and purer ingredient that can tolerate higher cooking temperatures.

Oils. Experiment with several until you find a brand of olive oil that you like. Extra virgin olive oil is heartily recommended for all uses, including sauces, sautés, and dressings. Canola is another good, basic, unsaturated cooking oil. Choose corn, peanut, clear sesame, and even grape seed oil over nonspecific vegetable oil. Oils should always be fresh, and in hot weather it's okay to store fine oils in the refrigerator. Never reuse oil.

Infused Oils. Infused oils are a great way to add flavor without extra steps or ingredients. *To prepare:* place the ingredients in a covered jar or bottle with 1 to 4 cups of extra virgin olive oil. Cover tightly and allow to marinate a few days in the refrigerator before straining. Try any of these combinations: rosemary and garlic; fresh thyme and a bay leaf; peppercorns and oregano sprigs; porcine mushrooms and pink peppercorns; a few slivers of truffle; citrus zests; just garlic cloves. For best results, make in small manageable batches, use it fast and make new infused oils often. Store in the refrigerator.

Vegetable Oil Cooking Spray. Vegetable oil cooking spray is readily called for throughout this book, especially in those recipes created overall with reduced amounts of fat and oil. Sprays also can be used with non-stick pans in recipes where a small amount of butter or oil is added strictly for taste. Sprays are an easy way to keep chicken from sticking to the grill indoors or outdoors. Try to find the pure and unflavored sprays. If you have a can sitting on the shelf and can't remember when you bought it, invest in a new can as this type of oil doesn't last in the can as long as oils in the bottle.

WINES & LIQUORS

The clear, dry characteristics of good white wine, especially chardonnay, are almost always a match with chicken breasts (although certain recipes' ingredients, like artichokes, can put a damper on the taste of any wine). Other drier whites, such as sauvignon blanc are great substitutions for chardonnay in many recipes, and very drinkable alongside Thai and Chinese dishes. Besides a sampling of white wines, consider the following for splashes of full flavors, especially in sautés and sauces: a good cognac, champagne, dry and medium sherry, dry vermouth, dark rum, Grand Marnier, port, or Madeira. Light red wines, like California pinot noir, Italian dolcetto and French beaujolais, are perfect for more complex, earthier chicken breast dishes. Sweet late-harvest wines and most full-bodied red wines are overwhelming to this delicate part of the chicken. Ultimately, it's a matter of taste. Good-quality wine is recommended for both cooking and drinking. The rule: If you can enjoy a glass of it, then it deserves to be an ingredient in the dish you are making. Avoid buying supermarket wines labeled "cooking wine," which are for the most part poor in quality and undrinkable.

WET & DRY MARINADE INGREDIENTS

These are not to be confused with barbeque sauces, rather, they are flavor-enhancing combinations of spices and herbs or other ingredients such as minced onion or garlic. Some contain liquids and oil and are applied wet; others are applied dry and contain no liquids. Rubbed onto the chicken breast, dry marinades usually have more ground spices and herbs mixed with just a little bit of oil. When using a dry marinade for roasted, grilled, or broiled chicken breasts there is no need to add any additional oil to the recipe. The breasts absorb the flavors of wet marinades in 1 to 2 hours. Lightly pat dry before adding to the hot pan.

HERBS, SPICES, & AROMATICS

Certain herbs and spices work especially well with chicken breasts and by altering the seasonings of the recipe you can create new versions. Try to use fresh herbs whenever called for in the recipe. But there are times when it's dried or nothing, so be sure to replenish your dried herb supply at least every six months as herbs lose their potency very quickly. As a rule of thumb (if one is possible since the strength of herbs varies so much), use one-half the amount of dried as fresh.

Herbs. Be prepared for any recipe with a supply of fresh (and certain dried) herbs, including flat-leaf parsley, basil, tarragon, chervil, marjoram, thyme, bay leaf, fresh ginger root, and cilantro.

Spices and Seasonings. Keep on hand: curry powder, dried red pepper flakes or whole chiles, peppercorns, kosher salt, coriander seed, dry mustard, and allspice berries. A pepper mill should be used any time freshly ground black or white pepper is called for in a recipe.

Aromatics. These members of the lily family add depth to recipes; their flavor intensity depends on the type of aromatic, the cooking method, and time. A whole fresh head of garlic is a must-have staple. Shallots, with their mild onion taste, add a flavor dimension that is well suited to the quick-cooking chicken breast. Many longer-cooking and ethnic-flavored dishes instead require white or yellow onions. Try cooking with the sweet onion family. New crops are popping up in Florida, though Maui, Vidalia, and Walla Walla are the best known in this group. Also keep scallions on hand at all times. From the farmer's market, spring onions are seasonal, and similar to scallions, but stronger in character.

DAIRY PRODUCTS

Sour cream now comes in both regular and light versions, as does mayonnaise. All of these new and improved products have slight differences in taste and textures; do a taste to find your favorites. Don't use products called "imitation" as these tend to break apart or separate into a curdled mess when heated. What's more, these products do not have the delicate richness and creaminess required for a creamy base recipe. As far as yogurts are concerned, it's best to taste-test these, too, as there are many choices to match your preferences, ranging from thick and creamy to sour and thin in consistency. Creams can include heavy or whipping cream, and crème fraîche, the French cultured cream. Milk can be whole, 2%, or even 1% milk as desired. Various hard cheeses and soft cream cheese can be used successfully in small quantities to thicken sauces. Hard aged cheeses (including Parmesan) usually take more time to melt and bind with other ingredients. Low-fat cheeses including Neufchatel and classic cream cheese are great additions to improve the texture and add a creamy quality to a sauce. Fat-free cheeses are not recommended for cooking but are great chilled and chopped in salads and as toppings. Very finely grated cheeses like pecorino, Romano, and Parmesan provide big flavor in small amounts. All these and other reduced-fat dairy products are readily available in supermarkets and health food stores.

BREAD CRUMB & CRUST COMBINATIONS

Make your own crumbs and coatings with melba toast, cornflakes, or other breakfast flakes, any yeast bread, calorie-reduced breads, and cornmeal. Make fresh or dried breadcrumbs in a food processor fitted with the metal blade. Add dried seasonings, or ground spices, citrus zests, pepper, and salt as desired. Store in the refrigerator or freezer. Create flavor combinations that complement or intensify the predominant flavor in the recipe.

TOOLS OF THE TRADE

How to handle any chicken breast with equipment that fits every recipe in this book and then some

Cookware. Many of the quick and easy recipes for chicken breasts start with a simple sauté. The proper sauté pan has a flat bottom and sides that go straight up (unlike frying pans which have slanted or slightly rounded sides) and should be made of heavy-gauge and highly conductive metal that transmits heat evenly and steadily, without "hot spots." The best sauté pans are copper-lined and tin or heavy-gauge aluminum lined with stainless steel. A good strong handle, one that is made separately and bolted on the pan, is recommended. The pan should also have a tight-fitting lid. One good professional sauté pan (such as All-Clad) or other professional quality, heavy-bottomed pan is essential in the kitchen. Several sizes would be a great addition to an enlarged selection of kitchen equipment. Saucepans of this same type are essential for reducing, and one large high-sided skillet can double for a poacher. A heavy bottom is the key to even heat distribution. Tight-fitting lids are also required for many recipes.

Nonstick Cookware. This is, in part, the key to more healthful low-fat cooking. There are many new nonstick surfaces from a variety of manufacturers, all are much improved over the early versions. They are higher-quality and no longer have chipping problems or require special nylon utensils. Coating a nonstick surface lightly with vegetable oil cooking spray is a simple way to further reduce the amount of butter or oil required to prevent food from sticking (if it's an issue).

Steaming Pots. Handmade Chinese steam baskets and stainless steel pans with separate steaming inserts are just two of the variety of possibilities. Turn to the "Steam" section on page 364 for the complete picture.

Woks. A carbon steel forged Chinese wok is only one way to go with stir-fry. Once it is seasoned (or broken in, so to speak) and well used, the surface gets slippery and the food slides off with very little oil needed. Woks with nonstick surfaces are okay for low-fat cooking in general; however, the high heat required for a quick cooking stir-fry is usually too hot for many of these surfaces. Check instructions for your nonstick wok before placing it over a high flame.

Grills. The "Grill, Broil, & Smoke" section beginning on page 180 is filled with specifics on grilling and smoking. So check it out for lots of useful tips and instructions for outdoor cooking over coals and wood on backyard grills. For indoors, one new and very improved aide to grilling is the now-popularized countertop electric grill which can accommodate chicken breasts and vegetables all at the same time. It's a great way to shave off fat calories while the cooking process encourages full flavors from added sauces or marinades (many great ones are found throughout the various chapters of this book). These new grills de-smoke as they cook. As with any electrical device, the heat is harder to control, so use at your own risk!

Pepper Mills. Though a matter of taste, pepper is a very important ingredient in many types of cooking. Almost all the recipes in this book call for white or black pepper. Both should be freshly ground from a separate pepper mill, which is the only way to get that special punch from the spice. Keep your supply as fresh as possible for the best flavor.

Basting Brush. For grilling or basting, a long-handled brush will help distribute a sauce or marinade over the meat's surface. See page 192 for advice on creating your own brush out of fresh herbs and kitchen string.

Boning Knife. A stainless steel coated blade made of high-carbon steel is best. The blade, five to five and a half inches (with a total length of about eleven inches including the handle), should be flexible.

Mallet. A flat-edged wooden mallet, a pounding bat, or a rolling pin is recommended for flattening chicken breasts, though some use the bottom of a heavy skillet (see page 4 for the process).

Chicken Breast Recipes for Every Occasion

This section will help, inspire, and put *The New Chicken Breast Cookbook* to work for you. So, you're planning a brunch for Sunday. Why not make a buffet? Perhaps on the patio or under the trees? Selecting recipes that are easily prepared in advance, and can be arranged on an outdoor buffet without further attention to detail will allow you to entertain in the most relaxed manner. **Alfresco & Picnic Fare** lists quite a few recipes that are perfect for outdoor entertaining anywhere people gather, from the patio to a beach blanket on the sand. With the recipes listed under **Dinner Soirées,** you'll get your fill of dishes of substance, from hearty everyday casseroles to full-flavored sautés, for a simple weeknight get-together or a fancy Saturday night gathering around your dining room table.

Shop through this section not only with a specific situation or occasion in mind, but with a taste on the tip of your tongue. For instance, when you want it "hot," the Southwestern, Asian and other recipes with hefty amounts of chiles are all listed under, what else, **Hot! Hot! Hot!** And when you find a recipe listed here that suits whatever your occasion or situation . . . look it up in the index. Or dive into the contents of the book by chapters to discover the perfect approach; there's certain to be a recipe that's perfect for your taste and timing. *Note:* When you find more personal picks throughout the chapters of this book, add them to the appropriate list below for quick and easy recall.

FAST FARE
Five-Minute Miracles

DINNER SOIRÉES
Casual & Dressed Up

PARTY FARE
Hot & Cold Buffets and Appetizers

HOT! HOT! HOT!
Southwestern, Asian, and Others with Chile Peppers

ENTERTAINING SLIM STYLE
Some Calorie Conscious Choices

FINGER FOOD
Hand-Held Delicacies

ETHNIC
A World of Flavors

HERBS & SPICES
Well-Seasoned Selections

VEGGIES & FRUITS

Fresh from Under the Farm Stand Canopy

ALFRESCO & PICNIC FARE

For Baskets, Boxes, and Anything Under the Sun

RECIPES FOR THE WAY WE *EAT!*

Appetizers & Starters

Call them alfresco finger foods, grazing fare, first courses, cocktail accompaniments, or hors d'oeuvres. Starters are plan-ahead, pre-prepared tidbits that are appropriate passed on a silver platter at wedding parties or served in a basket at the seaside. We invented this concept (yes, you out there) when we stopped eating to live and made food fit into our lives and fit to eat! Whatever these small munchies are called, throughout the pages of this book, they are lovely bits of flavorful and sometimes fanciful foods with chicken breasts as their main ingredient. Chicken and Cheese Quesadillas with a lively Tomato Corn Salsa on the side and Summer Rolls with Spicy Mint Dipping Sauce are among the delectable recipes you'll encounter in this section.

CHICKEN AND CHEESE QUESADILLAS

Long a favorite in Mexican restaurants on both sides of the border, this quick-to-fix starter can be made using the following hearty ingredient or a few of your own choosing along with plenty of chopped grilled chicken breast pieces. These are best served sizzling from the frying pan and shared with friends. Beer, sangria, or margarita are libations of choice; use only fresh limes, of course. Quesadillas are frequently served with a dollop of guacamole and sour cream on top and salsa passed on the side.

4 Quesadillas or 8 Servings

METHOD: PAN FRY

Tomato Salsa

½ small sweet red pepper, finely diced
½ small green pepper, finely diced
¾ cup frozen corn kernels, thawed under warm running water and blanched for 1 minute in boiling water and drained
2 medium plum tomatoes, peeled, seeded, and chopped
2 tablespoons minced fresh cilantro
4 medium scallions, chopped
1 tablespoon red wine vinegar
½ teaspoon ground cumin
2 tablespoons vegetable oil
Salt and freshly ground black pepper to taste

Quesadillas

1½ cup chopped grilled chicken breast (see recipe on page 180)
½ cup coarsely chopped mild green chiles (canned)
2 cups grated Monterey Jack cheese
8 10-inch flour tortillas
Vegetable oil for frying

1. To make the salsa, combine the red and green bell pepper, corn, tomatoes, cilantro, and green onion in a pottery or glass bowl. Let stand 1 hour. Drain well and set aside at room temperature.

2. Place 4 tortillas on a work surface. Evenly distribute the chicken, cheese and chiles over the tortillas. Cover with the remaining tortillas. Pinch the ends together slightly to keep the ingredients from falling out.

3. In a heavy 12-inch skillet, heat just enough oil to coat the bottom of the pan to keep the tortillas from sticking. Carefully transfer the quesadillas to the pan one at a time. Over medium-high heat, cook until the cheese is melted and the quesadilla is lightly browned on both sides. Turn with a large spatula. Use two skillets and cook several at a time.

4. Cut into pie-shaped wedges and serve immediately with the salsa.

GARDEN-FRESH HERBED CHICKEN BREAST ROUNDS

The special fragrance fresh herbs impart, as well as intensity of color, is essential to the success of this dish. The pretty pinwheel design the herb stuffing creates when the rolls are sliced makes a spectacular presentation on an appetizer platter. Serve as a light dinner from a buffet table, especially alfresco.

20 appetizer or starter servings
METHOD: BAKE

4 cups fresh bread crumbs, lightly toasted
½ small onion, minced
1 clove garlic, pressed
1 cup minced fresh herbs to taste, including a combination of basil, thyme, rosemary, flat-leaf parsley, sage, and marjoram
4 eggs, lightly beaten
½ teaspoon salt
¼ teaspoon freshly ground black pepper
3 skinless, boneless chicken breasts (about 3 pounds), halved and flattened to half-inch thickness
1 teaspoon canola or other vegetable oil
Freshly ground black pepper to taste
Fresh herb sprigs for garnish

1. Preheat the oven to 350°F.

2. Combine the bread crumbs, onion, garlic, minced herbs, eggs, salt, and pepper in a large bowl. Mix well.

3. Lay the chicken breasts, skinned side down, on a work surface and cover with the bread crumb mixture. Roll the breasts, tucking in the edges. Secure the ends with toothpicks.

4. Lightly coat the bottom or an ovenproof dish with cooking spray. Place the rolls close together in the dish but not touching. Sprinkle lightly with pepper and cover the rolls with a sheet of parchment paper cut to fit just inside the dish. The paper should rest gently on the rolls.

5. Bake the rolls for 20 to 25 minutes or until firm to the touch. Let cool to room temperature and chill. Remove the toothpicks, and with a very sharp knife, cut the rolls at a slight angle into half-inch thick slices and arrange on a platter, garnished with sprigs of fresh herbs.

SUSHI BAR CALIFORNIA ROLL WITH CHICKEN BREAST

A dozen of these hand rolls (as they're called at the sushi bar) arranged on a platter make an extraordinary display on a buffet table at cocktail time. Serve with a bowl of soy sauce (try tamari—naturally fermented Japanese soy sauce) flavored with wasabi (Japanese horse-radish).

8 servings
METHOD: POACH (CHICKEN)

1 cup chicken stock (see page 8)
16 chicken breast fillets, tendons removed
4 sheets of toasted nori* (dried sea-weed) cut into pieces approximately 7 × 8 inches
2 cups steamed sushi rice (sticky rice)*
2 teaspoons powdered wasabi,* mixed with 1 teaspoon water
½ to 1 avocado, peeled and cut length-wise into thin strips
8 1-inch strips of peeled, seeded cucumber
2 teaspoons toasted sesame seeds
4 ounces gari* (pickled ginger), drained
Soy sauce mixed with 2 teaspoons wasabi powder and 1 teaspoon water

***Available in Asian markets and some grocery stores**

1. In a medium saucepan, heat the stock. Add the chicken breast fillets and poach over medium heat until slightly underdone, about 3 minutes. Do not overcook. Remove the fillets and place on a platter to cool.

2. Lay a sheet of nori, rough side up, long side at the top and bottom, on a bamboo sushi mat. Dip your finger in cold water and pick up a little of the rice at a time, patting it down in a thin layer on the lower half of the nori, all the way to the right and left edges. Spread a small amount of wasabi paste across the rice in a streak. Then arrange a fourth of the avocado slices and cucumber strips in the center of the rice. Sprinkle with ½ teaspoon sesame seeds. Lay 4 chicken breast fillets end to end across the rice.

3. Starting at the edge closest to you, roll up the nori tightly, pressing down on the mat to shape the roll; leave a 1-inch margin of nori at the far end. Moisten the end of the flap with a little water to seal. Remove the roll from the mat and with a very sharp knife, cut into 8 slices, about l inch thick. Repeat with the remaining sushi ingredients.

4. Serve with bowls of gari and the soy sauce and wasabi mixture for dipping.

MEDITERRANEAN CHICKEN BREASTS PHYLLO TART

Though phyllo dough may seem intimidating with its great golden puffs of paper-thin layers enclosing mixtures of both sweet and savory contents, it is fairly easy to work with if you know this secret: always keep the sheets covered with a lightly dampened dish towel to keep the dough from drying and cracking, which makes it unusable.

12 appetizer servings
METHOD: BAKE

3 cups chicken stock (see page 8)
3 chicken breasts (about 3 pounds)
2 tablespoons extra-virgin olive oil
1 large onion, diced
3 cloves garlic, chopped
1 small red bell pepper, seeded and julienned
1 small green bell pepper, seeded and julienned
1 tablespoon dried oregano, finely crumbled
2 pounds fresh plum tomatoes, peeled and sliced
Salt to taste
1 cup sliced mushrooms
2 to 3 tablespoons unsalted butter, melted
1 1-pound package phyllo dough (24 sheets)
1 cup fine dry bread crumbs
½ pound boiled lean ham, finely diced
1 avocado, peeled and mashed
1 cup chopped pitted Kalamata or Niçoise olives
1 teaspoon anchovy paste (optional)
Extra-virgin olive oil and melted butter, for basting

1. In a 2-quart saucepan, heat the chicken stock to a simmer and poach the breasts for 10 minutes or until done throughout. The breasts will be firm when pressed with the back of a fork. Remove to a plate and cool. Remove the skin and bones. Tear the meat into bite-size pieces and set aside.

2. Heat 1½ tablespoons of the oil in a saucepan over medium heat. Add the onion, garlic, peppers, and oregano and cook about 4 minutes, or until tender. Add the tomatoes and salt and cook for 5 minutes or until soft. Remove to a bowl and set aside.

3. In the same pan, heat he remaining olive oil. Over medium heat, cook mushrooms for 2 minutes. Set aside.

4. Preheat the oven to 375°F.

5. Lightly brush a metal baking sheet with melted butter. Lay 2 sheets of phyllo dough on the baking sheet, covering the remaining sheets with a dampened dish towel. Brush the sheets with plenty of melted butter and sprinkle with bread crumbs. Distribute the chicken pieces over the phyllo. Lay two more sheets of phyllo on top, brush with butter and sprinkle with the bread crumbs. Continue with a layer of ham, a layer of cooked vegetables, a layer of avocado, a layer of olives, and dots of anchovy paste (if using), all with two sheets of phyllo in between, brushed with melted butter and sprinkled with bread crumbs. Top with the 2 more sheets of phyllo, brushed with butter but no bread crumbs. (*Note:* The ingredients may also be combined and distributed on each layer.) Roll any remaining phyllo dough and store well wrapped and freeze.

6. Score the top layer of dough into 12 pieces, but leave the tart whole. Brush the top with more melted butter and extra-virgin olive oil. Baste several times during cooking.

7. Bake for 30 minutes or until the phyllo is golden brown. Let the tart cool on a rack. Cut the score marks through and create 12 individual pieces. Serve warm or at room temperature.

CHILE SAUCE

Why buy bottled chile sauce when you can make a superior one in minutes? The difference in flavor is astounding and it keeps in the refrigerator or freezer for future use. Here's how:

Preheat the oven to 400°F. While wearing heavy rubber gloves, seed and stem 8 to 10 dried chiles (about ½ ounce total of either ancho, chipotle, or mulato chiles, or a combination of all three). Place the chiles on a baking sheet and bake for 4 minutes. Let cool. Put 1½ cups of filtered water in a saucepan. Add the chiles, ½ cup coarsely chopped onion, and 3 chopped cloves of garlic. Bring to a boil, lower the heat, and simmer, covered for 25 minutes or until the chiles are very soft. Let cool, then strain the liquid into a bowl. In a food processor, purée the solids with just enough of the reserved liquid to make a thickened sauce. Force the sauce through a fine metal sieve. Add salt and freshly ground black pepper to taste. Refrigerate, covered, for up to 1 month, or freeze in small amounts for future sauces, marinades, dressings, dipping sauces, stir-frying, etc.

CAJUN CHICKEN PIECES WITH APRICOT SAUCE

If it's sweet and spicy you want, try this fine old Cajun combination, influenced by the flavors of New Orleans.

8 to 10 appetizer servings
COOKING METHOD: SAUTÉ

Apricot Mustard Sauce

1½ cups apricot preserves—homemade or best quality
6 tablespoons Creole-style mustard (Dijon may be substituted)
3 tablespoons chicken stock (see page 8)
2 teaspoons ground cayenne pepper or to taste
2 teaspoons freshly ground black pepper
1 teaspoon freshly ground white pepper
2 teaspoons garlic powder
1 teaspoon salt

Chicken Fillets

2 pounds chicken breast fillets, tendons removed
2 tablespoons unsalted butter
2 tablespoons vegetable oil

1. To make the apricot-mustard sauce, heat the preserves, mustard, and stock in a small saucepan over low heat, stirring constantly until the preserves melt. Set the sauce aside and let cool to room temperature.

2. Combine the cayenne, black and white pepper, thyme, garlic powder, and salt in a small bowl. Mix well. Sprinkle the chicken with this mixture and let stand for 30 minutes.

3. In a sauté pan or heavy skillet, melt the butter oil over medium high heat. Sauté the chicken about 1 to 2 minutes per side or just until done.

4. Remove with a slotted spoon and drain briefly on a paper towel. Serve immediately with apricot mustard sauce on the side.

MINI CHICKEN CAKES WITH TOMATO CHILE SAUCE

The slightly-hot dipping sauce lends a tasty surprise to the crispy mini chicken cakes—just the right size for one sumptuous bite. These can easily be passed on a tray with the sauce on the side. Who needs crab?

24 "mini-sized" cakes or more

METHOD: PAN-FRY AND OVEN WARM

3 skinless, boneless chicken breasts (about 3 pounds each) coarsely chopped
3 tablespoons unsalted butter
1 cup chopped celery, inner stalks only
4 scallions, finely chopped, white part only
2 cups fine dry unseasoned bread crumbs
2 eggs, lightly beaten
½ cup heavy cream
2 tablespoons Dijon mustard
¼ minced flat-leaf parsley
2 tablespoons minced fresh tarragon, or 2 teaspoons finely crumbled dried tarragon
Salt and freshly ground black pepper to taste

Tomato Chile Sauce

4 tablespoons unsalted butter
2 shallots, minced
1½ pounds (about 6) ripe tomatoes, peeled, seeded, and chopped
½ cup dry white wine
½ cup minced flat-leaf parsley
2 tablespoons chile sauce (see page 29) or to taste
Salt to taste

Vegetable oil for frying
Fresh tarragon or parsley sprigs for garnish

1. Process the chicken breast meat in a food processor until finely chopped.

2. In a sauté pan or heavy skillet, melt the butter over medium heat. Cook the celery and scallions about 5 minutes or until tender. Transfer to a medium bowl. Mix in the chicken, bread crumbs, eggs, cream, mustard, parsley, tarragon, salt, and pepper to taste and chill for at least 2 hours.

3. To make the sauce, in a medium sauté pan or skillet, melt the butter over medium heat. Add the shallots and cook about 5 minutes or until tender. Add the tomatoes and cook 6 minutes more or until very tender. Mix in the wine and continue cooking about 15 minutes or until the sauce is reduced and thickened. Stir in the parsley, chile sauce, and salt. Set aside to cool.

4. Preheat the oven to 300°F.

5. Meanwhile, using about 1 rounded tablespoon of the chicken mixture for each, make small bite-size patties about ½ inch thick.

6. In a sauté pan or heavy skillet, heat about 2 tablespoons of vegetable oil (or enough to just cover the bottom of the pan) over medium-high heat. Carefully fry the patties in batches for about 3 minutes per side or until golden brown. Add a few drops more oil as needed between batches.

7. Transfer the patties to an ovenproof dish and continue cooking about 4 to 6 minutes or just until done.

8. Rewarm and sauce. Drain the chicken cakes on a paper towel. Transfer to a serving platter and garnish with herb sprigs. Serve with the warm sauce on the side for dipping.

GRAZING

The tasters of this world invented this method of consuming food now known as *grazing*—a word borrowed from the way cows consume the grasses of the field. A little here, a little there! Plates in motion, spoons reaching into a neighboring bisque or mousse are familiar sights at the table these days, even in the poshest restaurants. The French responded to this plate passing and food sampling phenomenon with a *menu degustation* (lots of little tasting courses usually pre-arranged by the chef), while Californians saw grazing more as a buffet concept, similar to the tapas bars of Spain.

Above all, grazing has given respect to the eating style of nibblers, and for those possessing insatiable appetites for variety. Grazers usually are still going strong while most have turned their attention to other activities (and they usually show up in the kitchen when it's time to clean the plates).

Imagine sinking a fork into inventive tastes like sautéed shiitake mushrooms, sliced smoked chicken breast (see page 00), aromatic olive oil-basted grilled radecchio dressed with lemon and freshly snipped chives. Besides being more interesting, these little meals are a boon for savvy dieters, who know that three appetizers or salads often constitute a lighter, healthier meal than an average main course with its side dishes.

When serving grazing courses, consider dishes with a variety of tastes, textures, and colors. It is perfectly acceptable to serve Chinese stir-fry alongside Japanese, Thai, or Italian-inspired dish. Just remember, no dish should overpower another.

CALIFORNIA CHICKEN NACHOS

A classic appetizer up and down the coast of California, it's rarely served without an accompanying bottle of Dos Equis Mexican beer.

4 to 6 appetizer servings
METHOD: BAKE

1 8-ounce bag blue or white corn tortilla chips (large triangle shapes)
6 ounces fresh goat cheese (chevre) at room temperature
1 free-range grilled chicken breast (about 1 pound), julienned
1 ripe avocado, peeled, pitted, and chopped
8 oil-packed sun-dried tomatoes, drained and julienned
3 tablespoons canned jalapeño chiles, drained and thinly sliced
¼ cup fresh cilantro, chiffonade cut

1. Preheat the broiler to 500°F. Separate the corn chips and select 32 or more whole chips. Arrange on a baking sheet.

2. Spread the cheese evenly over each chip, top with the chicken pieces. Bake 3 minutes. Arrange on a serving platter. Top with, avocado, tomatoes, chiles, and cilantro and serve.

SUMMER ROLLS WITH SPICY MINT DIPPING SAUCE

These make great anytime appetizers. The rice-paper wrappers are fun to work with but a bit fragile, so be prepared for a few sheets to tear as you get the hang of handling it.

4 to 8 generous appetizer servings or first course
METHOD: POACH

2 skinless, boneless chicken breasts (about 1½ pounds), halved
2 cups chicken stock (see page 8)
Salt to taste
1½ to 2 cups fresh sprouts, such as bean, sunflower, broccoli, and onion, cut into l-inch pieces
2 thin carrots, cut into 1½-inch matchsticks and blanched for 30 seconds in boiling water

3 large scallions, white and green parts, chopped
2 tablespoons minced fresh mint leaves
1 tablespoon fish sauce*
1 tablespoon fresh lime or lemon juice
18 to 24 8-inch rice paper wrappers*
20 to 24 long strips of scallion, green part only, blanched for 15 seconds in boiling water and dried on a paper towel

Mint Sauce

⅓ cup very strong mint tea (boil mint leaves in filtered water for 5 minutes and steep for 30 minutes and strained if necessary)
¼ cup rice wine vinegar
1 teaspoon Chinese hot chile paste*
2 cloves garlic, finely minced
1 tablespoon sugar
2 tablespoons soy sauce or tamari

*** Available in Asian markets and some grocery stores**

1. In a medium high-sided skillet, bring the stock and a scant amount of salt to a boil. Add the chicken breasts, reduce the heat, and simmer 8 to 10 minutes or until done. The chicken breasts will be firm to the touch when pressed with the back of a fork. Remove the chicken to a plate.

2. Tear the meat into very thin strips, then chop with a cleaver.

3. Combine the chopped chicken, sprouts, carrot, chopped scallions, fresh mint, fish sauce, and lime juice in a medium bowl. Toss to mix.

4. To make the mint sauce, place the mint tea, vinegar, chile paste, garlic, sugar, and soy sauce in a jar with a tight-fitting lid. Shake to mix well. Place in a small bowl.

5. In a shallow bowl filled with very hot water, dip two or three rice-paper wrappers at a time. When soft and pliable, after about 30 seconds, remove the wrappers to a work surface covered with a clean cotton dishcloth and pat off the excess water with paper towel.

6. Place a rounded tablespoon of the filling in the center of each wrapper. Fold in the left and right sides, fold the bottom flap and cover with the top flap. The bundle should form a rectangular log shape. Tie each roll in the center with a scallion strip.

7. Serve immediately with the sauce on the side. If not serving immediately, place the rolls on a serving platter and cover the bundles with a moistened dish towel so the rice paper does not dry out.

OREGANO CHICKEN WITH HERBED TOMATOES BRUSCHETTA

This is the ever-popular open-face Italian appetizer which can change flavors with the ingredients that top it. For this recipe, if you can't find yellow tomatoes, two red ones will work just fine. There's plenty of flavor atop to make these satisfying within.

8 servings

METHOD: POACH (CHICKEN), BROIL (BREAD)

4 shallots, chopped
1 cup dry white wine or champagne
1 cup chicken stock (page 8)
½ bunch fresh oregano leaves, or 2 teaspoons dried
Juice of 2 lemons
2 skinless, boneless chicken breasts (about 1½ pounds), halved
Salt to taste
1 large yellow tomato, seeded, sliced, then coarsely chopped
1 large red tomato, seeded, sliced, then coarsely chopped
1 teaspoon dried oregano or *herbes de Provence* or more to taste
3 tablespoons fresh finely chopped basil
1 clove garlic, finely minced
1 tablespoon extra-virgin olive oil
Freshly ground white pepper to taste
8 thick slices country or peasant bread
1 large clove garlic, peeled and halved
Extra-virgin olive oil for brushing
2 tablespoons chopped fresh parsley

1. Combine the shallots, champagne or wine, chicken stock, oregano, lemon juice, and a pinch of salt in a medium skillet. Bring to a boil, add the chicken breasts, reduce the heat to low, and simmer 8 to 10 minutes, or just until the chicken breasts are done. The breasts will be firm when pressed with the back of a fork. Remove the breasts to a plate and cool to room temperature.

2. Meanwhile, combine the tomatoes, oregano or *herbs de Provence,* garlic, and olive oil in a shallow glass or pottery bowl. Season lightly with salt and pepper. Marinate for 20 minutes at room temperature. Slice the chicken against the grain on an angle into thin rounds. Cover with plastic wrap.

3. Preheat the broiler on high.

4. Rub the bread slices with the garlic clove halves and broil on both sides to light golden. Brush each piece on top with the olive oil and return to the broiler for a few seconds. Arrange the bread on a serving platter and lay slices of chicken breast on top. Spoon on the tomato mixture, sprinkle with chopped parsley and a turn of the peppermill, and serve crowded on a platter.

MANGO CHUTNEY CHICKEN SPREAD

There are many commercial chutneys available that can be substituted for the mango in this recipe. Try peach or pineapple chutney which is made with sweet Maui or Vidalia onions. For a tarter vegetable alternative, try tomato chutney. Each chutney has a distinct and explosive flavor and will partner well with poached or grilled chicken breasts. Serve this delicate fare with assorted baby garden greens.

4 to 8 servings
METHOD: POACH

2 cups chicken stock (see page 8)
Salt to taste
2 skinless, boneless chicken breasts (about 1½ pounds), halved
⅓ cup homemade lemon mayonnaise or ⅓ cup commercially made mayonnaise with 1 tablespoon fresh lemon juice (reduced fat if desired)
¼ cup Major Grey's mango chutney, chopped
Freshly ground white pepper to taste
10 or more very thin slices whole wheat bread, crusts removed, cut in triangles and toasted just before serving
Parsley sprigs, for garnish

1. In a medium high-sided skillet, add the stock and a scant amount of salt and bring to a boil. Add the chicken breasts, lower the heat, and simmer 8 to 10 minutes or until done. The chicken breasts will be firm to the touch when pressed with the back of a fork. Remove the chicken to the bowl of a food processor, reserving several tablespoons of the poaching liquid.

2. Process the chicken to a smooth paste, adding a little liquid as needed. Add the mayonnaise and chutney and process to a smooth spread. Adjust seasoning with salt and pepper to taste.

3. Either spread the mango chicken on all the toast pieces and serve open face, or spread over only half of the toast triangles, place a parsley sprig on each, and top with the remaining toast pieces, or serve the spread in a bowl with the toast surrounding. Use the parsley sprigs to garnish the bowl.

BALSAMIC CHICKEN SKEWERS

The taste of balsamic vinegar has become a part of the American palate and the real Italian balsamic vinegar from Modena is readily available is almost any grocery store. There are so many ways to use it—in marinades and dressings of many different characters and flavors. In this case, start by firing up the grill. Then baste the chicken skewers with this deeply flavored, tart and sweet balsamic marinade and throw them on the grill. Baste and grill some vegetable slices, such as eggplant, large pieces of red bell pepper, sweet potato, and onion slices. The combination works in any season of the year and it is great for outdoor appetizers or grilled for an inside buffet assortment, served hot or at room temperature.

8 servings

METHOD: GRILL OR BROIL

½ cup dry white wine
½ cup chicken stock (see page 8)
½ cup balsamic vinegar
¼ cup dark raisins, chopped
1 tablespoon canola or extra-virgin olive oil
1 tablespoon grated orange zest
1 tablespoon grated lemon zest
2 teaspoons chopped fresh tarragon
2 skinless, boneless chicken breasts (about 2 pounds), halved, flattened slightly between plastic wrap and cut into 2½-inch chunks
20 or more 6-inch wooden skewers, soaked in water for 1 hour
Salt and freshly ground black pepper to taste

1. Fire up the grill or preheat the broiler.

2. In a small saucepan, combine the wine, chicken stock, balsamic vinegar, raisins, oil, orange and lemon zests, and tarragon. Bring to a boil, lower the heat to medium and reduce 8 minutes, or to one third of the original amount. Cool, then transfer to a blender. Blend until smooth and pour into a dish.

3. Thread each chicken chunk onto 2 parallel skewers placed 1 inch apart so that the meat stays flat on the grill. Lightly season with salt and pepper to taste. Place the skewered chicken in a shallow glass dish. Brush with the marinade on all sides and let stand for 20 minutes.

4. Lightly coat the grilling rack or broiler pan with cooking spray.

5. Grill or broil the skewers for 4 minutes per side, or until done throughout. Baste during cooking with the remaining marinade. Serve on the skewers hot or at room temperature.

THAI CHICKEN SATAY WITH PEANUT DIPPING SAUCE

Two dipping sauces are included in this recipe. Use one or both.

6 to 8 servings

METHOD: GRILL OR HIBACHI

2 skinless, boneless chicken breasts (about 2 pounds), halved and pounded between plastic wrap to ¼-inch thickness (or use chicken fillets) and cut into 1 by 4-inch strips
16 or more 6-inch wooden skewers, soaked in water for 1 hour
Salt and freshly ground black pepper to taste
Juice of 1 lemon

Sesame Peanut Dipping Sauce

3 tablespoons unsalted smooth peanut butter (natural style, avoid using the oil that collects on the top)
1 tablespoon tahini (sesame paste)
4 tablespoons soy sauce or tamari
4 tablespoons low-fat or nonfat yogurt or more to taste
5 tablespoons dark or light brown sugar
2 cloves garlic, finely minced
2 tablespoons crushed red pepper or pepper flakes, or more to taste
1½ tablespoons finely chopped toasted peanuts for garnish
¼ cup chopped fresh cilantro leaves

Coconut Peanut Dipping Sauce

½ cup smooth peanut butter (natural style, avoid the oil on top)
1 clove garlic, minced
1 tablespoon brown sugar
1 cup fresh coconut milk
1 tablespoon lemon juice
Salt to taste
2 tablespoons chopped toasted unsweetened coconut

1. Thread the chicken breast pieces onto the skewers. Season with salt and pepper. Splash with the lemon juice.

2. To make the *sesame dipping sauce,* whisk together the peanut butter, tahini, soy sauce, 4 tablespoons of the yogurt, brown sugar, garlic, vinegar, and red pepper in a small bowl until very smooth. Add 1 tablespoon more yogurt for a thinner sauce. Cover with plastic wrap and let stand for 1 hour at room temperature before serving.

To make the *coconut dipping sauce,* whisk together the peanut butter, garlic, brown sugar, coconut milk, lemon juice, and a pinch of salt in a small bowl until smooth. Transfer to a small saucepan and bring the sauce to a boil over medium-high heat. Reduce the heat and simmer 2 minutes. Pour into a bowl and stir in the coconut. Cool to room temperature.

3. Fire up the hibachi or grill. Lightly coat the grilling rack with cooking spray and place 4 to 5 inches from the hot coals. Grill the chicken skewers for 2 minutes per side, or until done throughout. Do not overcook. Arrange on a tray and serve with the sauces in small bowls.

SOFT TACOS FILLED WITH GRILLED CHICKEN, BLACK BEANS, AND JULIENNE VEGETABLES

These are great served on a buffet.

4 servings

2 skinless, boneless chicken breast (about 2 pounds), halved and flattened between plastic wrap to ¼-inch thickness.
Salt and freshly ground black pepper to taste
1 red onion, finely chopped
1 red bell pepper, roasted, seeded, and julienned
1 yellow bell pepper, roasted, seeded, and julienned
2 cloves garlic, finely minced
1 cup cooked black beans, drained and rinsed
1 cup julienned jicama
1 cups fresh cilantro leaves
2 tablespoons red wine vinegar
1 tablespoon fresh lime juice
1 tablespoon fresh lemon juice
3 tablespoons fresh orange juice
1 teaspoon honey
1 teaspoon ground coriander
2 tablespoons extra-virgin olive oil
¼ cup sour cream, regular or low-fat
8 or more 6-inch fresh corn tortillas

1. Fire up the grill or preheat the broiler. Lightly coat the grilling rack with cooking spray. Season the chicken with salt and pepper. Grill for about 2 minutes per side or until done throughout. Do not overcook. Cut into thin strips and set aside.

2. Combine half the red onion, the bell peppers, half the minced garlic, the black beans, the jicama, and ¼ cup of the cilantro leaves in a mixing bowl. Toss just to mix.

3. Place the remaining garlic, red onion, cilantro, vinegar, lime, lemon and orange juice, honey, and coriander in a blender, and blend until smooth. Place in a bowl and stir in the sour cream. Adjust the seasoning with salt and pepper to taste.

4. Pour the vinaigrette over the black bean mixture and toss to mix well.

5. Spread out the tortillas on a work surface. Spoon equal amounts of the black bean mixture and chicken in the center of each tortilla, drizzle on some sauce and roll. Use toothpicks to hold the rolls closed. Serve at room temperature with any remaining sauce on the side.

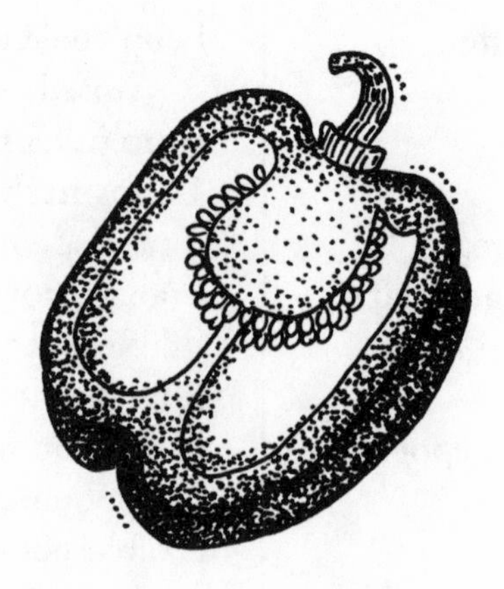

Salads

CLASSIC CURRIED CHICKEN SALAD

Fresh and delicious, this light recipe that makes a great lunch platter to pass around the table or set on a buffet. A good alternative to Salad Niçoise.

2 to 4 servings
METHOD: POACH OR BAKE

4 cups chicken breasts (about 2 pounds) poached or baked, chopped into bite-size pieces, and chilled for 1 hour
½ cup homemade lemon mayonnaise (see page 123)
½ cup white raisins
½ cup sliced almonds
¾ teaspoon white pepper
2 tablespoons curry powder
½ cup Major Grey's chutney, chopped
2 teaspoons fresh lemon juice

1. Combine the chicken, raisins, and almonds in a bowl and toss together.

2. Combine the white pepper, curry powder, chutney, mayonnaise, and lemon juice in a small bowl.

3. Add to the chicken mixture, gently toss to mix, cover and refrigerated. Serve cold, sprinkled with a few drops of lemon juice.

ASIAN CHICKEN, POTATO, AND AVOCADO SALAD

4 servings

METHOD: POACH

2 cups chicken stock (see page 8)
Poaching bouquet containing: 2 pieces smashed lemon grass, l-inch piece fresh ginger, quartered, ¼ teaspoon coriander seeds, 5 black peppercorns
2 skinless, boneless chicken breasts (about 1½ pounds) halves

Dressing

¼ cup fresh lime juice
2 tablespoons dry white wine
2 tablespoons chopped fresh cilantro
2 teaspoons honey
1 tablespoon soy sauce or tamari
2 teaspoons fish sauce*
2 tablespoons extra-virgin olive oil
3 tablespoons chopped scallion, green part only
1½ pounds new red potatoes, boiled to tender, cooled, quartered, and peeled
2 tablespoons reserved poaching liquid
Salt and freshly ground black pepper to taste
1 medium ripe avocado, peeled and thinly sliced

*Available in Asian markets and some grocery stores

1. Bring the stock and poaching bouquet to a boil in a medium high-sided skillet, reduce the heat to low, and simmer, covered, for 5 minutes. Add the chicken and simmer 8 to 10 minutes or just until done. The chicken will be firm when pressed with the back of a fork. Remove the chicken to a plate, cool to room temperature, wrap in plastic wrap, and refrigerate until chilled. Reserve 2 tablespoons of the liquid.

2. To make the dressing, whisk the lime juice, white wine, cilantro, honey, soy sauce and fish sauce together in a bowl. Whisk in the oil in a thin, steady stream until well combined. Stir in 2 tablespoons of the scallion.

3. Toss the potatoes with the reserved poaching liquid and remaining scallion in a medium bowl. Season with salt and pepper to taste.

4. Slice the chicken into thin rounds across the grain. Place in a bowl, drizzle on half of the dressing, and toss gently. Mound the potatoes in the center of a platter and arrange the chicken and avocado slices around the mound of potatoes. Top with a few turns of the pepper mill. Pass the remaining dressing on the side.

BASIL CHICKEN AND PASTA SALAD

It's another great any-season salad that gets attention in the center of the table as a lunch course or on a buffet table—indoors or *alfresco!*

4 servings
METHOD: POACH

2 cups chicken stock (see page 8)
1 cup dry white wine
6 black peppercorns
1 bay leaf
2 cloves garlic, smashed
3 skinless, boneless chicken breasts (about 2½ pounds), halved
Salt to taste
½ cup mayonnaise, regular or reduced-fat
½ cup plain yogurt, low or nonfat
1 tablespoon white wine vinegar
1 clove garlic, finely minced
¼ cup poaching liquid (reserved from poaching the chicken) or stock
Freshly ground black pepper to taste
½ pound fusilli pasta, cooked *al dente* according to package instructions, cooled to room temperature
10 fresh basil leaves, chiffonade cut
1 head red leaf lettuce, leaves separated
1 large ripe tomato, seeded, peeled, and diced for garnish
Fresh basil leaves for garnish

1. Bring the chicken stock, wine, peppercorns, bay leaf, and smashed garlic to a boil in a medium high-sided skillet. Lower the heat and simmer, covered, for 5 minutes. Lightly salt the liquid, add the chicken breasts, and poach 8 to 10 minutes, or just until done. Remove to a work surface. Reserve ¼ cup of the poaching liquid.

2. Strain the reserved poaching liquid. Cut the chicken into bite-size pieces. Set aside.

3. Whisk together the mayonnaise, yogurt, vinegar, and minced garlic in a small bowl. Thin with the poaching liquid to the desired consistency. Season with salt and pepper.

4. Combine the chicken and pasta in a large mixing bowl. Drizzle on the dressing, sprinkle with basil, and toss to mix well. Line a deep serving platter with the lettuce leaves. Mound on the chicken salad and garnish with tomato and basil leaves.

VIETNAMESE SHREDDED CHICKEN AND CABBAGE SALAD

A visit to the Asian market can turn up all sorts of interesting and tasty tidbits to serve on the side of this salad, including crunchy wasabi-coated peas, tiny spicy rice crackers, even shrimp puffs that melt in your mouth!

4 servings

METHOD: POACH

2 cups chicken stock (see page 8)
Asian poaching bouquet (see page 354) containing: 1-inch piece peeled fresh ginger, 1 star anise, 1 scallion cut in pieces
1 small clove garlic, peeled
2 skinless, boneless chicken breasts (about 1½ pounds), halved
Salt to taste
2 to 3 serrano or jalapeño chilees, seeded and very finely minced
2 large cloves garlic, crushed
2 tablespoons sugar
½ cup fish sauce*
¼ cup fresh grapefruit juice
¼ cup fresh lime juice
3 large carrots, peeled and grated
½ small head red cabbage (about ½ pound, finely shredded)
1 medium head napa cabbage (about 1 pound), finely shredded
2 tablespoons finely chopped fresh mint
3 tablespoons chopped fresh cilantro leaves
¼ cup toasted sesame seeds
Grapefruit sections, peeled, pith and membrane removed, for garnish
Fresh cilantro and mint sprigs for garnish

***Available in Asian markets and some grocery stores.**

1. Bring the chicken stock and the poaching bouquet to a boil in a medium high-sided skillet. Lower the heat, simmer, cover, and cook 5 minutes. Lightly salt the liquid, add the chicken breasts, and poach 8 to 10 minutes or until chicken is done. The breasts will be firm to the touch when pressed with the back of a fork. Remove to a plate and cool slightly.

2. Shred the breast meat with 2 forks and chill, covered with plastic wrap.

3. Place the chiles, garlic, and sugar in

the bowl of a blender or mini food processor. Process to a spreadable consistency. Transfer to a small bowl, stir in the fish sauce, grapefruit, and lime juice.

4. Combine the carrots, cabbages, chicken, mint, cilantro, and sesame seeds and toss to mix in a large mixing bowl. Drizzle on the dressing and toss to coat well. Marinate for 15 minutes.

5. Turn the salad onto a serving platter. Garnish with grapefruit sections, cilantro, and mint sprigs.

DRUNKEN CHINESE CHICKEN SALAD

Though a fairly simple recipe, a lengthy marinating time is required, so plan ahead accordingly. This recipe also lends itself to a highly flavored chicken salad spread (which is great for chicken sandwiches on whole-wheat toast) when the chicken is chopped and a few dollops of mayonnaise or sour cream are stirred in.

3 to 6 servings
METHOD: BROIL, ROAST, OR POACH

2 chicken breasts, (about 2 pounds), poached, broiled, or roasted (see pages 118, 128, and 180), quartered
4 scallions, chopped, white and green parts
1 cup Chinese rice wine or medium sherry (or a combination of both)
1 teaspoon salt
½ teaspoon sugar
1 bunch fresh coriander leaves, stems removed
3 tablespoons toasted sesame seeds

1. Add the chicken and half the scallions to a large bowl.

2. Combine the rice wine or sherry with the salt and sugar in a jar with a tight fitting lid. Shake well to mix. Add to the chicken mixture, toss to mix, cover with plastic wrap, and marinate in the refrigerator for 12 hours.

3. Drain off the marinade and discard. Arrange the coriander leaves on a serving platter. Place the chicken pieces in the center and sprinkle with sesame seeds and the remaining scallions.

PINEAPPLE CHICKEN SALAD IN PITA WITH PEANUTS

This recipe is a great appetizer, light lunch, or *alfresco* or evening supper overlooking the garden, with a glass (or two) of white wine on the side. Wrap this salad in lettuce leaves instead of pita bread (as called for in this recipe) for a super low-calorie appetizer and a perfect snack when every calorie (you don't eat) counts!

4 to 6 servings

METHOD: POACH

2 cups of chicken stock (see page 8)
1 cup fresh pineapple juice
3 skinless, boneless chicken breasts (about 2 ½ pounds) halved
Salt to taste
1 cup fresh pineapple chunks
1 celery stalk, thinly sliced
3 scallions, thinly sliced
½ cup chopped, unsalted, roasted peanuts
3 tablespoons Major Grey's mango chutney or pineapple chutney, chopped
2 tablespoons fresh lemon juice
1 teaspoon grated lemon zest
1 teaspoon medium or hot curry powder, or to taste
¼ cup mayonnaise, regular or reduced fat
½ cup sour cream, regular or light
2 tablespoons poaching liquid (reserved from poaching the chicken)
1 tablespoon finely chopped parsley
Freshly ground white pepper to taste
4 6-inch or 8 mini-size whole-wheat pita breads

1. Bring the chicken stock and pineapple juice to a boil in a medium high-sided skillet. Reduce the heat, lightly salt the liquid, add the chicken breasts, and simmer about 8 to 10 minutes or just until done. Remove to a work surface to cool. Reserve 2 tablespoons of poaching liquid.

2. Coarsely chop the chicken and place in a large mixing bowl. Add the pineapple chunks, celery, scallions, and peanuts. Toss to combine.

3. Combine the chutney, lemon juice, lemon zest, curry powder, mayonnaise, sour cream, poaching liquid, and parsley in a small bowl and mix well.

4. Drizzle dressing over the chicken mixture and toss to coat. Season with salt and pepper to taste. Cover tightly with plastic wrap and chill for 1 hour before serving with the pita bread.

SHREDDED CHICKEN AND WILD RICE SALAD IN LETTUCE POCKETS

Calorie-conscious by design, this salad, wrapped up in soft leaves of Boston or Bibb lettuce makes delicious low-fat finger food.

6 to 8 servings

METHOD: POACH

6 cups chicken stock (see page 8)
1 clove garlic, peeled
Salt to taste
2 ounces uncooked wild rice, soaked in hot tap water for 30 minutes and drained
2 skinless, boneless chicken breasts (about 2 pounds)
Poaching bouquet including: 1½-inch piece peeled ginger, 4 peppercorns, 1 stalk celery with tops (halved), 1 clove garlic, 2 parsley sprigs, 1 fresh tarragon sprig
3 tablespoons soy sauce or tamari
3 tablespoons rice wine vinegar
1 tablespoon dark sesame oil
1 tablespoon light canola or other vegetable oil
1 red bell pepper, seeded and finely chopped
2 cups (about 2 bunches) loosely packed arugula leaves, chiffonade cut
3 scallions, thinly sliced, white and green parts
¼ cup toasted sesame seeds
2 heads Boston or Bibb lettuce leaves separated, left whole, and chilled

1. Bring 4 cups of the chicken stock and the garlic to a boil in a heavy medium saucepan. Lightly salt the liquid, reduce the heat to low, add the wild rice, cover, and cook about 45 minutes or until tender. Remove from the heat, and let stand 15 minutes, covered. Drain thoroughly and remove the garlic clove. Fluff the wild rice and place it in a large mixing bowl to cool.

2. Bring the remaining chicken stock and poaching bouquet to a boil in a medium high-sided skillet. Lower the heat and simmer, covered, for 5 minutes. Lightly salt the liquid, add the chicken breasts, and simmer about 8 to 10 minutes or just until done. Remove to a work surface to cool.

3. Shred the breast meat with two forks into very thin strips, then cut the strips in half. Cover with plastic wrap and refrigerate until well chilled.

4. Combine the soy sauce, vinegar, and oil. Shake vigorously to combine in a glass jar with a tight-fitting lid.

5. Combine the chicken breast, wild rice, bell pepper, arugula, scallion, and half the toasted sesame seeds in a large mixing bowl. Toss to mix.

6. Drizzle on the dressing and toss to mix well. Arrange the lettuce leaves as cups on a platter or individual plates. Fill the lettuce cups about one-third full and sprinkle on the remaining sesame seeds. Serve while the lettuce is still cold, fold over the leaves to form pockets.

TEQUILA-MARINATED CHICKEN CEVICHE SALAD

These flavors are reminiscent of those used in the marinated seafood salads served in Mexico and Spain.

4 to 6 servings

METHOD: POACH

1 cucumber, halved lengthwise, seeds scraped out with a spoon and thinly sliced
Salt to taste
2 skinless, boneless chicken breasts (about 2 pounds), halved
2 cups chicken stock (seepage 8)
½ cup fresh lime or lemon juice
Pinch ground cumin
1 cup fresh orange juice
2 to 3 tablespoons light tequila
½ small red onion, halved and thinly sliced
½ small onion, halved and thinly sliced
2 small cloves garlic, finely minced
3 tablespoons finely minced fresh cilantro
½ teaspoon Tabasco sauce, or 2 teaspoon seeded, finely minced jalapeño
1 teaspoon finely chopped orange zest
1 teaspoon finely chopped lime or lemon zest
¼ teaspoon salt
1 green bell pepper, seeded, half finely diced and half cut into very thin matchsticks
1 red bell pepper, seeded, half finely diced and half cut into very thin matchsticks
Large romaine lettuce leaves, chilled
12 cherry tomatoes, halved (red and yellow)

1. Sprinkle a scant amount of salt on the cucumber slices and drain in a strainer for 30 minutes. Rinse and pat dry.

2. In a medium high-sided skillet, bring the chicken stock and cumin to a boil. Lightly salt the liquid, reduce the heat to low, add the chicken breasts, and simmer about 8 to 10 minutes or just until done. Remove to a work surface to cool.

3. Chop the chicken in ½-inch bite-size chunks and place in a large glass or pottery bowl. Add the lime or lemon juice, orange juice, tequila, both onions, garlic, cilantro, Tabasco or jalapeño, orange and lime or lemon zest, bell peppers, and cucumbers. Mix well and cover tightly with plastic wrap and marinate, refrigerated, for 2 hours.

4. Drain the salad in a fine mesh strainer and discard the marinade. Arrange several lettuce leaves on a serving plate. Fill the individual leaves in the center with salad to form individual servings and garnish with the bell pepper matchsticks and tomatoes.

SHREDDED GINGER-SOY CHICKEN SALAD

This salad is great served on a bed of finely grated cabbage and carrot slaw.

4 lunch salad servings

METHOD: POACH

2 cups chicken stock (see page 8)
2 one-inch slices fresh ginger, peeled
3 tablespoons sherry vinegar
2 scallions, green part only
3 black peppercorns
Salt to taste
2 skinless, boneless chicken breasts (about 1½ pounds), halved

Dressing

1 tablespoon finely minced, peeled fresh ginger
1 tablespoon rice wine vinegar
4 tablespoons red wine vinegar
1 tablespoon honey
1 teaspoon sugar
1 tablespoon soy sauce or tamari
1 tablespoon chopped fresh basil leaves
2 tablespoons chopped scallion, white part only
⅛ teaspoon crushed red pepper, or more to taste
2 tablespoons reserved poaching liquid
2 tablespoons peanut oil

2 tablespoons toasted sesame seeds
2 tablespoons chopped scallion, green part only
Salt to taste

1. In a medium high-sided skillet, bring chicken stock, ginger, vinegar, scallions, and peppercorns to a simmer and cook, covered, for 5 minutes. Lightly salt the liquid, add the chicken breasts, and poach 8 to 10 minutes or until done throughout. Remove to a work surface to cook. Reserve 2 tablespoons of the liquid. Shred the chicken and place it in a bowl.

2. To make the dressing, combine the ginger, vinegars, honey, sugar, soy sauce, basil, white part of the scallion, red pepper and reserved stock in a blender or mini food processor and process until smooth. With the motor running, add the oil in a thin steady stream until smooth.

3. Add the sesame seeds and the green part of the scallion to the chicken, and toss to combine. Drizzle on the dressing and toss to mix well. Adjust seasoning with salt to taste.

SUBSTITUTIONS ALLOWED!

So you looked a recipe over and several of the required ingredients are not in your cupboard . . . and there's just no way you're going back to the store. What to do? Substitute! Pastas, for instance: use any thin dried or fresh pasta for cappellini in the Dilled Chicken with Sweet Peppers and Cappellini Salad on page 65. Less virgin olive oil can be substituted in a pinch if need be when the extra-virgin bottle runs out unexpectedly. Simply exchange it for any fresh olive oil you may already have on hand, or even corn or sesame oil in a pinch. Nuts can always be exchanged in a recipe; try toasted sesame seeds or crunchy homemade croutons instead. What's more, a creative substitution can often lead to a whole new recipe—so take a chance!

A SALAD SUGGESTION: TOAST SESAME SEEDS FOR ADDED FLAVOR

Toasted sesame seeds make a glorious two-minute garnish for many chicken salad combinations. Toasting is essential to bring out that uniquely nutty and somewhat smoky flavor found deep within the sesame seeds. It also changes the color of the seeds from white to toasty brown, and creates a tiny crunch that bursts with flavor.

How to: To toast, set a small, dry, non-stick sauté pan over moderate heat. Add the sesame seeds and stir or shake the pan constantly until light to medium brown in color, 2 to 3 minutes. No need to cool, just sprinkle right onto the salad. Such little things. Such big flavor!

SHREDDED FRESH ARTICHOKE, CHICKEN, & PARMESAN SALAD

The shredded raw artichoke in the salad is a wonderful change from salad greens. It's very crunchy and has a hearty texture with a delicate and interesting taste. This is a classic Italian salad combination.

4 servings

METHOD: POACH

2 cups chicken stock (see page 8)
2 whole skinless, boneless chicken breasts (about 2 pounds)
Salt to taste
1 1 × 2-inch slice lemon rind
4 fresh baby artichokes
⅓ cup plus 1 tablespoon fresh lemon juice
2 tablespoons balsamic vinegar
1 tablespoon chopped fresh oregano, or 1 teaspoon dried
⅓ cup extra-virgin olive oil
Salt and freshly ground black pepper to taste
2 cups mixed baby lettuce
2 cups coarsely chopped aurgula leaves
¼ cup freshly shaved Parmesan pieces
¼ cup chiffonade-cut fresh basil leaves
Large shavings of Parmesan for garnish (1 ounces for each serving)

1. In a medium high-sided skillet, bring the chicken stock to a simmer. Lightly salt the liquid, add the chicken breasts, and poach about 8 to 10 minutes or just until done throughout. Remove to a plate and cool slightly. Shred the meat, cover with plastic wrap, and chill well.

2. Working quickly so the artichokes do not discolor, snap off the tough outer leaves from each, trim the ends, cut through the center lengthwise, and remove the purple inner leaves and hairy choke with a spoon.

3. With a very sharp stainless steel knife, a mandolin, or the sharp side of a stainless steel grater, shred or shave the artichokes very thinly. Place all the shaved artichokes in a large non-reactive glass or pottery mixing bowl with ⅓ cup lemon juice and immediately toss to coat well in order to keep the artichoke from discoloring. Marinate for 5 minutes in the juice.

4. Combine the remaining 1 tablespoon of lemon juice, vinegar, oregano, and olive oil in a glass jar with a tight-fitting lid. Shake well.

5. Place the shredded chicken in a small bowl. Drizzle on the balsamic dressing and toss to coat well. Adjust the seasoning with salt and pepper.

6. Add the lettuce, arugula, the ¼ cup shaved Parmesan, and basil to the artichokes; gently toss to mix well.

7. Divide the artichoke salad among individual bowls. Mount the shredded chicken breast in the center. Top with the large shreds of Parmesan and a turn of the pepper mill.

MEDITERRANEAN CHICKEN & GREEN BEAN SALAD

A classic *alfresco* lunch or picnic choice.

4 servings

METHOD: POACH

1¼ cups chicken stock (see page 8)
¾ cup dry red wine
2 black peppercorns
2 whole garlic cloves
4 fresh basil leaves
Salt to taste
2 skinless, boneless chicken breast (about 2 pounds), halved
⅔ cup reduced poaching liquid
1 pound green beans, trimmed
¾ cup nonfat plain yogurt
2 tablespoons fresh lemon juice
1 teaspoon dried oregano
2 teaspoons dried basil
½ teaspoon dried thyme
Salt to taste
Freshly ground black pepper
2 small red onions, halved and thinly sliced
2 tablespoons chopped toasted almonds
2 tablespoons coarsely chopped French, Italian, or oil-cured Greek olives
12 cherry tomatoes

1. Bring the chicken stock, wine, peppercorns, garlic, basil leaves, and a pinch or salt to a simmer in a medium high-sided skillet. Add the chicken breasts and poach 8 to 10 minutes or until done throughout. Transfer the chicken with a slotted spoon to a plate to cool. Cover with plastic wrap and refrigerate to chill.

2. Strain the remaining poaching liquid into a small saucepan and reduce by two thirds over high heat. Set aside to cool.

3. Steam the green beans just to crisp tender, about 4 minutes. Immediately plunge into a bowl of ice water or run under cold water to stop the cooking process. Cover and chill.

4. Combine the yogurt, lemon juice, oregano, dried basil, thyme, reduced poaching liquid, and a pinch of salt and pepper in a jar with a tight-fitting cover. Shake well to mix.

5. Combine the beans, onions, almonds, and olives in a large mixing bowl. Drizzle on three-quarters of the dressing and toss to mix well. Adjust the seasoning with salt and pepper to taste. Marinate for 15 minutes.

6. Slice the chicken breasts on the diagonal across the grain into quarter-inch slices. Arrange on 4 individual serving plates. Mound the bean salad beside the slices and garnish with the tomatoes. Drizzle the remaining dressing on the chicken slices and top with a turn of the pepper mill.

FOUR OAKS WARM CHICKEN SALAD WITH ORANGE VINAIGRETTE

It is often said that restaurants today are part substance and part showmanship, and not always in equal portion. Nowhere is the theater of dining more vibrant than on the floral trimmed patio of an outdoor café. Especially one reminiscent of patios in the south of France but 6,000 miles west. This particular spot in Los Angeles combines a delightful atmosphere with light, fresh fare. Perched along a narrow residential road that snakes through the jagged canyon of Bel Air, this establishment—which dates back to the turn of the century—has previously been a train station, a brothel, a speakeasy, a gas station, and a sandwich shop owned by "Ma" all before it became the Four Oaks Café, then later, a fine-dining restaurant. The Four Oaks is what energetic, innovative Swiss-born chef/owner, Peter Roeland, calls his home away from home. If you can't get there anytime soon, then try his famous chicken breasts over green beans, artichoke hearts, radicchio, and mâche drizzled with truffle vinaigrette or the recipe listed below. It's best eaten on the patio under the giant oak tree.

4 servings
METHOD: SAUTÉ

Vinaigrette

½ cup white wine vinegar
1 tablespoon chopped shallots
Juice of 1 orange, reduced by half
Salt and freshly ground black pepper to taste
Juice of 1 lemon
3 tablespoons extra-virgin olive oil
2 tablespoons lemon juice in 2 cups of cold water
Rind of 1 orange, julienned

4 Belgian endives, julienned very thin
1 tablespoons extra-virgin olive oil
2 skinless, boneless chicken breasts (about 2 pounds) cut into ¾-inch cubes
4 to 6 cups mâche (lamb's lettuce, field greens, or Bibb lettuce) washed, dried in a salad spinner, and chilled
1 small tomato, peeled, seeded, and diced (about 3 tablespoons total)
1 orange, peeled, membrane removed, and cut into small cubes for garnish

1. To make the vinaigrette, combine the vinegar, shallots, orange juice, and a pinch of salt and pepper in a small saucepan. Over low heat, simmer for 10 minutes to infuse the flavors. Remove from the heat, stir in the lemon juice, and whisk in the oil in a thin steady stream. Season with salt and pepper and set aside.

2. Refresh the endive leaves in the lemon juice and water. Spin dry in a salad spinner and chill.

3. In a small pan of boiling water, parboil the orange peel twice, changing the water each time. Drain and set aside.

4. In a skillet or sauté pan, heat the oil over medium-high heat. Cook the chicken breast for about 2 minutes on each side or until lightly browned and crispy. Let cool.

5. Meanwhile, mix the lettuce and endive in a bowl. Drizzle on vinaigrette to taste and toss to coat well. Divide the salad greens among four plates. Sprinkle the chicken and the oil in the pan delicately over the lettuce.

6. Top with the diced tomato and garnish with the orange peel and orange cubes.

HERBED CHICKEN SALAD WITH TOMATO TABBOULEH

4 to 6 servings
METHOD: GRILL OR BROIL

Tabbouleh Salad

½ cup bulgar
1 ¼ cups boiling spring water
2 tablespoons peeled, seeded, and finely diced plum tomato
1 tablespoon minced scallion
1 tablespoon minced flat-leaf parsley
1 tablespoon minced fresh mint leaf
1 tablespoon minced fresh basil
2 tablespoons extra-virgin olive oil
Salt and freshly ground black pepper to taste

Chicken Breast & Herb Marinade

¼ cup low-fat or nonfat yogurt
2 ripe plum tomatoes, peeled, seeded, and finely diced
2 tablespoons finely chopped scallion, white part only
1 tablespoon minced flat-leaf parsley
1 teaspoon minced fresh basil
½ teaspoon grated lemon zest
4 cups (about 2 pounds uncooked) shredded grilled or broiled chicken breast (see page 180)

Roasted Scallions & Cherry Tomatoes

8 large scallions
Extra-virgin olive oil for basting
12 cherry tomatoes for garnish
Salt and freshly ground black pepper to taste

1. To make the tabbouleh, heat a medium skillet over high heat and add the bulgar and toast, shaking the pan and stirring constantly until lightly browned, about 4 to 5 minutes. Transfer to a medium bowl and add the water. Cover tightly with plastic wrap and let stand about 30 minutes. When tender but still a bit chewy, transfer to a strainer and press to remove any excess water. Return to the bowl and add the tomato, scallion, parsley, mint, basil, and oil and toss to combine. Season with salt and pepper. Cover tightly with plastic wrap and marinate for 1 hour at room temperature.

2. Meanwhile, to make the chicken breast and herb marinade, combine the yogurt, tomatoes, scallion, parsley, basil, lemon zest, and chicken in a large bowl. Season with salt and pepper and toss gently to mix. Cover tightly with plastic wrap and marinate, refrigerated, for 1 hour.

3. To make the roasted scallions and cherry tomatoes, preheat the oven to 450°F, brush with the olive oil. Place on a baking sheet and roast 6 to 8 minutes, or until the scallions are browned slightly and the tomatoes are tender. Remove any excess oil with paper towel. Season lightly with salt and pepper.

4. To assemble the salad, toss the tabbouleh to fluff up the bulgar. Toss the marinated chicken to mix. On a large serving platter, make a nest of tabbouleh. Pile the chicken in the center. Garnish with the roasted scallions and cherry tomatoes.

CHICKEN & FENNEL SALAD WITH THYME-MUSTARD DRESSING

These poached chicken breasts are permeated with smoky tones from the ham and freshened with the anise-flavored fennel. Interesting!

4 servings
METHOD: POACH

3 cups chicken stock (see page 8)
4 ounces thick slices of smoked ham, diced
2 skinless, boneless chicken breasts (about 1½ pounds), halved
1 tablespoon Dijon mustard
1 tablespoon coarse-grain mustard
½ teaspoon minced garlic
2 tablespoons minced onion
14 cup plain yogurt, low-fat or nonfat
¼ sour cream, regular or light
2 teaspoons extra-virgin olive oil
2 tablespoons reserved poaching liquid
3 teaspoons chopped fresh thyme leaves
Salt and freshly ground black pepper to taste
2 medium fennel bulbs, trimmed, quartered, cored, and very thinly sliced
2 tablespoons fresh lemon juice

1. In a medium high-sided skillet, bring 3 cups of the chicken stock and the ham to a simmer and cook, covered, for 10 minutes. Add the chicken breasts to the liquid and poach 8 to 10 minutes or until done throughout. Remove from the poaching liquid, cool to room temperature. Reserve 2 tablespoons of the liquid. Discard the ham and liquid. Transfer to a work surface to cool.

2. Process the mustard, garlic, onion, yogurt, sour cream, oil, reserved poaching stock, and 2 teaspoons of the thyme in a blender or a mini food processor until smooth.

3. Cut the chicken into bite-size chunks and transfer to a large mixing bowl. Drizzle on the dressing and toss to mix well. Adjust seasoning with salt and pepper to taste.

4. In another large bowl, toss together the fennel, lemon juice, and a scant amount of salt and pepper. Divide the fennel evenly among 4 large plates. Mound the chicken chunks on top and sprinkle with the remaining thyme. Top with a turn of the pepper mill.

PICKING HERBS AND AROMATICS FOR FLAVORFUL SAUTÉS

Chicken breasts, herbs, and spices can be partnered in many ways. Lots of shallots and garlic show up in the sauté pan. Fresh basil, marjoram, parsley, sage, oregano, thyme, tarragon, cilantro, dill, rosemary, and chives are all high on the list. Fresh herbs should be selected over dried if possible since the cooking time, in general, is so short for chicken breasts, meaning the fresh garden flavors won't be cooked out of the food. When dried are substituted in a recipe, use only half the amount called for with fresh.

CHINESE CHICKEN SALAD WITH WARM SZECHUAN-STYLE DRESSING

Szechuan-style Chinese cooking is noted for its heat—from chile peppers in various forms! This wonderfully spicy flavored recipe is no exception. The ingredients can be assembled in advance, then the dressing is warmed just before serving. Toss this one right at tableside!

4 servings

METHOD: POACH

2 cups chicken stock, (see page 8)
2 chicken breasts (about 2 pounds), halved
2 cups leeks, green part only, or scallions
1-inch piece fresh peeled ginger, sliced very thin

Warm Dressing

2 tablespoons peanut oil
⅓ cup chopped scallion, white part and a little of the green
2 teaspoons minced peeled fresh ginger
1 small jalapeño, seeded, deveined, and finely chopped
½ teaspoon ground Szechuan peppercorns*
2 tablespoons soy sauce
1 tablespoon hoisin sauce
2 tablespoons fresh orange juice, reduced to 1 tablespoon
1 teaspoon honey
2 cloves garlic, minced
1 to 2 teaspoons Chinese hot chile oil*
6 cups shredded Shantung or Napa cabbage

*Available in Asian markets and some grocery stores.

1. In a high-sided skillet or saucepan, combine the chicken stock, leeks, and ginger and bring to a boil. Lower the heat, lightly salt the liquid, add the chicken breasts, and simmer 8 to 10 minutes or until done. The breasts will feel firm when pressed with the back of a fork. Transfer to a strainer to cool. Remove the bones and skin. Shred the meat, cover tightly with plastic wrap, and chill.

2. Combine the peanut oil, scallion, ginger, jalapeño, and ground peppercorns in a small saucepan. Set aside.

3. Combine the soy sauce, hoisin sauce, orange juice, honey, garlic, and chile oil in a small bowl. Set aside.

4. Combine the cabbage and chicken in a large mixing bowl. Toss to mix.

5. Over high heat, bring the peanut oil mixture to a boil, reduce the heat to low and cook for 1 minute. Stir in the soy sauce mixture and simmer just to warm through. Remove from the heat.

6. Drizzle the warm dressing over the chicken and cabbage, toss gently to coat well, divide onto four individual plates, and serve immediately.

HOW TO COOL IT WITH THE CHILES!

There's always someone picking the chile peppers out of the dish you just slaved over. Or perhaps it's you picking them out?

Q: How do you adjust the heat of a hot chile pepper?

A: The small, hottest red chile peppers are the serranos. Jalapeños are not as hot. If you want a dish to be generally flavored by the chile pepper but not a tongue-burner, use the larger peppers with the seeds and veins removed or a small amount of jalapeños, sliced paper-thin and minced. *Note:* Always wear rubber gloves when handling hot peppers and wash your hands after to remove the hot chile oils. Be careful not to touch your face or eyes before washing the potent chile oil off your gloves. Wash work surfaces and knives as well.

CHICKEN, AVOCADO, & WILD RICE SALAD

2 to 4 servings
METHOD: GRILL OR BROIL

6 cups chicken stock (see page 8)
Salt to taste
4 ounces uncooked wild rice, soaked in hot tap water for 30 minutes and drained
1 large ripe avocado, peeled, sliced into half-inch pieces, and chilled
1 tablespoon fresh lemon juice
4 scallions, white and some of the green part, coarsely chopped
12 pitted black olives, sliced
3 cups bite-size pieces of grilled or broiled chicken breast (see page 180)

Dressing
¼ cup red wine vinegar
2 teaspoons Dijon mustard
½ cup canola or other light vegetable oil
½ teaspoon sugar
1 tablespoon chopped fresh parsley
¼ cup slivered almonds or toasted pine nuts for garnish
12 cherry tomatoes for garnish

1. Bring 4 cups of the chicken stock and the garlic to a boil in a heavy medium saucepan. Lightly salt the liquid, add the wild rice, cover, reduce the heat to very low, and cook until tender, about 45 minutes. Remove from the heat, and let stand, covered, for 15 minutes. Drain thoroughly. Fluff the rice and place it in a large mixing bowl, cover with plastic wrap and refrigerate until cold.

2. Drizzle the lemon juice onto the avocado pieces to keep from turning brown.

3. Combine the scallions, olives, chicken, and rice in a large mixing bowl. Toss gently just until mixed.

4. Combine the vinegar, mustard, vegetable oil, sugar, and parsley in a small bowl or jar with a tight-fitting lid. Shake to mix well.

5. Add the avocado slices to the chicken and rice mixture. Pour on the dressing and toss gently to combine thoroughly. Divide between individual plates and serve sprinkled with toasted nuts; arrange the tomatoes around the salad.

CHICKEN, BROCCOLI & ARTICHOKE HEART PASTA SALAD WITH CREAMY BASIL DRESSING

4 to 6 servings

METHOD: POACH, GRILL, OR BROIL

3 cups bite-sized chunks chicken breast (about 1 ½ pounds) poached, grilled or broiled (see pages 118 and 180), chilled
½ pound pasta shells or tubes, cooked according to package directions to *al dente,* rinsed, drained and cooled
1 ½ cups quartered marinated artichoke hearts (jarred), drained
1 ½ cups small broccoli florets, cooked until crisp-tender, drained, and chilled
4 scallions, white and green parts, cut into half-inch pieces
Salt and freshly ground black pepper to taste

Creamy Basil Dressing

¼ cup best quality white wine vinegar
2 tablespoons Dijon mustard
1 egg yolk
2 garlic cloves, peeled
⅓ cup extra-virgin olive, canola, or other light vegetable oil
1½ cup sour cream, regular or low-fat
½ cup tightly packed chopped fresh basil leaves
2 tablespoons chopped fresh chives for garnish

1. Combine the chicken breast chunks, artichoke hearts, broccoli, scallions, and salt and pepper in a large bowl. Cover with plastic wrap and refrigerate until well chilled.

2. To make the dressing, combine the vinegar, mustard, egg yolk and garlic in a blender or mini food processor. Blend until smooth. Leave the machine running and pour in the oil in a slow but steady stream. Add the sour cream and blend thoroughly. Remove to a bowl and fold in the chopped basil. Adjust seasoning with salt and pepper to taste. Refrigerate 1 hour before serving.

3. To the chicken mixture, add the pasta, drizzle on the dressing and toss gently. Turn onto a large platter and garnish with chives.

MANDARIN ORANGE CHICKEN SALAD

2 to 4 servings
METHOD: POACH

3 cups fresh orange juice
2 skinless, boneless chicken breasts (about 2 pounds), halved
6 to 8 pitted dates, chopped
¼ cup coarsely chopped blanched almonds
1 cup canned mandarin orange segments, drained (reserve ⅓ cup juice)
4 scallions, julienne cut into 1-inch strips
½ cup fresh peas, blanched and chilled
2 teaspoons fresh lemon juice
4 to 6 cups torn Boston, Bibb, and red leaf lettuce leaves

Cinnamon Vinaigrette

⅓ cup reserved juice from mandarin orange sections
3 tablespoons extra-virgin olive oil
3 tablespoons canola or other light vegetable oil
3 tablespoons champagne or white wine vinegar
Salt and freshly ground white pepper to taste
2 teaspoons ground cinnamon

1. Bring the orange juice to a boil in a large, high-sided saucepan. Reduce the heat to low, lightly salt the liquid, add the chicken breasts, and simmer 8 to 10 minutes or until done throughout. Remove the breasts to a work surface and discard the poaching liquid.

2. Cut the chicken into 1-inch strips, cover with plastic wrap, and chill.

3. Combine the chicken, dates, almonds, mandarin oranges, scallions, fresh peas, and lemon juice in a large bowl. Toss gently.

4. To prepare the cinnamon vinaigrette, combine the reserved mandarin orange juice, olive oil and vegetable oil, vinegar, salt, pepper, and cinnamon. Whisk until thoroughly mixed. Drizzle over the chicken breast mixture, toss gently.

5. Arrange the salad greens on a large platter. Place the mandarin chicken in the center and chill before serving.

CHICKEN & FRESH VEGETABLE PRIMAVERA SALAD

6 servings

METHOD: POACH OR GRILL

4 cups bite-size pieces chicken breast (about 2 pounds), grilled or poached (see pages 118 and 180)
⅓ cup extra-virgin olive oil
2 tablespoons canola or other light vegetable oil
3 teaspoons sherry wine vinegar
1 garlic clove, minced
2 scallions, white and green parts, minced

Vegetable Marinade

⅓ cup extra-virgin olive oil
¼ cup white wine vinegar
2 tablespoons sherry wine vinegar
Salt and freshly ground black pepper to taste

Vegetables

8 asparagus spears, trimmed, cooked to crisp-tender, and cut into 1-inch pieces
2 cups small broccoli florets, cooked to crisp tender
1 cup green beans, cooked to crisp-tender, sliced on the diagonal into half-inch pieces
4 coarsely chopped scallions, white and some of the green part
½ cup finely diced red bell pepper
1 head radicchio, leaves separated
1 bunch large fresh spinach leaves, washed, stems removed, dried
1 pound small tube pasta, such as penne or ziti, cooked according to package directions to *al dente*, rinsed, drained, and chilled
2 minced scallions, white and green parts
10 cherry tomatoes for garnish

1. Place the chilled chicken breast pieces in a large bowl. Combine half the olive oil and the vegetable oil, vinegar, garlic, and scallions in a jar with a tight fitting lid. Shake to mix. Drizzle on the chicken and toss gently. Cover with plastic wrap and chill for one hour.

2. Place the vegetables in a large bowl. To make the vegetable marinade, combine the remaining olive oil, white wine vinegar, sherry wine vinegar, and a pinch of salt and pepper in a jar with a tight-fitting lid. Shake to mix well. Drizzle onto vegetables and toss to coat well. Cover with plastic wrap and chill for one hour.

3. To prepare the platter, ring the outer edge with the radicchio and spinach leaves. Toss the pasta and the vegetables together and place inside of the leaves. Place the chicken in the well, sprinkle with minced scallions, and garnish with tomatoes. Keep refrigerated until serving. Top with freshly ground black pepper if desired.

CHILLED LIME & BASIL MARINATED CHICKEN BREASTS

2 to 4 servings

METHOD: POACH

4 poached skinless, boneless chicken breast halves (about 2 pounds) (see page 118), chilled

Marinade

½ cup fresh lime juice
2 large cloves garlic, crushed
2 tablespoons packed fresh basil or 1 tablespoon crushed and dried
2 large shallots, minced
½ cup extra-virgin olive oil
⅓ cup canola or other light vegetable oil
¾ teaspoon sugar
½ teaspoon salt
1 teaspoon freshly ground black pepper or more to taste

Assorted salad ingredients including torn lettuce, arugula, or baby spinach leaves or a combination of the above

1. Combine the lime juice, garlic, basil, shallots, olive and vegetable oils, sugar, and salt and pepper in a small bowl.

2. Slice the chicken breasts into half-inch wide strips. Place in a shallow glass or pottery dish and pour in the marinade. Cover tightly with plastic wrap and marinate in the refrigerator for 24 hours.

3. Drain off the marinade. Place the salad greens on a serving platter making a bed in the center. Arrange the chicken in the center and serve chilled.

CHICKEN "COBB" (THE ORIGINAL!)

This fine combination of ingredients created at the (former) Brown Derby in Hollywood, gained its own fame and lives on at restaurants everywhere. The world's first Cobb salad was made up *à la minute* when Derby owner Robert Cobb raided his refrigerator seeking a midnight snack for theater magnate Sid Gruman (the original owner of the Hollywood Boulevard landmark, Grauman's Chinese Theater). Cobb's late-night culinary extravaganza was so tasty he added it to the Derby's menu where it became a star, and now a legend in its own time.

4 to 8 servings

METHOD: POACH

2 cups chicken stock, (see page 8)
1 stalk celery
1 parsley sprig
Salt to taste
2 skinless, boneless chicken breasts (about 2 pounds), halved
¼ pound bacon, cooked to crispy, drained, and crumbled
1½ avocados, peeled and diced
1½ large ripe tomatoes, diced
½ cup Danish or domestic blue cheese, crumbled

Vinaigrette
¼ cup champagne vinegar
½ cup corn oil or other light vegetable oil
½ cup extra-virgin olive oil
2 cloves garlic, minced
2 teaspoons minced fresh oregano leaves, or 1 teaspoon dried
Freshly ground black pepper to taste
8 to 10 cups shredded lettuce (the classic was made with iceberg lettuce, or use romaine cut chiffonade)

1. In a high-sided skillet or saucepan, bring the chicken stock, celery, and parsley to a boil. Reduce the heat to low, lightly salt the water, add the chicken breasts, and simmer for 8 to10 minutes or just until done. The breasts will be firm when pressed with the back of a fork.

2. Transfer to a plate to cool. Julienne the chicken, then cut the strips in half.

3. Combine the chicken, bacon, avocado, tomato, and blue cheese in a medium bowl. Set aside.

4. Combine the vinegar, corn and olive oil, garlic, oregano, and salt and pepper in a jar with a tight-fitting cover. Shake to mix well.

5. Drizzle half the dressing over the chicken mixture, toss to coat well.

6. Mound the shredded lettuce on individual plates, top with the chicken and a few turns of the pepper mill. Pass the remaining vinaigrette.

DILLED CHICKEN, SWEET PEPPERS, & CAPPELLINI SALAD

Here's another perfect salad for lunch or dinner. Also a great "make ahead" pasta salad that is anything but run-of-the-mill.

4 servings
METHOD: POACH

¾ pound dried cappellini pasta, cooked according to package directions to *al dente*, rinsed, and chilled
2 cups chicken stock (see page 8)
2 sprigs flat-leaf parsley
2 dill sprigs
Salt to taste
1 chicken breasts (about 1 pounds), halved
¼ cup white wine vinegar
2 tablespoons fresh lemon juice
1 tablespoon medium dry sherry
1 teaspoon honey
½ cup extra-virgin olive oil
Freshly ground black pepper to taste
1 large red bell pepper, seeded and julienned
1 large yellow bell pepper, seeded and julienned
1 large cucumber, peeled, seeded, and sliced into thin rounds
½ cup dill threads (not chopped)
5 scallions, chopped, green and white parts

1. Combine the chicken stock, parsley, and dill sprigs in a high-sided skillet or saucepan and boil. Lightly salt the liquid, add the chicken breasts, lower the heat, and simmer for 8 to 10 minutes or just until done throughout. The breasts will be firm when pressed with the back of a fork.

2. Transfer to a strainer, remove the skin and bones. Tear the meat into large pieces and set aside.

3. In a small bowl, whisk the vinegar, lemon juice, sherry, honey, and salt and pepper. Add the oil in a thin steady stream, whisking until the dressing emulsifies.

4. Combine the pasta with the chicken, peppers, cucumber, dill, and scallions in a large bowl. Drizzle on the dressing and toss to coat well. Cover the bowl with plastic wrap and chill at least 1 hour before serving.

MOROCCAN-STYLE CHICKEN BREAST SALAD

6 to 8 servings

METHOD: GRILL

2 skinned, boned chicken breasts (about 2 pounds each), flattened slightly
2 green bell peppers, seeded and cut into ¼-inch strips
2 small red onions, thinly sliced
¼ cup chopped flat-leaf parsley
¼ cup chopped fresh cilantro
2 cloves garlic, finely minced
2 bunches watercress, stems removed

Vinaigrette

¼ cup lemon juice
¼ cup red wine vinegar
1 teaspoon paprika
1 teaspoon ground cumin
¼ teaspoon cayenne pepper
Salt and freshly ground black pepper to taste
⅔ cup extra-virgin olive oil
12 chopped black olives for garnish

1. Fire up the grill. Lightly coat the grill rack with cooking spray. Grill the chicken breasts 4 minutes per side or just until done. Cool and cut into ¼-inch wide strips.

2. Combine the chicken strips, bell peppers, onions, parsley, cilantro, garlic, and watercress in a large mixing bowl.

3. Combine the lemon juice, vinegar, paprika, cumin, cayenne, and salt and pepper in a small bowl. Whisk in the oil in a thin steady stream until well mixed.

4. Drizzle half the vinaigrette over the chicken mixture, gently toss to coat well. Divide the chicken salad among individual plates and garnish with the chopped olives. Pass the remaining vinaigrette.

THAI CHICKEN SALAD

Thai food offer incredibly interesting flavor combinations, which might explain its popularity these days. With so many creative ways to prepare chicken breasts, from appetizers to salads and main courses, here is one salad that offers two different, interesting Thai dressing approaches to add to your repertoire. Try both to find your favorite and remember to adjust the heat to your palate.

6 servings

METHOD: POACH

3 cups chicken stock (see page 8)
2 threads lemongrass
1 l-inch piece lime rind
1 tablespoon fresh lime juice
Salt to taste
3 chicken breasts (about 3 pounds), halved
5 ounces cellophane noodles*
1 cup finely grated carrots
2 cucumbers, peeled, seeded and chopped
½ cup coarsely chopped dry-roasted, unsalted peanuts

Dressing #1

4 large cloves garlic, blanched, mashed to a paste with ½ teaspoon salt
¼ cup soy sauce
½ cup fresh lime juice
1 teaspoon grated lime zest
1 tablespoon sugar
1 tablespoon peanut butter
1½ teaspoon red pepper flakes or to taste
¼ cup light sesame oil

Dressing #2

⅓ cup extra-virgin olive oil
2 tablespoons Asian chile oil or to taste*
1 large clove garlic, minced
¼ cup rice wine vinegar
3 tablespoons soy sauce
1 serrano chile, seeded and finely minced
¼ cup shredded unsweetened coconut, toasted in the oven to light brown

*Available in Asian markets and some supermarkets

1. In a high-sided skillet or saucepan, combine the stock, lemongrass, lime rind, and juice and bring to a boil. Reduce the heat to low, lightly salt the water, add the chicken breasts and simmer 8 to10 minutes or just until the done. The breasts will be firm when pressed with the back of a fork. Transfer to a strainer, remove the skin and bones. Shred the chicken into bite-size pieces and let cool to room temperature.

2. Place the noodles in a heatproof glass bowl. Pour on boiling water to cover completely and let stand for 10 minutes. Drain well.

3. Combine the chicken, carrots, and cucumbers in a large mixing bowl.

4. *For dressing #1:* Combine the garlic paste, soy sauce, lime juice and zest, sugar, peanut butter, and pepper flakes in a blender. With the motor running, add the oil in a thin steady stream and blend until very thick. Continue with step 5. *For dressing #2:* In a small bowl, whisk together the olive oil, chile oil, garlic, vinegar, and soy sauce and combine well. Stir in the chile. Continue with step 5.

5. Drizzle half the dressing over the chicken mixture and toss to coat well. Place the noodles in the center of a serving platter. Top with the chicken mixture. If using dressing #1, top with the peanuts, or shredded coconut if using Dressing #2. Serve the remaining dressing on the side.

TARRAGON CHICKEN BREAST SALAD WITH TOASTED PECANS

4 to 6 servings

METHOD: POACH

4 cups chicken stock (see page 8)
1 celery top with leaf
1 sprig parsley
3 tablespoons fresh lemon juice
½ teaspoon dried tarragon
3 chicken breasts (about 2½ pounds), halved
Salt to taste
1 cup finely chopped celery hearts
Freshly ground black pepper to taste
⅓ cup homemade lemon mayonnaise (see page 123) or best quality mayonnaise mixed with 1 tablespoon fresh lemon juice added 4 hours prior to using
⅓ cup plain yogurt, regular or low-fat
2 tablespoons tarragon white wine viengar
1 tablespoon chopped fresh tarragon or 1½ teaspoon dried, crumbled
1 cup chopped toasted pecans

1. In a high-sided skillet or saucepan, combine the stock, celery top, parsley, lemon juice, tarragon, and salt and bring to a boil. Reduce the heat to low, lightly salt the water, add the chicken breasts and simmer 8 to 10 minutes or until done. The breasts will be firm when pressed with the back of a fork. Transfer to a strainer, remove the skin and bones. Shred the chicken breasts and chop into bite-sized pieces. Place in a mixing bowl.

2. Add the celery, salt, and pepper to the chicken. Toss to combine.

3. Whisk together the mayonnaise, yogurt, vinegar, and tarragon in a small bowl. Pour the dressing onto the chicken and toss to mix well. Chill for 1 hour. Toss in the pecans before serving, reserving a few tablespoons to sprinkle on each salad for garnish.

SPICY MEXICAN GARBANZO BEAN & CHICKEN SALAD

6 servings

METHOD: BAKE

2 chicken breasts (about 2 pounds), halved
Salt and freshly ground black pepper to taste
¼ cup red wine vinegar
Dash of Tabasco
1 16-ounce can garbanzo beans, drained and rinsed well
1 red bell pepper, seeded and diced
1 green bell pepper, seeded and diced
3 celery stalks, diced (use only inner stalks)
1 small red onion, finely diced

Dressing

1½ cups sour cream, regular or light
2 tablespoons chile sauce
2 teaspoons cumin
2 jalapeño peppers, or more to taste, stemmed, seeded and finely chopped
½ cup chopped cilantro
Salt and freshly ground black pepper to taste

1. Preheat the oven to 375°F.

2. Arrange the chicken breasts in a baking dish in a single layer. Sprinkle with a scant amount of salt and pepper. Bake 8 to10 minutes or just until done. Place on a rack and let cool. Remove the skin and bones and cut into ¼-inch strips. Transfer to a large mixing bowl.

3. Combine the vinegar and Tabasco in a small bowl.

4. Drizzle the vinegar over the chicken and toss. Add the garbanzo beans, red and green bell peppers, celery, and onion and toss to combine.

5. Combine the sour cream, chile sauce, cumin, jalapeños, cilantro, and salt and pepper in a bowl. Mix well.

6. Add the dressing to the chicken mixture and toss to coat the ingredients. Chill for 1 hour before serving.

CHICKEN & VEGETABLES PASTA SALAD

Serve this very modern Italian dish with a glass of dry pinot grigio. This salad is also recommended for a lunch buffet, but not necessarily in the heat of an outdoor dining experience as the mayonnaise can go bad in a very short time when the weather is too hot.

4 to 6 servings

METHOD: POACH

2 cups chicken stock (see page 8)
1 celery top with leaf
1 sprig flat-leaf parsley
1 tablespoon chopped fresh basil
Salt to taste
2 chicken breasts (about 1½ pounds), halved
1 pound rotelle pasta (spinach, tomato, and egg combination), cooked according to package instructions to *al dente*, rinsed, and cooled
¾ cup cubed zucchini
¾ cup seeded, peeled, and diced tomatoes
½ cup thinly chopped celery, inside stalks
½ cup sour cream, regular or light
⅓ cup homemade mayonnaise (see page 123), or best quality commercial
1½ teaspoons lemon juice
3 tablespoons chopped fresh basil, or 2 teaspoons dried
1 teaspoon dried oregano
Freshly ground black pepper to taste
2 tablespoons chopped fresh parsley for garnish
¼ cup toasted pine nuts

1. In a high-sided skillet or saucepan, combine the stock, celery leaf, parsley, and basil. Reduce the heat to low, lightly salt the liquid, add the chicken breasts, and simmer 8 to 10 minutes or just until done. The breasts will be firm when pressed with the back of a fork. Transfer to a strainer, remove the skin and bones. Shred the chicken breasts and set aside.

2. Combine the chicken, pasta, zucchini, tomatoes, and celery in a large bowl.

4. Combine the sour cream, mayonnaise, lemon juice, basil, oregano, and salt and pepper in a small bowl. Fold the dressing into the chicken mixture, sprinkle on the parsley and pine nuts, and mix well. Chill for 2 hours before serving. Pass the pepper mill.

CHICKEN WITH BLACK BEAN SALAD & CUMIN VINAIGRETTE

6 servings

METHOD: GRILL OR BROIL

2 cups black beans, soaked in water for 12 hours or overnight, drained, and well rinsed
½ onion, chopped
Salt and freshly ground black pepper
3 skinless, boneless chicken breasts (2½ pounds), halved
6 cups filtered water (or more)

Marinade

¾ cup extra-virgin olive oil
¼ cup white wine vinegar
1 tablespoon fresh lemon juice
2 teaspoons Dijon mustard
1 tablespoon minced fresh parsley
2 teaspoons cumin
½ teaspoon salt
2 large tomatoes, peeled, seeded, and coarsely chopped
½ red bell pepper, seeded, and finely chopped
½ green bell pepper, seeded, and finely chopped

1. In a medium saucepan, combine the beans, onion, and a pinch of salt and pepper with cold filtered water. Bring to a boil, reduce the heat to low, and simmer the beans until tender but not soft, about 30 to 40 minutes. Drain and let cool to room temperature.

2. Place the chicken in a shallow glass dish. Season with a scant amount of salt and pepper.

3. In a small bowl, whisk together the olive oil, vinegar, lemon juice, mustard, parsley, cumin, pepper, and ½ teaspoon of salt. Pour two-thirds of the vinaigrette over the chicken breasts and toss to coat. Cover with plastic wrap and marinate at room temperature for 30 minutes.

4. Fire up the grill or prepare the broiler.

5. Place the beans in a mixing bowl. Add the tomatoes, bell peppers and the remaining vinaigrette. Adjust the season with salt and pepper. Toss to combine well and set aside.

6. Lightly coat the grill rack with cooking spray. Grill the chicken breasts for 4 to 5 minutes on each side, basting once, just until done. Let cool to room temperature.

7. Tear the chicken meat into bite-size pieces and toss with the beans. Cover and refrigerate until ready to serve.

NOTE: Instead of combining the chicken with the beans, try serving the bean salad alongside grilled chicken breast halves.

APPLE & WALNUT CHICKEN SALAD

Serve this classic fruit and chicken salad on a bed of shredded red and white cabbage. In addition, note the variations on the fruit and chicken breast salad concept below—each one as easy and delicious as the original.

4 to 6 servings
METHOD: POACH

4 cups chicken stock (see pge 00)
1 celery top with leaf
1 sprig flat-leaf parsley
2 tablespoons fresh lemon juice
Salt to taste
3 chicken breasts (about 2 ½ pounds), halved
2 tart green apples, cored, peeled, and julienned
¼ cup fresh lemon juice
⅔ cup chopped pitted dates
1 cup finely chopped celery, tender inner stalks only
⅓ cup sour cream, regular or light
⅓ cup homemade mayonnaise (see page 123), or best quality commercial
Salt and freshly ground white pepper to taste
½ cup chopped toasted walnuts

1. In a high-sided skillet or saucepan, bring the stock, celery top, parsley, and lemon to a boil. Reduce the heat to low, lightly salt the liquid, add the chicken breasts, and simmer 8 to 10 minutes or just until done. The breasts will be firm when pressed with the back of a fork. Transfer the chicken to a strainer, remove and discard the skin and bones. Shred or chop the chicken breasts into bite-size pieces.

2. Combine the apples with half of the lemon juice in a large bowl. Add the chicken, dates, and celery and toss to mix well.

3. Whisk together the sour cream, mayonnaise, and remaining lemon juice in a small bowl. Add the chicken mixture, season with salt and pepper and toss to coat well.

4. Cover with plastic wrap and chill for 1 hour or more. Just before serving, toss in the walnuts.

VARIATIONS:

With Red & Green Grapes

1 cup each red and green seedless grapes, halved
4 scallions, chopped, white and green parts
⅓ cup toasted slivered almonds
1 cup chopped celery, tender inside stalks only

Prepare the chicken as in step l; combine the dressing ingredients as in step 3. Substitute the ingredients above and toss with the chicken until well combined.

With Mango

2 mangoes, peeled, pitted, and cut into ¾-inch pieces
½ teaspoon mild curry powder
¼ teaspoon cumin
1 cup coarsely chopped toasted cashews
2 tablespoons chopped cilantro

Follow step 1 as above. Combine the sour cream, mayonnaise, curry powder and cumin. Substitute the ingredients above and toss with the chicken until well combined. Top with chopped cilantro just before serving.

With Grapefruit

1 pink grapefruit, peeled, sectioned, and membranes removed
1 endive, finely chopped
¼ cup chopped fresh dill
1 teaspoon fresh lemon juice
¼ cup fresh pink grapefruit juice
1 cup chopped roasted hazelnuts

Follow step 1 as above. Follow step 3, using the lemon and grapefruit juice. Substitute the ingredients above and toss with the chicken to mix well. Toss in the hazelnuts just before serving.

GRILLED VEGETABLES AND CHICKEN BREAST SALAD WITH THYME VINAIGRETTE

When the coals are hot, throw anything you like around the outer rim of the grill. Wrap a whole head of garlic, drizzled with some olive oil, in aluminum foil and grill for 1 hour. Just before it's ready, grill some thick slices of crusty peasant bread to spread with the baked garlic instead of butter, or mix the roasted garlic and soft butter together and serve with the hot bread along with cold wine. It's a delicious amusement for the mouth while the chicken breasts sizzle over the embers. This recipe can travel from the backyard to the beach to the brunch table . . . it's a basic.

4 to 6 servings

METHOD: GRILL

3 skinless, boneless chicken breasts (about 3 pounds), halved
Vegetable oil for basting
Salt and freshly ground black pepper to taste
4 ears of corn, shucked and boiled
2 large zucchini, scrubbed, blanched in boiling water for 3 minutes, quartered lengthwise
¾ cup finely chopped red onion, soaked in ice water 10 minutes and patted dry with paper towels
2 red bell peppers, seeded and quartered
12 scallions, 6 reserved for garnish

Vinaigrette

2 tablespoons white wine vinegar
2 teaspoons grainy mustard
1 clove garlic, minced
1 tablespoon minced fresh thyme, or 1 teaspoon dried thyme
Salt and freshly ground black pepper to taste
3 tablespoons extra-virgin olive oil
3 tablespoons canola oil or other light vegetable oil
3 tablespoons chopped cilantro or flat-leaf parsley for garnish

1. Fire up the grill. Lightly coat the grill rack with cooking spray.

2. Salt and pepper the chicken breasts. Grill for 4 to 5 minutes per side. Do not overcook. Cool to room temperature.

3. Brush the corn with oil, season with a scant amount of salt and pepper and place on the grill toward the outer rim away from the intense heat, cook for about 10 minutes. Turn occasionally until it is lightly colored and grill marks appear all around. Grill the zucchini, onion, bell peppers, and scallions in the same manner. Exact grilling time will be different for each vegetable. Each is done when it reaches crisp-tender, but not soft.

4. Transfer the chicken breasts to a work surface and cut each into 6 strips. Cut the vegetables into hearty sized pieces. Let cool to room temperature.

5. Whisk together the vinegar, mustard, garlic, thyme, salt, and pepper in a small bowl. Whisk in the oils in a thin steady stream until well combined.

6. Arrange the chicken strips and vegetables on one large platter. Drizzle on half the vinaigrette. Sprinkle with cilantro or parsley. Serve at room temperature. Or serve the dressing on the side as a dipping sauce.

NOTE: In the event that the an outdoor grill filled with white-hot coals is not available, don't fret. Try a counter top electric grill, or grill the ingredients on a well-seasoned cast-iron grill pan with ridges, over moderate heat on the stove top. Of course, the overall taste will lack the flavor only burning wood and coals can provide, but the look will be similar.

CHICKEN BREASTS & BROCCOLI FLORETS WITH TANGY CARROT DRESSING

4 servings

METHOD: POACH

3 cups chicken stock (see page 8)
1 sprig parsley
Salt to taste
2 chicken breasts (about 2 pounds), halved
2 cups broccoli florets, blanched
1 red bell pepper, seeded and chopped

Dressing

6 to 8 carrots (about ½ pound), peeled and thinly sliced
4 cloves garlic, minced
1 teaspoon chopped fresh thyme, or ½ teaspoon dried thyme
2 tablespoons chopped fresh basil, or 1 tablespoon dried basil
1 cup rich chicken stock (see page 9)
¼ cup tarragon vinegar
2 tablespoon extra-virgin olive oil
Freshly ground white pepper to taste

1. Bring the stock and parsley sprig to a boil in a high-sided skillet or saucepan. Reduce the heat to low, lightly salt the water, add the chicken breasts, and simmer 8 to 10 minutes or just until done throughout. The breasts will be firm when pressed with the back of a fork. Transfer to a strainer and cool to room temperature. Remove the bones and skin. Shred or tear the chicken into bite-size pieces.

2. Combine the broccoli florets, red pepper, and chicken in a large mixing bowl. Cover with plastic wrap and chill.

3. Combine the carrots, garlic, thyme, basil, and stock in a saucepan. Bring to a boil, stirring occasionally. Reduce the heat to low and simmer for 10 minutes or until the carrots are very tender. Let cool slightly. Put the mixture in a blender or food processor. Add the vinegar, oil, salt, and pepper. Process until smooth.

4. Pour the dressing over the chicken mixture and toss to combine well. Refrigerate at least 2 hours before serving.

For a variation, combine broccoli and cauliflower florets.

BROILED CHICKEN BREAST & ASPARAGUS SALAD WITH HAZELNUT BALSAMIC VINAIGRETTE

Chicken breasts can be transformed into tasty envelopes for almost any type of stuffing. Since the pocket is small, stuffing with intensely flavored ingredients is best.

6 servings
METHOD: BROIL

3 skinless, boneless free-range chicken breasts (about 3 pounds), halved
⅓ cup white wine vinegar
2 tablespoons extra-virgin olive oil
1 medium onion, sliced into rounds
2 cloves garlic, quartered
3 tablespoons chopped fresh parsley
Salt and freshly ground black pepper to taste
15 thin asparagus spears, trimmed
¼ cup rich chicken stock (se page 9)
6 to 8 cups torn heads lettuce, including red leaf, Boston, or Bibb lettuce, washed and dried in a lettuce spinner and chilled

Vinaigrette

3 tablespoons balsamic vinegar
⅓ cup extra-virgin olive oil
1 teaspoon minced shallots
¼ teaspoon Dijon mustard
¼ teaspoon honey
¼ cup very finely chopped toasted hazelnuts
2 tablespoons coarsely chopped toasted hazelnuts for garnish
12 cherry tomatoes, halved, for garnish

1. To create a pocket for the stuffing, cut an opening, using a sharp knife, along the outside of each breast half without cutting all the way through. Stop cutting ½ inch before the top and bottom. Place the breasts in a shallow glass dish.

2. Whisk together the vinegar, oil, onion, garlic, parsley, and a scant amount of salt and pepper in a small bowl. Pour over the breasts, cover with plastic wrap, and marinate, refrigerated, for 2 hours or more.

3. Preheat the broiler.

4. Cook the asparagus in boiling water about 3 minutes or just until crisp-tender and still firm. Drain and let cool. Cut into 2-inch pieces, reserving the tips separately.

5. Remove the chicken from the marinade. Strain the onion, garlic, and parsley out of the marinade, chop together. In a small bowl, combine the onion, garlic, and parsley with 1 tablespoon of the stock, mash to form a paste. Divide the mixture evenly between the breasts and stuff into the pockets. Press the ends together. Arrange the breasts on a broiler pan lined with aluminum foil. Broil 4 to 5 minutes per side or just until done. Let cool slightly and cut into 1-inch slices.

6. Combine the lettuce and the asparagus in a large bowl.

7. To make the vinaigrette, whisk together the vinegar, oil, stock, shallots, mustard, honey, and the finely chopped hazelnuts in a small bowl.

8. Briefly warm the vinaigrette in a small saucepan over low heat. Immediately drizzle half over the lettuce and asparagus and toss to coat well. Arrange the chicken breasts slices in the center of a platter and then arrange the lettuce around the chicken. Garnish with the chopped hazelnuts and asparagus tips. Arrange the tomatoes around rim of the platter. Serve the remaining dressing on the side and pass the pepper mill.

A TRIO OF VINAIGRETTES FOR CHICKEN SALAD

Here are three delicious vinaigrettes to create a quick meal with your favorite leftover chicken breast (poached, grilled, broiled or baked), greens and salad fixings. Use these flavor combinations as marinades as well for surprisingly tasty results from grilled, baked, or broiled chicken breasts.

Sesame Ginger

4 cloves garlic, minced
2 tablespoons minced fresh ginger
1 cup Oriental-style sesame paste
5 tablespoons soy sauce or tamari
1 tablespoon sugar
1 tablespoon chile oil
3 tablespoons dark sesame oil
3 tablespoons white wine or dry vermouth
6 scallions, cut into ½-inch thick slices, white and green parts
2 tablespoons chopped fresh cilantro

Anchovy Mustard

1½ tablespoons Dijon mustard
1 2-ounce can anchovies, drained and minced
¼ cup red wine vinegar
⅔ cup extra-virgin olive oil
2 small shallots, minced
1 ½ teaspoons crumbled dried thyme
Freshly ground black pepper to taste

Raspberry Walnut Vinaigrette

½ cup plus 2 tablespoons raspberry vinegar
½ cup extra-virgin olive oil
2 tablespoons walnut oil
1 cloves garlic, minced
2 tablespoons chopped fresh parsley
⅓ cup finely minced shallots

To make any of the above vinaigrettes, combine the ingredients in a jar with a tight-fitting lid and shake to mix well, or place in a blender and blend until smooth. Dress any combination of salad vegetables with the vinaigrette and serve cooked chicken breasts on the side.

BRAZILLIAN CHICKEN BREAST SALAD

4 servings

METHOD: BAKE

2 skinless, boneless chicken breasts (about 2 pounds), halved
Salt and freshly ground black pepper to taste
2 green bell peppers, seeded and julienned
1 red bell pepper, seeded and julienned
4 hearts of palm cut into ½-inch slices
1 banana, cut into ¼-inch slices

Dressing

⅓ cup extra-virgin olive oil
⅓ cup orange juice
2 tablespoons lime juice
4 tablespoons red wine vinegar
1 teaspoon red chile flakes
Pinch of cayenne
1 teaspoon Tabasco
Pinch of sugar

1. Preheat the oven to 375°F.

2. Place the chicken breasts in a baking pan and sprinkle with a scant amount of salt and pepper. Bake 8 to 10 minutes or just until done. Let cool and cut julienne.

3. Combine the chicken, peppers, hearts of palm, and banana in a mixing bowl, tossing gently. Season with salt and pepper to taste.

4. For the dressing, combine the oil, juices, vinegar, chile, cayenne, Tabasco, sugar, and a pinch of salt in a blender.

5. Drizzle half the dressing over the chicken mixture and toss to coat well. Chill well before serving. Pass the remaining dressing on the side.

CHICKEN, TOFU, & TARRAGON WILD RICE SALAD

4 servings
METHOD: BROIL

1 cup uncooked wild rice, soaked in hot tap water for 30 minutes and drained
4 cups chicken stock (see page 8)
2 teaspoons chopped fresh tarragon, or 1 teaspoon dried tarragon
1 clove garlic, unpeeled
Salt to taste
1 tablespoon canola or other light vegetable oil
4 half-inch thick slices solid tofu, diced
Freshly ground black pepper to taste
2 chicken breasts (about 1½ pounds), halved

Vinaigrette
2 tablespoons extra-virgin olive oil
2 tablespoons rice wine vinegar
2 tablespoons fresh lime juice
1 tablespoon grainy mustard
2 tablespoons minced shallots
1 tablespoon chopped fresh chives
Pinch fresh ground white pepper
20 endive spears (2 to 3 whole endives)
2 large carrots, peeled and shredded
10 cherry tomatoes
¼ cup chopped fresh chives
3 tablespoons chopped flat-leaf parsley
1 small red onion, minced
½ green bell pepper, seeded and minced

1. In a 5-quart stock pot or saucepan, combine the stock, tarragon, garlic, and a pinch of salt. Bring to a boil, add the wild rice, stir reduce the heat to low, and simmer for 45 minutes, adding more boiling water if necessary. Remove from the heat and let stand, covered, for 15 minutes. Drain thoroughly. Remove the garlic and fluff the wild rice. Transfer to a large bowl to cool. Set aside.

2. Preheat the broiler.

3. Sprinkle the chicken breasts with a scant amount of salt and pepper. Broil 4 minutes per side or until done. Remove the skin and bone, tear the meat into bite-size pieces and let cool to room temperature.

4. Heat the canola oil in a sauté pan over medium-high heat. Add the tofu and cook, turning gently, until slightly browned and crispy. Transfer to paper towel to drain briefly, set aside.

5. To make the vinaigrette, combine the olive oil, vinegar, lime juice, mustard, shallots, chives, salt, and pepper in a small bowl. Whisk to mix well.

6. Add the chicken, chives, parsley, onion, and bell pepper to the wild rice. Drizzle on the dressing and toss gently until well combined. Let marinate, refrigerated, for 2 hours.

7. On a serving platter, arrange the endive spears with mounds of shredded carrots in the center of each. Toss the tofu with the chicken and mount in the center of the platter. Garnish with cherry tomatoes and a few turns of the pepper mill.

CHICKEN NIÇOISE SALAD

The chicken breast fillets called for in this recipe are the delicate strips of white-meat chicken on the underside of the breast. Also sold as "chicken tenders," each one is about two bites. Remove the tendon from each fillet (see page 4), and reduce the cooking time as these morsels cook very quickly. The *haricots verts* called for in this salad, are very slender French green beans. Regular green beans can easily be substituted.

6 servings
METHOD: SAUTÉ

Dressing

2 anchovy fillets packed in olive oil, well drained and rinsed, 2 teaspoons of the oil reserved
½ cup extra-virgin olive oil
¼ cup chicken stock (seepage 8)
3 tablespoons red wine vinegar
2 cloves garlic, peeled and chopped
1 teaspoon chopped fresh rosemary
½ teaspoon freshly ground black pepper

Salad

24 chicken breast fillets (about 2 pounds), tendons removed
Salt and freshly ground black pepper to taste
1 teaspoon extra-virgin olive oil
10 small red potatoes, well scrubbed
½ pound *haricot verts,* or regular green beans, choose the thinnest ones
1 small red onion, cut into very thin rings
12 cups mixed lettuce (such as mâche, mixed baby lettuces, romaine, or Boston)

18 or more tiny Niçoise olives
4 hard-boiled eggs, halved
12 cherry tomatoes, halved
1 tablespoon capers, drained

1. To make the dressing, combine the anchovy fillets, the 2 teaspoons of reserved anchovy oil, olive oil, chicken stock, vinegar, garlic, rosemary, and pepper in a blender or food processor and process until smooth. Transfer to a bowl and let stand for hour before using.

2. Place the chicken in a shallow bowl. Drizzle on 2 tablespoons of the dressing and coat well. Season with a scant amount of salt and pepper. Marinate for 10 minutes.

3. In a large skillet or sauté pan, heat 1 teaspoon of olive oil over medium high heat. Add the chicken fillets and cook about 2 minutes per side or until lightly browned and done. Do not overcook. Place on paper towels to drain. Let cool to room temperature. Cut into strips lengthwise. Set aside.

4. Meanwhile, boil the potatoes in a stockpot filled with lightly salted boiling water about 12 to 15 minutes or just until tender. Remove the potatoes with a slotted spoon and reserve the boiling water. Let cool, quarter, and place in a bowl. Drizzle on 2 tablespoons of the dressing, season with salt and pepper to taste, and gently toss to coat.

5. Add the green beans to the boiling water, reduce the heat to low, and simmer about 2 minutes or until crisp-tender. Do not overcook. Drain and run cold water over the beans to stop the cooking process. Let cool to room temperature. Place the beans in a bowl, drizzle on a scant amount of dressing and toss to coat well.

6. Place the red onion and lettuces in a large bowl and drizzle on 2 tablespoons of the dressing. Toss to coat.

7. Mound the salad greens in the center of a large platter. Place the green beans, potatoes, chicken, olives, and boiled egg halves around the greens. Drizzle 1 tablespoon of dressing over the egg halves. Top with a few turns of the pepper mill. Serve the remaining dressing on the side.

PEANUT AND SESAME CHICKEN SALAD

An Asian steamer with two layers (made of woven bamboo) placed over a water filled wok is the cooking method called for to cook this recipe. (See the Steam section on page 363 for more information). An alternative is a steaming basket that fits into a stockpot or a vegetable steamer. In either case, it must be large enough to hold a dish containing the chicken. If neither is available, poach the chicken fillets in the sake and chicken stock.

4 servings

METHOD: STEAM OR POACH

18 chicken breast fillets (about 1½ pounds), tendons removed
¼ cup sake
Salt and freshly ground white pepper
2 tablespoons chicken stock (see page 8)
1 tablespoon Oriental sesame paste*
1 tablespoon natural smooth peanut butter (avoid the oil on top)
2 tablespoons rice wine vinegar
1 tablespoon soy sauce or tamari
1 teaspoon fresh lemon juice
½ teaspoon honey
1 large head Romaine lettuce, tough outer leaves removed, chiffonade cut
½ head Napa cabbage, shredded
¼ cup finely chopped scallion, green part only
2 tablespoons toasted sesame seeds
¼ cup tablespoons roasted peanuts, coarsely chopped

***Available in Asian markets and some supermarkets**

1. Place the chicken fillets in a shallow ovenproof dish that loosely fits in a bamboo steamer and pour in the sake. Season with a scant amount of salt and pepper. Let marinate 10 minutes.

2. In a wok, add water, bring to a boil, then reduce the heat to low.

3. Position the steamer on top of the over the water. Place the dish with the chicken and sake in a steamer basket on the top tier. (*Note:* The chicken should be in a single layer while cooking so it may be necessary to steam in two batches.) Cover the steamer with a tight-fitting lid and steam the chicken for about 8 minutes or until done. Remove the steamer basket and uncover to cool about 10 minutes. Remove the dish from the basket, discard the sake, and reserve 2 tablespoons of the steamer liquid and set aside.

4. Cut the chicken into strips, cover with plastic wrap, and chill.

5. Meanwhile, to make the dressing, combine the stock, sesame paste, peanut butter, vinegar, soy sauce, lemon juice, honey, and the reserved steaming liquid in a glass jar with a tight fitting lid. Shake to mix well.

6. Place the chicken in a bowl. Drizzle dressing over the chicken; toss to mix well.

7. On individual plates or a serving platter, make a bed of lettuce and cabbage. Mound the chicken breast in the center. Sprinkle with scallions and toasted sesame seeds and the chopped peanuts.

SMOKED CHICKEN SALAD WITH GOLDEN CAVIAR CREAM

You can smoke your own chicken for this salad by using the instructions on page 215. Or, buy smoked chicken breasts at most specialty food stores, delis, or fine meat counters in a gourmet market.

4 servings
METHOD: SMOKE

1 jar (2 ounces) American golden caviar, 1 teaspoon reserved for garnish
¾ cup sour cream, regular or light
1 teaspoon Dijon mustard
2 tablespoons very finely chopped fresh chives
5 large lemon wedges
4 cups choice salad greens, washed and dried in a salad spinner, chilled
4 smoked skinless, boneless chicken breast halves (about 1 ½ pounds)
Salt and freshly ground white pepper to taste

1. In a small bowl, gently fold together the caviar, sour cream, mustard, and 1 tablespoon of the chopped chives. Transfer to a serving bowl and refrigerate until ready to serve.

2. Divide the salad greens on individual plates. Place one lemon wedge on each.

3. On a work surface using a very sharp knife, thinly slice the smoked chicken breasts. Season with salt and pepper to taste. Arrange the chicken over the greens. Squeeze a few drops of lemon juice over the chicken slices from the remaining lemon wedge.

4. Place 2 tablespoons of the caviar cream across the top of the slices. Dot each serving with a few of the reserved caviar eggs and one twist of the pepper mill. Serve with the remaining caviar cream on the side.

CHICKEN AND PORTOBELLO MUSHROOM SALAD

This salad is served warm, which makes it a perfect fall or winter dish for a hearty first course, or a main course salad.

4 servings
METHOD: STEAM

2 skinless, boneless chicken breasts (about 1½ pounds), halved
1 teaspoon dried basil
Salt and finely ground black pepper to taste
4 teaspoons fresh lemon juice
2 tablespoons extra-virgin olive oil
2 large portobello mushrooms, stemmed and chopped in large chunks
2 tablespoons finely chopped flat-leaf parsley
⅓ cup chicken stock or steaming liquid
2 large cloves garlic, crushed
4 sun-dried tomato halves, softened in hot water for 15 minutes and drained
¼ cup peeled, seeded, and chopped plum tomatoes
2 tablespoons red wine vinegar
4 cups mixed baby lettuce or salad greens of choice

1. Cut 4 pieces of heavy-duty plastic wrap. Lay a breast half on each. Sprinkle on the basil, salt, pepper, and lemon juice. Wrap the chicken breast halves and tuck under the plastic wrap to make a pouch sealed at both ends.

2. Add water to a wok, bring to a boil, then reduce the heat to low. Place a bamboo steamer with a tight-fitting lid on top of the water. Place the wrapped chicken breasts in the steamer on the top tier. Cover and steam for 10 to 12 minutes or until done. Remove pouches from the steamer, and transfer them to a plate. Let the meat cool in the juices, reserving the juice. Unwrap the chicken and slice on the diagonal.

3. Meanwhile, heat 1 tablespoon of the oil in a large skillet or sauté pan over medium-high heat. Add the portobello chunks and cook, stirring occasionally, about 4 minutes or until the liquid from the mushrooms has almost evaporated. Add the parsley and ⅓ cup of stock and reserved cooking juice from the steamed chicken. Season with salt and pepper to taste and continue cooking over medium heat, stirring occasionally, until the liquid has evaporated, about 5 minutes more. Cool to room temperature.

4. To make the vinaigrette, place the garlic, sun-dried tomatoes, chopped plum tomatoes, vinegar, and a pinch of salt and pepper in a blender. Blend to a smooth consistency. With the motor running, add the remaining 1 tablespoon of oil in a thin steady stream.

5. Place the salad greens on individual salad plates. Arrange the chicken slices on the greens. Toss the mushroom pieces with half the vinaigrette and scatter over the chicken and greens. Pass the remaining vinaigrette on the side and the pepper mill.

CLASSIC ROSEMARY CHICKEN SALAD

Place a scoop of this salad on a bed of lettuce before dusting with chopped toasted walnuts, or use it to fill a whole wheat pita pocket, or make a sandwich on toasted crusty bread.

4 servings
METHOD: SAUTÉ

1 tablespoon plus 1 teaspoon extra-virgin olive oil
1 small clove garlic, minced
2 skinless, boneless chicken breasts (about 1½ pounds), halved
4 teaspoons finely chopped fresh rosemary
Salt and freshly ground black pepper to taste
⅓ cup dry white wine
½ cup chicken stock (see page 8)
1 stalk celery, very thinly sliced
2 scallions, white and green parts, thinly sliced
1 cup seedless red or green grapes, halved
¼ cup mayonnaise, regular or reduced fat, or plain yogurt
¼ cup sour cream, regular or reduced fat
2 teaspoons fresh lemon juice
1 to 2 tablespoons toasted, finely chopped walnuts for garnish

1. Heat the oil and garlic in a medium skillet or sauté pan over medium-high heat. Add the chicken and sauté until browned, about 2 minutes per side.

Sprinkle on 1 teaspoon of the rosemary and a scant amount of salt and pepper.

2. Add the wine and stock, partially cover the pan, reduce the heat to low, and simmer about 3 minutes or until the chicken is done. Cool slightly.

3. Chop the chicken into bite-sized chunks.

4. Combine the chopped chicken, celery, scallions, and grapes in a medium mixing bowl. Set aside.

5. Combine the mayonnaise or yogurt, sour cream, lemon juice, the remaining rosemary, and salt and pepper in a small bowl. Stir to mix well.

6. Fold the dressing into the chicken until well coated. Chill for 1 hour. Dust with the walnuts before serving.

GRILLED ROSEMARY CHICKEN & ASPARAGUS SALAD WITH STILTON VINAIGRETTE

The strongly flavored Stilton vinaigrette requires a surprisingly small amount of cheese to add dimension to this salad.

4 lunch servings
METHOD: GRILL OR BROIL

- 2 skinless, boneless chicken breasts (about 1½ pounds), halved
- 2 branches fresh rosemary leaves, pounded slightly
- 3 tablespoons dry white wine or vermouth
- 2 tablespoons fresh lemon juice
- 2 teaspoons Dijon mustard
- Salt and freshly ground black pepper to taste
- 1½ pounds thin asparagus, stems trimmed
- 1 tablespoon extra-virgin olive oil
- 1 red onion, peeled, quartered, and very thinly sliced
- 4 small heads Boston lettuce, leaves separated (one head per serving)

Vinaigrette
- 2 tablespoons crumbled Stilton cheese
- 1 tablespoon extra-virgin olive oil
- 1 tablespoon canola or other vegetable oil
- 2 tablespoons chicken stock (see page 8)
- 2 tablespoons milk, low or non-fat
- 2 tablespoons champagne vinegar

1. Place the chicken breasts in a small shallow dish. Nestle the rosemary branches in between the breasts.

2. In a small bowl, whisk together the wine or vermouth, lemon juice, Dijon mustard, and salt and pepper until well combined. Drizzle half the marinade over the chicken breasts, coating on all sides. Cover the dish tightly with plastic wrap and marinate, refrigerated, for 2 hours.

3. In a high-sided skillet or stockpot, bring enough water to cover all the asparagus to a boil, lower the heat to medium. Lightly salt the water, add the asparagus, and cook about 3 minutes or until crisp-tender. Drain the asparagus and place under cold running tap water to stop the cooking process. Set aside to drain. Cut into bite-sized pieces.

4. Fire up the grill or prepare the broiler. Remove the chicken from the marinade and discard. Grill or broil the chicken for 3 to 4 minutes per side, or until done. Cool slightly and slice into ½-inch pieces.

5. Heat the oil over medium-high heat in a skillet or sauté pan. Cook the onion, stirring frequently, for about 3 minutes or until brown and crisp. Do not burn. Remove from the pan with a slotted spoon. Place on paper towels to drain.

6. To make the vinaigrette, combine the blue cheese, olive oil, vegetable oils, chicken stock, milk, vinegar, and salt and pepper, and process in a blender or food processor until smooth.

7. Place the lettuce in a large mixing bowl and drizzle on dressing to taste. Toss gently. Divide among 4 plates.

8. Place the chicken breast pieces and the asparagus tips in a clean, medium mixing bowl, and toss dressing to taste. Adjust the seasoning with salt and pepper to taste. Place the chicken and asparagus on the lettuce. Top with the crispy onions and a few turns of the pepper mill.

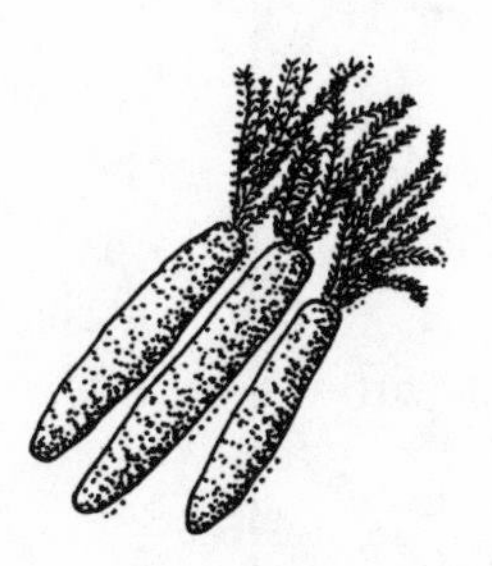

CILANTRO CHICKEN SALAD

6 servings
METHOD: POACH

3 skinless, boneless chicken breasts (about 3 pounds), halved
4 tablespoons chopped fresh cilantro
2 cups crème fraîche or heavy cream whipped just to stiffen slightly
Salt and freshly ground black pepper to taste
½ cup homemade lemon mayonnaise (see page 123) or best quality mayonnaise with 1 tablespoon fresh lemon juice added 4 hours prior to using
½ cup sour cream, regular or light
2 celery stalks, cut into l-inch long pieces and julienned
1 cup very coarsely chopped walnuts
¼ cup finely chopped scallion, white and some of the green parts
10 cups or more assorted salad greens (including Boston, Bibb, red leaf, romaine, watercress, radicchio etc.)

1. Arrange the chicken breasts in a shallow dish just large enough to hold the chicken in a single layer. Sprinkle on 2 tablespoons of the cilantro and cover with crème fraîche or heavy cream. Season with salt and pepper. Cover and marinate at room temperature for 1 hour.

2. Transfer the chicken and the marinade to a high-sided skillet or large sauté pan. Over medium heat, bring the marinade to a boil, reduce the heat to medium low, cover partially, and simmer for 8 to 10 minutes or until done. Remove the chicken from the liquid, let cool, and cut into bite-sized pieces. Place in a bowl.

3. Combine the mayonnaise and sour cream in a small bowl.

4. Add the celery, ¾ cup of the walnuts, 1 tablespoon of the cilantro, and the scallion to the chicken. Fold the mayonnaise mixture in gently. Adjust the seasoning with salt and pepper to taste. Chill for at least 2 hours.

5. Place the greens on a serving platter. Spoon on the chicken mixture and sprinkle with the remaining tablespoon of cilantro and the remaining chopped nuts.

ROASTED CHICKEN, ARUGULA, AND BASIL SALAD

Take the ingredients commonly used in pesto sauce and create a salad dressing with bursting flavors and the crunch of toasted pine nuts on top. Serve it with crispy croutons made from a French or Italian peasant loaf. Try using grilled chicken for this recipe instead of roasted chicken.

4 servings

METHOD: ROAST

2 boneless, chicken breasts (about 1½ pounds), halved
Salt and freshly ground black pepper to taste
1 cup chiffonade cut fresh basil leaves
3 tablespoons red wine vinegar
1 tablespoon extra-virgin olive oil
2 bunches arugula, stemmed and cut chiffonade
1 tablespoon finely grated Parmesan cheese
1 tablespoon toasted pine nuts for garnish

1. Preheat the oven to 375°F.

2. Season the chicken breasts under the skin with salt, pepper, and ¼ cup of the basil. Place in a baking dish and roast for 18 to 20 minutes or just until done. Cool and remove the skin. Cut into bite-sized pieces, set aside.

3. Combine the vinegar and oil in a jar with a tight-fitting lid. Shake well to mix.

4. In a large mixing bowl, combine the arugula, the remaining ¾ cup basil, and the chicken pieces. Drizzle on the dressing and toss to mix. Adjust the season with salt and pepper. Sprinkle on the grated Parmesan and toss again.

5. Divide the chicken among individual plates. Garnish with toasted pine nuts.

Sandwiches, Burgers, & Wraps

CHICKEN PARMESAN PANINI ON PEASANT BREAD

Make these big sandwiches out of a whole loaf of bread, then cut in 1½-inch wide strips just before serving on a buffet. Or wrap the whole sandwich loaf and cut individual servings once you've arrived under the trees or at the seaside.

4 to 8 servings

Spread

½ pound piece Parmesan cheese, 8 large shaved pieces (reserved) using the large side of a metal grater, then shave the remaining into small shavings
½ pound cream cheese, regular or fat reduced, softened
6 sun-dried tomato halves packed in olive oil
3 tablespoons milk
2 teaspoons white wine vinegar
1 teaspoon dried thyme, crumbled
Pinch of sugar
Salt and freshly ground black pepper to taste

Chicken Sandwich

1 large loaf crusty country bread such as focaccia or ciabatta, cut in half through the center (horizontally)

2 bunches arugula, stems removed, washed and dried in a salad spinner
1½ pounds cross-grain slices grilled, poached, or smoked chicken breast
1 red bell pepper, seeded and thinly sliced
1 red onion, sliced horizontally through the center, into very thin rounds

1. To make the spread, combine the small shavings of Parmesan, cream cheese, sun-dried tomatoes, yogurt, vinegar, thyme, and sugar in a food processor. Process to combine. Add the milk in a thin steady stream and process to a smooth spread.

2. Lay the bottom of the loaf of bread on a work surface. Cover both top and bottom with the spread.

3. On the bottom half, layer on the spread, arugula, chicken slices, bell pepper slices, and onion to taste and top with more arugula. Put spread on the top half and cover the sandwich. Press down slightly on the top. Wrap the loaf tightly in plastic wrap until ready to cut and serve.

CURRIED CHICKEN AND CRAB SALAD SANDWICHES

Serve this at luncheon or even at tea. The light little sandwiches are both tasty elegant.

4 servings
METHOD: POACH

½ cup sour cream, regular or light, or crème fraîche
2 tablespoons chopped fresh cilantro
1 teaspoon mild curry powder (Madras if available)
Pinch of cayenne
2 cups bite-sized pieces chicken breast poached with an herb poaching bouquet (see page 353)
½ pound fresh crab, all remaining shell pieces picked away
Salt and freshly ground black pepper to taste
8 fresh dinner-size rolls

1. Combine the sour cream or crème fraîche, cilantro, curry powder, cayenne, and salt and pepper to taste in a small bowl. Stir to mix well.

2. Stir in the chicken and crab and toss to coat well. Cover with plastic wrap and chill.

3. Assemble the chicken and crab salad sandwiches with bread or rolls of choice or serve in a bowl surrounded with the toast slices or rolls.

TRI-VINEGAR GLAZED WARM CHICKEN BREASTS SANDWICH

This warm sandwich is as hearty and satisfying as any. The mix of vinegar flavors makes it interesting as well as delicious.

4 servings

2 skinless, boneless chicken breasts (about 2 pounds), trimmed and flattened to ⅓-inch thickness
Salt and freshly ground black pepper to taste
2 tablespoons extra-virgin olive oil
¼ cup red wine vinegar
¼ cup herb-scented white wine or champagne vinegar
3 shallots, finely chopped
2 tablespoons chopped flat-leaf parsley
¼ cup balsamic vinegar
½ cup dry white wine
½ cup chicken stock reduced to ¼ cup
4 large crusty French or Italian rolls or onion rolls

1. Place the chicken breasts on a work surface. Season with salt and pepper.

2. In a sauté pan or heavy skillet, heat half the oil over high heat. Add one chicken breast to the pan and sauté 2 to 3 minutes per side or until browned and done. Transfer to a plate, keep warm. Repeat with the remaining oil and chicken breast.

3. Deglaze the pan with the red and white or champagne vinegar over high heat, stirring constantly and scraping up any bits on the bottom of the pan. Add the shallots and cook for 1 minute or until translucent. Add the balsamic vinegar, white wine, and stock, bring to a boil, reduce the heat to low, and simmer until 10 minutes or until reduced to a thickened sauce and only about ¼ cup liquid remains in the pan.

4. Return the chicken to the pan, rewarm, and coat each piece of chicken well with glaze. Place glazed chicken pieces on the rolls. Serve warm.

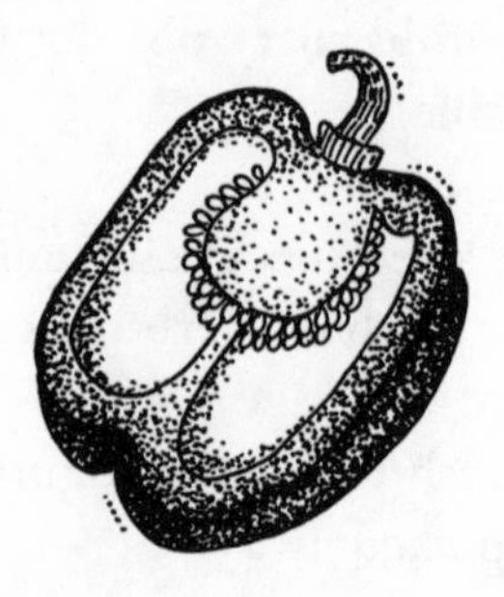

OPEN-FACE CHICKEN MELT

This is a close cousin to the beloved hot sandwich known as the "tuna melt."

2 to 4 servings
METHOD: BROIL

Spread

¼ cup mayonnaise, regular or light
2 tablespoons ketchup
1 tablespoon Dijon mustard
1 scallion, very thinly sliced

Sandwich

1 poached chicken breast (about 1 pound)
1 ripe avocado, peeled, cut lengthwise into 8 thin slices
4 large slices dark or sourdough bread, lightly toasted
4 thick slices Swiss or sharp Cheddar (large enough to cover the top of the sandwich—use several slices if necessary)
2 tablespoons finely chopped flat-leaf parsley or scallion, green part only

1. To make the spread, combine the mayonnaise, ketchup, mustard and scallion in a small bowl. Mix well and set aside.

2. Preheat the broiler.

3. On a work surface using a thin sharp knife, cut the chicken breast in half width-wise. Cut each half into 4 thin slices lengthwise.

4. Place the bread slices on a work surface and lightly coat with the spread. Layer each in the following order: chicken slices, spread, avocado, more spread, and sprinkle with parsley or scallion, reserving some for garnish. Top with the cheese slices.

5. Place the sandwiches in the broiler about 4 inches from the heat to melt the cheese about 1 to 1½ minutes. Sprinkle with parsley and serve.

CHICKEN CROQUE MONSIEUR

This traditional French warm sandwich, in which the cheese is literally meltingly delicious, is dipped in egg batter and fried in a skillet. But use a large, heavy skillet. A counter-top flat grill (with pull-down cover to enclose the ingredients while cooking) is an alternate, lower-fat method to make Croque Monsieur grilled sandwiches.

4 servings
METHOD: GRILLED OR SEARED

4 2-inch thick slices fresh French bread with crust
1 tablespoon Dijon mustard
1 teaspoon honey
1 skinless, boneless chicken breast (about 1 pound), flattened to ¼-inch and pan-seared until browned and done
8 slices Swiss cheese
½ cup milk
2 large eggs plus one egg white, beaten
Pinch of salt and freshly ground black pepper
2 tablespoons (or more) unsalted butter

1. With a sharp pointed knife, make a slit through the crust on one side and into the center of the breast to form a pocket, without cutting all the way through.

2. Mix the mustard and honey together in a small bowl. Spread even amounts inside each pocket.

3. Divide the chicken and cheese in four equal amounts. Handling gently to keep the bread intact, stuff the chicken and cheese into the bread pockets. Press the opening closed.

3. Combine the milk, eggs, salt, and pepper in a bowl. Whisk to mix well. Dip each sandwich in the mixture, turn to coat well.

4. Melt 1 tablespoon of butter in a heavy large skillet over medium-high heat. When the butter is bubbling, add the sandwiches to the pan and cook 3 to 4 minutes on each side or until golden brown. Use more butter if necessary. Press the sandwiches down gently with a metal spatula from time to time during cooking for better browning. Serve hot or keep warm in the oven until all the sandwiches are done. Serve whole or cut into halves.

GRILLED GREEK CHICKEN BREAST BURGERS WITH MARINATED CUCUMBERS

Though this book is dedicated to chicken breast cookery, this recipe calls for half chicken and ground half turkey for a slightly different flavor dimension. With turkey or without, it's highly satisfying and delicious.

Serves 4

METHOD: GRILL OR BROIL

Marinated Cucumbers

1 hot house cucumber, peeled and sliced thin
1 teaspoon salt
2 tablespoons best quality white wine vinegar
1 tablespoon honey
1 tablespoon lemon juice
1 teaspoon grated lemon zest
Pinch dried oregano for garnish

Burgers

1 pound coarsely chopped chicken breast
1 pound coarsely chopped turkey breast
1 teaspoon chopped fresh basil or ½ teaspoon dried
½ teaspoon dried oregano
2 cloves garlic (or more to taste), finely minced
Salt and freshly ground black pepper to taste
½ cup crumbled feta cheese
¼ cup coarsely chopped pitted Kalamata olives
4 pita halves or flatbread, cut open

1. To prepare the marinated cucumbers, place the sliced cucumbers in a strainer to drain. Sprinkle with salt. Let stand for 30 minutes. Rinse and pat dry.

2. Transfer the cucumbers in a bowl. In a separate bowl, combine the vinegar, honey, lemon juice, and zest. Pour over the cucumbers, cover with plastic wrap, and marinate, refrigerated, for 15 minutes. Discard the marinade, sprinkle the cucumbers with the oregano, and chill until ready to serve.

3. Fire up the grill or prepare the broiler.

4. To prepare the burgers, combine the chicken, turkey, basil, oregano, garlic, salt, and pepper in a food processor. Process 30 seconds or until coarsely ground.

5. Transfer the meat to a large mixing bowl, add the cheese and olives and mix well. Divide into 4 portions, shape into 1-inch thick rounds, and flatten slightly to make thick patties.

6. Grill or broil 4 to 5 minutes on each side or until done throughout. Do not overcook, but do not serve undercooked.

7. Heat the pitas or flatbread on the grill or broiler if desired, stuff the burgers into the bread and serve the cucumbers on the side.

GRILLED SCALLION CHICKEN BURGERS WITH TOMATO CHUTNEY

Several flavor combinations are particularly delicious in a grilled chicken breast burger: try freshly grated ginger root, soy sauce, and fresh cilantro leaves as alternative seasonings to the recipe below and exchange the tomato chutney for mango or whip up some homemade lemon mayonnaise (see page 123) and add a mashed avocado for an interesting burger spread.

4 to 6 servings

METHOD: GRILL

2 skinless, boneless chicken breasts (about 2 pounds), coarsely chopped
¾ cup fresh bread crumbs (from day-old French or sourdough)
3 tablespoons finely chopped flat-leaf parsley
1 cup chopped scallion, white and green parts
Salt and freshly ground white pepper to taste
1½ teaspoon grated lemon zest
4 tablespoons tomato chutney
Fresh rolls

1. Fire up the grill or hibachi, or use a countertop indoor grill. Lightly coat the grill rack with cooking spray.

2. Place the chopped chicken breast in a food processor and process until coarsely ground or about 30 seconds. Transfer to a large mixing bowl.

3. Add the breadcrumbs, parsley, scallion, zest, and salt and pepper to the bowl and mix well with the back of a wooden spoon. Divide into 4 to 6 portions, shape into 1-inch thick rounds and flatten slightly to make patties.

4. Place the burgers on a rack, cook 5 minutes per side, or until done throughout. Serve with a dollop of tomato chutney on a roll.

GRILLED ASIAN CHICKEN BURGERS

These burgers can easily be made on a countertop grill.

4 to 6 servings

2 pounds ground chicken breast
1 teaspoon hot or mild curry powder, or more to taste
1 teaspoon honey
2 to 3 tablespoons finely chopped cilantro
2 tablespoons finely chopped scallions, white and green parts
2 tablespoons finely chopped garlic
1 jalapeño chile, seeded, deveined, and minced
1 teaspoon cumin
Freshly ground black pepper to taste
1 teaspoon salt
¼ cup teriyaki sauce
1 tablespoon extra-virgin olive oil
12 scallions
4 large mushroom caps (about 3 inches across), stems removed, cut in two through the center (horizontally)
4 large sesame rolls, grilled

1. Fire up the grill, or prepare the broiler. Lightly coat the grilling rack with cooking spray.

2. In a large bowl, combine the chicken, curry, sugar, cilantro, chopped scallion, garlic, chile, cumin, salt, and pepper and mix together well.

3. Divide into 4 portions and make 1-inch thick rounds, flatten slightly to make patties.

4. Whisk together the teriyaki and olive oil in a small bowl. Cut the scallions in half. Brush the scallions and mushroom slices with the teriyaki sauce. Place on the outer rim of the grill. At the same time, grill the chicken burgers about 5 minutes per side or until done. Remove the mushrooms and onions when tender to a platter.

5. Just before the burgers are done, brush the buns with the olive oil. Place on the grill to toast on one side only. To serve, place a mushroom slice on a bun, top with the burger, lay criss-cross strips of onion over the burgers, top with another mushroom slice and top with the bun. Serve hot.

ITALIAN CHICKEN & TURKEY SAUSAGE BURGERS WITH PARMESAN SHAVINGS

This is a hearty meal with bursts of traditional Italian flavors. Make it a peasant-style dish by adding a whole loaf of fresh-baked ciabatta bread cut into squares large enough to envelope a burger.

4 servings

METHOD: GRILL OR BROIL

2 tablespoons extra-virgin olive oil
2½ cups red bell pepper, matchstick cut
1½ cups green bell pepper, matchstick cut
1½ cup thinly sliced then chopped onion
1 cup prepared best quality pasta sauce
¾ pound hot turkey Italian sausage, casings removed
1 pound chicken breast, coarsely chopped
Salt and freshly ground black pepper to taste
8 or more large shaved pieces of Parmesan (use a mandolin or the wide side of a metal grater), shaved from a large chunk of cheese
8 pieces of peasant or country style bread such as crusty ciabatta, or 4 freshly baked buns

1. Fire up the grill or prepare the broiler. Lightly coat the grill rack with cooking spray.

2. Heat the olive oil in a large skillet over medium-high heat. Add both bell peppers and the onion and cook 2 minutes stirring constantly. Lower the heat to medium and continue cooking 3 minutes more or until crisp-tender. Stir in the pasta sauce, and continue cooking 2 to 3 minutes until the sauce has reduced to a paste. Remove the pan from the heat, cover, and keep warm.

3. Combine the sausage, chicken breast, and salt and pepper in a food processor. Process until coarsely ground. Divide into 4 portions, shape into l-inch thick rounds, and flatten slightly to form patties.

4. Grill or broil the burgers 4 to 5 minutes per side or until done. Do not overcook but do not serve undercooked.

5. Open bread halves or buns. Place a shaving of Parmesan on the bottom piece and divide the pepper and onion mixture on the top. Place the burgers on the cheese, top with another slice of cheese, cover with the top, and serve immediately.

CHICKEN SLOPPY JOES

This all-American favorite tastes just as good with chicken breast meat.

4 servings

3 tablespoons extra-virgin olive oil
1 cup finely chopped onion
1 stalk celery, finely chopped
½ green bell pepper, seeded, deveined, and chopped
½ teaspoon dried oregano
2 pounds ground chicken breast
½ cup ketchup
½ cup tomato sauce (see page 126)
¼ cup chicken stock
2 tablespoons red wine vinegar
1 tablespoon Worcestershire sauce
1 teaspoon salt
1 tablespoon packed dark brown sugar
Freshly ground black pepper to taste
Tabasco sauce to taste
4 large poppy seed rolls, halved

1. Heat the oil on high heat in a heavy large saucepan or skillet. Add the onion, celery, bell pepper, and oregano and cook until the onion is translucent and the peppers are cooked to crisp-tender.

2. Add the chicken and, cook about 4 to 5 minutes or until the chicken is white, stirring constantly. Break up any large pieces with the back of the spoon.

3. Stir in the ketchup, tomato sauce, and stock, and cook 1 minute more. Add the vinegar, Worcestershire sauce, brown sugar, salt and pepper, and Tabasco. Lower the heat and simmer, partially covered, for 3 to 5 minutes more or until the sauce is very thick.

4. Place the bottom or the buns in shallow bowl, top with the chicken mixture and the bun.

GRILLED CHICKEN-LOAF BURGERS SMOTHERED IN ONIONS

The flavors in this chicken burger are reminiscent of homemade meatloaf, which makes them so moist, filling, and familiar. The caramelized onion topping is like an onion relish, adding just a bit of sweetness. Serve this with mashed potatoes or potato salad.

4 servings

METHOD: GRILL OR BROIL

Onions

2 teaspoon extra-virgin olive oil
2½ cups sliced onion
Salt to taste
1 tablespoon dark brown sugar
4 tablespoons balsamic vinegar, slowly reduced to 1 tablespoon

Burgers

1½ tablespoons canola oil or other light vegetable oil
1½ cup diced green bell pepper
1 cup finely chopped celery, tender inner stalks only
1½ pounds coarsely chopped chicken breast
1 cup fresh whole-wheat bread crumbs
2 eggs, beaten
2 tablespoons ketchup

1. Fire up the grill or prepare the broiler.

2. To prepare the onions, heat the olive oil over medium-high heat in a large skillet or sauté pan. Add the onions and a pinch of salt. Cook over medium heat until soft and nicely browned. Lower the heat, stir in the brown sugar and vinegar and continue cooking, covered, for 30 minutes until the mixture is cooked down to very thick sauce and no liquid remains in the pan. Stir occasionally.

3. Heat the oil in a skillet or sauté pan over medium high heat. Add the bell pepper and celery and cook 4 to 5 minutes or until crisp-tender.

4. Place the chicken breast meat in a food processor and process until coarsely ground. Add the pepper and celery mixture, bread, ketchup (reserving 1 tablespoon), thyme, and salt and pulse a few times or just until the ingredients are well combined.

5. Divide into equal portions, shape into l-inch rounds, and flatten slightly into patties. Baste the burgers with the ketchup.

6. Grill or broil 4 to 5 minutes per side or until done. Do not overcook. In the last 1 minute of cooking, baste with ketchup again.

7. Rewarm the onions. Top the burgers with onions and serve hot.

BROILED GARDEN BURGERS

4 servings

METHOD: BROIL OR PAN-FRY

2 pounds ground chicken breast
1 large egg, beaten
2 cups finely chopped fresh spinach
1 cup finely grated and peeled carrot
1 cup canned chick peas well washed, drained, and mashed with a fork
½ cup finely chopped onion
½ cup finely chopped scallion, white and green parts
1 ½ teaspoon lemon zest
Salt and freshly ground black pepper to taste
4 fresh onion rolls or French rolls, toasted
Lettuce leaves, left whole
Lemon avocado mayonnaise (see page 123)

1. Prepare the broiler.

2. In a large bowl, combine the chicken breast, egg, spinach, carrot, chick peas, onion, scallion, lemon zest, and salt and pepper. Mix together well.

3. Divide into 4 portions, form into 1-inch thick rounds, and flatten slightly into patties. Broil 5 minutes per side or until done. Serve on warmed rolls with lettuce leaves and mayonnaise on the side.

CHICKEN, TAPENADE, & GREENS WRAP

For those who absolutely adore olives, here's your wrap! Giant burrito-size flour tortillas now come in great flavors such as roasted red-pepper and garlic-pesto, among others, which add to the flavor of the finished wrap.

4 servings

Tapenade Spread

½ cup Kalamata olive, pitted
½ cup oil-cured black olives, pitted

1 teaspoon grated lemon zest
1 teaspoon extra-virgin olive oil

Chicken Wrap

2 skinless, boneless chicken breasts (about 1½ pounds), halved and pounded slightly, and cut into 2-inch strips
1 tablespoon canola or extra-virgin olive oil
1⅓ cup thinly sliced red onion
3 tablespoons balsamic vinegar
2 tablespoons fresh lemon juice
1 tablespoon red wine vinegar
1 tablespoon honey
1 teaspoon chopped fresh rosemary
2 teaspoons Dijon mustard
1 clove garlic, minced
Salt to taste
4 10-inch burrito size flour tortillas
4 cups salad greens including: baby spinach, whole baby romaine, sunflower sprouts, bean sprouts, watercress leaves, etc.)

1. To make tapenade, place the olives, lemon zest, and olive oil in a food processor. Pulse a few times until finely chopped. Do not over process. Set aside.

2. In a large skillet or sauté pan, heat half the oil over medium-high heat. Add the onion and cook until very lightly browned. Add the balsamic vinegar, cook 30 seconds more, transfer to a bowl.

3. Combine the lemon juice, vinegar, honey, rosemary, mustard, garlic, and a pinch of salt in a small bowl.

4. Reheat the pan and add the remaining oil over medium-high heat. Add the chicken breasts and cook about 3 minutes until the chicken is well browned on all sides. Lower the heat, add the lemon and vinegar mixture, and cook for 2 minutes more or until the sauce thickens and the chicken is done.

5. Warm the tortillas slightly. Spread tapenade on each. Top with chicken strips, balsamic onions, and the greens. Roll up, cut in half, and serve immediately.

SPICY FAJITA HAND ROLL

For a spectacular quick summer snack that suits any situation, grill the pounded chicken breasts and vegetables on a counter-top indoor grill, and slice them onto warmed flour tortillas, along with grilled vegetables, guacamole, sour cream, sautéed onions, fresh salsa, and chopped cilantro.

8 servings

¼ cup red wine vinegar
1 tablespoon extra-virgin olive oil
2 garlic cloves, peeled
½ teaspoon ground coriander
½ teaspoon cinnamon
½ teaspoon dried thyme
½ teaspoon salt
¼ teaspoon ground cloves
¼ teaspoon freshly ground black pepper
2 skinless, boneless chicken breasts (about 2 pounds), halved and flattened to ⅓-inch thickness
1 large red onion, cut into ¼-inch slices
8 corn or flour tortillas
1 cup fresh tomato salsa

1. Combine the vinegar, olive oil, garlic, herbs, salt, cloves, and black pepper in a food processor. Process until well blended. Pour into a shallow dish.

2. Add the chicken breasts and toss to coat well. Marinate for 1 to 4 hours in the refrigerator. Drain and let the chicken breasts stand at room temperature for half an hour before grilling.

3. Fire up the grill or prepare the broiler. Lightly coat the grill rack with cooking spray. Grill 5 minutes per side or until done.

4. While the chicken is grilling, place the onion slices around the outer rim of the grill, and cook until tender. Slice the chicken breasts into strips. Place the tortillas on the grill and warm for one minute. Place several slices of chicken and onion on each tortilla and roll up. Serve with salsa.

CHICKEN AND VEGETABLE TAMAKI HAND ROLL

A hand roll is traditional at any sushi bar and can contain a variety of ingredients, depending on the chef. Try some sake on the side.

Makes 4 rolls
METHOD: POACH

2 cups cooked sushi rice
4 nori (seaweed) sheets, cut in half
1 to 2 teaspoons sesame seeds
1 teaspoon prepared wasabi
1 poached chicken breast (about 1 pound) cut into thin strips
24 snow peas, steamed and trimmed
1 red bell pepper, cut into thin strips

1 ripe avocado, peeled and cut into 8 or more wedges
Soy sauce or tamari

1. Lay the nori sheets out on a flat surface. Spread ¼ cup rice on the bottom half of each sheet. Sprinkle with a few sesame seeds. Spread a tiny amount of the wasabi on each from top to bottom.

2. Arrange an even number of chicken breast strips, snow peas, pepper strips, and avocado over the rice. Roll the nori over the ingredients to form a roll or a cone. Serve with soy sauce or tamari mixed with wasabi.

QUICK CHICKEN WRAPS

Individual serving

Tex-Mex

1 10-inch burrito-size roasted red-pepper flour tortilla
½ avocado, mashed
Salt and freshly ground black pepper to taste
1 half grilled chicken breast, sliced on the diagonal or cut into strips
2 to 3 slices pepper-Jack cheese
½ cup shredded lettuce

1. Place the tortilla on a work surface.

2. Add salt and freshly ground black pepper to the avocado. Spread on the tortilla.

3. Top with a layer of chicken, cheese, lettuce, and freshly ground black pepper to taste.

4. Fold the top and bottom of the tortilla over the ingredients, wrap, cut in half and serve.

Chicken Caesar

1 10-inch burrito-size garlic-pesto flour tortilla
2 tablespoons creamy Caesar salad dressing (bottled)
1 half chicken breast, grilled and sliced on the diagonal or cut into strips
1 cup chiffonade cut romaine lettuce

1. Place the tortilla on a work surface.

2. Spread on the Caesar dressing.

3. Lay on the chicken breast slices or strips and top with the lettuce

4. Fold the top and bottom of the tortilla over the ingredients, wrap, cut in half, and serve.

SWEET THAI CHICKEN SALAD WRAPS

These are wrapped individually right when they're about to be eaten. An enticing platter of ingredients offers the opportunity for a create-your-own wrap with what you want inside a chilled large lettuce leaf.

6 to 8 servings

Sauce

½ cup rice wine vinegar
⅓ tablespoon fish sauce
1 tablespoon sugar
2 cloves garlic, finely minced
6 scallions, white and green parts, finely chopped
½ teaspoon red pepper flakes or more to taste

Chicken and Filling

1½ pounds skinless poached or smoked chicken breast, sliced very thin across the grain
1 small bunch fresh mint leaves, stemmed, rinsed, and dried
2 cups cooked white or brown rice
2 heads butter lettuce and 1 head romaine (inner leaves), leaves separated, trimmed of the thick ribs, washed, dried, and chilled
1 container sprouts, including: sunflower, bean, broccoli, onion, or a combination
¼ cup toasted sesame seeds

1. Combine the vinegar, fish sauce, sugar, half the scallions, and pepper flakes in a small bowl.

2. Place the chicken slices in a shallow dish. Drizzle on ⅓ of the sauce and toss to coat. Cover with plastic wrap and marinate, refrigerated, for 30 minutes.

3. Finely chop enough of the mint to equal 2 tablespoons, leaving the remaining leaves whole. Add the chopped mint to the sauce and place in a serving bowl. Set aside.

4. On a large platter, place the lettuce leaves all around the edge. Mound the chicken slices, the rice, and sprouts in the center. In small bowls, place the scallions, the sauce, sesame seeds, and pepper flakes if desired. Wrap ingredients of choice inside lettuce leaves. Drizzle on some sauce and eat immediately after wrapping.

CHICKEN AND ASIAN VEGETABLES SALAD WRAP

There's no bread or rice wrappers involved here. Instead, the delicate ingredients are wrapped within a lettuce leaf. This recipe is influenced by the light and fresh tasting Asian summer roll. However, the vegetables are first stir-fried before wrapping.

4 to 8 servings
METHOD: WOK

Sauce

2 tablespoons teriyaki sauce
3 tablespoons rice wine vinegar
1 tablespoon honey
½ teaspoon crushed red pepper or more to taste
½ teaspoon cornstarch

Chicken

3 teaspoons peanut oil
1 skinless, boneless chicken breast (about 1 pound), halved and cut into thin strips
2 tablespoons grated peeled fresh ginger
1½ cup grated carrot
1 cup fresh sprouts, including bean, sunflower, and radish
1 cup snow peas, trimmed and cut lengthwise into thin strips
½ cup scallions, mostly green parts, sliced lengthwise and cut into 2-inch strips
⅓ cup sliced almonds
2 to 3 heads Boston lettuce, leaves separated, chilled

1. Whisk together the teriyaki sauce, rice vinegar, honey, red pepper, and cornstarch in a bowl.

2. In a wok or large skillet, heat the olive oil over medium high heat. Add the chicken and ginger and stir-fry for 3 minutes or until the chicken is no longer white.

3. Add the sauce, carrot, bean sprouts, snow peas, and scallions to the wok. Stir-fry 3 minutes more or until the sauce thickens slightly. Transfer to a serving bowl to cool to room temperature. Stir in the almonds.

4. Place the lettuce leaves on plates or a platter. Spoon on even amounts of chicken mixture into each leaf cup and fold over. Serve immediately.

Spa Cuisine

ORANGE & BASIL CHICKEN

4 servings

2 skinless chicken breasts (about 2 pounds) halved, trimmed of all traces of fat and flattened slightly to even thickness
Salt and freshly ground black pepper to taste
½ cup fresh basil leaves, stemmed
1 cup fresh orange juice, reduced to ½ cup
1 navel orange, peeled and cut into thin rounds for garnish
Fresh basil or parsley for garnish

1. Preheat the oven to 375°F.

2. Sprinkle the chicken breasts with salt and pepper and place in a single layer an ovenproof pan.

3. Put a basil leaf beneath and on top of each breast. Pour on the orange juice.

4. Cut a piece of parchment paper to fit just inside the pan. Lightly oil the paper and place the oiled side on the chicken. Bake 8 to 10 minutes or until done throughout. Do not overcook. The breasts will be firm when pressed with the back of a fork. Let cool to room temperature.

5. Arrange on a platter and decorate with orange rounds and basil leaves.

POACHED CHICKEN BREASTS WITH BABY VEGETABLES

Baby vegetables are readily available in both gourmet stores and upscale grocery markets. They are usually more expensive than regular-size vegetables. Use the smallest of the regular vegetables as an economical substitute. Organics are the best for the purist's version of a spa cuisine dishes.

4 servings

METHOD: POACH

6 baby zucchini
6 baby crookneck yellow squash
¼ pound very tiny pearl onions
⅔ cups cooked fava, edamame (soy beans), or others to taste
2 cloves garlic, minced
2 tablespoons fresh chopped chives
2 skinless, boneless chicken breasts (about 2 pounds), halved, well trimmed of all traced of fat, flattened to even thickness
1¼ cups defatted chicken stock (see page 9)
1 bunch watercress, washed and stemmed
2 teaspoons pesto sauce (see page 108), or 2 tablespoons fresh basil and ½ small clove garlic, pressed, mixed with 2 tablespoons extra-virgin olive oil
Salt and freshly ground black pepper to taste

DOWN WITH CALORIES, UP WITH FLAVOR

A spa is a place where everyone willingly submits to a program of exercise and special cuisine—Spa Cuisine. This upgraded diet fare can be defined as follows: It is made up of a great variety of dishes prepared with ingredients low in fat, free of saturated fat and cholesterol, with low or no added sodium or sugar. They are high in protein, complex carbohydrates, and fiber. Add to this the challenge many home cooks and professional chefs have taken upon themselves, which is to be creative within these constraints, and Spa Cuisine begins to look like some kind of *miracle!* The spa-style recipes in this section contain some flavors that might sound unfamiliar, or difficult to predict flavor-wise at first, but each one is a delectable creation. Spa Cuisine is a welcome approach when it's time to take off those excess pounds without suffering bland uninteresting food at lunch or dinner!

1. Combine the zucchini, yellow squash, carrots, onions, and beans in a heavy skillet or sauté pan. Sprinkle on the garlic and chives. Arrange the chicken on top.

2. Combine the stock, watercress, pesto sauce, and salt and pepper in a blender or food processor. Blend to a purée.

3. Pour the sauce over the chicken breasts and vegetables. Over low heat, simmer, covered, for 20 to 25 minutes, or until the chicken and vegetables are tender.

4. Arrange on a platter, pour on the remaining pan sauce. Serve immediately.

BREAST OF CHICKEN WITH PEACH AND PINK PEPPERCORN SAUCE

A splash of peach brandy or other fruit liqueur adds depth to the flavors in this recipe. Use fresh apricots instead of peaches in the sauce for an interesting variation.

4 servings

METHOD: SAUTÉ (IN A NONSTICK PAN)

2 large ripe peaches, blanched for 30 seconds in boiling water, peeled, halved, and pitted
1¾ cup dry white wine such as sauvignon blanc
1 tablespoon unsalted butter
2 skinless, boneless chicken breasts (about 2 pounds), halved and trimmed of all traces of fat
Salt and freshly ground black pepper to taste
1 teaspoon pink peppercorns
1 tablespoon chopped fresh basil
1 ripe peach, sliced for garnish
4 fresh basil sprigs for garnish

1. Purée the peaches with ¾ cup of the wine in a blender or food processor.

2. Melt the butter in a nonstick sauté pan over medium-high heat. Add the chicken breasts, a scant amount of salt and pepper, and peppercorns and sauté on both sides just until opaque. Transfer to a plate. Over high heat, deglaze the pan with the remaining wine, scraping any bits off the bottom of the pan and reduce the wine by half. Lower the heat, add the basil, return the chicken breasts to the pan, partially cover, and simmer for 3 minutes or until most of the liquid in the pan is reduced.

3. Stir in the peach purée and simmer for 5 minutes more or just until the chicken is done. Do not overcook.

4. Arrange the chicken breasts on individual plates and garnish with the peach slices and basil sprigs. Spoon the pan sauce over the chicken breasts.

ROSEMARY CHICKEN ROLLS WITH ORANGE NUT STUFFING

2 to 4 servings

METHOD: POACH

4 tablespoons fine fresh whole-wheat bread crumbs
1 small onion, finely minced
Salt and freshly ground black pepper to taste
1 tablespoon finely chopped fresh rosemary
3 tablespoons chopped pecans
1 egg, beaten
2 skinless, boneless chicken breasts (about 2 pounds), trimmed of all traced of fat, flattened to about ½-inch thick and edges evenly trimmed
1 cup defatted chicken stock (see page 9), reduced to ⅔ cup
1 cup fresh orange juice, reduced to ⅔ cup
Fresh rosemary sprigs for garnish

1. Combine the bread crumbs, onion, salt, pepper, chopped rosemary, pecans, and the egg in a mixing bowl. Press together to make a paste.

2. Place the chicken breasts on a work surface. Spread the paste evenly over the breasts. Roll the breasts, tucking in the edges. Secure the ends with toothpicks.

3. Bring the stock and juice to a boil in a saucepan or skillet. Add the chicken rolls, reduce the heat to low, cover, and simmer for 8 to 10 minutes or until the chicken is tender and done throughout. Do not overcook. The rolls will be firm when pressed with the back of a fork.

4. Transfer the rolls to a serving platter, remove the toothpicks, and keep warm.

5. Reduce the liquid in the pan by half over high heat. Spoon the sauce over the chicken rolls. Garnish with rosemary sprigs and serve immediately.

WHITE CHILI

The Canyon Ranch Spa (located in the Berkshires of Massachusetts and in Tucson, Arizona), a fantastic health and fitness resort, is known for its health regimen as well as for its imaginative cuisine and organic gardens. Cooking classes are offered daily in order to send ranch visitors home with all the basics of Spa Cuisine. This unusual one-pot, one-dish delight is quick and delicious. You can go to the Canyon Ranch to sample it for a mere $5,000 per week, or try it at home with equally good results. This one is also a great make-ahead for guests.

4 servings
METHOD: STOVE TOP

1 pound dried Great Northern beans (white beans), soaked overnight in lightly salted water, drained
4 cups defatted chicken stock (see page 9)
2 medium onions, coarsely chopped
3 cloves garlic, finely chopped
1 teaspoon salt
½ cup chopped canned green chiles
2 teaspoons ground cumin
1½ teaspoons crushed dried oregano (use a mortar and pestle)
1 teaspoon ground coriander
⅛ teaspoon ground clove
¼ teaspoon cayenne pepper, or more to taste
3 cups cooked chicken breast chunks (from 2 breasts, poached or grilled)
1 cup grated Monterey Jack cheese, reduced fat, optional

1. Rinse the beans. Combine the beans, stock, half of the onions, the garlic, and a pinch of salt in a large heavy saucepan or stockpot. Bring to a boil. Reduce the heat to low, cover, and simmer for 2 hours or until the beans are very tender, adding more stock as needed. (More stock should not be needed if you use a heavy pot.)

3. When the beans are tender, add the remaining onions and the chiles, cumin, oregano, coriander, cloves, and cayenne. Mix well and continue to cook, covered, for 30 minutes.

4. Add the chicken and heat through. Spoon 1 cup of chile into each serving bowl and top with 2 tablespoons of the cheese, passing the remaining.

CHICKEN BREASTS SCALOPPINI WITH WILD MUSHROOM SAUCE

Use dried wild mushrooms such as morels, porcines, chanterelles, oyster mushrooms, or a combination.

4 servings

METHOD: PAN-SEARED

1 tablespoon extra-virgin olive oil
1 tablespoon walnut oil
2 skinless, boneless chicken breasts (about 2 pounds), halved, trimmed of all fat, and flattened to ½-inch thickness between plastic wrap
2 tablespoons unsalted butter
2 ounces fresh shiitake or wild mushrooms, or dried mushrooms rehydrated in 1 cup hot water for 30 minutes, drained, cleaned well, water reserved
¼ pound fresh mushrooms, cleaned and thinly sliced
4 shallots, finely shopped
2 cloves garlic, finely minced
2 cups defatted chicken stock (see page 9)
1 teaspoon chopped fresh thyme, or ¼ teaspoon dried
¼ teaspoon salt
¼ teaspoon freshly ground black pepper
1 teaspoon arrowroot, mixed with 1 tablespoon chicken stock

1. Heat the olive and walnut oils in a heavy skillet or sauté pan over high heat. Add the chicken breasts and sear for 30 seconds on each side. Remove to a platter and set aside.

2. Lower the heat to medium, and melt the butter. Add the mushrooms, shallots, and garlic. Cook, stirring frequently, for 5 minutes or until softened.

3. Turn the heat to medium high and add the stock, thyme, and salt and pepper. Bring to a boil, reduce the heat to medium, and continue cooking to reduce the liquid by half. Add the arrowroot mixture, stir to mix thoroughly, and simmer for 1 minute or more, or until the sauce is slightly thickened.

4. Return the chicken to the pan just long enough to heat through. Serve with the sauce drizzled on the chicken.

COLD POACHED CHICKEN BREASTS WITH FRESH PAPAYA CHUTNEY

The papaya chutney can be made up to two days in advance and stored, covered, in the refrigerator.

4 servings
METHOD: POACH

2 cups defatted chicken stock (see page 9)
Salt to taste
2 chicken breast (about 2 pounds), halved
1 clove garlic, finely minced
1 one-inch piece of peeled fresh ginger, grated
1 tablespoon mustard seed
¼ cup dark brown sugar
¼ cup sherry vinegar
1 large papaya (about 1 pound), peeled, seeded, and diced

1. Bring the stock to a boil in a skillet or saucepan. Lightly salt the liquid, add the chicken breasts, lower the heat, and simmer 9 to 10 minutes or just until done throughout. The breasts will be firm when pressed with the back of a fork. Transfer to a strainer and let cool to room temperature. Remove the bones and skin and discard. Cover with plastic wrap and chill.

2. In a heavy saucepan over medium heat, bring the garlic, ginger, mustard seed, sugar, and vinegar to a boil, reduce the amount of liquid by half.

3. Add the papaya and cook for about 2 minutes. Quickly remove the papaya with a slotted spoon, drain, and place in a bowl. Increase the heat to high and reduce the pan juices by half. Pour over the papaya. Refrigerate until well chilled, about 2 hours.

4. Slice the chicken breasts on the diagonal. Arrange the chicken breasts on individual plates and serve with the papaya chutney on the side.

SPA-STYLE CHICKEN BREASTS AND VEGETABLE LASAGNA

6 servings

2 skinless, boneless chicken breasts (about 2 pounds), trimmed of all fat and flattened to ⅓-inch thickness
8 ounces part-skim ricotta cheese
1 teaspoon chopped fresh oregano
1 tablespoon chopped fresh basil
8 ounces fresh whole wheat lasagna noodles, cooked, drained, and cooled
4 cups simple tomato and fresh herb sauce (see page 126)
1 pound carrots, scraped, thinly sliced on the diagonal, and blanched
1 pound zucchini, peeled and sliced into long thin strips
12 ounces spinach, stems removed, steamed for 1 minute and drained
½ cup grated part-skim mozzarella cheese

1. Preheat the oven to 150°F.

2. In a nonstick frying pan or a stovetop grilling pan, quickly sear the chicken for about 1 minute on each side. Set aside.

3. Mix the ricotta, oregano, and basil in a small bowl. Line the bottom of a 9 × 11-inch glass or ovenproof baking dish with a layer of tomato herb sauce. Top with a layer of noodles and tomato sauce. Add a layer of carrots, followed by layers of zucchini and spinach. Cover with half of the ricotta mixture, then layer the chicken pieces over the ricotta. Repeat, finishing with a layer of pasta. Cover with aluminum foil and bake for 30 to 45 minutes.

4. When the lasagna is nearly finished, heat the remaining tomato until bubbling.

5. Remove the lasagna from the oven, discard the foil and cut into portions. Top with the heated tomato sauce and sprinkle with mozzarella. Place the baking dish in the broiler set on high for 1 minute or just until the cheese melts. Serve immediately.

CREOLE CHICKEN

This dish can be served either hot or at room temperature.

4 servings

2 skinless, boneless chicken breasts (about 2 pounds), halved, all traces of fat removed and flattened to 1-inch thickness
Salt and freshly ground black pepper to taste
1 tablespoon extra-virgin olive oil
¾ cup finely chopped onion
¾ cup finely chopped celery
⅔ small green bell pepper, seeded, ribbed and finely chopped
2 large cloves garlic, minced
Pinch of cayenne pepper
¾ cup white wine
2 cups canned tomatoes, drained and coarsely chopped
¼ cup tomato paste
½ to 1 teaspoon Tabasco sauce to taste
3 tablespoons chopped flat-leaf parsley
½ teaspoon dried thyme
¼ teaspoon salt

1. Sprinkle the chicken with salt and pepper. Set aside.

2. Heat the oil in a sauté pan over medium-high heat. Add the onion, celery, green pepper, garlic, and cayenne and cook, stirring frequently, for 5 minutes, or just until the onion is wilted.

3. Add the chicken, wine, tomatoes, tomato paste, Tabasco, parsley, thyme, and salt. Bring to a boil, partially cover the pan, and cook for 6 to 8 minutes or just until the chicken is done. Do not overcook. Remove the chicken to a platter and cover to keep warm.

4. Raise the heat to high and reduce the sauce by half, stirring frequently and scraping up the bits on the bottom of the pan. Arrange the chicken on individual plates and spoon on the sauce, or serve at room temperature with warm sauce on the side.

SPA VINEGAR CHICKEN BREASTS

4 servings

1 small jalapeño pepper, seeded, stemmed, and minced (wear rubber gloves)
3 cloves garlic, minced
Juice of 1 lemon
2 large chicken breasts with upper wing and bones attached, skin and all traces of fat removed
1 cup defatted chicken stock (see page 9)
1 cup dry white wine
1 tablespoon extra-virgin olive oil
¼ cup red wine vinegar
2 tablespoons best quality white wine or champagne vinegar
1 tablespoon balsamic vinegar
Bouquet garni: 1 sprig fresh rosemary or 1 teaspoon dried, 1 tablespoon fresh tarragon or 1 teaspoon dried, 1 bunch parsley with stems, tied in a cheesecloth bag
2 tablespoons minced shallots
2 teaspoons tomato paste

1. Combine the jalapeño, garlic, and lemon juice. Spread over the chicken breasts and marinate, covered with plastic wrap, for 2 hours at room temperature.

2. Combine the stock and wine in a saucepan. Over high heat, reduce by half. Set aside.

3. Heat the olive oil in a nonstick skillet over medium heat. Add the chicken pieces, skinned side down, and cook about 3 to 5 minutes or until the breasts are well browned on one side. Turn over and cook, covered for 2 minutes more. Remove the chicken from the pan and set aside.

4. Pour any excess fat out of the pan. Over medium-high heat, deglaze the pan with the red, white, and Balsamic vinegars, stirring and scraping to loosen any browned bits on the bottom of the pan. Stir in the shallots, bouquet garni, tomato paste, and the stock and wine reduction. Raise the heat to high and reduce the liquid slightly.

5. Lower the heat, add the chicken breasts, and cook, partially covered, for about 5 minutes, or until the chicken is done and the sauce is thick.

Sauces & Purées

. . . TO SERVE WITH HOT AND COLD COOKED CHICKEN BREASTS

What can you add to stocks to create low-fat and non-fat sauces so rich in flavor that butter-laden sauces will never be missed again? This list of ingredients is long and wonderful, including puréed carrot, artichoke, spinach, watercress, tomato, beet, white corn, and fresh peas. Even aromatics such as oven roasted or smoked onions, roasted garlic, leeks, and shallots can be incorporated.

Here's How: The vegetables should be well peeled, cut, and pre-cooked before transferring to a blender or food processor. Add wine or vegetable stock (see recipes on pages 9–11), or equal amounts of both, and blend to a smooth purée. For a silky finish, add a teaspoon of butter or extra-virgin olive oil and season with a pinch of salt and freshly ground white pepper to taste. To thicken, heat and reduce slightly, or add ½ teaspoon of arrowroot to hot sauces and cook a few seconds longer, just until thickened. Don't overcook a purée-based sauce. Flavored stock sauces tend to be thinner then flour-thickened sauces or butter-based sauces. The real difference is the intensity and purity of flavor, and lack of fat or butter is a great bonus health wise. These sauces are at their best when paired with simply cooked chicken breasts (poach, roast, broil, grill, or sauté in a non-stick pan with just stock and a hint of added fat such as a teaspoon or two of extra-virgin olive oil or unsalted butter). Adjust the seasoning with salt and pepper to taste after the sauce is fully prepared, just before serving.

PERFECT POACHED CHICKEN BREASTS

When you intend to poach a chicken breast, here is a no-fail method that is also used in the recipes calling for poached breasts throughout this book. Think ahead and poach several at a time for the next day or for the freezer (wrapped tightly in plastic wrap and stored in a plastic freezer bag). This is the perfect high-protein food, easy to take to work (just grab a cooked one from the freezer), and ideal for a quick-fix dinner that incorporates chicken and one of the sauce or vinaigrette recipes in the section. See page 354 for optional poaching liquids that add a variety of stocks and flavor essences, such as white wine, lemon juice, herbs, peppercorns, and allspice berries, to the delicate white breast meat while gently simmering to the perfect poach:

ADVANCE PREPARATION

Many of the sauces in this section can be made in advance. They are especially delicious as chicken salad dressings, as dipping sauces, on sandwiches, pastas, grilled, broiled, and especially on hot and cold poached chicken breasts. To say the very least, this chapter contains a versatile group of recipes you will enjoy again and again, for many occasions.

Poaching Liquid

2 cups or more chicken stock (see page 8)
1 sprig flat-leaf parsley
1 celery top with leaf
Pinch of salt

2 chicken breasts (about 2 pounds), halved (skin and bone on or off)

1. In a high-sided skillet or saucepan, combine the chicken stock, parsley sprig, celery top, and salt. Reduce the heat to low and add the chicken breasts arranged in a single layer. Simmer and cook 8 to 10 minutes or just until done. The breasts will be firm when pressed with the back of a fork. Transfer to a strainer and, if on, remove the skin and bones and discard.

2. Serve hot with sauce, cool to room temperature, or chill for salad and other recipes. Or wrap tightly with plastic wrap and refrigerate to chill well.

FRESH TARRAGON SAUCE OR MARINADE

As a marinade: Marinate 1 to 1½ pounds cold poached chicken breast strips, refrigerated, for an hour. Remove the chicken and drain off the excess marinade before serving.

Makes about 3/4 cup

3 tablespoons tarragon wine vinegar
2 tablespoons minced fresh tarragon leaves
2 teaspoons Dijon mustard
Salt and freshly ground black pepper to taste
¾ cup extra-virgin olive oil

1. Combine the vinegar, tarragon, mustard, and salt and pepper to taste in a bowl. Whisk in the olive oil in a thin steady stream until well combined. Serve at room temperature or well chilled.

PURÉED FRESH VEGETABLE SAUCE

Makes about 1½ cup

¼ cup chicken stock (see page 8)
¾ cup dry white wine, (sauvignon blanc or chardonnay)
⅓ cup peeled, chopped carrot
⅓ cup sliced celery
⅓ cup chopped zucchini
½ cup chopped onion
½ cup peeled, seeded, and chopped tomato
Salt and freshly ground white pepper to taste

1. In a medium saucepan, bring the stock, wine, carrot, celery, zucchini, and onion to a boil. Reduce the heat to low, cover, and simmer for 10 minutes. Cool slightly.

2. Transfer to a blender or food processer, add the tomato, and blend until smooth.

3. Return the sauce to the pan, bring to a simmer, and reduce by half. Season with salt and pepper to taste. Serve warm or at room temperature.

CHARDONNAY AND YELLOW PEPPER PURÉE

This can be served hot or cold.

Makes 1 cup or 1½ cups with sour cream

1 large yellow bell pepper, cored, seeded, and coarsely chopped
¾ cup dry white wine (sauvignon blanc or chardonnay)
¾ cup defatted chicken stock (see page 9)
3 cloves garlic, chopped
Salt and freshly ground black pepper to taste
½ cup sour cream (optional), regular or light, at room temperature

1. Combine the yellow pepper, wine, chicken stock, and garlic in a medium saucepan. Over medium-low heat, simmer about 10 minutes, or until soft. Remove the peppers with a slotted spoon, set aside, and continue simmering until the stock is reduced by half. Cool.

2. Combine the reduced stock and peppers in a blender or a bowl of a food processor and process until smooth. Season with salt and pepper to taste. Return to the pan, stir in the sour cream, and swirl the pan over very low heat to warm through. If serving cold, chill the sauce thoroughly. Stir in chilled sour cream before serving.

APRICOT-MUSTARD SAUCE

Makes about 1 cup

1 cup best quality apricot preserves
2 teaspoons white wine or champagne vinegar
2 tablespoons Dijon mustard
Salt and freshly ground black pepper to taste

1. In a small saucepan, heat the preserves, vinegar, mustard, pepper, and salt over low heat until warmed through and the preserves melt.

2. Transfer to a blender and blend until smooth. Transfer to a serving bowl and serve warm or at room temperature.

HOMEMADE JALAPEÑO MAYONNAISE

Makes about 1 cup

2 jalapeño chiles, roasted, peeled, seeded, deveined, and finely minced
1 tablespoon fresh lime juice
1 tablespoon fresh lemon juice
⅔ to 1 cup mayonnaise, regular or reduced fat, or homemade (see page 123)
1 tablespoon finely chopped fresh cilantro

1. Mix together the jalapeños, lime and lemon juices, and the mayonnaise in a bowl.

2. Cover and chill. Fold in the cilantro just before serving.

YOGURT HORSERADISH SAUCE

Makes 1½ cups

½ cup sour cream, regular or light
½ cup plain yogurt, regular or low fat
3 tablespoons grated horseradish, freshly grated or jarred and drained
2 tablespoons coarse-grain mustard
Salt to taste
1 tablespoon clover blossom honey

1. In a medium bowl, whisk the sour cream, yogurt, horseradish, mustard, salt, and honey together until well combined.

2. Chill well before serving.

FRESH DILL AND DIJON SAUCE

Makes about 1 cup
3 tablespoons spicy brown mustard
3 tablespoons Dijon mustard
3 tablespoons white wine vinegar
1 tablespoon sugar
Salt and freshly ground white pepper to taste
½ cup canola or other light vegetable oil
½ cup chopped fresh dill leaves

1. Combine both mustards, the vinegar, sugar, and salt and pepper to taste in a bowl. Whisk in the oil in a thin steady stream until smooth and well blended.

2. Stir in the dill. If you're not using the sauce immediately, whisk again before serving.

WATERCRESS SAUCE

Makes about 1 cup

Salt to taste
4 bunches fresh watercress, stems removed, well washed, dried in a salad spinner
2 tablespoons sour cream, regular or light
1 tablespoon fresh lemon juice
Freshly ground black pepper to taste

1. In a large sauce pan or stockpot of lightly salted boiling water, blanch the watercress leaves for 3 minutes. Drain, reserving ½ cup of the liquid.

2. Transfer the watercress to a blender, and adding 1 tablespoon of the reserved cooking liquid at a time, blend to a purée. Transfer to a bowl, cover, and chill.

3. Just before serving, stir in the sour cream until well combined, and then stir in the lemon juice. Adjust the seasoning with salt and pepper to taste.

SPICY BLACK MUSHROOM SAUCE

Makes about 1 cup

12 dried black Oriental or oyster mushrooms, softened in 1 cup of hot water, drained and liquid reserved, cleaned with a brush of all dirt particles
2 teaspoons peanut oil
½ cup chile sauce (see page 29)
½ cup medium dry sherry
2 tablespoons soy sauce or tamari, regular or reduced sodium
2 tablespoons red wine vinegar
2 tablespoons dark brown sugar
2 teaspoons Szechuan chile paste with garlic*

***Available in Asian markets and some supermarkets**

1. Wash the mushrooms well, pat dry, and chop finely.

2. Heat the peanut oil in a small skillet. Cook the mushrooms over low heat about 5 minutes or until tender and the moisture has almost evaporated.

3. Combine the chile sauce, sherry, soy sauce, vinegar, brown sugar, chile paste, and the reserved mushroom liquid in a small saucepan, bring to a boil, then reduce the heat to medium. Cook 7 to 8 minutes, or until thickened as desired. Serve warm or at room temperature. (*Note:* This can be processed to a smooth mushroom sauce in a food processor or blender.)

HOMEMADE LEMON MAYONNAISE

Makes about 3 cups

1 whole egg plus 2 egg yolks
½ cup fresh lemon juice
Salt and freshly ground white pepper to taste
2 ½ cups extra-virgin olive oil, canola oil, or other light vegetable oil

1. Combine the egg, yolks, lemon juice, a scant amount of salt and pepper in a blender or food processor, and blend until smooth.

2. With the motor running, pour in the olive oil a few small drops at a time at first, and then in a thin steady stream until thoroughly incorporated and emulsified. Adjust seasoning with salt and pepper to taste. Refrigerate in a glass jar until ready to use.

FRESH TOMATO & SHERRY VINAIGRETTE

Makes about 2½ cups

1 shallot, minced
⅓ cup sherry wine vinegar
2 sprigs fresh tarragon leaves
1 tablespoon tomato paste
¼ cup rich chicken stock (see page 8)
1 large ripe tomato, peeled, seeded, and diced
½ cup extra-virgin olive oil
2 cups tomato juice (unsalted)
Salt and freshly ground black pepper to taste

1. Combine the shallot, vinegar, tarragon, tomato paste, and water in a saucepan. Over medium-high heat, cook until the mixture is reduced by two-thirds. Let cool to room temperature.

2. Put the cooked mixture in a blender of food processor bowl. Add the tomato and process until very smooth.

3. With the machine running, add the olive oil in a thin steady stream until well incorporated. Add the tomato juice and blend thoroughly. Season with salt and pepper to taste. Refrigerate until well chilled. Stir before serving.

CHILLED ANCHOVY MUSTARD SAUCE

Makes about 1 3/4 cups

2 egg yolks
3 tablespoons Dijon mustard
1 2-ounce can anchovies, soaked in water for 30 minutes, drained, and dried
Juice of 1 lemon
1 shallot, peeled and chopped
1 cup canola oil or other light vegetable oil
¼ cup crème fraîche or sour cream
Salt and freshly ground black pepper to taste

1. Combine the egg yolks and mustard in a blender or food processor until smooth. Add in the anchovies, lemon juice, and shallot and blend until light and foamy.

2. With the blender running, add the oil in a thin steady stream until well incorporated. Transfer the mixture to a bowl. Fold in the crème fraîche or sour cream. Season with salt and pepper to taste. Chill well before serving.

YOGURT CUCUMBER SAUCE

Makes about 2 1/2 cups

1 ½ cups plain yogurt, regular or low-fat
2 teaspoons chopped fresh dill
1 tablespoon sugar
2 tablespoons canola or other light vegetable oil
Juice of 2 lemons
2 tablespoons white wine vinegar
1 cucumber, peeled, seeded, quartered lengthwise, and very thinly sliced
4 scallions, white and some of the green parts, coarsely chopped
Salt and freshly ground white pepper to taste

1. Combine the yogurt, dill, sugar, oil, lemon juice, and vinegar in a blender and blend until smooth. Transfer to a bowl.

2. Add the cucumber and scallion. Chill well before serving.

SWEET CURRY SAUCE

Makes about 2 cups

1 cup plain yogurt, regular or fat-reduced
1 clove garlic, minced
2 tablespoons mild curry powder (Madras if available)
3 tablespoons extra-virgin olive oil
2 teaspoons sugar
Juice of 2 medium oranges
2 tablespoons fresh lemon juice
2 tablespoons chopped fruit chutney (such as Major Grey's mango chutney; peach, apple-spice, pineapple chutney, etc.)
Salt and freshly ground white pepper to taste
1 ounce best-quality gin

1. Combine the sour cream and the yogurt in a small bowl.

2. In a saucepan over very low heat, cook the garlic and curry powder in the olive oil for 5 minutes. Remove from the heat and stir into the sour cream. Add the sugar, orange and lemon juice, chutney, and salt and pepper to taste, stir until well combined. Over very low heat, swirl the pan just to warm the ingredients.

3. Transfer the mixture to a bowl and stir in the gin. Or, chill before serving and stir in the gin.

LEMONY HORSERADISH CREAM

Makes about 2 cups

¾ cup heavy cream
½ cup grated horseradish, fresh or jarred, well drained
2 teaspoons Dijon mustard
½ cup homemade lemon mayonnaise (see page 123), or best quality mayonnaise mixed with ¼ cup lemon juice 4 hours prior to using
1 teaspoon lemon zest
Pinch of sugar
Salt and freshly ground white pepper to taste

1. In a high-sided bowl, whip the cream with a whisk or electric blender until soft peaks form.

2. Combine the horseradish, mustard, and mayonnaise in another bowl. Using a rubber scraper, gently fold the mixture into the whipped cream. Add the zest, sugar, and salt and pepper, stir gently to combine well. Serve chilled.

TOMATO HERB SAUCE OR VINAIGRETTE

Makes about 2 cups

Tomato Sauce

1 tablespoon extra-virgin olive oil
½ cup chopped onion
2 cloves garlic, finely minced
½ teaspoon sugar
1 teaspoon dried basil
1 teaspoon dried oregano
1 teaspoon freshly ground black pepper
1 teaspoon salt
1 can (8 ounces) plum tomatoes, drained and chopped

Vinaigrette

1 tablespoon red wine vinegar
1 teaspoon chopped fresh basil
1 tablespoon extra-virgin olive oil
Salt and freshly ground black pepper to taste
Few drops Tabasco sauce (optional)

1. To make the sauce, heat the oil over medium heat in a small saucepan. Add the onion and garlic and cook about 3 minutes or until tender but not brown.

2. Stir in the sugar, basil, oregano, pepper, salt and tomatoes. Cook 8 to 10 minutes or over medium heat, partially covered, to desired thickness. Serve hot

3. To make the vinaigrette, make the sauce as in steps 1. At the end of step 2, continue reducing the sauce to a thicker consistency. Cool the tomato sauce to room temperature. In a food processor or blender, combine the sauce with the vinegar, basil and the olive oil. Pulse a few times to mix well. Adjust seasoning with salt and pepper to taste. Add a few drops of Tabasco sauce if desired.

RECIPES FOR THE WAY WE *COOK!*

Bake & Roast

Baking and roasting are high atop the list of cooking methods for the quick- cooking chicken breast. Many recipes in this section can even be prepared ahead of time and then popped in the oven just before the dish is served. These recipes tend to take a little longer on the preparation end of the process than a stir-fry or sauté, but the baking or roasting time is usually under 30 minutes. Little attention is required once the baking pan has entered the oven. The variety of different baking and roasting recipes is extraordinary. Just think of bubbling, homey, one-dish casseroles filled with lots of flavorful ingredients, time-saving, even calorie-saving dishes, all with lots of flavor.

Some of the recipes in this chapter are ideal for special occasions and for entertaining. Olive and Feta-Stuffed Chicken Rolls are fancy enough to be served on your best china. Chicken Pot Pie with bubbling tender chicken breast pieces, spring vegetables, and a potato topping is definitely "comfort gourmet," if there is such a thing. Even the everyday favorites found in this chapter, like Glazed Chicken Loaf, Chicken, Rice, and Spinach-Filled Cabbage Rolls, Pizza with the Works!, and tantalizing Layered Chicken Enchiladas are excellent fare and appeal to almost everyone with an appetite. Just set the oven to 350°F (or as directed) and dig into these wonderful opportunities.

SPICE-RUBBED CHICKEN BREASTS WITH PINEAPPLE SALSA

Though these flavors may seem Southwestern in nature, they are influenced by typical Southern barbecue with a touch of the tropics on the side. The pineapple or mango relish adds a balance to the spicy chicken and is a natural complement to the chicken. See the recipe for a Mango Salsa variation below.

4 servings

Pineapple Salsa

1 cup finely chopped fresh pineapple
¼ cup pineapple preserves or ½ cup fresh pineapple, 2 tablespoon pineapple juice and 1 tablespoon sugar cooked until soft and reduced to ¼ cup
⅓ cup finely chopped red onion
¼ cup finely chopped cilantro
1 tablespoon finely chopped seeded jalapeño (optional)
½ teaspoon freshly ground black pepper
2 skinless, boneless chicken breasts (about 2 pounds), halved
½ teaspoon salt
½ teaspoon garlic powder
1 teaspoon each: chile powder, paprika, onion powder, ground cumin
¼ teaspoon dried thyme

1. To make the salsa, combine the pineapple, pineapple preserves or reduced cooked pineapple, red onion, cilantro, jalapeño (if using), and black pepper in a medium glass bowl. Stir to mix well, cover with plastic wrap, and chill before serving.

2. To prepare the chicken, place the chicken breasts on a flat work surface. Season with salt. In a small bowl, combine the chile powder, paprika, onion powder, cumin, and thyme. Rub the chicken with the spice mixture on all sides. Marinate, refrigerated, for 30 minutes. Let the chicken come to room temperature before baking.

3. Preheat the oven to 325°F.

4. Transfer the chicken breast to a baking pan coated lightly with a cooking spray. Bake for about 18 to 20 minute or until done throughout. Do not overcook.

5. With a sharp knife, cut into ⅓ inch slices. Arrange on plates and serve with salsa on the side.

Variation: Mango Salsa

1 large fresh ripe mango, peeled, flesh removed, and chopped
¼ cup red bell pepper
½ small serrano or jalapeño chile, seeded, deveined, and finely chopped
2 shallots or ½ small red onion finely chopped
2 tablespoons finely chopped cilantro or flat-leaf parsley
2 tablespoons fresh lime juice
Pinch of salt

Combine all the ingredients in a medium pottery or glass bowl. Cover the bowl with plastic wrap and chill before serving.

FRESH GINGER AND COCONUT BAKED CHICKEN BREASTS

This sweet and spicy Asian-style chicken breast recipe can be made with the bone left on or removed. If leaving the bone on the breast, turn the breast meat in the marinade and spoon some over the bone portion. This recipe also works well cooked on the grill over hot coals. Ultimately, chicken and the coconut-ginger flavor combination marry well, especially with the long marinating time. Serve with parsley or cilantro rice, tossed with toasted sesame seeds.

4 servings

2 skinless, boneless chicken breasts (2 pounds), halved
1 tablespoon grated peeled fresh ginger
2 tablespoons chopped fresh cilantro or flat-leaf parsley
2 tablespoons chopped peeled fresh lemongrass*
⅓ cup bottled or fresh coconut milk
3 tablespoons honey
2 ½ tablespoons Asian fish sauce*
1 tablespoon Thai chile sauce*
2 cloves garlic

***Available in Asian markets or some specialty stores**

1. Place the chicken breasts in a glass dish.

2. Place the ginger, cilantro or parsley, lemongrass, coconut milk, honey, fish sauce, chile sauce, and garlic in a blender or mini food processor. Blend or process until smooth. Pour over the chicken breasts, cover tightly with plastic wrap, and marinate, refrigerated, for 1 to 2 hours, turning in the marinade several times.

3. Preheat the oven to 350°F.

4. Transfer the breasts to a baking pan coated with cooking spray. Bake for about 25 to 30 minutes or until the breasts are done throughout. Serve hot or room temperature.

BAKED CHICKEN BREASTS WITH ONION PARSLEY SAUCE

This is similar to a classic Spanish sauce which can be served beside the baked chicken or, as in this recipe, baked on the chicken.

4 servings

2 skinless, boneless chicken breasts (about 1½ pounds), halved and flattened slightly between plastic wrap
Salt and freshly ground black pepper to taste
2 cups flat-leaf parsley leaves, stems removed
1 small sweet Vidalia or Maui onion, chopped
1 small red onion, chopped
⅓ cup clam juice or dry white wine
2 tablespoons fresh lime juice
2 cloves garlic
1 scallion, mostly green part, finely chopped

1. Preheat the oven to 350°F.

2. Arrange the chicken breasts on a baking pan lightly coated with cooking spray. Season with a scant amount of salt and pepper.

3. In a blender or mini food processor, add the parsley, both onions, clam juice or wine, lime juice, a scant amount of and garlic. Process until smooth.

4. Spoon the parsley sauce over the chicken breasts and bake 18 to 20 minutes or until done throughout. Sprinkle with chopped scallion and serve hot.

OVEN FRIED CHICKEN

It's a surprising twist on traditional skin-on stove-top fried chicken. This approach creates equally juicy and tender chicken, eliminating the mess and calories of the deep-fried type.

4 to 6 servings

2 cups buttermilk, regular or low-fat
3 boneless chicken breasts (about 3 pounds), skin on, halved
¾ cup all-purpose flour
1½ teaspoon salt
1 teaspoon ground red pepper
½ teaspoon freshly ground white pepper
1 teaspoon paprika, hot or sweet

1. Combine the chicken pieces and buttermilk in a shallow glass or pottery dish. Marinate, refrigerated, for 1 hour.

2. Preheat the oven to 450°F.

3. In a shallow dish or pie plate, combine the flour, salt, red and white peppers, and paprika, and mix well. Remove the buttermilk from the chicken breast pieces and discard. Dredge the chicken one piece at a time through the flour mixture coating well and shaking any excess flour back into the dish. Place the pieces bone side down on a baking sheet lined with parchment paper. When all the pieces are coated with flour, lightly coat with cooking spray on the top.

4. Bake for 10 minutes at 450°F, then lower the heat to 300°F and keep baking for 15 to 18 minutes more or until chicken is crispy, browned, and done throughout. Serve hot or at room temperature.

GRAPE LEAVES, FIG LEAVES, AND CHICKEN BREASTS

These two types of leaves add both good looks and great taste to your chicken breasts. Their flavor is subtle, but comes right through. When you wrap a chicken breast in either of these leaves, tie it shut, and cook it (either on a grill or in the oven), the essence from the grape or fig leaf imparts a distinctive flavor. Begin by washing the leaves well. Lightly spray one side with vegetable oil cooking spray. Place the chicken breast, salt and pepper to taste, and a few of your favorite fresh herbs in the center of the leaf and fold in the edges to make a package. Place them opening side down on an ovenproof baking sheet lightly sprayed with cooking spray, and bake at 350°F for 15 to 20 minutes, or until the chicken is done throughout. Serve in the leaves and let each person remove the chicken breast from its natural package. You begin to sense Napa, Provence, or Tuscany in every bite. And, naturally, a leaf doesn't add a drop of fat to your feast.

CHICKEN BREAST BAKED WITH MIXED OLIVES

Use a mix of Mediterranean olives, including dark plum Kalamatas, green Picholines, the tiny, red, tart Niçoise olives, or brine-cured Italian Gaetas olives that are usually packed in oil and drained well before using. This is a dish for olive aficionados. Serve with fluffy rice, couscous, or oven-fresh country bread.

4 to 6 servings

1 cup finely chopped onion
1 large onion, very thinly sliced
¾ cup chopped fresh flat-leaf parsley
2 tablespoons extra-virgin olive oil
2 teaspoons finely chopped garlic
½ teaspoon ground oregano
1 ½ teaspoon paprika, sweet or hot to taste
½ saffron thread crumbled
3 chicken breasts (about 3 pounds) halved, (skinned and boned if desired)
1 cup white wine (chardonnay)
1 cup rich chicken stock (see page 9)
2 cups mixed olives (see note above), drained, rinsed, pitted, and left whole or in large pieces
¼ cup lemon juice
2 tablespoons flat-leaf parsley leaves for garnish

1. Preheat the oven to 350°F.

2. In a Dutch oven or large, covered oven-proof skillet, combine the chopped and sliced onion, parsley, olive oil, garlic, pepper, salt, oregano paprika, saffron, wine, stock, and the chicken. Bring to a boil, transfer the pan to the oven and cook, uncovered, for 5 minutes.

3. Add the olives and the lemon juice. Cover and continue baking for 30 minutes more.

4. Transfer the chicken pieces into individual large pasta bowls, divide the olive mix among the bowls. Garnish with parsley.

A WARNING ABOUT WARMING

Leaving the chicken breasts in the oven to keep them warm can be a disaster. When they're done, they're done! This delicate meat can quickly reach the point of no return. To serve the chicken hot, remove the chicken breasts from the oven, tent with a piece of aluminum foil, and try to serve the breasts within 5 minutes.

ROASTED CHICKEN BREAST, POTATO, AND VEGETABLE PLATTER

There nothing like roasting to bring out the deep flavors of vegetables, and no more perfect accompaniment for roasted chicken breasts. This is a quick and easy one-pan version of a very basic dish.

6 servings

1 pound fingerling potatoes, scrubbed and halved lengthwise
1 pound Yukon Gold potatoes, scrubbed and halved lengthwise
¼ cup extra-virgin olive oil
Salt and freshly ground black pepper to taste
3 boneless chicken breasts (about 3 pounds), halved
1 pound medium asparagus spears, trimmed and halved
6 ripe plum tomatoes, halved
¼ cup pitted black Kalamata olives, rinsed
2 teaspoons fresh thyme or 1 teaspoon dried

1. Preheat the oven to 400°F.

2. Combine all the potatoes in a large mixing bowl. Drizzle on 1 tablespoon olive oil. Toss to coat the pieces well, add a generous amount of salt and pepper, and toss again.

3. Transfer the potatoes to a baking sheet and roast 15 minutes.

4. Meanwhile, place the chicken breasts in the same bowl, drizzle on 1 tablespoon of the olive oil, sprinkle with salt and pepper, and toss to coat well. Place the chicken around the outside of the potatoes on the same baking sheet, cook 5 minutes, then lower the heat to 350°F.

5. In the same bowl, toss the asparagus with 1 tablespoon of the olive oil and a scant amount of salt and pepper. Add to the chicken and potatoes in the oven. Continue roasting 10 minutes.

6. In the same bowl, combine the tomatoes, olives, and thyme with the remaining tablespoon of olive oil. Add to the roasting potatoes and chicken, cut side down, and continue roasting 5 minutes more or until the tomatoes are softened and the chicken is done throughout.

7. Transfer to a serving platter and arrange the roasted vegetables in the center and the chicken breast pieces around the side. Serve hot.

CHICKEN POT PIE WITH A POTATO TOP

Try this wonderful looking, and tasting, dish for a special family dinner.

4 servings

2 pounds boiling potatoes, peeled and cubed

2 cups milk, low or non-fat

Salt and freshly ground white pepper to taste

½ cup buttermilk, regular or lowfat

1 tablespoon finely grated Parmesan cheese

4 skinless, boneless chicken breast (about 1½ pounds), halved and cut into bite-sized pieces

3 teaspoons canola or other light vegetable oil

4 shallots, very thinly sliced

1 garlic clove, minced

1 small leek, white part only, washed, quartered lengthwise, and thinly sliced

2½ cups chicken stock (see page 8)

½ pound mushrooms, stemmed and sliced

½ cup dry white wine

2 medium carrots, peeled, cut into matchsticks

1 cup peas, fresh or frozen, and defrosted

2 tablespoons cornstarch dissolved in 3 tablespoons chicken stock

½ tablespoon finely chopped flat-leaf parsley

1 teaspoon finely chopped fresh thyme

1 tablespoon finely chopped fresh chives for garnish

1. In a large saucepan, combine the potato cubes, milk, and 2 cups water, or more to cover. Bring to a boil over medium-high heat, lightly salt the water, and cook until the potatoes are tender, about 12 to 15 minutes. Drain thoroughly. In a mixing bowl, mash the potatoes, adding the buttermilk a little at a time until no lumps remain. Season with salt and pepper. Add ½ tablespoon of the Parmesan. Stir to mix well and set aside.

2. Lightly season the chicken with salt and pepper. In a large sauté pan or skillet, heat 1 teaspoon of the oil over medium-high heat. Add the chicken and sauté 2 to 3 minutes per side or just until browned. Remove to a platter and set aside.

3. In the same pan, heat 1 more teaspoon of the oil over medium heat. Add the shallots, garlic, and leek and cook, stirring frequently, until tender. Add 1¼ cups of the chicken stock, bring to a boil, and cook for 3 minutes to reduce slightly. Transfer to a bowl.

4. In the same pan, heat the remaining 1 teaspoon of oil over medium heat. Add the mushrooms and cook until the mushroom liquid has evaporated, about 5 minutes. Add the remaining 1¼ cups stock, wine, carrots, and peas and lower the heat and simmer about 4 minutes or until the vegetables are just crisp-tender. Remove the vegetables with a slotted spoon and set aside.

5. Increase the heat to high and reduce the stock by one third or about 8 minutes. Lower the heat, stir in the cornstarch mixture, and simmer about 3 to 4 minutes or until the sauce is thick. Remove from the heat.

6. Add the chicken, parsley, and thyme to the pan. Season with salt and pepper to taste.

7. Preheat the oven to 350°F. Lightly coat a one-quart, high-sided, ovenproof baking dish (such as a soufflé dish) with cooking spray. Fill with the chicken, all the vegetables, and the sauce.

8. Top with the mashed potatoes and smooth to cover the surface of the chicken mixture completely. Set the dish on a larger baking sheet and bake for 20 to 25 minutes or until the chicken and vegetables are bubbling hot and done.

9. Turn the heat to broil. Sprinkle the potato top with the remaining Parmesan and brown under the broiler for about 20 to 30 seconds. Watch carefully not to burn the Parmesan. Sprinkle the top with the chopped chives.

FREE-RANGE FOR FANCY FARE

Free-range chickens are the top of the line, so to speak. Buy them at Whole Foods Markets, a wonderful healthy and organic food emporium filled with gourmet and everyday items (this store is located coast to coast). Discover the flavor of free-range birds for yourself. Cage-free are a definite cut above the commercially raised chickens. The taste and texture of the meat is noticably different, and, in fact, free-range chickens are leaner than those that just stand around eating and getting fat. These chicken breasts tend to be larger and plumper, a plus for making elegant meals, especially for stuffed dishes. And they roast beautifully! Yes, as you might have guessed, the price is higher. In this case it's worth it, just like fresh herbs, good wine, hearth-baked bread, farm-fresh cheeses, and extra-virgin olive oil are worth their higher price tags.

CHICKEN, RICE, AND SPINACH-FILLED CABBAGE ROLLS

This updated version of a classic cabbage roll is surprisingly hearty though calorie-conscious.

4 servings

12 large green cabbage leaves
1 skinless, boneless chicken breast (about 1 pound), finely chopped
¼ medium onion, finely chopped
½ medium carrot, peeled and finely chopped
¼ teaspoon dried rosemary
¼ teaspoon salt
½ teaspoon freshly ground black pepper
1 pound fresh spinach leaves, stemmed
1½ cups cooked brown or white rice
1 large egg, beaten
2 tablespoons finely grated Parmesan cheese
Pinch of nutmeg
½ to 1 cup chicken stock (see page 8)
Freshly cracked black pepper

1. Fill a large bowl with ice-cold water. In a stockpot, bring lightly salted water to a boil. Blanch the cabbage leaves 4 at a time for about 1 minute, or until the thickest part bends easily. Plunge into the cold water. Drain on paper towels and pat dry.

2. In a sauté pan or nonstick skillet, heat the oil over medium heat. Add the chicken in a single layer and cook for 3 minutes. Add the onion, carrot, rosemary, and salt and pepper, and cook, stirring frequently, about 5 minutes or until the vegetables are tender. Add the spinach, spreading it evenly over the other ingredients, cover, and cook about 2 to 3 minutes more or until wilted.

3. Transfer the chicken mixture to a large bowl to cool slightly. Add the cooked rice, egg, Parmesan, and nutmeg, and stir to combine.

4. Preheat the oven to 350°F. Lightly coat a 9 × 13-inch glass baking dish with cooking spray.

5. Place the cabbage leaves, hard rib side up, on a flat work surface. Using a paring knife, trim off the thick portion of the rib down the center but without cutting through to the other side, so the leaves can easily be rolled over. Turn the leaves over.

6. Divide the stuffing into 12 equal portions and place in the center of the leaves. Fold the trimmed end over the stuffing, fold in each side, and then roll up the top to form a bundle about 3 inches long. Place the bundles, seam side down, in the baking dish. The bundles should be touching but not tightly packed together.

7. Pour over the chicken stock. Bake for 20 to 25 minutes, or until the stuffing is cooked through. Sprinkle with freshly cracked pepper before serving.

BAKED CHICKEN-STUFFED ZUCCHINI

Buy zucchini that are all the same size and length so that they cook evenly. Your choice of squash need not be limited to zucchini. Try stuffing round patty pan and crookneck yellow summer squash to make a trio of interesting presentation. Serve piping hot or warm on a buffet with equal success.

4 to 6 servings

Salt to taste
9 medium zucchinis
2 tablespoons extra-virgin olive oil
2 shallots, minced
1 pound mushrooms, stemmed and finely chopped
1 pound ground skinless, boneless chicken breast
1 cup fresh bread crumbs
⅓ cup finely grated Parmesan cheese
¼ cup chopped flat-leaf parsley
Freshly ground black pepper to taste

1. Finely chop one of the zucchini. Halve the remaining eight zucchini lengthwise, scrape out the seeds, and discard, leaving a center well in each half.

2. Place the chopped zucchini in a small strainer. Sprinkle with a pinch of salt and let drain for 30 minutes. Sprinkle a scant amount of salt on the inside of each of the zucchini halves and place, cut side down, on paper towels to drain for 30 minutes. Pat both the chopped zucchini and the zucchini halves dry with paper towels.

3. Preheat the oven to 325°F.

4. In a large sauté pan or nonstick skillet, heat 1 tablespoon of the oil over medium heat. Add the shallots and cook, stirring constantly, for about 4 minutes or until translucent. Add the mushrooms, sprinkle with salt, and cook about 7 minutes or until the liquid has evaporated and the mushrooms are brown. Transfer to a bowl and set aside.

5. Add the ground chicken breast to the skillet and cook over medium-high heat, stirring constantly, about 4 minutes or just until browned. Add to the mushrooms. Set aside.

6. In a clean, large nonstick skillet, heat the remaining 1 tablespoon of oil over medium heat. Add the chopped zucchini and cook about 3 minutes or until tender. Add to the chicken mixture, along with the breadcrumbs, half of the Parmesan, and half of the parsley. Adjust the seasoning with salt and pepper to taste.

7. Mound the mixture evenly into the well of each zucchini half. Arrange in a decorative ovenproof baking dish. Bake for 20 minutes, or until the zucchini is tender. In the last 5 minutes of baking, sprinkle the tops with the remaining Parmesan, parsley, and a few grinds of the pepper mill. Serve hot or warm.

HERB AND MUSTARD BAKED CHICKEN WITH FAVA BEANS

4 to 6 servings

1 pound fava beans, removed from pods
3 tablespoons coarse-grain Dijon mustard
2 tablespoons extra-virgin olive oil
2 shallots, minced
3 large garlic cloves, minced
1 tablespoon chopped fresh thyme
1 teaspoon finely chopped fresh rosemary leaves
2 skinless, boneless chicken breasts (about 2 pounds), halved, quartered
2 teaspoons unsalted butter
¼ cup red wine vinegar
¼ cup light red wine (such as pinot noir or beaujolais)
2½ cups chicken stock (see page 8)
2 tablespoons tomato paste
Salt and freshly ground black pepper to taste
Fresh thyme sprigs for garnish

1. Bring lightly salted water to a boil in a saucepan. Drop in the fava beans all at the same time and blanch for 3 minutes. Drain, cool, and peel off the skins.

2. Combine 2 tablespoons of the mustard, 1 tablespoon of the oil, shallots, garlic, thyme, and rosemary in a small mixing bowl and mix to a paste.

3. Place the chicken pieces in a baking dish and rub all sides evenly with the mixture. Cover tightly with plastic wrap and marinate, refrigerated, for 1 hour.

4. Preheat the oven to 350°F. In a large sauté pan or nonstick skillet, heat the remaining 1 tablespoon of oil and 1 teaspoon of the butter over medium-high heat. Add the chicken pieces and sauté about 2 to 3 minutes or until brown on all sides. Transfer to a baking dish, cover tightly with foil, and bake for 8 to 10 or until the chicken pieces are tender and done throughout.

5. Meanwhile, add the vinegar to the skillet and boil until the liquid is almost evaporated. Over high heat, add the red wine and deglaze the pan scraping up any bits in the bottom of the pan, and reduce by half. Add the chicken stock and tomato paste and continue cooking for 5 to 6 minutes more or until the sauce has reduced by half. Pour into a clean saucepan.

6. Heat the remaining 1 teaspoon of butter in the skillet over medium heat. Add the beans and cook for 2 to 3 minutes. Add to the sauce, lower the heat, and stir in the remaining tablespoon of mustard. Simmer until the beans are tender. Adjust the seasoning with salt and pepper to taste.

7. To assemble, use a large decorative platter. Remove the beans from the sauce with a slotted spoon and place on the platter. Nestle the chicken pieces over the beans and spoon over the sauce, and garnish with sprigs of parsley.

CHICKEN BREASTS IN A PAPER POUCH

Or, as the French say, *en Papillote*. In searching out methods and techniques of cooking chicken breasts that are intrinsically quick but also fun, I found one that is becoming more popular in my kitchen and now all over the country. Properly called *en papillote*, this French technique is cooking food in a parchment paper pouch. (Aluminum foil may be substituted, but it isn't as romantic, so the French would definitely give this suggestion the thumbs down.) The delicate, lean, skinless, boneless chicken breast meat cooks in its own juices and joins with the other ingredients *en papillote*, bubbling together in the no-leak pouch. The pouch puffs up or inflates during cooking, which is a distinct trademark of this method of baking chicken breasts. When each *papillote* is slit through the top to reveal the cooked food within, the unique presentation is enhanced by a burst of enticing aromas. (Try tying the ends with kitchen string, the package makes its own attractive serving dish.) Remember to fill the pouch with quick cooking ingredients, like matchstick cut vegetables and fresh chopped herbs, so that everything is perfectly done at the same time.

PIZZA WITH THE WORKS!

2 to 4 servings

¾ pound ground skinless, boneless chicken breast
¾ cup chopped onion
¼ cup chopped green or red bell pepper
1 cup thinly sliced mushrooms
2 small cloves garlic, minced
1 tablespoon cornmeal
Salt and freshly ground black pepper to taste
2 9-inch, pre-made frozen pizza dough, thawed
2 cups Tomato-Herb Sauce (see page 126), reduced to very thick
1½ cups grated mozzarella
⅓ cup finely grated Romano cheese
Red pepper flakes to taste

1. In a large sauté pan or nonstick skillet lightly sprayed with cooking spray, cook the chicken over medium-high heat for 2 to 3 minutes. Add the onion, bell pepper, mushrooms, and garlic and cook, stirring constantly for about 3 to 4 minutes or until the chicken is done. Pour into a fine mesh strainer and let drain over a bowl. Season with salt and pepper to taste. Set aside.

2. Preheat the oven to 400°F.

3. Spray 2 9-inch round pizza pans (or baking sheets) with cooking spray. Sprinkle the cornmeal evenly onto the two pans. Place the pizza dough on the pans and push into the inner rim to secure. Spoon the sauce evenly over the dough and spread it all around. Divide the chicken mixture over the sauce. Distribute the mozzarella on top and sprinkle with the Romano cheese and red pepper flakes.

4. Bake in the center of the oven for 10 to 12 minutes, or until the crust is browned and the edges are crisp. Serve with more cheese and red pepper flakes on the side.

HOW TO STUFF CHICKEN BREASTS

Chicken breasts conveniently become envelopes for almost any type of tasty stuffing. Since the pocket is small, stuffing the breasts with intense flavorings is best. First, put a skinned and boned chicken breast in the freezer for 30 minutes. Remove it to a work surface, skin side up. Insert the tip of a sharp boning knife into the thickest part of the breast. Make a slit in the meat that runs about three-quarters of the length of the breast and about 1- to 1½-inches deep. Fill with your choice of stuffing and press the edges together to seal before baking.

GLAZED CHICKEN LOAF

To make homemade bread crumbs, place 7 slices of home-style white bread in the bowl of a food processor fitted with the metal blade and process until crumbled. Place the crumbs on a baking sheet and dry in the oven at 250°F for 15 minutes.

6 servings or 4 servings with leftovers

1 tablespoon canola or other light vegetable oil
½ cup minced onion
½ cup minced scallion, green and white parts
2 teaspoons minced garlic
½ cup minced celery
½ cup minced red bell pepper
½ cup minced peeled carrot
2 pounds ground skinless, boneless chicken breast
5 large egg whites, beaten
¾ cup ketchup
1 cup unseasoned dried bread crumbs (homemade if possible)
½ teaspoon ground nutmeg
½ teaspoon ground cumin
½ teaspoon ground coriander
1 teaspoon freshly ground white pepper
1 teaspoon salt
3 tablespoons dark brown sugar

1. Preheat the oven to 350°F.

2. In a large sauté pan or nonstick skillet, heat the oil over medium heat. Add the onion, scallions, garlic, celery, bell pepper, and carrot and cook about 10 minutes or until soft. Set aside to cool.

3. Combine the ground chicken breast, egg whites, 4 tablespoons of the ketchup, and the bread crumbs in a large bowl. Mix well by hand.

4. In a small bowl, combine the nutmeg, cumin, coriander, and pepper. Stir into the cooled vegetable mixture. Combine with the chicken mixture until very well mixed.

5. Combine the remaining ½ cup ketchup and brown sugar in a small bowl and stir to mix well. Set aside.

6. Lightly coat two 9 × 5-inch loaf pans with cooking spray and spoon in the chicken mixture. Spread the glaze on top to cover completely. Bake for 30 to 40 minutes or until firm to the touch.

7. Let stand 10 minutes before removing the loaves to a cutting board. Slice thin and serve hot or cold. *Note:* All the vegetables can be minced in a food processor fitted with the metal blade.

PAPRIKA CHICKEN WITH EGG NOODLES

The combination of hot and sweet paprika makes this dish incredibly flavorful.

4 to 6 servings

2 skinless, boneless chicken breast (about 1¾ pounds), halved
2 tablespoons all-purpose flour
Salt and freshly ground black pepper to taste
1 tablespoon extra-virgin olive oil
1 small onion, quartered, thinly sliced
3 large cloves garlic, crushed and minced
4 to 5 teaspoons sweet Hungarian paprika
½ teaspoon hot Hungarian paprika
1½ cups chicken stock (see page 8)
6 to 8 plum tomatoes, peeled and chopped (about 2 cups)
½ tablespoons tomato paste
2 teaspoons unsalted butter, melted
2 to 3 tablespoons minced parsley
1 pound fresh egg noodles, cooked al dente, rinsed, drained and kept hot

1. Preheat the oven to 350°F. Dust the chicken with the flour and season with salt and pepper on all sides.

2. In a large sauté pan or skillet lightly coated with cooking spray, heat the oil over high heat. Add the chicken breasts and sauté about 2 minutes on each side or until lightly browned. Transfer to an ovenproof baking dish.

3. To the same skillet over medium heat, add the onion and garlic and cook until tender. Lower the heat, sprinkle on both paprikas, stirring constantly, and cook for 2 minutes more. Pour in the chicken stock and tomatoes and stir in the tomato paste until well mixed. Simmer, uncovered, for 2 to 3 minutes to reduce slightly.

4. Pour the sauce over the chicken and bake for 10 minutes, or until the chicken is tender and done throughout.

5. Meanwhile, add the butter and 1 tablespoon of the parsley to the noodles and toss. Rewarm in the sauté pan. Serve the chicken breasts over the noodles, sprinkled with the remaining parsley. Drizzle a little more sauce over the chicken and pass the remaining sauce on the side.

SPICY SZECHUAN BAKED CHICKEN

This regional Chinese dish is hot (from the heat of chile peppers) and offers a complex flavor. It's also a great picnic lunch or alfresco dinner since it can be served hot (from the oven) or at room temperature. For those interested in a high-flavor, low-fat dish, this recipe has only 1 tablespoon of oil in the ingredient list.

1½ tablespoons Szechuan peppercorns, toasted
⅛ teaspoon dried crushed red pepper
1½ tablespoons coriander seed, toasted
½ teaspoon coarse salt
½ cup fresh cilantro leaves (not packed)
¼ cup parsley leaves
2 teaspoons chopped orange or lemon zest
4 large cloves garlic, chopped
3 large shallots, chopped
2 teaspoons dark sesame oil
1 teaspoon vegetable oil
4 tablespoons soy sauce or tamari
2 skinless boneless chicken breast (about 2 pounds), halved

1. Preheat the oven to 350°F.

2. Combine the peppercorns, red pepper, coriander, and salt in the bowl of a food processor and process for 30 seconds. Scrape down the sides, add the cilantro, parsley, orange or lemon zest, garlic, shallots, and sesame oil and continue processing for 30 seconds. Scrape into a small bowl.

3. In another small bowl, whisk together the vegetable oil and soy sauce. Dip the chicken breasts in the soy mixture. Place on a baking sheet lightly coated with cooking spray. Spread the herb mixture evenly on the chicken to cover completely. Marinate for 30 minutes.

4. Bake 20 minutes, or until done throughout. Serve hot or room temperature.

RULES OF THE ROAST

So you're really tight on time. You don't even have time to read this, but you want to cook some chicken breasts and don't want to have to keep an eye on the oven. Check out the quick and easy marinades on page 187 and drop a plump whole chicken breast in a flavorful bath in a Ziploc bag for a few minutes. Or just squeeze on some lemon juice and chop up a few different kinds of fresh herbs and throw them on along with salt and freshly ground pepper to taste. Preheat the oven to 350°F. Lightly coat a nonstick ovenproof skillet (no plastic handles, please) with vegetable oil cooking spray, heat over medium-high heat, and add a teaspoon of olive oil or unsalted butter. Sear the breasts, about 2 minutes per side to seal in the juices and lightly brown. Place the skillet in the oven. Then, go and do something constructive. Come back in 8 to 10 minutes and eat! Easy? Always! That's the nature of the beast.

BAKED CHEESE AND MUSHROOM QUESADILLAS WITH SALSA AND CREAMY GUACAMOLE

This creamy rich dish will really satisfy your craving for a hearty and delicious meal or snack, yet it still can be designated as moderately low-fat if you choose non-, low-, or reduced-fat ingredients (and remember, the fat in avocado is good for us).

4 to 6 servings

Creamy Guacamole

1 large avocado, peeled and cubed (about 1½ cups), pit reserved
1½ cup low-fat sour cream, regular or light
½ cup nonfat ricotta, thinned with ½ tablespoon nonfat milk
3 tablespoons finely chopped red onion
2 tablespoons fresh lime juice
5 tablespoons finely chopped fresh cilantro
½ teaspoon salt
½ teaspoon freshly ground black pepper

Salsa

4 ripe plum tomatoes, chopped
½ small red onion, chopped
1 small jalapeño pepper, seeded, deveined, and minced
Pinch of salt
2 teaspoons canola or corn oil

Quesadillas

½ pound mushrooms, stemmed and sliced
Salt and freshly ground black pepper to taste
2 skinless, boneless chicken breast (about 1½ pounds), halved and cut into ½-inch wide strips
8 eight-inch flour tortillas
1½ cups shredded Monterey Jack cheese, regular or reduced fat
½ small red onion, very thinly sliced
¾ cup sour cream, regular or light, at room temperature

1. To make the guacamole, combine the avocado, sour cream, and ricotta in a food processor and process until smooth. Transfer to a mixing bowl, stir in the red onion, 1 tablespoon of the lime juice, 2 tablespoons of the cilantro, salt, and pepper. Place the pit in the center, drizzling the remaining 1 tablespoon lime juice over the guacamole to prevent it from turning brown. Cover tightly with plastic wrap. Chill until ready to serve.

2. To make the salsa, combine the tomatoes, onion, jalapeño in a small bowl and season with salt to taste. Set aside.

3. To make the quesadillas, preheat the oven to 375°F.

4. In a heavy nonstick skillet, lightly coated with cooking spray, heat 1 teaspoon of the oil. Add the mushrooms and cook over medium-high heat, stirring occasionally, for about 7 minutes or until the mushrooms are lightly browned and the moisture has evaporated. Season with salt and pepper. Transfer to a bowl.

5. Wipe the skillet clean. Lightly coat with cooking spray and heat the remaining teaspoon of oil over medium-high heat. Add the chicken breast strips and cook, stirring, about 4 to 5 minutes or until done. Season with a pinch of salt.

6. Lightly coat a baking sheet with cooking spray. Place 2 or more tortillas on the baking sheet. Sprinkle each tortilla with equal amounts of the cheese, chicken strips, mushrooms, onion, and the remaining chopped cilantro. Top each with another tortilla. Pinch the edges together. Bake for 5 to 7 minutes, or until the cheese is melted.

7. Remove the pit from the guacamole and stir. Place the quesadillas on a wooden cutting board and cut into quarters. Serve hot with of dollop of salsa, guacamole, and sour cream on the side. Pass the remaining sauces.

BALSAMIC CHICKEN BREASTS WITH VEGETABLES *EN PAPILLOTE*

Substitute aluminum foil only if parchment paper is not available. Parchment makes a wonderful presentation, as it puffs up during cooking.

4 servings

2 skinless, boneless chicken breasts (about 2 pounds), halved
3 tablespoons balsamic vinegar
Salt and freshly ground black pepper to taste
3 tablespoons dry white wine or chicken stock
2 cloves garlic, minced
1 tablespoon chopped fresh basil, or 1½ teaspoons dried

2 teaspoons chopped fresh thyme, or 1 teaspoon dried
1 tablespoon chopped flat-leaf parsley
2 shallots, sliced
2 tablespoons extra-virgin olive oil
2 medium carrots, peeled and cut into 2-inch matchsticks
1 medium leek, white and light green parts, washed and cut into 2-inch matchsticks
½ red bell pepper and ½ yellow bell pepper, seeded and cut into 2-inch matchsticks

1. Place the chicken in a shallow glass baking dish and pour on the balsamic vinegar, salt, and pepper. Cover with plastic wrap and marinate for 15 to 20 minutes.

2. In a jar with a tight-fitting lid, combine the wine or stock, garlic, basil, thyme, parsley, shallots, and oil. Shake to mix well.

3. Combine the carrots, leek, and bell peppers in a mixing bowl and pour on the herb and oil mixture. Toss to coat the vegetables and marinate for 10 minutes.

4. Preheat the oven to 375°F.

5. Cut four 15 × 15-inch squares of parchment paper. Fold in half and crease to mark the center. Place the paper on a flat work surface.

6. In the centers of the halves, place one quarter of the vegetables in a flat layer, reserving the remaining marinade. Remove a chicken breast from the marinade and place on top of the vegetables. Stir the chicken and vegetable marinades together. Drizzle over the chicken. Top with a grind of pepper from the pepper mill.

7. To close the parchment pouches, make an envelope by drawing the top flap of the paper over the filling and folding in the edges together all around. Seal the packet with several more narrow folds around the edges too completely close. The package should seal tightly with the paper still loose over the filling to allow for expansion during cooking. Repeat with all the pouches.

8. Place the packets on a baking sheet lightly coated with cooking spray. Bake for 20 to 25 minutes, or until the chicken is done and the parchment is puffed. Serve the packages in 4 shallow bowls and cut them open at the table.

CHICKEN WITH MUSTARD-CREAM SAUCE

This sauce should be served warm. Heat it slowly in a small saucepan over low heat just long enough to warm throughout. Do not allow it to even come to a simmer.

4 to 6 servings

2 skinless, boneless chicken breast (about 2 pounds), halved
1 tablespoon unsalted butter, melted
4 tablespoons light brown sugar
¼ cup soy sauce or tamari
2 tablespoons fresh lemon juice
3 tablespoons dry white wine
½ teaspoon freshly ground white pepper
Salt to taste
1 cup sour cream, regular or light
½ cup plain yogurt, regular or low-fat
1 teaspoon Worcestershire sauce
½ cup coarse-grain Dijon mustard
2 teaspoons dried basil
1 tablespoon finely chopped fresh basil

1. Line a baking pan with enough foil hanging over the sides to fold over the chicken to form a closed package. Place the chicken breasts in the foil, just touching but not crowded.

2. Combine the melted butter, 3 tablespoons of the brown sugar, soy sauce, lemon juice, wine, ¼ teaspoon of the pepper, and a pinch of salt in a small bowl. Brush the mixture onto the chicken breasts and marinate, refrigerated, for 1 hour.

3. Meanwhile, combine the remaining 1 tablespoon brown sugar, sour cream, yogurt, Worcestershire sauce, mustard, the remaining ¼ teaspoon pepper, and dried basil in a saucepan and mix well. Adjust the seasoning with salt. Set aside.

4. Preheat the oven to 375°F. Let chicken come to room temperature before putting in the oven.

5. Fold the foil into a tight package over the chicken breasts and bake for 10 minutes. Open the foil, baste with the pan juices, and continue baking for another 7 to 8 minutes or until done.

6. Slice the breasts and arrange on 4 plates. Gently heat the sauce over the very lowest heat, swirling the pan above the heat. Do not let the sauce simmer. Remove from the heat, stir in the fresh basil, and spoon some sauce next to each piece of chicken. Pass the remaining sauce on the side.

LAYERED CHICKEN ENCHILADA PIE

6 servings

2 teaspoons vegetable oil
1 ½ pounds ground skinless, boneless chicken breast
1 teaspoon finely minced garlic
Salt and freshly ground black pepper to taste
½ cup chopped onion
2 tablespoons all-purpose flour
¾ cup chicken stock (see page 8)
¼ cup low-fat or nonfat milk
1 can (4 ounces) chopped green chiles
1 teaspoon ground cumin
4 8-inch corn tortillas
1 can (10 ounces) enchilada sauce
3 cups chopped tomatoes
½ cup grated sharp cheddar cheese
½ cup crumbled white Mexican cheese or feta
½ cup chopped fresh cilantro
½ cup picante sauce (bottled)
6 tablespoons sour cream, regular or light

1. Preheat the oven to 350°F.

2. In a medium sauté pan or nonstick skillet lightly coated with cooking spray, heat 1 teaspoon of the oil over medium-high heat. Add the ground chicken and garlic and cook about 5 minutes or until brown and crumbly. Remove from the pan. Drain in a strainer.

3. In the pan, heat the remaining 1 teaspoon oil over medium heat. Add the onion and cook, stirring frequently, about 5 minutes or until tender. Transfer to a bowl.

4. Sprinkle the flour into the pan. Whisk in the stock and milk in a thin, steady stream until well mixed. Bring to a boil, reduce to a simmer, and continue cooking about 3 minutes or until the sauce has thickened. Remove from the heat and add the chicken and onion to the sauce. Stir in the chiles and cumin until well combined.

5. Coat the bottom and sides of an 8-inch spring-form pan or round baking pan with cooking spray. Place one of the tortillas on the bottom. Spread on one quarter of the enchilada sauce and layer on one third of the tomatoes and then the chicken mixture. Repeat with two more layers, reserving one quarter of the cheddar and Mexican cheese and chopped cilantro. Cover with the remaining tortilla. Spread enchilada sauce over the top tortilla, cover with foil, place on a baking sheet, and bake for 20 minutes.

6. Remove the foil cover, sprinkle on the remaining cheese, and return to the oven for about 5 minutes or just until the cheese is melted and bubbling.

7. Let the layered enchilada sit for 10 minutes before cutting into 6 wedges. Top each serving with chopped cilantro, picante sauce, and sour cream.

CRISPY OVEN-FRIED CHICKEN BREASTS

This recipe can also be used to make bite-size chicken breast fried tenders (better than McDonald's by a long shot) using the fillets. Serve them as an appetizer or main dish. Create a Mediterranean version using Parmesan cheese instead of sesame seeds, oregano for the thyme, and switch the butter for extra-virgin olive oil.

4 to 6 servings

1½ cups cereal flakes (cornflakes or Special K or with no sugar added), coarsely crushed into crumbs
⅓ cup sesame seeds, toasted and ground
1 teaspoon dried thyme, crumbled
2 teaspoons finely grated lemon zest
½ teaspoon salt
½ teaspoon freshly ground black pepper
2 medium egg whites
1 tablespoon fresh lemon juice
2 skinless, boneless chicken breasts (about 1½ pounds), halved
1 tablespoon unsalted butter, melted and warm

1. Preheat the oven to 450°F. Lightly coat a metal baking sheet with cooking spray.

2. Combine the cereal crumbs, ground sesame seeds, thyme, lemon zest, and salt and pepper in a large plastic bag. Shake to mix, pour onto a plate, and spread out in a thin even layer.

3. In a large shallow dish, whisk together the egg whites and lemon juice until frothy. Coat the chicken breasts with the egg mixture on all sides letting the excess drip back into the dish. Roll the chicken breasts in the crumbs, firmly pressing the crumbs into the surface.

4. Place the breasts on the baking sheet. Put the warm melted butter in a spray bottle and coat the breasts, or use a pastry brush to gently dab the butter onto the tops of the breasts. Place in the oven and bake for 10 to 15 minutes, or until golden brown and done throughout.

OLIVE AND FETA-STUFFED CHICKEN ROLLS

4 servings

2 skinless, boneless chicken breasts (about 2 pounds), flattened between plastic wrap to ⅓-inch thickness
Salt and freshly ground black pepper to taste
½ cup dry bread crumbs or panko flakes
1 teaspoon dried oregano
1 large egg white, beaten
½ cup crumbled feta cheese
2 tablespoons finely chopped fresh basil
1 cup packed chopped fresh spinach leaves, stem removed
2 tablespoons finely chopped oil-cured Kalmata olives, drained
2 teaspoons unsalted butter, melted

1. Preheat oven to 400°F. Lightly season the chicken breasts with salt and pepper.

2. Combine the bread crumbs, oregano, ¼ teaspoon salt, and ¼ teaspoon pepper in a shallow bowl, stir to mix well. Transfer to a plate.

3. Place the egg white in a bowl. Dip the chicken breasts in the egg white, allowing the excess to drip back into the bowl. Dredge through the bread crumbs, shaking off any excess. Place the chicken breasts on a flat work surface.

4. Combine the feta, basil, olives, and spinach in a small mixing bowl. Mix with a fork to a paste. Divide the stuffing evenly and place in the center of each chicken breast half. Fold in the two sides and roll up to enclose the stuffing.

5. In a shallow glass baking pan lightly coated with cooking spray, place the chicken breast bundles seam side down, not touching. Using a spray bottle, spray on the melted butter evenly, or use a pastry brush to dab butter on the chicken. Bake for 18 to 20 minutes, or until brown and done throughout. Serve hot or at room temperature.

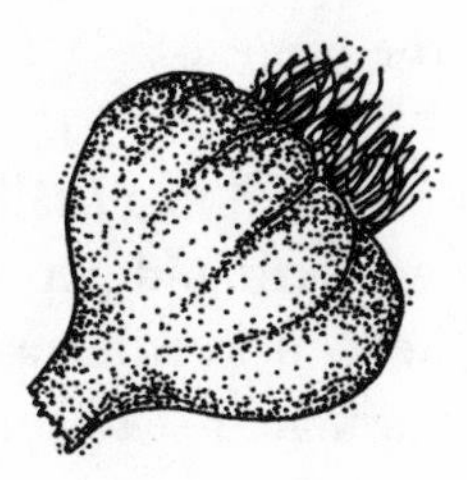

TARRAGON CHICKEN BREASTS WITH ARTICHOKES

Baking *en papilotte* can be an essentially fat-free cook method. See page 140 for the full description.

4 servings

4 skinless, boneless chicken breast (about 1½ pounds), halved and flattened slightly between plastic wrap
Salt and freshly ground black pepper to taste
4 tablespoons chicken stock (see page 8)
4 tablespoons dry white wine
1½ tablespoons chopped fresh tarragon, or 2½ teaspoons dried
4 teaspoons unsalted butter, melted
8 large white mushrooms, thinly sliced
2 six-ounce packages frozen artichoke hearts, thawed, bottoms trimmed flat

1. Preheat the oven to 375°F.

2. Place the chicken in a shallow dish and season with salt and pepper. Drizzle on the chicken stock, wine, and tarragon, cover, and marinate for 15 minutes.

3. In a sauté pan or nonstick skillet, heat 1 teaspoon of the butter over medium heat. Add the mushrooms and cook about 5 minutes or until the liquid has evaporated. Season lightly with salt and pepper. Set aside.

4. Cut four 15 × 15-inch squares of parchment paper. Fold in half, crease, and open on a baking sheet lightly coated with cooking spray. In the center of one of the halves place one quarter of the artichokes. Place a chicken breast on the artichokes and top with one quarter of the mushrooms. Drizzle the marinade and remaining melted butter over the chicken and vegetables. Season with a turn of the pepper mill.

5. Draw the top flap of the paper over the filling and fold in the edges. Seal the packet with several more narrow folds around the edges. The package should be sealed tightly with the parchment still loose to allow for expansion.

6. Bake for 20 to 25 minutes, until the chicken is done and the parchment is puffed. Serve on individual shallow bowls and cut open at the table.

BAKED CHICKEN WITH TOMATO-MUSTARD CREAM SAUCE

This recipe offers an opportunity to show off your culinary skills. The sauce, tangy yet creamy, is a perfect complement to the delicate meat of the chicken breast. Using crème fraîche in the sauce makes it a bit lighter than with heavy cream, though the calories are almost the same.

4 servings

2 skinless, boneless chicken breasts (about 2 pounds), halved
Salt and freshly ground black pepper to taste

Sauce

3 tablespoons extra-virgin olive oil
5 large ripe tomatoes, peeled, seeded, and finely diced
1 tablespoon minced fresh thyme, or 1 teaspoon dried thyme
Salt and freshly ground black pepper to taste
3 tablespoons white wine (chardonnay)
3 tablespoons white wine or champagne vinegar
1½ tablespoons finely chopped shallots
1 tablespoon grainy mustard
1½ cups crème fraîche or heavy cream
6 tablespoons cold unsalted butter, cut into small pieces

1. Cut the chicken breasts at a 30-degree angle across the grain into ½-inch thick slices. Sprinkle with salt and pepper. Place on a baking sheet lightly sprayed with cooking spray. Refrigerate until ready to cook.

2. In a sauté pan or nonstick skillet, heat the oil over medium-high heat. Add the tomatoes and cook, stirring constantly, for about 7 minutes or until thick and well reduced. Add the thyme and salt and pepper. Remove from the heat and set aside.

3. Preheat the oven to 375°F.

4. In a heavy non-reactive saucepan, combine the wine, vinegar, and shallots and bring to a boil over medium-high heat. Continue boiling until almost all the liquid has evaporated. Remove the pan from the heat and whisk in the mustard and crème fraîche. Return to the heat, cooking until reduced by half. Over low heat, add the butter one piece at a time, whisking constantly. When the mixture is thick and foamy, add the tomato reduction. Adjust the seasoning with salt and pepper. Keep warm.

5. Place the chicken on a baking sheet and bake 18 to 20 minutes or just until done. Rewarm the sauce over very low heat.

6. Arrange the chicken breasts on individual plates and spoon on the sauce.

ONION, LEEK, CHICKEN, & CHEESE TORTE

This take-along torte is positively picnic perfect. For potluck affairs, this can be easily reheated in a microwave, or served just slightly warmed. Add a salad and serve piping hot from the oven for a lovely Sunday brunch selection instead of old standards like quiche.
Note: Though the recipe for a quick homemade pastry is listed herein, if you can buy good pre-made pastry dough in the freezer of your grocery story, by all means do so and save a few minutes in the process.

1 9-inch torte

Pastry

2 cups sifted all-purpose flour
½ teaspoon salt
½ cup cold unsalted butter, cut into small pieces
1 egg yolk
¼ cup milk
Pinch of salt
2 tablespoons chopped fresh parsley

(Begin the recipe here if you are using frozen pre-made dough, defrosted. Start with Step 3.)

Filling

2 tablespoons unsalted butter
2 cups chopped leeks (white part only)
1 large onion, coarsely chopped
4 shallots, chopped
Salt and freshly ground black pepper to taste
1 skinless, boneless chicken breast (about 1 pound), thinly sliced against the grain
1½ cups ricotta cheese
1 cup chopped fresh parsley
8 pieces green leek tops, blanched for 15 seconds in boiling water

1. Combine the flour, salt, and butter in a food processor. Pulse the mixture until very coarse (it will look like cornmeal).

2. Add the egg and yolk and mix well. Add the milk, salt and parsley and continue pulsing until the pastry forms a ball on the sides of the bowl. Remove and refrigerate for at least 2 hours.

3. To make the filling, melt the butter over medium low heat in a heavy saucepan. Add the chopped leeks and cook until soft. Add the shallots and continue cooking for 2 or 3 minutes more. Season with salt and pepper. Remove from the pan and set aside. Increase the heat to medium, add the chicken to the pan, and cook heat for 2 to 3 minutes. Do not cook completely. Season with salt and pepper. Set aside.

4. Preheat the oven to 375°F.

5. Remove the pastry dough from the refrigerator and roll into a circle large enough to cover the bottom and sides of a 9-inch spring-form pan. Put the dough in the pan and refrigerate again.

6. Mix together the eggs, ricotta, and parsley in a small bowl. Layer the leek mixture, chicken pieces, and the ricotta mixture in the torte pan. Decorate the top of the torte with the leek tops (try a lattice pattern or as the spokes of a wheel).

7. Bake for 50 minutes to 1 hour, or until the cheese is set and the crust is golden. Serve warm or at room temperature.

CALIFORNIA-STYLE HERB AND GOAT CHEESE- FILLED CHICKEN BREASTS

Elegant party fare!

4 servings

2 boneless chicken breasts (about 2 pounds), cartilage removed, skin on
½ pound fresh goat cheese (chevre), at room temperature
1 tablespoon finely chopped fresh oregano
1 tablespoon finely chopped fresh thyme
1 large clove garlic, finely minced
¼ teaspoon salt
½ teaspoon freshly ground white pepper
1 tablespoon extra-virgin olive oil
1 cup dry white wine (chardonnay)

1. Preheat the oven to 375°F.

2. Loosen the skin from the chicken breasts just enough to form a pocket but leaving the skin partially attached.

3. Combine the goat cheese, oregano, thyme, garlic, salt, and pepper in a small bowl. Stir until well combined.

4. Divide the filling between the breasts and tuck under the skin. Pull the skin over the filling and around, tucking all the edges of the meat under to form a neat little package. Arrange the breasts in an ovenproof skillet or sauté pan lightly coated with cooking spray.

5. Sprinkle the breasts with salt and pepper to taste and brush the tops with olive oil. Roast for 25 to 35 minutes, or until golden brown and done throughout. Transfer the breasts to a platter and keep warm.

6. Pour off any excess fat from the pan. Place the pan over medium-high heat on the stove top. Add the wine and deglaze, scraping up any brown bits from the bottom of the pan. Reduce the sauce slightly or until it thickens. Strain the sauce if desired.

7. Slice the breasts crosswise with a sharp knife, arrange on plates, and spoon on the sauce; or split the breasts and serve sauce on the side.

CHICKEN BREAST ENCHILADAS WITH MILD GREEN CHILE SAUCE

This green sauce version of the classic Mexican dish is piquant and interesting.

6 servings

Poaching liquid

2 cups (or more) chicken stock (see page 8)
1 cilantro sprig
1 parsley sprig
1 bay leaf
2 chicken breasts (about 2 pounds)
Pinch of salt

Green Chile Sauce

20 fresh tomatillos (Mexican green tomatoes), or two 1- to 3-ounce cans tomatillos
¼ cup vegetable oil
1½ cups chopped onion
6 Anaheim chiles, or one 7-ounce can mild chile peppers, drained and chopped

2 large cloves garlic, pressed
2 tablespoons minced fresh oregano, or 2 teaspoons finely crumbled dried
2 tablespoons freshly squeezed lemon juice
1 teaspoon sugar
1 teaspoon salt
2 cups chicken stock (see page 8) or strained poaching liquid
2 bay leaves

2 cups shredded Monterey Jack cheese
1 tablespoon minced fresh oregano or 1 teaspoon dried
12 corn tortillas
Vegetable oil for frying

Garnish and Side Dishes
Avocado slices or guacamole
Chopped ripe tomatoes or salsa (see page 25)
Finely chopped scallion, green and white parts
Sour cream, regular or low-fat
Ripe olives
Cilantro leaves

1. In a large saucepan or stockpot, bring the poaching liquid to a boil. Add the chicken breasts and simmer for 8 to 10 minutes or just until the done throughout. The breasts will be firm when pressed with the back of a fork. Transfer to a strainer, remove the skin and bones, and shred the chicken into bite-size pieces.

2. Put the tomatillos in a saucepan and cover with water. Over medium-high heat, bring to a boil and cook until almost tender, about 5 minutes. Drain in a colander, rinse, and drain again. Set aside. (If using canned tomatillos, just drain and set aside.)

3. Heat the oil in a heavy skillet over medium-high heat. Add the onion and cook about 5 minutes or until translucent. Transfer to a blender or a food procesor. Add the tomatillos, chiles, garlic, oregano, lemon juice, sugar, salt, and half the stock. Process until smooth.

4. Transfer the mixture to a saucepan, add the remaining stock and the bay leaves, and bring to a boil. Reduce the heat to low, cover, and simmer until the sauce is slightly thickened, about 30 minutes. Remove the bay leaves. Set aside.

5. Preheat the oven to 350°F.

6. Combine the chicken, 1½ cups cheese, and 1 tablespoon fresh oregano in a bowl. Set aside.

7. Reheat the chile sauce. Pour vegetable oil into a 10-inch skillet to a depth of ½ inch. One at a time over medium heat, fry the tortillas for just a few seconds, then dip immediately and briefly in the chile sauce, and let the excess drip off.

Lay each tortilla on a flat surface, spoon ⅓ to ½ cup of the chicken filling down the center, roll up into a cylinder, and place, seam side down, in an ovenproof dish. Spoon a little of the sauce over the tops of the enchiladas. Cover with foil.

8. Bake about 15 minutes, or until the filling is heated through. Remove the foil, sprinkle the remaining cheese over the enchiladas, and bake about 10 minutes, or until the cheese is melted.

9. Heat 6 plates. Spoon some chile sauce onto each and put 2 hot enchiladas on the sauce. Garnish with avocado slices, chopped tomatoes, sour cream, olives, and cilantro. Pass the salsa on the side.

MEXICAN CHILEQUIDES

This casserole recipe travels well and is delicious served hot or at room temperature. Up to step 5, you can prepare this casserole-type dish one day in advance. Just cover with plastic wrap and refrigerate. One hour before you're ready to cook the chilequides, remove the dish from the refrigerator to come to room temperature. Consider using this as a starter dish.

4 to 6 servings

2 tablespoons unsalted butter
1 onion, coarsely chopped
5 medium tomatoes, peeled, seeded, and coarsely chopped
1 cup fresh cilantro leaves
2 cloves garlic
2 serrano chiles, stemmed and seeded
Salt to taste
Vegetable oil for frying
9 6-inch corn tortillas
2 skinless, boneless chicken (about 2 pounds), broiled and julienned
1 cup sour cream, at room temperature
1½ cups freshly grated white Mexican cheese
⅔ cup chicken stock (see page 8), heated

1. Melt the butter over medium heat in a large heavy saucepan. Add the onion and cook about 5 minutes or until translucent. Transfer to a food processor and add the tomatoes, cilantro, garlic, and chiles and process to a chunky salsa consistency.

2. Return the mixture to the saucepan, bring to a boil, reduce the heat to low and simmer, stirring occasionally, for about 20 minutes or until slightly thickened. Add salt to taste.

3. Preheat the oven to 350°F.

4. In a large heavy skillet, heat half an inch of oil over high heat. Fry the tortillas one at a time until golden brown, about 2 minutes per side. Drain on paper towel.

5. In the bottom of a 9 × 13-inch baking dish, overlap 3 of the tortillas. Top with a third of the salsa, a third of the sour cream, a third of the chicken, and a third of the cheese. Repeat with two more layers.

6. Pour the stock over the layers and bake about 35 minutes, or until the top is brown and bubbling. Serve immediately or warm.

SPINACH CHICKEN LOAF

A great buffet dish as well as a light main course. This looks wonderful when placed in the center of a white plate and garnished with sprigs of herbs all around. It can also be served as a starter.

6 to 8 servings

2 skinless, boneless chicken breasts (about 2 pounds), chopped
2 pounds fresh spinach, washed, stemmed, and chopped, or one 10-ounce package frozen chopped spinach, thawed and drained well
¾ cup finely chopped carrots
1 cup finely chopped onion
5 eggs, lightly beaten
1½ cup tomato paste
1 teaspoon salt
¾ teaspoon freshly ground black pepper
1 cup seasoned, fine, dry bread crumbs

1. Preheat the oven to 350°F.

2. Combine the chicken, spinach, carrots, and onion in a large mixing bowl.

3. In another bowl, beat together the eggs, tomato paste, salt, and pepper. Stir into the chicken mixture to combine well. Fold in the bread crumbs.

4. Line 2 loaf pans with parchment paper and gently spoon in the chicken mixture, being careful not to pack it down, making the mixture too dense.

5. Bake 40 to 50 minutes, or until the internal temperature reaches 140°F. on a meat thermometer.

6. Let cool slightly and serve from the pan or wait 15 minutes before unmolding.

STUFFED FREE-RANGE CHICKEN BREASTS FLORENTINE

A recipe from Chef Michael Saragueta, formerly of New York's 21 and the Polo Lounge at the Beverly Hills Hotel. Now you'll know how to treat your guests like celebrities.

4 servings

2 skinless, boneless chicken breasts (about 2½ pounds), halved
¼ cup extra-virgin olive oil
2 bunches spinach, washed, dried, stemmed, and chopped
Salt and freshly ground black pepper to taste
½ cup freshly grated Monterey Jack cheese, regular or fat reduced
1 cup heavy cream
2 tablespoons minced fresh basil
2 tablespoons minced fresh chives

1. With a sharp, pointed knife, make an incision in the thickest end of the breast. Do not cut all the way through.

2. Heat 1 tablespoon of the oil over medium-high heat in a skillet. Add the spinach, salt, and pepper and cook just until the spinach is wilted, about 2 minutes. Remove to a plate to cool. Press the moisture out of the spinach. Mix in the cheese.

3. Arrange the breasts on a work surface. Fill the pockets carefully with the spinach mixture. Roll each breast in plastic wrap to make a sausage shape. Remove the plastic wrap.

4. Preheat the oven to 375°F.

5. Heat the remaining oil over medium-high heat in a sauté pan. Add the chicken breasts and sauté 4 to 5 minutes or until golden brown on all sides. Transfer to a baking dish and bake 10 minutes, or until done. Slice before serving

PARMESAN-CRUSTED PICNIC BASKET CHICKEN BREASTS

Positively perfect picnic or backyard lunch fare, and it's as good hot as it is at room temperature.

6 pieces

½ cup Dijon mustard
¼ cup dry white wine (chardonnay)
1 cup fresh bread crumbs
1 cup finely grated Parmesan cheese
Salt and freshly ground black pepper to taste
3 skinless, boneless chicken breasts (about 3 pounds), halved

1. Preheat the oven to 375°F.

2. Whisk the mustard and wine together in a shallow bowl. The mixture should be a dipping consistency. Set aside.

3. Combine the bread crumbs, Parmesan, and a scant amount of salt and pepper. Dip the chicken breasts in the mustard mixture, then roll in the crumbs.

4. Bake on a greased baking sheet for 30 minutes, or until the chicken is cooked through and the coating is brown and crispy. Serve hot or at room temperature.

CHICKEN MOUSSE WITH TOMATO BASIL SAUCE

This recipe can easily be doubled, and baked in a loaf pan rather than in individual cups. Allow a terrine to rest for at least 30 minutes before slicing.

4 servings

1 skinless, boneless free-range chicken breast (about 1¼ pounds, coarsely chopped)
5 large eggs
4 large egg yolks
1 cup heavy cream
½ teaspoon salt
½ teaspoon freshly ground white pepper
Pinch of freshly grated nutmeg
1 ounce prosciutto, finely chopped
Melted unsalted butter

8 very thin slices boiled ham (about ¼ pound)

Tomato Basil Sauce

1 tablespoon extra-virgin olive oil
4 ripe tomatoes (about 2 pounds), peeled, seeded, and diced
Bouquet garni (see page 354) including: 1 sprig thyme sprig, 1 bay leaf, 1 sprig flat-leaf parsley
½ cup chicken stock (see page 8), reduced by half
Salt and freshly ground white pepper to taste
3 tablespoons chopped fresh basil or parsley (or a combination of both)
1 tablespoon chopped fresh parsley for garnish
1 tablespoon chopped fresh chives for garnish

1. Preheat the oven to 325°F.

2. To make the mousse, combine the chicken with the eggs, egg yolks, cream, salt and pepper, and nutmeg and process to a smooth paste in two batches in a blender or a food processor. Add the prosciutto and pulse to mix well.

3. Brush 4 individual 1-cup custard cups with melted butter. Press 2 slices of ham into each cup so the edges hang a bit over the sides. Pour in the mousse and fold the ham over the top to cover it. Cut 4 rounds of parchment paper to fit the molds. Butter the parchment paper and put it buttered side down over the ham.

4. Put the molds in a large baking pan and add hot water halfway up the sides of the cups. Bake for 40 to 45 minutes, or until the mousse is set.

5. Combine the oil, tomatoes, bouquet garni, and stock in a saucepan. Bring to a simmer and reduce for 15 minutes. Remove the bouquet garni and pour the sauce through a strainer into another saucepan. Add salt and pepper to taste and stir in the basil. Set aside.

6. Remove the molds from the oven and take off the parchment paper. Let cook slightly. Unmold onto shallow soup bowls.

7. Add the 1 tablespoon butter to the warm tomato sauce, whisking constantly until it melts. Pour the sauce around the base of the mousse molds. Sprinkle on the parsley and chives. Serve immediately.

ROASTED PESTO CHICKEN BREASTS

4 to 6 servings

2 cups tightly packed fresh basil leaves
⅓ cup finely chopped toasted pine nuts
3 cloves garlic, finely chopped
¾ cup freshly grated Parmesan cheese
½ cup extra-virgin olive oil
3 boned chicken breasts (about 3 pounds), halved, skin on
Salt and freshly ground black pepper to taste

1. Preheat the oven to 350°F.

2. Process the basil in a food processor until finely chopped. Add the pine nuts, garlic, and cheese and pulse a few times. With the motor running, pour in the oil in a thin stream and pulse just until the ingredients are combined.

3. Loosen the skin of each chicken breast enough to form a pocket, leaving the skin partially attached. Divide the pesto evenly among the breasts and tuck it under the skin. Pull the skin around the filling and toward the underside to form a neat package.

4. Arrange the chicken breasts, pesto side up in a baking dish lightly coated with cooking spray. Sprinkle with salt and pepper and brush with a little olive oil. Bake 30 to 35 minutes, or until golden brown. Serve hot or at room temperature.

HOT AND SPICY OVEN-FRIED HERBED CHICKEN BREASTS

The crispy coating on the chicken is really hot stuff! If you prefer milder flavors, choose another recipe.

4 to 6 servings

¾ cup fine dry bread crumbs
1½ teaspoons ground cumin
1½ teaspoons crumbled dried oregano
1½ teaspoons salt
¼ teaspoon freshly ground black pepper
½ teaspoon chile powder
⅛ teaspoon cayenne pepper
1 cup all-purpose flour

3 eggs
3⅓ tablespoons fresh lime juice
3 skinless, boneless chicken breasts (about 3 pounds), halved
3 tablespoons unsalted butter
3 tablespoons canola or other light vegetable oil
Flat-leaf parsley for garnish
Lime wedges for garnish

1. Preheat the oven to 350°F.

2. Combine the bread crumbs, cumin, oregano, salt, black pepper, chile powder, and cayenne in a small bowl. Put the mixture in a shallow dish.

3. Put the flour in another shallow dish.

4. Beat the eggs and lime juice together in a medium shallow bowl.

5. Roll the chicken breasts in the flour, then dip in the egg mixture, allowing any excess to drip back into the dish. Roll in the bread crumb mixture, coating completely. Refrigerate the breasts for at least 30 minutes.

6. In a large heavy skillet, melt half the butter with half the oil over medium heat. Add the chicken breasts and sauté about 2 minutes per side or until lightly browned. Repeat with the remaining butter and oil. Transfer to a baking dish lightly coated with cooking spray.

7. Bake the breasts until cooked throughout and crispy on the outside, 20 to 25 minutes. Garnish with parsley and lime wedges for squeezing.

CHICKEN BREASTS RELLENO

6 servings

4 skinless, boneless chicken breasts (about 3½ pounds), flattened between plastic wrap to ⅓-inch thickness thick
⅛ teaspoon cumin
⅛ teaspoon oregano
Pinch freshly grated nutmeg
1 green bell pepper, seeded and quartered
8 quarter-inch slices Monterey Jack cheese
4 thin slices smoked or boiled ham
8 pimiento-stuffed green olives, halved lengthwise
3 eggs, separated
2 tablespoons all-purpose flour
⅛ teaspoon salt

Pinch of cayenne pepper
Light vegetable oil for frying
2 tablespoons chopped parsley
Lemon wedges for garnish
Salsa (see page 25)

1. Preheat the oven to 350°F.

2. Place the chicken breasts on a work surface. Combine the cumin, oregano, nutmeg in a small bowl and sprinkle onto the chicken breasts.

3. In a large saucepan filled with lightly salted boiling water, cook the bell pepper pieces for 4 minutes. Drain and let cool to room temperature and dice.

4. On half of each piece of chicken breast, layer a piece of bell pepper, a slice of cheese, a slice of ham, and 4 olive halves. Fold over to cover all the ingredients and seal the edges by pressing down with the tines of a fork.

4. Lightly coat the bottom of a shallow oven-proof baking dish with cooking spray. Arrange the chicken breasts in a single layer, loosely cover with foil, and bake for 4 to 6 minutes, or until they just begin to turn white. Do not overcook. Remove the pan from the oven, uncover, and allow the chicken breasts to cool (they will continue to cook to done).

5. In a bowl, beat the egg whites until stiff and dry. In a fairly large bowl, beat the yolks well. Beat in the flour, salt, and cayenne pepper. Fold a third of the egg whites into the yolk mixture. When absorbed, fold in the remaining egg whites very gently. Do not beat. The mixture should remain stiff.

6. In a heavy skillet, heat the oil (½ inch deep) until very hot but not smoking. Spoon enough egg mixture onto a saucer to cover the bottom. Place one chicken breast in the center. Spoon on enough egg mixture to cover. Remove the excess from around the edges. Slide the chicken breasts into the hot oil and fry for 1 minute on each side or until golden brown and puffed. Turn only once during cooking. Repeat with all the breasts.

7. Place each on a plate after frying, sprinkle with parsley, garnish with a lemon wedge, and serve immediately with salsa on the side.

TARRAGON-MUSTARD CHICKEN BREASTS

4 servings

2 cups dry bread crumbs
1 teaspoon salt
1 teaspoon Hungarian paprika
Freshly ground black pepper to taste
1 egg
4 tablespoons Dijon mustard (or other prepared mustard)
2 shallots, peeled
1 tablespoon finely crushed dried tarragon
8 tablespoons melted butter
2 skinless, boneless chicken breasts (about 2 pounds), flattened slightly

Sauce

2 tablespoons Dijon mustard (or other prepared mustard)
2 shallots
1 teaspoon dried tarragon
¼ cup chicken stock (see page 8)
½ cup dry white wine (chardonnay)
2 tablespoons unsalted butter
2 teaspoons finely chopped fresh parsley

1. Preheat the oven to 375°F.

2. Combine the bread crumbs, salt, paprika, and black pepper in a small bowl.

3. Combine the egg, mustard, shallots, and tarragon in a blender or food processor. Add the melted butter in a thin but steady stream and blend until the mixture is light and fluffy. Transfer to a bowl.

4. Dip the chicken breasts in the mustard mixture, coating well. Roll in the bread crumbs. Place the breasts in a shallow oven-proof dish lightly coated with cooking spray. Bake for 15 to 18 minutes, or just until done.

5. Meanwhile, to prepare the sauce, combine the mustard, shallots, tarragon, stock, and wine in a blender. Transfer to a saucepan, bring to a boil, and reduce by half. Lower the heat and whisk in the butter, one tablespoon at a time. Keep warm.

6. Spoon the sauce on the bottom of dinner plates and place the chicken breasts on the sauce. Sprinkle with chopped parsley.

CHICKEN BREASTS WITH WILD MUSHROOMS

4 to 6 servings

2 ounces dried wild mushrooms (such as morels, porcine, cepes, chanterelles, trompettes des morts), rehydrated in enough boiling water to cover the mushrooms for 30 minutes or until soft, washed well, and sliced
8 tablespoons unsalted butter
2 shallots, finely minced
Pinch of allspice
Salt and black pepper to taste
1 cup chicken stock (see page 8), reduced to ½ cup
1 tablespoon fresh lemon juice
3 tablespoons dry sherry
1 cup heavy cream
2 tablespoons extra-virgin olive oil
1 large clove garlic, finely minced
3 skinless, boneless chicken breasts (about 3 pounds)
2 tablespoons medium sherry
3 tablespoons chopped fresh parsley
2 tablespoons chopped fresh chives

1. In a sauté pan or heavy skillet, melt 6 tablespoons of the butter over medium heat. Add the shallots and cook for about 3 minutes or until tender and lightly browned. Add the mushrooms, sprinkle on the allspice, salt, and pepper and continue cooking over medium heat, stirring occasionally, for about 4 to 5 minutes or until the liquid from the mushrooms has evaporated.

2. Add ¼ cup of the reduced stock, lemon juice, and dry sherry to the pan and continue cooking until the mushrooms are tender. Lower the heat, add half the cream, and simmer for 5 minutes, or until the sauce begins to thicken.

3. Lightly butter a shallow oven-proof baking dish. Spread the mushroom mixture evenly over the bottom. Set aside.

4. Preheat the oven to 350°F.

5. In a sauté pan or skillet, melt the remaining 2 tablespoons of butter with the olive oil over medium-high heat. Add the garlic and cook for about 1 minute or until lightly browned. Season the chicken breasts with salt and pepper, add to the pan, and sauté for about 2 to 3 minutes on each side or until lightly browned. Remove the chicken and arrange on the mushrooms. Cover tightly with foil and bake for 10 to 15 minutes or until done and tender. Remove the chicken breasts and mushrooms from the pan.

6. Add the remaining ¼ cup stock and the medium sherry to the baking pan and continue cooking over medium heat. Reduce the liquid in the pan until almost evaporated. Reduce the heat to low, pour in the remaining ½ cup cream and cook until the sauce thickens, stirring constantly and scraping any bits on the bottom of the pan. Add the parsley.

7. Place the chicken breasts and mushrooms on plates and spoon on the sauce. Sprinkle with chives.

SILVER-WRAPPED CHICKEN BREASTS

These tender morsels of chicken sometimes appear on menus in Chinese restaurants. Serve as an appetizer or main course.

4 to 6 servings

4 tablespoons sesame seeds
½ cup light soy sauce
2 tablespoons sugar
¼ cup sake
2 pounds chicken fillets, tendons removed (see page 4)
1 tablespoon canola or other light vegetable oil
¼ teaspoon black pepper
4 scallions (white and some of the green part), chopped
8 very thin round slices of lemon

1. In a heavy sauté pan or skillet over medium-high heat, toast the sesame seeds until they turn brown and start to pop. Remove from the heat and transfer to a plate to cool.

2. Combine the soy sauce, sugar, and sake in a small bowl. Add chicken breasts. Cover and marinate for at least 30 minutes.

3. Preheat the oven to 350°F.

4. Measure out pieces of aluminum foil large enough to make a loose package around each piece of chicken breast. Lightly brush each piece of foil with oil.

5. Remove the chicken fillets from the

marinade and place each piece on foil. (There should be some liquid still on the chicken breasts.) Sprinkle with black pepper, sesame seeds, and scallions.

6. Wrap the foil loosely around the chicken breast pieces, making sure to seal tightly so the moisture does not escape during cooking. Put the foil package on a baking sheet and bake for 10 to 12 minutes. Leave wrapped, and serve hot or room temperature.

ALMOND CHICKEN BREASTS

6 servings

2 eggs, lightly beaten
½ cup half-and-half
½ cup milk
½ teaspoon salt
1 teaspoon Hungarian paprika
¾ cup all-purpose flour
3 skinless, boneless chicken breasts (about 3 pounds), flattened between plastic wrap to ⅓-inch thickness
All-purpose flour for dredging
1 cup ground blanched almonds
½ cup dried bread crumbs
8 tablespoons unsalted butter
¼ cup sliced almonds
2 tablespoons melted butter

1. Preheat the oven to 350°F 15 minutes before you're ready to bake. Lightly butter an oven-proof baking dish.

2. Combine the eggs, half-and-half, milk, salt, paprika, and flour in a bowl and beat to form a pasty batter. Marinate the chicken breasts in batter for one hour.

3. Combine the ground almonds and bread crumbs and spread on a plate.

4. Remove the chicken breasts from the marinade and drain. Coat with bread crumbs. Allow to set for 15 minutes.

5. Melt the butter over medium heat in a heavy sauté pan or skillet. Add the chicken breasts and cook for about 2 to 3 minutes on each side or until lightly browned. Place in the baking dish, sprinkle with sliced almonds, drizzle on the melted butter, and bake for 15 minutes or until crisp and golden brown.

MANGO OR APRICOT GLAZED CHICKEN BREASTS

2 to 4 servings

1 tablespoon melted unsalted butter
2 chicken breasts (about 2 pounds), halved

Mango Glaze
1 clove garlic
Salt and freshly ground black pepper to taste
2 tablespoons unsalted butter
½ cup finely chopped Major Grey's mango chutney
1 to 2 teaspoons fresh lemon juice

1. Preheat the oven to 350°F.

2. Coat a shallow oven-proof baking dish with melted butter and put in the chicken, skin side down. Bake for 10 minutes.

3. In a blender, combine the garlic, salt and pepper, 2 tablespoons of the butter, and the chutney and blend until smooth.

4. Turn the chicken breasts to skin side up and coat with the glaze. Return to the oven for 10 minutes more or until golden brown and done throughout.

5. Drizzle lemon juice over each piece of glazed chicken breast.

Variation: Apricot Mustard Glaze
½ cup apricot preserves
1 tablespoon Dijon or other prepared French mustard
2 tablespoons unsalted butter
Salt and freshly ground white pepper

CLASSIC HERB CHICKEN POT PIE

This delicious pot pie is made with a rich chicken breast filling and sports a lighter-than-air pastry top.

6 to 8 servings

Pastry
1 cup all-purpose flour
1 teaspoon baking powder
½ teaspoon salt
4 tablespoons cold unsalted butter
1½ tablespoons lard
⅓ cup ice cold water

Filling
3 boneless, skinless chicken breasts (about 3 pounds), cut into bite-sized cubes

All-purpose flour for dredging
Canola or other light vegetable oil for frying
Salt and freshly ground black pepper to taste
2 tablespoons dried *herbes de Provence*

Sauce

6 tablespoons unsalted butter
7 tablespoons all-purpose flour
3 cups rich chicken stock (see page 9), warmed
½ cup heavy cream
Salt and freshly ground black pepper to taste
Dash of mace
1 egg mixed with 1 tablespoon water for pastry glaze

1. To make the crust, combine the flour, baking powder, and salt in a large bowl. Cut in the butter and lard with a pastry cutter or fork to form pea-sized pieces. Add the ice water all at once and stir quickly with a fork just until mixed. Refrigerate, covered, for 1 to 2 hours.

2. Coat the chicken pieces with flour.

3. In a large heavy sauté pan or skillet, heat just enough oil to cover the bottom of the pan over medium-high heat. Sauté the chicken until lightly brown. Transfer to a bowl and sprinkle with salt, pepper, and *herbes de Provence.*

4. To make the sauce, melt the butter over low heat in a 4-quart saucepan. Stirring constantly, sprinkle the flour into the pan and cook to form a roux (mixture should be slightly browned). Continue stirring and slowly add the stock, starting with ¼- to ½-cup amounts. Cook the mixture over low heat until it thickens. Stir in the cream. Add salt, pepper, and mace. Combine the chicken with the sauce and put the mixture in an ovenproof casserole dish.

5. Preheat the oven to 350°F.

6. On a lightly floured board or pastry cloth, roll out the pastry to ⅛-inch thick. Shape the pastry to match the casserole dish and carefully lay on top of the chicken breast mixture to cover the chicken completely with extra pastry to tuck under. Tuck any overlapping pastry into the casserole. Decorate the top with pastry scraps cut into leaf shapes. Cut a slit in the middle of the pastry to allow the steam to escape during cooking.

7. Brush the pastry with the egg glaze. Bake for 40 to 45 minutes, until the crust is golden and the filling is bubbling hot.

BAKED GREEN CHILES AND CHICKEN

2 to 4 servings

4 tablespoons canola or other light vegetable oil
2 boneless chicken breasts (about 2 pounds), halved
1 cup minced onion
20 mild green chiles (canned)
1 ½ cups heavy cream
1 teaspoon Tabasco
2 teaspoons fresh lemon juice
½ teaspoon salt
Freshly ground black pepper to taste
1 cup grated Monterey Jack cheese

1. In a sauté pan or heavy skillet, heat the oil over medium-high heat. Add the chicken breasts and sauté about 2 to 3 minutes or until lightly browned on the skin side only. Put them in a single layer in an ovenproof casserole just large enough for the breasts to be touching, skin side up.

2. Add the onion to the sauté pan and cook until translucent. Add half the chiles, heat through, and pour the mixture over the chicken breasts. Preheat the oven to 350°F

3. Combine the remaining chiles, cream, Tabasco sauce, lemon juice, salt, and black pepper in a blender or food processor and blend until smooth and slightly thickened. Pour over the chicken and sprinkle on the cheese.

4. Bake for 25 to 30 minutes or until done. Serve hot.

NORTH AFRICAN BASTILLE

This relatively easy-to-prepare dish is perfect for a buffet with cocktails. The flavors are nothing short of unique, complex, and, some would say, unforgettable.

4 to 6 servings

4 tablespoons unsalted butter
1 cup rich chicken stock (see page 9)
1 teaspoon curry powder
1 onion, finely chopped
1 sprig of cilantro
1 teaspoon ground ginger
¼ teaspoon cinnamon

Pinch of allspice
1 tablespoon chopped parsley
2 chicken breasts (about 2 pounds)
¾ cup finely chopped blanched almonds
4 tablespoons sugar
1 tablespoon lemon juice
4 eggs, lightly beaten
8 sheets phyllo dough
8 tablespoons melted unsalted butter
Powdered sugar
Cinnamon

1. In a small saucepan, combine 2 tablespoons of the butter, stock, curry powder, onion, coriander, ginger, cinnamon, allspice, and parsley and bring to a boil. Reduce the heat to medium and continue cooking, uncovered, for 15 minutes.

2. Add the chicken breasts to the saucepan, cover, and simmer for 10 minutes or until firm to the touch. Let cool to room temperature. Remove the chicken to a strainer, reserving the stock in its saucepan. Discard the bones and skin and cut the meat into small bite-sized pieces. Set aside.

3. Melt the remaining 2 tablespoons of butter in a small sauté pan. Cook the almonds for 2 to 3 minutes or until lightly browned. Remove from the heat and add the sugar. Stir and set aside.

4. Place the reserved stock over medium-low heat. Add the lemon juice and bring to a low simmer. Add the eggs, cooking until done. (This mixture will be somewhat curdled and have the appearance of scrambled eggs.) Remove from the heat immediately and set aside.

5. Preheat the oven to 450°F.

6. Brush a lightly dampened dish towel (not terry cloth) with melted butter and place a sheet of phyllo dough on the towel. Coat the phyllo generously with melted butter. Continue layering all the sheets of the phyllo dough, brushing each with a generous amount of melted butter before topping with the next.

7. Brush a baking pan with melted butter.

8. Layer the chicken mixture, the egg, and the nuts over the phyllo dough, spreading evenly. Carefully roll up the dough like a jelly roll. Place in a shallow baking pan seam side down. Brush with melted butter all over the top and sides and tuck the ends under. Bake immediately or cover with a dampened kitchen towel to keep the phyllo from drying out.

9. Bake 23 to 30 minutes or until the phyllo is deep golden brown. When done, sprinkle generously with powdered sugar and a small amount of cinnamon. Let cool slightly and slice just before serving. Serve hot or warm.

CHICKEN BAKED IN CLAY

Claypot cooking is quick and versatile, and just about any ingredients in the pot will taste terrific with chicken breasts once the flavors get together. Remember, always put the tightly closed clay pot in a cold oven, then turn on the heat. The clay could crack if the pot is put in a hot oven. When done, this type of cooked chicken breast is meltingly tender and delicious.

2 to 4 servings

2 skinless, boneless (optional) chicken breasts (about 2 pounds)
4 tablespoons unsalted butter, cut into pieces
¼ teaspoon dried oregano
1 teaspoon chopped fresh basil or ½ teaspoon dried basil
3 cloves garlic, peeled and minced
Salt and freshly ground black pepper to taste
¼ cup chicken rich stock (see page 9)
½ cup dry sherry, vermouth, or white wine
2 green apples, cored and sliced

1. Put the chicken in a clay pot, bone side up. Dot with butter and sprinkle with oregano, basil, garlic, and salt and pepper.

2. Warm the stock and wine slightly. Pour over the chicken pieces. Arrange the apple slices around the chicken breasts. Close the clay pot tightly. Place in the center of the cold oven, directly on the oven rack. Close the door and turn the heat to 450°F. Bake 45 to 50 minutes, or until the chicken is very tender.

Variation: Greek Chicken Breasts
Rub the chicken breasts with garlic and olive oil and sprinkle with salt, pepper, and oregano. Make a layer of thinly sliced lemon rounds on the bottom of the clay pot. Put the chicken breasts on the lemon and surround with Greek olives. Bake as directed.

Variation: Orange Chicken Breasts Baked in Clay
Put ½ cup slightly warmed orange juice, 2 medium onions, quartered, 2 teaspoons fine herbs, 4 tablespoons butter, ½ teaspoon white pepper, salt to taste, 1 teaspoon dry dill, and 2 tablespoons Cointreau (orange liqueur) in the clay pot along with the chicken breasts, breast side down. Seal and bake as directed.

***** 3-1-2005

CHICKEN BREASTS PARMESAN

½ cup all-purpose flour
2 skinless, boneless chicken breasts (about 2 pounds), halved and flattened between plastic wrap to ½-inch thickness
½ teaspoon salt
¼ teaspoon white pepper
2 eggs, well beaten
1 cup freshly grated Parmesan cheese (or more to taste)
8 tablespoons unsalted butter
1 cup finely chopped fresh parsley

1. Sprinkle the flour on a plate. Dredge the chicken breasts in the flour, shaking off the excess. Sprinkle the breasts with salt and pepper.

2. Beat the eggs into the Parmesan cheese in a bowl, making a stiff batter. Dip the breasts in the batter until well coated. Allow to stand at room temperature for about 1 hour to set.

4. Preheat the oven to 325 F.

5. In a sauté pan or skillet melt the butter over medium-high heat Add the chicken breasts and sauté for 2 to 3 minutes on each side or until the batter is golden brown.

5. Place in an oven-proof dish in one layer and bake for 10 to 12 minutes or until done. Sprinkle with parsley before serving.

add sauce

CHICKEN BREASTS WITH CHICKEN LIVER STUFFING

4 servings

6 tablespoons unsalted butter
2 tablespoons pine nuts
⅓ pound chicken livers
1 clove garlic, minced
2 tablespoons finely chopped shallots
2 tablespoons minced fresh parsley
Pinch of freshly grated nutmeg
Salt and freshly ground black pepper to taste
4 tablespoons white wine (chardonnay)
4 large springs of parsley for garnish
2 skinless, boneless free-range chicken breasts (about 2½ pounds), halved, slit open to form a pocket (see page 239)
3 tablespoons melted unsalted butter

1. Melt 2 tablespoons of the butter over medium heat in a sauté pan or skillet. Add the pine nuts and cook until browned. Remove from the pan and set aside.

2. In the same sauté pan, melt 2 tablespoons of the butter over medium heat. Add the chicken livers and cook about 3 to 4 minutes; the livers will still be slightly pink inside. Set aside.

3. Add the garlic to the pan and cook 1 minute or until lightly browned. Increase the heat to medium-high, add the shallots, and cook until soft. Add the minced parsley, nutmeg, salt, pepper, and 2 tablespoons of the wine. Continue cooking about 2 minutes more or until the wine has evaporated completely. Remove from the heat and let cool slightly.

4. Coarsely chop the pine nuts. Mash the chicken livers with the tines of a fork to form a paste. Combine the chicken livers with the parsley and shallot mixture; fold in the pine nuts. Place equal amounts of the stuffing in the prepared chicken breast. Press the edges together to seal.

5. Preheat the oven to 325°F.

6. Melt the remaining 2 tablespoons of butter over medium-high heat in a sauté pan or skillet. Add the chicken breasts and sauté for 2 to 3 minutes per side, or just until lightly browned. When turning the breasts, be very careful that the stuffing does not come out. Transfer to an ovenproof baking pan.

7. Over high heat, deglaze the pan with the remaining 2 tablespoons of wine, stirring constantly and scraping to loosen any bits on the bottom of the pan. Reduce the liquid slightly and pour over the chicken breasts. Cover the pan tightly with foil and bake for 10 to 12 minutes or until done. Transfer to a serving platter and garnish with parsley.

Variation: Italian Sausage Stuffing

In a sauté pan, melt 2 tablespoons of butter over medium heat. Add ¼ pound finely ground Italian sausage meat removed from the casings and cook until almost done. Add ¼ cup finely chopped onion and continue cooking until the onion is tender. Add black pepper to taste and ¼ teaspoon dried oregano. Combine ½ cup fresh bread crumbs, ¼ cup chopped parsley, and salt to taste. Mix into the sausage. Stuff the chicken breasts and bake as directed.

ACAPULCO ENCHILADA

4 servings

3 cups shredded poached chicken breast meat (see page 353)
½ cup minced scallion, white and some of the green part
½ cup chopped blanched almonds
½ teaspoon salt
3 cups Enchilada Chile Sauce (see recipe following)
8 fresh corn tortillas
¾ cup sour cream
1 cup shredded cheddar cheese
½ cup sliced pitted ripe olives
Additional sour cream and scallion for garnish

Enchilada Chile Sauce

2 tablespoons vegetable oil
⅔ cup chopped onion
¼ cup chopped green bell pepper
1 clove garlic, minced
1 cup tomato paste
1 cup water
¼ cup chile powder
1 teaspoon salt
½ teaspoon dried oregano

1. Toss together the shredded chicken, scallions, almonds, and salt and pepper in a small bowl. Toss to mix.

2. To prepare the sauce, heat the oil in a sauté pan over medium-high heat. Add the onion, bell pepper, and garlic and cook until the vegetables are soft. Stir in the tomato paste, water, chile powder, salt, and oregano and combine well. Lower the heat, cover, and simmer for 5 minutes.

3. Preheat the oven to 350°F.

4. To assemble the enchiladas, lightly oil the bottom of a decorative shallow ovenproof casserole. Dip a tortilla in the hot sauce until partially saturated and place the tortilla in the casserole dish. Fill the tortilla with one eighth of the chicken mixture and top with 1 tablespoon each of sour cream and cheese. Roll the tortilla into an enchilada, seam side down. Repeat with the remaining tortillas. When the casserole is filled, drizzle the remaining sauce over the enchiladas, sprinkle with cheddar cheese, and top with olives.

5. Bake the enchiladas for 15 minutes or until the cheese and sauce are hot and bubbling. Serve with additional sour cream and chopped scallions on the side.

SPICY INDIAN CHICKEN BREASTS

4 to 6 servings

3 chicken breasts (about 3 pounds), halved
¼ teaspoon dry mustard
1 teaspoon filtered water
½ teaspoon crushed red pepper flakes
½ teaspoon freshly ground black pepper
½ teaspoon ground cardamom
½ teaspoon ground ginger
½ teaspoon cumin seed
1 teaspoon curry powder
2 cloves garlic, peeled
1 tablespoon salt
¼ cup cider vinegar
2 tablespoons fresh lemon juice
2 cups plain yogurt, regular or low-fat
½ cup canola or other light vegetable oil

1. Arrange the chicken breasts in a single layer in a shallow glass or ceramic dish.

2. Combine the mustard, water, red pepper, black pepper, cardamom, ginger, cumin, curry powder, garlic, salt, vinegar, lemon juice, and yogurt in a food processor or blender; blend thoroughly.

3. Pour the mixture over the chicken, cover with plastic wrap and marinate, refrigerated, for 12 hours.

4. Preheat the oven to 325°F when you are ready to cook the chicken breasts. Let the chicken come to room temperature for 30 minutes before cooking.

5. Heat the oil over medium high heat in a sauté pan or heavy skillet. Remove the chicken breasts from the marinade, letting the excess drain back into the dish. Reserve the marinade. Cook the chicken breasts for 2 to 3 minutes on each side, or just until lightly browned. Do not overcook.

6. Arrange the chicken breasts in an oven-proof baking dish and pour the reserved marinade over the chicken. Bake, uncovered, for 1 hour, basting with the marinade several times. Serve hot or at room temperature.

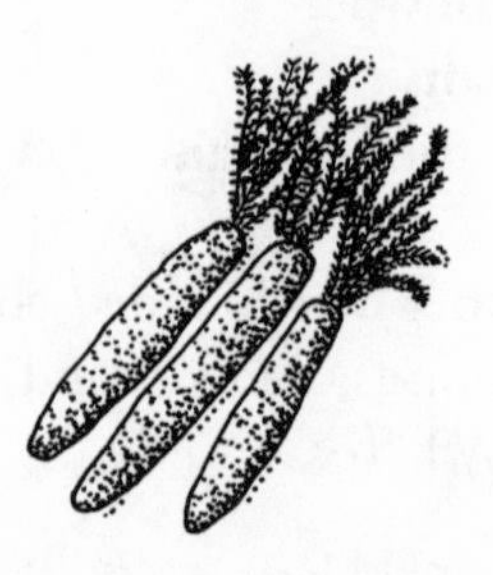

APRICOT-ALMOND CHICKEN BREAST PAUPIETTES

Consider this dish for a buffet or as an appetizer as well as another of the many great ways to serve the endlessly versatile chicken breast.

4 to 6 servings

4 cloves garlic, peeled
1 cup finely chopped dried apricots, marinated in 1 cup apple juice, drained (reserve ½ cup apple juice)
½ cup finely minced fresh parsley
Salt and freshly ground white pepper to taste
¼ cup extra-virgin olive oil
3 skinless, boneless chicken breasts (about 3 pounds), halved and flattened between plastic wrap to ½-inch thickness
½ cup white raisins
1 cup sour cream, regular or light
¼ cup sliced almonds, toasted in a 350°F oven for 10 minutes, until brown and crispy

1. Preheat the oven to 350°F. Lightly oil the bottom of a 7 × 11-inch baking pan.

2. Add the garlic, apricots, parsley, and salt and pepper to a food processor or blender and process to a smooth paste.

3. Heat the oil over medium-low heat in a sauté pan. Add the apricot mixture and cook for about 5 minutes, stirring constantly.

4. Spread half the mixture on the flattened chicken breasts, roll into paupiettes (like jellyrolls), and place, seam side down, in the baking pan. Tent the pan with foil and bake for 10 to 12 minutes or just until done. Do not overcook.

5. To make the sauce, put the reserved apple juice and the raisins in the sauté pan over medium-high heat. Cook, stirring occasionally, until the liquid has almost completely evaporated. Remove the pan from the heat and stir in the sour cream until thoroughly blended. Return to very low heat, just to warm through. Pour the sauce over the paupiettes and sprinkle with toasted almonds.

Variation: Walnut and Garlic Chicken Breast Paupiettes

In place of the apricots, use 1 cup walnuts, and walnut oil instead of olive oil. Eliminate the raisins. Prepare in the same way and cook as directed.

Grill, Broil, & Smoke

These days, with fast, easy, and low-fat cooking at the forefront of the food scene, the broiler is making a comeback. This modern-day, all-weather, 100% reliable, fast, and fat-free cooking machine is always ready when you are. But when the weather is great and you have to choose between broiling and grilling out in the backyard with friends and neighbors, the hands-down choice is to go for the grill! It's not just a charcoal and lighter-fluid affair anymore. A barbecue grill is now an all-in-one grill and smoker. It's also a great way to toast peasant bread slices and roast a whole head of garlic as well as vegetables, like tomatoes for a smoked tomato sauce, or grilled Maui Onion Marmalade (see page 222). When cooked in this manner, chicken breasts are especially flavorful. First, make a marinade of complex essences and then let the lean white meat soak up the flavors (see page 187 for a variety of great marinades). A basting sauce, such as Texas Bar-B-Q on page 189, can transform the chicken breast into a flavor-packed entrée with very little effort. Simply baste, grill, and eat! Once you've chosen a cooking method, whether it's grilling, smoking, or broiling, that's where the fun begins. Serve the cooked chicken breasts with an endless number of dishes, such as pastas, alongside garlic-mashed potatoes, in salads, on couscous, between a bun, wrapped in a tortilla, or with papaya-mango salsa on the side. In addition, for those who want to start smoking foods, this is the place to light your fire! In this chapter, you'll find lots of easy tips to get going. The only foreseeable problem is which recipe to try first. You pick!

BROILED CHICKEN BREASTS WITH WARM SEEDLESS GRAPE RELISH

This relish is also delightful with sliced smoked chicken breasts.

4 servings

Relish

½ cup chopped onion
½ cup red wine vinegar
½ cup dry red wine
¼ cup chopped dried figs
2 tablespoons sugar
2 teaspoons mild or hot paprika
1 teaspoon grated peeled fresh ginger
1 3-inch piece cinnamon stick
1 cup seedless green grapes, halved
1 cup seedless red grapes, halved

2 skinless boneless chicken breasts (about 2 pounds), halved
1 teaspoon canola oil
Salt and freshly ground black pepper to taste

1. Prepare the broiler.

2. To make the relish, combine the onion, vinegar, red wine, dried fig, sugar, paprika, ginger, and cinnamon stick in a heavy saucepan. Bring to a boil and cook 10 minutes. Stir in the grapes, reduce the heat to low, and simmer 20 minutes more. Remove the cinnamon stick and transfer to a bowl, keep warm.

3. Place the chicken breasts on the broiler pan and brush with oil on both sides. Sprinkle with salt and pepper. Broil for 5 minutes per side or until done throughout.

4. Slice the breasts across the grain into rounds, arrange on plates, and top with a dollop of the relish. Serve the remaining relish on the side.

RAISE YOUR GLASS TO A NEW WAY OF GRILLING AND SMOKING – SPIKED WOOD CHIPS!

The Jack Daniels whiskey distillery in Lynchburg, Tennessee, is now licensing Nature-Glo Brand Charcoal Briquettes and Barrel Chunks—briquettes formed out of local sugar maple wood and pulverized white oak barrels once used to age their famous alcohol. The briquettes, which sell for about $3.25 per seven-pound bag, lend an outdoorsy flavor to food grilled over the spiky aromatic embers, and with nary a trace of whiskey breath!

ROSEMARY MARINATED CHICKEN AND SUMMER SQUASH KEBABS

Soaking the wooden skewers in a flavorful liquid instead of water adds a surprising burst of flavor to the inside of the chicken pieces. Try white wine or lemon juice for this recipe, or rum, red wine, or soy sauce.

4 servings

2 tablespoons chopped fresh rosemary
4 tablespoons extra-virgin olive oil
2 cloves garlic, minced
Rind of ½ a lemon, cut in thin strips
2 boneless skinless chicken breasts (about 2 pounds), cut into 1-inch cubes
2 tablespoons fresh lemon juice
1 tablespoon honey mustard
Salt and freshly ground black pepper to taste
1 pound yellow squash, cut into 1-inch pieces
2 small onions, cut in half through the center lengthwise and separated
1 pound zucchini, cut into 1-inch pieces
Extra-virgin olive oil for brushing
8 to 10 10-inch wooden skewers soaked in water for 30 minutes

1. Combine the rosemary, lemon rind, and half the olive oil and garlic in a shallow dish. Add the chicken and turn to coat on all sides. Cover tightly with plastic wrap and marinate, refrigerated, for 1 hour.

2. Fire up the grill or prepare the broiler.

3. Combine the remaining oil and garlic, lemon juice, honey mustard, and salt and pepper in a small bowl, whisk to mix well.

4. Thread the chicken, zucchini, and yellow squash on the skewers alternately with pieces of the onion in between each chicken or squash piece. Grill for 5 minutes per side or until done throughout.

5. Place the skewers on a platter, drizzle on the lemon mixture or serve it on the side as a dipping sauce.

Q: When is it best to leave the bone and/or skin intact?

A: When grilling, leaving on the bone and skin is optional and just a matter of taste. Those who eat the grill-crisped skin will let you know of their expectations, so leave a few pieces intact. However, when the chicken breasts require flattening, the skin and bone must go!

PEPPER-CRUSTED CHICKEN BREASTS WITH CARAMELIZED ONIONS

This dish can easily be accompanied by grilled bread spread with roasted garlic.

4 servings

2 skinless, boneless chicken breast (about 2 pounds), halved, flattened slightly
2 teaspoons extra-virgin olive oil
2 cloves garlic, minced
½ teaspoon salt
4 tablespoons cracked black pepper or more to taste
¼ cup brandy (best quality)
2 tablespoons unsalted butter
4 cups vertically sliced onions
3 tablespoons balsamic vinegar
1 teaspoon dried thyme

1. Prepare the broiler.

2. Place the chicken breasts in a broiler pan.

3. Heat the olive oil over medium heat in a small sauté pan. Add the garlic and cook until lightly browned. Remove from the heat. Add the salt, pepper, and brandy and stir. Pour over the chicken breasts. Cover loosely with plastic wrap and marinate for 15 minutes.

4. To make the onions, melt the butter over medium-high heat in a sauté pan. Lower the heat, add the onions and sweat them for 5 minutes until they lose their juices. Add the vinegar and thyme, stir to mix well, and cover. Continue cooking 5 to 7 minutes more or until tender. Uncover and continue cooking until all the liquid has evaporated and the onions are a nicely browned. Keep warm.

5. Broil the breasts for about 5 minutes per side or until done throughout. Serve with the onions spooned over the top. Serve the remaining caramelized onion on the side.

POP YOUR TOAST ON THE GRILL!

Just about any bread benefits from grilling. Try thick slices of a crusty peasant loaf, baguette, pita pockets, corn bread, biscuits, or tortillas. Lightly brush both sides of the bread with a fruity olive oil (using a bunch of herbs as a brush adds more flavor) and sprinkle with coarse salt. Rub slices with the cut side of a garlic clove, if desired. Grill over gentle heat on the perimeter, with the entrée cooking in the center.

MOJO GRILLED CHICKEN

Here's a Cuban-Latin flavor combination which is a staple from the Caribbean to Havana. It's growing in popularity in the U.S. as Latin flavors gain greater attention.

4 to 6 servings

½ cup chopped garlic
½ cup extra-virgin olive oil
¼ cup white wine vinegar
¼ cup fresh lime juice
3 tablespoons chopped flat-leaf parsley
2 tablespoons chopped cilantro
2 teaspoons paprika
½ teaspoon cayenne
Salt and freshly ground pepper to taste
3 chicken breasts (about 3 pounds), halved, skin and bone on or off

1. Heat the olive oil over medium heat in a sauté pan. Add the garlic, lower the heat, and cook for 10 minutes. Remove from the heat and let cool. Strain, reserving the oil.

2. To make the marinade, combine the vinegar, lemon juice, parsley, cilantro, paprika, cayenne, salt and pepper, and garlic in a small bowl. Add the oil in a thin steady stream whisking constantly until well incorporated.

3. Brush the chicken pieces on the breast and bone sides with the marinade. Let stand for 20 to 30 minutes.

4. Fire up the grill or prepare the broiler.

5. Grill the chicken breasts 5 to 6 minutes per side or until done throughout. Serve hot or at room temperature.

PATIENCE, PLEASE!

Mythology tells us mankind has been cooking gourmet grilled food over glowing embers since Prometheus (who might have been the first grill chef on earth). The technique has reached a very high level of proficiency except for one typical failing—lack of patience.

There's no such thing as an instant grill, except if it's on the countertop and fired by electricity. But for the delicious taste of outdoor grilling, patience is the primary ingredient for mastery of this ancient cooking technique: You must wait for the coals to catch, for the flames to die down, for slow cooking that will ensure aromatic succulent smoke-flavored food, which only grilling over glowing ash-covered embers can impart.

Timing, too, is crucial. The charcoal will not be ready to use for at least 30 minutes after the fire is started. There is no way that this process can be speeded up, so allow yourself plenty of time. This method can provide a leisure cooking experience at its best. Why rush? Have a beer!

LEMON THYME BROILED CHICKEN BREASTS WITH ROASTED RED POTATO SALAD

This recipe easily translates to the grill or broiler with no adjustments.
This potato salad recipe is influenced by the cooking of Provence, where it is usually dressed simply, *sans* mayonnaise.

4 to 6 servings

3 skinless free-range chicken breasts (about 3½ pounds)
1 teaspoon grated lemon zest
Juice of 4 lemons (about 1 cups)
¼ cup chopped fresh thyme
2 tablespoons extra-virgin olive oil
2 tablespoons honey
Salt and freshly ground black pepper to taste

Potato Salad

8 medium red new potatoes, well washed, and pricked with a fork
2 tablespoons extra-virgin olive oil
1½ teaspoons lemon juice
3 tablespoons white wine (chardonnay)
2 tablespoons finely chopped fresh flat-leaf parsley
1 small clove garlic, finely minced
Salt and freshly ground black pepper to taste

1. To make the potato salad, preheat the oven to 350°F.

2. Place the potatoes in a baking dish and bake for 45 to 50 minutes or until done throughout. Let cool.

3. Cut the potatoes into thin slices, skin on, and place in a bowl.

4. Place the olive oil, lemon juice, wine, parsley, and a scant amount of salt and pepper in a jar with a tight-fitting lid. Shake to mix. Pour over the potatoes and toss to mix well. Adjust the seasoning with salt and pepper and chill. Remove from the refrigerator 20 minutes before serving. (This salad is best served at room temperature with hot chicken.)

5. Fire up the grill or preheat the broiler.

6. Arrange the chicken pieces in a glass dish large enough to hold the chicken in a single layer.

7. Combine the lemon zest, juice, thyme, olive oil, and honey in a bowl. Pour over the chicken and turn to coat well. If using boneless chicken, place the chicken breast side down into the marinade. Marinate, refrigerated, 1 to 2 hours. Allow the chicken to come to room temperature before cooking.

8. Grill or broil the chicken for 6 minutes per side, turning twice, or until done throughout. Serve hot or at room temperature.

SPICY PEANUT CHICKEN

2 to 4 servings

½ cup smooth peanut butter (all peanuts with no salt or sugar added)
5 tablespoons soy sauce or tamari
1 tablespoon brown sugar
2 tablespoons filtered water
2 cloves garlic, minced
1 tablespoon fresh lemon juice
1 teaspoon dried crushed red chiles or ½ teaspoon red pepper flakes
½ teaspoon cinnamon
4 tablespoons unsalted butter
1 onion, chopped
2 chicken breasts (about 2 pounds), halved, skinless, and boneless if desired

1. Combine the peanut butter, soy sauce, brown sugar, water, garlic, lemon juice, chiles, and cinnamon in a blender or food processor. Transfer the mixture into a saucepan.

2. Heat the ingredients in the saucepan over low heat. Add the butter and melt, stirring occasionally. Cool to room temperature.

3. Place the onion and chicken breasts in a shallow glass dish or ceramic dish in a single layer. Pour on the marinade, cover tightly with plastic wrap, and marinate refrigerated for 12 hours.

4. Fire up the grill or prepare the broiler. Cook the chicken for about 5 to 6 minutes on each side, turning several times during grilling, until done throughout.

Q: How should bone-in breasts be prepared so they lie flat on the grill?

A: When the breasts are left whole and the bone in, crack the bone to flatten it with a few strong smacks directly in the center (skin side up, bone side on a flat, hard surface), using the palm of your hand or a heavy cast-iron skillet.

SESAME-LEMON CHICKEN

4 servings

½ cup soy sauce or tamari
½ cup fresh lemon juice
2 teaspoons light sesame oil
1 teaspoon sugar
¼ teaspoon salt
2 chicken breasts (about 2 pounds), halved, skinless and boneless if desired

1. In a bowl, combine the soy sauce, lemon juice, sesame oil, sugar, and salt.

2. Arrange the chicken in one layer in a shallow glass or ceramic dish. Pour on the marinade and let sit at room temperature for 1 hour, turning and basting frequently.

3. Fire up the grill or prepare the broiler. Cook the chicken breasts, starting with the bone side up for 5 to 6 minutes per side or until done throughout. Baste and turn several times during cooking.

QUICK MARINADES—A REFERENCE GUIDE TO ETHNIC FLAVOR COMBINATIONS

Thai: Juice of 2 limes, 2 tablespoons fish sauce, 3 tablespoons soy sauce, 1 minced shallot, 2 to 3 tablespoons cold-pressed peanut oil, and 3 hot green chiles, such as jalapeños, seeded and minced.

Southwestern: Juice of 2 limes, ½ cup tequila, 2 tablespoons extra-virgin olive oil, ¼ cup balsamic vinegar, 1 chopped onion, 5 minced cloves garlic, 1 large chopped tomato, ¼ teaspoon red pepper flakes, 1 tablespoon chopped fresh oregano, 3 tablespoons chopped flat-leaf parsley, and a pinch of salt and pepper.

Mediterranean: 3 tablespoons extra-virgin olive oil, ¼ cup balsamic vinegar, 1 chopped onion, 5 minced cloves garlic, 1 large chopped tomato, ⅛ teaspoon red pepper flakes, 1 tablespoon chopped fresh oregano, and 3 tablespoons chopped flat-leaf parsley.

East Indian: ½ cup plain non-fat yogurt, 2 tablespoons vegetable oil, juice of 1 lime, juice of 1 lemon, ½ chopped onion, 3 minced cloves garlic, 2 tablespoons Indian tandoori spice, and a pinch of salt.

Provencal: 1 cup dry white wine, juice of 1 lemon, 1 chopped onion, 1 tablespoon Dijon mustard, 1 teaspoon honey, 5 tablespoons herbes de Provence, and salt and freshly ground black pepper.

Chinese: 1 head garlic, cloves peeled and minced; 1 tablespoon plum sauce; ¼ cup dry sherry; 1 tablespoon soy sauce; 1 tablespoon Chinese chile paste; and 1 tablespoon minced fresh cilantro.

Texas: 4 minced cloves garlic, 1 small, hot, seeded red chile, 1 teaspoon chopped fresh cilantro, ¼ teaspoon ground cumin, ½ teaspoon ground anise seed, pinch of salt, 2 tablespoons brown sugar, 1 tablespoon Worcestershire sauce, 1 cup cider vinegar, 2 cups ketchup, and 1 to 2 tablespoons Tabasco sauce.

CHINESE MARINADE FOR GRILLED CHICKEN

2 to 4 servings

2 chicken breasts (about 2 pounds), halved, skinless, and boneless if desired
3 tablespoons soy sauce or tamari
2 tablespoons honey
2 tablespoons hoisin sauce
2 tablespoons white wine vinegar
2 tablespoons rice wine
2 tablespoons pale dry sherry
1 teaspoon crushed garlic
1 teaspoon minced fresh peeled ginger
1 teaspoon sugar
2 tablespoons chicken stock (see page 8)
2 tablespoons Chinese plum sauce*

*Available in Asian markets and some grocery stores

1. Place the chicken in a shallow dish.

2. To prepare the marinade, combine the soy sauce, honey, hoisin sauce, vinegar, rice wine vinegar, sherry, garlic, ginger, sugar, stock, and plum sauce in a small bowl. Whisk to mix well.

3. Pour the marinade over the chicken and let set at room temperature for 1 hour or up to 2 hours refrigerated.

4. Fire up the grill or prepare the broiler. Grill 5 to 6 minutes per side, turning several times during cooking. Serve hot or at room temperature.

SMOKING, SOAKING, AND BASTING FOR MORE FLAVOR

To produce more flavorful smoke from your grill, water-soak aromatic wood chips for 15 minutes and toss onto the coals. Moisture increases the smolder effect, sending more flavor up to the food. Or soak herbs, dried apples, or peaches and toss them onto the coals for extra-interesting aromatic smoke. Covering the grill for part of the cooking time creates even more intense flavor results.

Marinating foods in flavorful, slightly acidic liquids before grilling serves the threefold purpose of tenderizing, moisturizing (to prevent grill dry-out), and enhancing the flavor. Even oil-based marinades add minimal calories, because most of the marinade drips off during grilling.

For a quick shot of flavor (without the hours required for marinating meat), infuse ½ cup olive oil with a generous tablespoon of chopped fresh herbs, orange peel, cracked pepper, red pepper flakes, cumin, or shallots. Brush on the chicken breasts before grilling for instant and fantastic flavor.

For paillards, cutlets, or thin boneless pieces of poultry, marinate for at least 30 minutes. Watch carefully and baste frequently while cooking, as they overcook easily.

LONE STAR BBQ SAUCE

The favorite of Lone-Star native Mark Erwin.

4 to 6 servings

3 chicken breasts (about 3 pounds), halved
¼ cup red wine vinegar
1 teaspoon salt
½ teaspoon crushed garlic
1 tablespoon brown sugar
¼ teaspoon black pepper
8 tablespoons unsalted butter
1 medium onion, chopped
1 tablespoon prepared mustard (such asDijon-style)
Juice of ½ lemon
1 teaspoon chile powder
¼ cup chile sauce (see page 29)
3 tablespoons Worcestershire sauce
¼ bottle beer

1. Place the chicken breasts skin side up in a shallow glass or ceramic dish in a single layer.

2. Combine the vinegar, salt, garlic, brown sugar, black pepper, butter, onion, mustard, lemon juice, and chile powder in a small saucepan over low heat. Simmer for 5 minutes and remove from the heat.

3. Add the chile sauce, Worcestershire sauce, and beer to the saucepan. Bring to a boil and remove from the heat.

4. Brush the chicken breasts with the barbecue sauce and let stand at room temperature for 30 minutes.

5. Fire up the barbecue grill or prepare the broiler. Place the chicken breasts on the grill or broiler, 6 to 8 inches from the heat source, starting with the bone side toward the heat. Baste frequently and turn several times during the cooking process. Cook for 8 to 10 minutes, or until the barbecue sauce turns very brown and crispy and the chicken is done throughout. Serve hot or at room temperature.

MESQUITE OR PINE BOUGH-SCENTED SMOKED CHICKEN BREASTS

Mesquite or pine boughs add a rich and woody flavor to the chicken breasts. Served hot or cold, this recipe is excellent. The flavor is an unexpected treat in salads and sandwiches.

2 to 4 servings

1 cup dry white wine (chardonnay)
½ cup dry Spanish sherry
5 garlic cloves, coarsely chopped
1 medium onion, chopped
1 tablespoon brown sugar
Salt and black pepper to taste
2 chicken breasts (about 2 pounds), halved
4 to 5 pine boughs or ½ pound mesquite wood chips soaked in water for 30 minutes

1. Process the wine, sherry, garlic, onion, sugar, and salt and pepper in a food processor or blender until liquefied.

2. Arrange the chicken in a single layer in a shallow glass or ceramic dish. Pour on the marinade, cover, and refrigerate for 4 to 6 hours, turning several times.

3. Fire up the grill. Lightly coat the grill rack with cooking spray. When the coals are white-hot and ready, toss on the pine boughs or mesquite chips to the fire, and let burn for 2 minutes with the grill lid closed.

4. Arrange the chicken breasts on the grill, 7 to 9 inches from the coals. Cook, with the lid of the grill closed, for 5 to 6 minutes on each side. The chicken will cook and smoke at the same time. Cook the chicken until it is done throughout.

IT MAY BE RAINING ON THE GRILL, BUT THE BROILER IS DRY!

Preheat the broiler for at least 15 minutes before beginning to cook. The breast meat should be at least ½-inch thick. If it's thinner, there is a good chance it will dry out too quickly. Place the chicken breasts in a shallow broiler-proof pan and add just enough liquid—such as wine, vermouth, lemon juice, stock, or water—to keep the meat from drying out. (Marinated chicken breasts are more likely to stay moist throughout broiling.) Set the broiler grill so the chicken breasts are 5 to 6 inches from the direct flame. Turn once during cooking, about 4 to 6 minutes per side, or just until done throughout. Don't overcook.

SHARPEN YOUR OUTDOOR GRILL SKILLS

It doesn't really matter whether you're using a simple hibachi or a fancy outdoor custom cooker-smoker, here are surefire tips for success:

1. The coals: Use wood chips and hardwood charcoal to fuel your fire. Mesquite, oak, hickory, beech, fruitwoods (cherry, apple, pecan), and grapevine cuttings infuse foods with robust to delicate smoky flavors. Charcoal briquettes may be included along with wood chips for up to half of the total fuel. Of course, the ideal grilling fire would be composed completely of aromatic wood.

2. Building the fire: Successful grilling depends on steady cooking; coals that are not hot enough to give even heat will char food before cooking it through. Here are two fire-building methods guaranteed not to fizzle out:

- For a hardwood fire, make a roll of tightly crumbled newspaper (about 10 sheets) top with a layer of wood kindling and 15 to 25 hardwood chunks (depend on grill size). Light the paper in several places but don't start cooking until the wood coals glow red under a coating of white ash, about 30 minutes. To check whether coals are ready, hold the palm of your hand 5 or 6 inches above the grill. If you can tolerate the heat for only 3 or 4 seconds, your fire is ready. Don't rush!
- As a cheap alternative to the all-wood fire, mound 10 to 15 briquettes on a bed of crumbled newspapers, ignite, and let them burn down to red-hot coals, about 25 minutes. Add some vine clippings or wood chips just before grilling and throughout the cooking process. (Soak the chips in water first.)

3. Adjusting the heat: Food that's not browning needs a heat increase. But food that chars, blackens, or loses juices too quickly needs less heat. To get the heat just right:

- Push coals closer together to increase heat output. Spread coals out to reduce the heat.
- Also, raise the heat by opening the grill vents or lowering the grill height. To reduce heat, simply do the reverse: close the vents and raise the grill.
- Moving food to the center of the grill exposes it to higher temperatures; moving it to the periphery takes some heat off.

HERB AND FRENCH MUSTARD-BASTED CHICKEN BREASTS

4 to 6 servings

3 skinless, chicken breasts (about 3 pounds), halved
Salt and black pepper to taste

Mustard Herb Basting Sauce
3 tablespoons coarse French mustard (such as Moutarde de Meaux or Pommery)
2 egg yolks
1 scallion, white and some green part, chopped
1 teaspoon chopped fresh marjoram or ¼ teaspoon dried marjoram
2 tablespoons lemon juice
1 cup extra-virgin olive oil
½ cup heavy cream
1½ tablespoons capers, rinsed and drained
8 branches of fresh marjoram for scattering on the coals

1. Season the chicken breasts with salt and pepper.

2. Combine the mustard, egg yolks, scallions, marjoram, and lemon juice in a food processor or blender. With the motor running, gradually add the oil and mix well. Add the cream and capers and blend well.

3. Put the chicken breasts in a single layer in a shallow glass or ceramic dish. Pour on the marinade and let stand for 30 minutes.

4. Fire up the grill and strew the marjoram branches over the coals. Lightly coat the grilling rack with cooking spray. When the coals are white-hot, cook the chicken breast pieces 6 to 8 inches from the coals for 4 to 5 minutes on each side, turning and basting several times, until done throughout.

USE A HANDFUL OF HERBS AS A BASTING BRUSH, NATURALLY!

It looks great and this natural basting brush imparts its own particular flavor in the process. To make a natural herb brush, line up the herbs in even 6- to 7-inch lengths. Wind raffia or kitchen string around one end and tie to forma handle. Dip the brush in the basting or barbecue sauce and apply liberally to chicken breasts cooking on the grill. When you're tired of it and want to move on to another favored brush, just drop it in the fire and start over.

TANDOORI CHICKEN

4 to 6 servings

3 chicken breasts (about 3 pounds), halved
⅓ cup plus 2 tablespoons fresh lemon juice
1 teaspoon salt
½ teaspoon powdered saffron or 2 saffron threads, minced
2 teaspoons crushed coriander seeds
¼ teaspoon dried red pepper flakes
1 teaspoon cumin
2 large garlic cloves, coarsely chopped
1 teaspoon finely chopped fresh peeled ginger
1 cup plain yogurt, regular or low-fat
4 tablespoons unsalted butter or ghee

1. Prick the chicken breasts all over with a fork several times so the marinade can penetrate the meat.

2. Arrange the chicken breasts in a single layer in a shallow glass or ceramic dish.

3. Combine ⅓ cup of the lemon juice, salt, and saffron in a bowl. Rub this mixture into the chicken breasts with your hands.

4. Toast the coriander seeds, red pepper flakes, and cumin for about 2 minutes in a small skillet over medium heat, stirring constantly. Place in a food processor; add the garlic, ginger, and 4 tablespoons of the yogurt, and blend for 30 seconds. Add the remaining yogurt, mix well, and pour over the chicken breasts. Cover tightly and marinate, refrigerated, for at least 12 hours, turning the breasts several times.

5. Fire up the grill or prepare the broiler. Melt the butter in a small saucepan over medium heat. Remove the chicken from the marinade and drain off the excess. Discard the marinade. Baste the chicken breasts with the butter or ghee and grill 6 to 8 inches from the hot coals for 4 to 5 minutes per side, starting with the bone side toward the heat.

6. When the chicken breasts are done, sprinkle with the remaining 2 tablespoons of lemon juice.

SPICY SESAME CHICKEN BREAST

4 to 6 servings

3 boneless chicken breasts (about 3 pounds), halved
Salt and black pepper to taste

Marinade
4 tablespoons melted unsalted butter
¼ cup soy sauce
¼ cup dry white wine
1 teaspoon dried tarragon
1 teaspoon dry mustard
8 ounces sesame seeds

1. Salt and pepper the chicken breast.

2. Mix together the melted butter, soy sauce, wine, tarragon, and mustard in a bowl. Arrange the chicken breasts in a single layer in a shallow glass or ceramic dish. Pour on the marinade, and let stand at room temperature for 2 hours.

3. Fire up the grill or heat the broiler. Starting with the bone side toward the heat, cook the chicken 6 to 8 inches from the coals for 4 to 5 minutes per side. Baste the chicken breasts and turn several times during the cooking process.

4. Just before the chicken is done, remove from the fire and roll in the sesame seeds until well coated. Return the chicken breasts to the fire for 1 or 2 minutes or until the seeds are browned but are not burned. Serve hot or cold.

GRILLED FRUIT

Many fruits (except delicate soft berries) cook very well on the grill. Their flavors intensify, yet the sweetness is cut by the aromatic smoke. While grilled fruit makes a spectacular ending to any grilled dinner, don't limit it to dessert. Once grilled, the fruit can become a side dish, or quickly made into great puréed condiment for all types of poultry and meats when processed in a blender or food processor. The basic technique is to brush fruits (halved peaches, nectarines, plums, papayas, apricots, or pears) with melted butter or light vegetable oil. Sprinkle with a dusting of nutmeg, ground cloves, or ground cinnamon. For easy handling, grill in a wire basket. Start testing for doneness (fruit should be soft but not mushy) after 3 to 5 minutes per side. Other fruity grillables to try are apples (cored and cut into ½-inch rings), oranges, pineapple, mango (cut into ½-inch-thick slices), and bananas (grilled whole in their peel for 5 minutes per side until very soft, then sliced open and scooped out). Whole peaches, apples, nectarines, and apricots can be wrapped in foil and cooked directly on the coals. Cook these about 20 minutes, turning occasionally.

RED WINE MARINADE GRILLED CHICKEN BREASTS

2 to 4 servings

2 chicken breasts (about 2 pounds), halved, skinless and boneless if desired
Salt and black pepper to taste

Marinade

¼ cup extra-virgin olive oil
2 medium onions, chopped
1 cup tomato purée
1 tablespoon finely chopped fresh basil or 1 teaspoon dried basil
⅓ cup honey
¼ cup chicken stock (see page 8)
3 tablespoons Worcestershire sauce
1 teaspoon dry mustard
1 cup Italian dry red wine

1. Sprinkle the chicken breasts with salt and pepper.

2. Heat the olive oil over medium heat in a sauté pan or heavy skillet. Sauté the onions until soft. Add the tomato puree, basil, honey, stock, Worcestershire sauce, and mustard. Mix together well. Reduce the heat to low and simmer for 15 minutes. Add the wine in the last minute of cooking and heat through. Let cool to room temperature.

3. Arrange the chicken in a single layer in a shallow glass or ceramic dish. Pour on the marinade, cover with plastic wrap, and refrigerate for 3 hours, turning several times to coat well. Let the chicken come to room temperature before cooking.

4. Fire up the grill or prepare the broiler. Beginning bone side down, cook the chicken breasts for 5 to 6 minutes per side, basting several times during cooking until done throughout.

Q: When is a grilled chicken breast ready?

A: To grill perfectly, place the chicken breasts on the grill when the coals are glowing red hot and covered with a top layer of white ash and cook for 5 minutes to insure perfect grill marks. In some cases, it will be necessary to lightly brush or spray the grilling rack with oil. Turn the chicken breasts several times during the 10- to 15-minute cooking process. To test for perfect doneness, pierce a breast with a knife. The meat should be white and slightly opaque throughout but still juicy. Or, press on the breasts, which are not squishy but firm when done. Do not overcook. Basting with a marinade during grilling helps to seal in the moisture and keep the chicken from drying out. Remember, the chicken continues to cook once it has left the grill so eat it right away or take the breasts off the grill a minute early to compensate.

SOY-GINGER CHICKEN BREASTS TERIYAKI

Though we associate the word teriyaki with a particular sweet sauce that is frequently used as a marinade; to the Japanese, it is the technique of grilling food while basting with flavored soy sauce and sweetened rice wine. In this recipe, the chicken breasts are cooked slower and farther away from the coals to keep the soy sauce from caramelizing. Adjust your grill or broiler, too.

2 to 4 servings

2 chicken breasts (about 2 pounds), halved, skinless, and boneless if desired
½ cup peanut oil
½ cup tamari (Japanese soy sauce)
2 tablespoons grated fresh peeled ginger
2 cloves garlic, finely chopped
1 tablespoon orange zest
¼ cup sweet cooking rice wine or medium sherry

1. Arrange the chicken breasts in a single layer in a shallow glass or ceramic dish.

2. Combine the oil, tamari, ginger, garlic, orange zest, and rice wine in a bowl. Pour over the chicken, cover, and marinate, refrigerated, for 12 hours. Let the chicken breasts come to room temperature before cooking.

3. When you are ready to cook the chicken breasts, fire up the grill or heat the broiler. Cook the chicken breasts at least 8 to 10 inches away from the fire for 8 to 10 minutes per side, beginning bone side away from the heat. Turn and baste at least twice during the cooking process.

SWEET AND SOUR CHICKEN

4 to 6 servings

3 tablespoons vegetable oil
1 cup sugar
6 tablespoons soy sauce or tamari
2 cups red wine vinegar
2 tablespoons cornstarch
1 large onion, minced
3 tablespoons finely chopped fresh peeled ginger
3 chicken breasts (about 3 pounds), halved, skinless, and boneless if desired

1. Combine the oil, sugar, soy sauce, vinegar, and cornstarch in a saucepan. Over medium-high heat, cook for 2 minutes to reduce by half.

2. Add the onion and ginger; continue to boil for 4 minutes more. Remove the sauce from the heat and let cool slightly.

3. Place the chicken breasts in a single layer in a shallow glass or ceramic dish and pour on the sauce. Marinate for 30 minutes to 1 hour at room temperature.

4. Fire up the grill or prepare the broiler. Grill or broil the chicken breasts for 5 to 6 minutes per side, basting several times until done throughout. Serve hot or cold.

Variation: Sweet and Sour Plum Marinade

In step 1, add 1 cup pitted fresh plums. Strain the mixture before pouring over the chicken.

WHAT'S THAT SMOKING?

It's none other than mozzarella cheese. Just wrap fresh mozzarella loosely in an aluminum foil pouch with an open top and smoke for 2 to 3 hours. The fire should be very low. Use hickory, apple, mesquite, and other wood chunks and chips along with the charcoal. For smoking, it is very important the fire be as low as possible, giving off almost no heat, just smoke. Soak wood chips in water for 30 minutes and add to the smoker from time to time during the smoking time of 2 to 3 hours. The cheese will melt slightly. Mold it back into a round with your hands while still warm, then chill for several hours. Cut into ¼-inch slices and serve with ripe tomatoes, fresh oregano, and basil, drizzled with extra-virgin olive oil. Also, consider smoking whole tomatoes, whole heads of garlic, onions, bell peppers, and even bread slices. They usually smoke in 30 minutes, but need to be turned. Make a tomato sauce of the smoked tomatoes. The taste difference will be surprising, especially on pasta or a pizza.

WATT A GRILL!

Undoubtedly, backyard grills have always worked overtime on weekends, especially in summer. But where can we take this cooking methods on a freezing Tuesday evening in the middle of February? Well, these days, you can grill in your kitchen—everything from papaya to pizzas—with no smoke and not even any fire, as long as there's an electrical outlet nearby. I'm talking about mini-indoor grills, which come in a variety of sizes and fit on the countertop. The one used to test some of these recipes is none other than the George Foreman countertop grill (if you watch TV these days, it's hard to miss the former boxing champ as pitchman). These grills are easy to use and easy to clean, and it looks quite "electric" in aqua! An entire meal, from chicken breast to an array of vegetables, fit nicely inside all at the same time (if you own the supersize grill), and marinades and/or basting sauces can be used to enhance flavors exactly as if you were grilling in the great outdoors.

GRILLED CHICKEN BREASTS WITH HERBS

The herbs are stuffed under the skin so as the breasts grill to tender doneness; the herbs, garlic, and lemon impart their wonderful perfume into the meat.

4 to 6 servings

3 boneless free-range chicken breasts (about 3½ pounds)
Fresh herbs: 3 tablespoons of either fresh tarragon leaves, basil, or crushed dried rosemary, or a combination of all of these
3 cloves garlic, peeled and quartered
1½ large lemons, thinly sliced into rounds
6 tablespoons melted unsalted butter
Salt and black pepper to taste

1. Place the chicken breasts on a work surface. Press down firmly with your palm to break the breastbone. Carefully, without detaching the skin, place equal amounts of the herbs under the skin of each chicken breast. Push the pieces of garlic under the skin. Place lemon slices over the herbs and the garlic. Place the chicken breasts in a shallow dish and cover tightly; refrigerate for 12 hours. Let the chicken breasts come to room temperature before cooking.

2. Fire up the grill or prepare the broiler. Remove the garlic and lemon slices from under the chicken skin, then rub the skin with butter and sprinkle with salt and pepper.

3. Grill or broil the chicken for 6 to 8 minutes on each side, basting with melted butter several times during cooking.

GRILLED GRAND MARNIER CHICKEN

Grand Marnier is a cognac-based orange liqueur.

6 servings

¾ cup Grand Marnier
1 ¼ cups apricot jam
¾ cup distilled white vinegar
4 ½ tablespoons Worcestershire sauce
3 tablespoons Dijon mustard
3 tablespoons honey
I tablespoon dried red pepper flakes
3 skinless, boneless chicken breasts (about 3 pounds), halved

Extra-virgin olive oil for basting

1. Combine the Grand Marnier, jam, vinegar, Worcestershire sauce, mustard, honey, and red pepper flakes in a saucepan. Simmer over medium-low heat until the honey and jam are melted. Remove from the heat and let cool to room temperature.

2. Place the chicken breasts in a single layer in a shallow glass baking dish. Pour on the marinade and refrigerate, covered with plastic wrap, for at least 4 hours. Let the chicken come to room temperature before grilling.

3. Fire up the grill or prepare the broiler. Grill the chicken breasts 5 to 6 minutes per side, basting several times with olive oil during cooking, or until done throughout. Slice and serve hot or at room temperature.

THE PERFECT GRILLED CHICKEN BREAST ACCOMPANIMENT—A SALAD ON THE SIDE

Simple marinated and grilled chicken breasts with an interesting assortment of salad greens on the side create the perfect low-cal meal. Here's a peppery hot yet sweet dressing and salad greens combination, and it's dressed to kill!

Mixed Greens with Warm Jalapeño Vinaigrette

Salad

1½ heads Boston lettuce
1 cup arugula
1 cup radicchio
2 bunches watercress with stems trimmed
2 chopped fresh mint leaves with stems trimmed

Dressing

¼ cup vegetable oil
½ cup finely chopped red or sweet onion
½ tablespoon chopped jalapeño peppers (stem, seed, and deveined)
¼ cup rice wine vinegar
1½ tablespoons honey
1 jalapeño pepper stemmed, seeded, deveined, and thinly sliced, for garnish (optional)

1. Wash the greens, spin dry, and tear into bite-sized pieces. Divide evenly on 6 plates. Sprinkle on the mint.
2. Heat the oil in a small saucepan. Add the onion and chopped jalapeño and cook over medium-high heat, swirling the pan until the onion is translucent, about 3 minutes. Stir in the vinegar and honey.
3. Immediately pour the dressing over the salads, garnish with a jalapeño slices if desired, and serve immediately with grilled chicken breasts.

Note: Romaine lettuce, endive, lambs or field lettuce, baby red leaf lettuce, or red cabbage may also be used.

WORCESTERSHIRE BASTING SAUCE FOR CHICKEN BREASTS

This recipes makes enough for 4 to 5 pounds of chicken breasts and can be stored in a glass jar with a tight-fitting lid in the refrigerator for four weeks or more.

1 cup Worcestershire sauce
1 teaspoon pickling spice
½ teaspoon sugar
1 celery stalk (including top), chopped
1 onion, thinly sliced
1 clove garlic, minced
1 cup filtered water
½ cup vegetable oil
¼ cup dry sherry
2 to 3 chicken breasts (2 to 3 pounds), halved, skinless and boneless if desired

1. Combine the Worcestershire sauce, pickling spice, sugar, celery, onion, garlic, and water in a non-reactive saucepan. Over low heat, simmer for 25 minutes. In the last 5 minutes of cooking, add the oil and sherry. Let cool to room temperature. Store in the refrigerator until ready to use.

2. Place the chicken breasts in a single layer in a shallow glass or ceramic dish, pour on ¼ cup of the marinade per pound of chicken breasts the basting sauce, cover, and marinate for at least 1 hour.

3. Fire up the grill or prepare the broiler. Cook the chicken breasts for 5 to 6 minutes per side, basting during the cooking process, or until done throughout.

HONEY MUSTARD GRILLED CHICKEN BREASTS

4 to 6 servings

8 tablespoons unsalted butter
½ cup honey
2 tablespoons Dijon mustard
2 medium cloves, crushed
¼ cup fresh lime juice
⅛ teaspoon dried savory
⅛ teaspoon crumbled dried rosemary
3 chicken breasts (about 3 pounds), halved
Salt and black pepper to taste

1. Combine the butter, honey, mustard,

garlic, lime juice, savory, and rosemary in a skillet large enough to marinate the chicken breasts. Cook over medium-high heat. Mix well. Remove the skillet from the heat, let cool to warm.

2. Season the chicken breasts with salt and pepper; place in the warm marinade, and set aside at room temperature for half an hour.

3. Fire up the grill or prepare the broiler. Lightly coat the grill rack with cooking spray. Remove the chicken breasts from the marinade and cook 6 to 8 inches from the fire for 5 to 6 minutes per side or until done throughout. Baste several times during the cooking process.

CITRUS AND SPICE GRILLED CHICKEN BREASTS

4 to 6 servings

2 cups freshly squeezed orange juice, reduced to 1 cup or 1 cup frozen orange juice concentrate, thawed and diluted with ¼ cup water
½ cup tomato purée
3 tablespoons honey
2 teaspoons orange zest
1 teaspoon lemon zest
½ teaspoon lime zest
¼ cup fresh lemon juice
¼ cup fresh lime juice
3 large cloves garlic, pressed
1 teaspoon dried thyme
½ teaspoon cayenne pepper
¾ teaspoon freshly ground black pepper
½ teaspoon salt
3 chicken breasts (about 3 pounds), halved, skinless, and boneless if desired

1. Combine the orange juice, tomato puree, honey, all the zests, lemon and lime juice, garlic, thyme, cayenne, black pepper, and salt in a large bowl. Mix well.

2. Place the chicken breasts in a shallow glass baking dish. Pour on the marinade and refrigerate, covered with plastic wrap, for 12 hours. Let the chicken stand at room temperature before grilling.

3. Fire up the grill or prepare the broiler. Lightly coat the grilling rack with cooking spray.

4. Drain the chicken, straining the marinade into a small saucepan. Bring the marinade to a boil and cook for 2 minutes to reduce slightly.

5. Grill or broil the chicken breasts 5 to 6 minutes per side or until done throughout. Baste with the marinade several times during cooking. Serve hot or at room temperature.

GRILLED BALSAMIC CHICKEN BREASTS

6 to 8 servings

4 chicken breasts (about 4 pounds), skinned, halved, and flattened to about ¾-inch thickness
½ cup balsamic vinegar
4 shallots, chopped
1 teaspoon chopped fresh thyme
2 cloves garlic, pressed
Salt and freshly ground white pepper to taste

Balsamic Vinaigrette

1 cup chicken stock (see page 8), and ½ cup dry white wine, reduced to ¾ cup (*Note:* stock and wine should be reduced together over medium heat)
⅓ cup balsamic vinegar
3 shallots, minced
1 large clove garlic, finely chopped
1 teaspoon chopped fresh thyme, or ½ teaspoon crumbled dried thyme
1 small tomato, peeled, seeded, and very finely chopped
2 tablespoons chopped flat-leaf parsley

1. Place the chicken breasts in a shallow glass baking dish. Add the vinegar, shallots, thyme, garlic, salt, and pepper. Refrigerate, covered with plastic wrap, for at least 2 hours. Let stand at room temperature before grilling.

2. To make the balsamic vinaigrette, combine the reduced stock and wine with the vinegar, shallots, garlic, and thyme in a saucepan. Bring to a boil. Stir in the tomato. Season with salt and pepper. Cook over high heat for 2 minutes to reduce and thicken slightly. Set aside.

3. Fire up the grill or prepare the broiler. Lightly coat the grilling rack with cooking spray. Grill or broil the chicken breasts for 5 to 6 minutes per side, turning every 2 to 3 minutes, or until done throughout. In the last 2 minutes of cooking, reheat the balsamic vinaigrette, baste the chicken breasts well, and turn once more to caramelize the vinaigrette. Serve sprinkled with parsley and with the remaining vinaigrette on the side.

SHERRY-MARINATED CHICKEN BREASTS

4 to 6 servings

3 skinless, boneless (optional) chicken breasts (about 3 pounds), halved
1 ½ cups dry sherry
3 tablespoons fresh lemon juice
1 bay leaf
2 large cloves garlic, pressed
1 cup finely chopped onion
1 15-ounce can tomato purée
3 tablespoons honey
2 tablespoons light molasses
1 teaspoon salt
½ teaspoon cayenne pepper
½ teaspoon dried thyme
½ teaspoon freshly ground black pepper
3 tablespoons white wine vinegar

1. Place the chicken breasts in a shallow glass baking dish.

2. Combine the sherry, lemon juice, bay leaf, garlic, and onion in a large bowl. Pour over the chicken breasts and coat well. Cover with plastic wrap and marinate, refrigerated, for about 6 hours. Let the chicken come to room temperature before grilling.

3. Drain the chicken breasts, saving the marinade. In a heavy medium saucepan, combine the marinade with the tomato purée, honey, molasses, salt, cayenne, thyme, and black pepper and boil over moderate heat. Reduce the heat to low and simmer 30 to 35 minutes, stirring occasionally, until the sauce is thick and reduced to about 2 cups. Remove from the heat, discard the bay leaf, and stir in the vinegar. Set aside.

4. Fire up the grill or prepare the broiler. Lightly coat the grill with cooking spray. Grill the chicken breasts 5 to 6 minutes per side, basting several times with the tomato sauce during cooking, or until done throughout. Serve hot or at room temperature.

Q: Which woods fan the flames of flavor in your barbecue?
A: Hawaiian kiawe, mesquite, hickory, cherry, apple, maple, oak, walnut, and grapevine cuttings.

EAST INDIAN-STYLE GRILLED CHICKEN BREASTS WITH VEGETABLES AND MINTED-YOGURT SAUCE

For this great tasting recipe, get a bag of grapevine cuttings and soak them in water before beginning the grilling process.

4 to 6 servings

3 skinless, boneless chicken breasts (about 3 pounds) flattened
1¾ cups plain yogurt, regular or low-fat

Marinade
½ cup extra-virgin olive oil
¼ cup vinegar
1 3-inch piece of fresh ginger, peeled and cut into chunks
8 large cloves garlic, peeled
2 tablespoons ground cumin
2 tablespoons ground coriander
2 teaspoons ground cardamom
1½ teaspoons salt
1 teaspoon cayenne pepper
½ teaspoon ground cloves
2 tablespoons yellow food coloring (optional)
1 small cauliflower, cored, stemmed, and broken into large florets
2 to 4 medium carrots, peeled and quartered by cutting on the diagonal
2 onions, cut into ½-inch slices
1 to 2 zucchini, halved lengthwise

Minted-Yogurt Sauce
1 cup plain yogurt, regular or low-fat
1 cucumber, peeled, seeded, and grated
2 tablespoons chopped fresh mint
Fresh cilantro sprigs for garnish
Thin lemon slices for garnish

1. Place the chicken breasts in a large shallow bowl. Make slashes, one inch apart, along the grain. Push the yogurt into the slashes.

2. Combine the olive oil, vinegar, ginger, garlic, cumin, coriander, cardamom, salt, cayenne, garlic, and (if using) food coloring in a blender or a food processor. Process until smooth.

3. Pour the marinade over the breasts. Turn several times to coat well and push the marinade into the slashes. Cover with plastic wrap and marinate, refrigerated, for 12 hours. Or, marinate at room temperature at least 2 hours. Let the chicken come to room temperature before grilling.

4. Fire up the grill or prepare the broiler. Scatter soaked grapevine cuttings over the coals and allow the heat to subside to a moderate level. Lightly coat the grilling racks with cooking spray.

5. Remove the chicken breasts from the marinade and allow any excess to drain off. Brush the cauliflower, carrots, onions, and zucchini with the marinade and let dry.

6. Place the chicken breasts toward the center of the grill with the vegetables around the outer rim, and grill for 6 to 8 minutes per side, turning every few minutes, or until done throughout. Check the vegetables and turn frequently. They are done when slightly soft but still hold their shape.

7. To make the sauce, combine the yogurt, cucumber, and 1 tablespoon of the mint and chill. Just before serving, sprinkle with the remaining mint.

8. To serve, arrange the chicken breasts on a platter, surrounded with the grilled vegetables. Garnish the platter with cilantro and lemon slices. Serve with minted yogurt sauce on the side.

GRILLED GREENS AND OTHER VEGGIES

When it comes to grilling vegetables, you can cook them on the grill, sometimes right in the coals, at the same time as you cook your entrée. All grilled vegetables should be brushed with oil before hitting the rack. Heartier vegetables like radicchio and endive not only stand up to grilling but also become sweeter. Slice radicchio and endive in half lengthwise, brush with oil, and grill about 4 to 5 minutes per side. Slice tomatoes in half crosswise, brush with extra-virgin olive oil, sprinkle with herbs, and grill about 2 minutes per side. Grill corn on the cob right in the husk. Carefully peel the husk back, remove the silk, replace the husk, and soak 10 minutes in cold water. Then grill 15 minutes, turning frequently. And don't forget eggplant, sliced, brushed with oil, dusted with dried herbes de Provence, and salt and pepper before grilling. Baby veggies and onion slices (or standard-size varieties, sliced a half or a quarter inch thick) are also very "grillable." Place these in a wire grilling basket and grill about 4 to 5 minutes on each side or until soft but still holding their shape—mushy veggies are overdone and might better be made into a roasted veggie puree. Root vegetables (potatoes, sweet potatoes, onions, and garlic) taste awesome when cooked right in the coals. Just brush with oil, wrap in a double layer of heavy-duty foil, ventilated with a few punched holes, and bury in the coals. Most of these cook tender in 45 minutes.

GRILLED CHICKEN BREASTS AND EGGPLANT WITH THYME CREAM SAUCE

4 to 6 servings

Juice of 1 lemon
¼ cup extra-virgin olive oil
¼ cup soy sauce or tamari
3 cloves garlic, peeled and crushed
½ teaspoon freshly ground black pepper
1 sprig each: fresh marjoram, summer savory, thyme
3 skinned, boned chicken breasts (about 3 pounds), halved
1 large eggplant, ends trimmed off, cut into 4 lengthwise slices
2 tablespoons finely chopped fresh rosemary
2 tablespoons crumbled dried oregano
Salt and freshly ground black pepper to taste
2 slices pancetta (Italian bacon)
1 teaspoon extra-virgin olive oil
1 pound pearl onions, boiled for 30 seconds, peeled, and cut in half lengthwise
8 fresh thyme sprigs
2 cups heavy cream
Chopped fresh thyme for garnish

1. Combine the lemon juice, 2 tablespoons of the olive oil, soy sauce, garlic, salt, and black pepper in a small bowl. Mix well.

2. Pound or bruise the herbs lightly to release their oils and mix into the marinade. Let stand, covered, 3 to 4 hours at room temperature, stirring occasionally.

3. Place the chicken breasts in a shallow glass baking dish. Prick both sides several times with a fork or the tip of a paring knife.

4. Strain the marinade and pour enough over the chicken to coat both sides well, reserving the remaining. Cover with plastic wrap and marinate, refrigerated, for 4 hours.

5. Brush the eggplant slices on both sides with the marinade. Sprinkle on the rosemary, oregano, and salt and pepper. Cover with plastic wrap and set aside.

6. Cut the pancetta into ¼-inch pieces. Heat the remaining olive oil over medium heat in a saucepan or skillet. Add the pancetta and cook until well browned. Reduce the heat to low, add the onions, and continue cooking until translucent. Add the thyme sprigs and cream, and, over medium heat, reduce the liquid by one quarter. Season with black pepper and set aside.

7. Fire up the grill or prepare the broiler. Lightly coat the grill with cooking spray. Place the eggplant slices around the outer rim of the grill and not directly over the coals. Grill until slightly blackened and soft but still holding their shape. Turn once during grilling.

8. Remove the chicken from the marinade and let come at room temperature before grilling. Grill the chicken breasts 5 to 6 minutes per side, turning every few minutes, until done throughout.

9. Rewarm the sauce. Place the eggplant slices on individual plates, spoon on the sauce, top with a chicken breast, and sprinkle on the chopped thyme. Serve the remaining sauce on the side.

YOGURT-CUMIN MARINATED GRILLED CHICKEN BREASTS

4 to 6 servings

3 skinless, boneless chicken breasts (about 3 pounds), flattened
Salt and freshly ground black pepper to taste
2 cups plain yogurt, regular or low-fat
¼ cup honey
2 tablespoons cumin seeds
1 tablespoon ground cumin
2 tablespoons dry mustard
4 tablespoons chopped cilantro

1. Place the chicken breasts in a shallow glass baking dish. Season with salt and pepper.

2. Combine the yogurt, honey, cumin seeds, ground cumin, and mustard in a bowl.

3. Pour the marinade on the chicken breasts, coating both sides well. Cover with plastic wrap and marinate, refrigerated, for at least 4 hours or overnight. Let the chicken stand half an hour at room temperature before grilling.

4. Fire up the grill or prepare the broiler. Lightly coat the grill with cooking spray. Grill the chicken breasts 5 to 6 minutes per side, turning several times during cooking, or until done throughout. Sprinkle with cilantro and serve hot or at room temperature.

GRILLED CHICKEN WITH RANCHERO SAUCE

You've eaten eggs ranchero for brunch. In Tex-Mex cooking, ranchero-style simply means with tomato sauce of a particular type. This version uses another border classic, salsa, which can also be used for chip dipping.

2 to 4 servings

1 small onion, thinly sliced
1 large clove garlic, thinly sliced
½ cup chopped fresh cilantro
1 jalapeño pepper, seeded and thinly sliced
1 medium ripe tomato, cored and thinly sliced
2 skinless, boneless chicken breasts (about 2 pounds), halved and flattened to 1-inch thickness
Salt and freshly ground black pepper to taste

Salsa

2 large ripe tomatoes (about 1 pound), cored and diced
¼ cup chopped cilantro
2 tablespoons minced onion
1 small jalapeño pepper, seeded and minced
2 tablespoons extra-virgin olive oil
½ teaspoon salt
¼ teaspoon freshly ground black pepper
2 tablespoons fresh lemon juice

1. Layer half the onion, garlic, cilantro, jalapeño, and sliced tomato in a shallow glass baking dish. Season the chicken breasts with salt and pepper. Place on top of the ingredients in the baking dish. Cover with the remaining onion, garlic, cilantro, jalapeño, and tomato. Cover with plastic wrap and marinate, refrigerated, for 12 hours. Let the chicken breasts come to room temperature before grilling.

2. For the salsa, combine the diced tomatoes, cilantro, onion, jalapeño oil, salt, pepper, and lemon juice in a mixing bowl. Cover with plastic wrap and let stand at room temperature for 2 hours. Serve at room temperature.

3. Fire up the grill or prepare the broiler. Lightly coat the grilling rack with cooking spray. Grill the chicken breasts 6 to 8 minutes per side, turning every few minutes, or until done throughout.

4. Warm the salsa, partially covered, over low heat in a small saucepan. Serve the chicken breasts smothered in warmed salsa.

GRILLED CHICKEN KEBABS

Sprinkle the fire with sprigs of herbs that have been soaked in water. This creates an even more intense flavor.

4 servings

2 skinned, boned chicken breasts (about 2 pounds), cut into ½-inch strips
½ red bell pepper, stemmed, seeded, and cut into 2-inch pieces
½ green bell pepper, stemmed, seeded, and cut into 2-inch pieces
½ yellow bell pepper, stemmed, seeded, and cut into 2-inch pieces
¼ cup fresh lemon juice
¼ cup dry white wine (chardonnay)
2 tablespoons grated lemon zest
3 shallots, chopped
3 cloves garlic, minced
2 tablespoons chopped fresh basil, or 1 teaspoon dried basil
3 tablespoons chopped fresh parsley
2 tablespoons chopped fresh marjoram, or 1 teaspoon dried marjoram
¼ teaspoon freshly ground white pepper
8 to 10 pearl onions (cut into the root end, boil for 30 seconds, and peel)
8 cherry tomatoes
10 metal skewers, or bamboo skewers that have been soaked in water for 20 minutes

1. Combine the chicken, bell peppers, lemon juice, wine, zest, shallots, garlic, basil, parsley, marjoram, and white pepper in a shallow glass dish. Toss to mix and marinate, covered with plastic wrap, at room temperature for 1 hour or refrigerate for 2 hours. Let the chicken come to room temperature before grilling the chicken.

2. Drain the chicken strips and roll like a jelly roll into rounds. Skewer each round, alternating pepper pieces, onions, and cherry tomatoes onto the skewers.

3. Fire up the grill or prepare the broiler. Lightly coat the grilling rack with cooking spray. Grill the kebabs 6 to 8 inches from the heat for 10 to 12 minutes, turning frequently, or until done throughout. Serve hot or at room temperature.

COLD SMOKED CHICKEN BREASTS WITH SWEET PEPPER COULIS

Simple grilled chicken breasts and a dollop of tasty sauce make a wonderful starter or lunch course. For dinner, make an assortment of grilled vegetables as a side dish. To give it a Mexican or Southwestern flavor, brush the vegetables with a scant amount of oil with a dash of hot chile oil mixed in and serve the chicken breasts and vegetables with salsa on the side.

6 servings

2 cups dry white wine (chardonnay)
¼ cup chopped fresh rosemary
2 or 3 cloves garlic, minced
Salt and freshly ground black pepper to taste
3 chicken breasts (about 3 pounds), flattened (skinned and boned optional)

Coulis

1 red bell pepper, seeded and chopped
1 green bell pepper, seeded and chopped
1 orange bell pepper, seeded and chopped
1 cup chopped cilantro
¼ cup extra-virgin olive oil

1. Combine the wine, rosemary, garlic, and a scant amount of salt and pepper in a bowl. Place the chicken breasts in a shallow glass baking dish. Pour the marinade over the chicken breasts. Cover with plastic wrap and marinate in the refrigerator for 12 hours, turning several times to coat well. Let the chicken breasts stand at room temperature before grilling.

2. Combine the bell peppers, cilantro, and olive oil in a blender or a food processor. Blend to a fine purée. Press through a fine sieve and chill until ready to serve.

3. Fire up the grill. Add aromatic hardwood chunks that have been soaked in water for 2 hours.

4. Remove the chicken breasts from the marinade and pour the remaining marinade into the smoker pan. Place the chicken on a rack over the smoker pan and put the pan in place. Cover the smoker and cook 45 minutes to 1 hour, or until the chicken is opaque throughout. Test after 35 minutes by cutting into a breast along the bone. When done remove the skin and bones (if desired), chill and serve with coulis on the side.

GRILLED TERIYAKI MARINATED CHICKEN BREATS

This is an opportunity to make your own teriyaki sauce rather than relying on the commercially made kind, it's much more delicious. Remember, to create the perfect teriyaki-marinated chicken breasts, you must marinate for at least 2 hours.

2 to 4 servings

2 skinless, boneless chicken breasts (about 2 pound each), halved and flattened slightly to even thickness
¼ cup chopped fresh peeled ginger
2 tablespoons minced garlic
½ cup sugar
1 cup sake (Japanese rice wine)
½ cup soy sauce or tamari

1. Place the chicken breasts in a shallow glass baking dish.

2. Combine the ginger, garlic, sugar, sake, and soy sauce in a blender or food processor and process until smooth.

3. Pour the marinade over the chicken breasts and coat well. Cover with plastic wrap and marinate, refrigerated, for at least 2 hours or more. Turn to coat occasionally during marinating. Let the chicken come to room temperature before grilling.

4. Fire up the grill or prepare the broiler. Lightly coat the grilling rack with cooking spray. Grill the chicken about 8 to 10 inches further from the coals, turning every few minutes, for longer, slower cooking, about 7 to 10 minutes per side or until done throughout. Serve hot or at room temperature, sliced.

CHICKEN BREASTS MARINATED IN AROMATIC HERBS

Eating outdoors under the stars—though you might experience an array of bugs performing kamikaze dives into your salad or sangria—nothing beats it for the experience. Somehow your cares slip away and the world looks lovely again. Add grilled herbed chicken breasts and vegetables and all will be well with the world once again.

6 servings

3 chicken breasts (about 3 pound each), skinned and flattened slightly
3 tablespoons chopped cilantro
3 tablespoons chopped flat-leaf parsley
1 ½ cloves garlic, peeled
1 teaspoon ground paprika
¼ teaspoon ground cumin
⅛ teaspoon cayenne pepper
3 tablespoons lemon juice
1 teaspoon salt
½ teaspoon freshly ground black pepper
¼ cup extra-virgin olive oil

1. Place the chicken breasts in a single layer in a shallow glass baking dish.

2. Combine the cilantro, parsley, garlic, paprika, cumin, cayenne, lemon juice, and salt and pepper in a blender or a food processor. With the machine running, pour in the olive oil.

3. Pat the marinade onto both sides of the chicken breasts. Cover with plastic wrap and marinate in the refrigerator for 4 to 6 hours. Let the chicken come to room temperature before grilling.

4. Fire up the grill or prepare the broiler. Lightly coat the grilling rack with cooking spray or brush with oil. Remove the chicken breasts from the marinade. Grill the chicken breasts 5 to 6 minutes per side, turning several times, or until done throughout. Serve immediately or at room temperature.

CARIBBEAN GRILLED CHICKEN

You've heard of "jerk" chicken, haven't you? It's standard barbecue fare on most Caribbean islands and almost a daily event for Jamaicans. This is a version of that dish, with just as much Hot! Hot! Hot! as you'd find on any of the islands. The extra marinade can be stored in a glass jar with a tight-fitting lid.

6 to 8 servings

1 cup coarsely chopped onion
1 cup coarsely chopped scallion, white and green parts
1 or 2 Scotch bonnet chiles, stemmed, seeded, and coarsely chopped (or substitute 2 or 3 jalapeños, halved, seeded, chopped)
2 teaspoons ground allspice
1 teaspoon cracked black pepper
1 teaspoon dried thyme
1 teaspoon ground nutmeg
1 teaspoon ground cinnamon
1 teaspoon salt
¼ cup packed dark brown sugar
¼ cup fresh orange juice
¼ cup fresh lemon juice
2 tablespoons canola or other vegetable oil
3 to 4 chicken breast (about 3 to 4 pounds), skin and bone optional

1. Combine the onion, scallion, chiles, allspice, black pepper, thyme, nutmeg, cinnamon, salt, and brown sugar in a blender or food processor. Process to a coarse paste. With the motor running, pour in the orange and lemon juices, and then the oil, in a thin steady stream.

2. Place the chicken breasts in a shallow glass dish. Pour on the marinade and turn to coat well on all sides. Cover with plastic wrap and marinate in the refrigerator for 2 to 4 hours (the longer, the hotter). Let the chicken come to room temperature before grilling.

3. Fire up the grill or prepare the broiler. Lightly coat the grilling rack with cooking spray. Grill the chicken breast for 10 to 12 minutes, turning a few times to prevent burning. Cut open 1 breast to test for doneness. Serve hot off the grill.

ASIAN ORANGE-GLAZED CHICKEN BREASTS

4 servings

1 tablespoon dark brown sugar
1 tablespoon grated orange zest
2 tablespoons rice wine vinegar
2 tablespoons soy sauce or tamari
2 teaspoons canola or extra-virgin olive oil
2 medium cloves garlic, finely minced
1 tablespoon finely minced peeled fresh ginger
¼ teaspoon freshly ground white pepper
¼ teaspoon crushed star anise
2 skinless, boneless chicken breasts (about 2 pounds), pounded between plastic wrap to ½ inch thick

1. Reduce the orange juice by half, or about 4 to 5 minutes, in a small saucepan over medium heat. Cool to room temperature.

2. Combine the orange juice, brown sugar, zest, vinegar, soy sauce, oil, garlic, ginger, pepper, and star anise in a jar with a tight-fitting lid. Shake until well mixed.

3. Place the chicken breasts in a shallow glass dish. Pour the marinade over the chicken breasts and turn to coat well. Cover with plastic wrap and marinate in the refrigerator for 2 to 3 hours. Let come to room temperature before grilling.

4. Fire up the grill or prepare the broiler. Lightly coat the grilling rack with cooking spray. Grill the chicken breasts for 5 to 6 miutes or until done throughout.

FUSILLI WITH CHICKEN, HERBS, AND OVEN-DRIED TOMATOES

Any type of corkscrew or tubular shape pasta can be substituted, or try spinach, tomato, or other vegetable-based pastas to make this dish even more visually appealing. The oven-dried tomatoes, which are a milder homemade version of standard sun-dried tomatoes, are an interesting touch. Grill the chicken breasts in advance, so the dish can be easily tossed together in just minutes.

4 to 6 servings

2 large ripe tomatoes, thinly sliced
1 teaspoon dried basil or oregano
2 skinless, boneless chicken breast (about 2 pounds), pounded between plastic wrap to ½-inch thickness
Salt and freshly ground black pepper
1½ tablespoons extra-virgin olive oil
4 cloves garlic, very finely minced
3 shallots, minced
3 medium carrots, peeled and julienned
1 cup chicken stock (see page 8)
¼ cup dry white wine
5 tablespoons mixed chopped fresh herbs (such as parsley, thyme, basil, oregano, and rosemary)
1 pound dried fusilli or other corkscrew or tubular pasta, cooked in lightly salted water to al dente, rinsed and kept warm
1½ teaspoons unsalted butter

1. Preheat the oven to warm.

2. Sprinkle the tomatoes with the dried basil or oregano and place in the oven for 2 hours. Cool the tomatoes slightly and chop.

3. Fire up the grill or preheat the broiler. Lightly coat the grilling rack with cooking spray. Season the chicken breasts with salt and pepper. Grill or broil about 4 to 5 minutes per side, or until browned on both sides and done throughout.

4. Cut the chicken into large strips about ½-inch wide and 1½-inches long. Set aside.

5. In a large skillet or sauté pan lightly coated with cooking spray, heat 1 tablespoon of the olive oil over medium heat. Cook the garlic and shallots until tender but not browned. Over low heat, add the carrots, tomatoes, chicken stock, wine, fresh herbs, and salt and pepper and cook until the carrots are tender, about 5 minutes. Cover and keep hot.

6. In a large sauté pan or skillet, heat the remaining ½ tablespoon of olive oil and the butter over medium heat. Add the pasta and the chicken and toss to coat well, and heat through. Toss in the vegetables, adjust the seasoning with salt and pepper, and serve in large warmed pasta bowls.

TRY IT SMOKED . . . IT'S EASIER THAN YOU THINK!

Tending the fires is not necessary with this flavor-enhancing cooking method. Foods are slowly smoked and flavored in an enclosed barbecue/smoker by the direct, although low, heat of the smoldering hardwood charcoal embers—usually left over from grilling. Water-soaked hardwood chips provide the smoke. Once the food to be smoked is in place, just throw on some wood chops, slam down the lid of the smoker, and come back later. Then, finish the smoked chicken breasts in the oven for a few minutes before serving. This is low-fat, high-flavor cooking with no fuss or flames. Many other kinds of foods can be smoked, such as chicken breasts, chicken rolls (see page 197 for recipe), or just about anything that cooks fairly fast (not whole chickens or turkeys) and that won't disintegrate during smoking and fall into the bottom of the barbecue. Along with chicken breasts, try smoking tomatoes, eggplant, onion halves, squash, portobello mushrooms, whole heads of garlic, even mozzerella cheese, to use in an amazingly delicious smoked vegetable ragout or sauce.

CHICKEN WITH FIG AND PORT WINE SAUCE

This recipe can also be used with broiled or baked chicken breasts.

4 servings

6 large dried figs, chopped, or 8 to 10 fresh figs, peeled and chopped
2 cups port wine (best quality)
2 skinless, boneless chicken breasts (about 2 pounds), flattened between plastic wrap to ½-inch thickness
Salt and freshly ground white pepper to taste
2 cups rich chicken stock (see page 9)
4 large shallots, chopped
1 clove garlic, finely chopped
½ large onion, thinly sliced
1 teaspoon cornstarch, dissolved in 1 tablespoon cold stock

1. Combine the figs with enough water to cover in a small saucepan. Over low heat, bring to a simmer and immediately remove from the heat. Set aside for 30 minutes.

2. Fire up the grill or prepare the broiler. Lightly coat the grilling rack with cooking spray. Season the chicken breasts with salt and pepper. Grill 3 to 4 minutes per side or until done throughout. Remove to a platter and keep warm.

3. Meanwhile, combine 2 tablespoons of the chicken stock, the shallots, garlic, and onion in a medium saucepan and cook over medium-high heat about 5 minutes, adding a bit more stock if necessary, until tender and well browned. Add the remaining wine to the pan and reduce by half. Add the remaining stock and continue cooking over moderate heat about 5 minutes more or until reduced by one third. Remove the pan from the heat.

4. Add the cornstarch mixture to the pan and stir to mix in well. Cook over low heat until the sauce thickens, about 1 minute. Add the figs and wine, continue cooking over medium-low heat, stirring constantly, about 1 to 2 minutes more. Adjust the seasoning with salt and pepper to taste.

5. Place the chicken breasts on warmed plates and spoon equal amounts of the sauce over them. Serve hot.

SPICY MEXICAN GRILLED CHICKEN BREASTS WITH SWEET AND HOT CITRUS VINAIGRETTE

This chicken is particularly delicious when served chilled. While the grill is still hot, smoke some tomatoes for a sauce. This is great *alfresco* party fare and partners wonderfully with traditional mixed greens salad, or coleslaw and potato salad.

4 servings

¼ cup tomato paste
Juice of 1 lime
1 teaspoon dried chile powder (ancho if possible)
1 teaspoon ground cumin
1 teaspoon cinnamon
½ teaspoon salt
2 cloves garlic, minced
2 skinless, boneless chicken breast (about 2 pounds), halved

Vinaigrette

½ cup fresh orange juice
1½ tablespoons fresh lemon juice
1½ tablespoons fresh lime juice
1½ tablespoons finely chopped red onion
⅛ teaspoon dried chile powder
2 tablespoons red wine vinegar
1 tablespoon balsamic vinegar
1 tablespoon honey
1½ tablespoons extra-virgin olive oil

1. Combine the tomato paste, lime juice, chile powder, cumin, cinnamon, salt, and garlic in a small bowl. Press the ingredients with the back of a wooden spoon to form a smooth paste.

2. Rub the chicken breasts with the paste to coat completely and place in a dish. Cover with plastic wrap and marinate for 2 hours in the refrigerator. Let the chicken come to room temperature before cooking.

3. To make the vinaigrette, combine the orange, lemon, and lime juices, red onion, chile powder, both vinegars, and the honey in a blender. With the motor running, add the oil in a thin stream and blend until smooth. Transfer to a bowl and set aside.

4. Fire up the grill or prepare the broiler. Lightly coat the grilling rack with cooking spray. Grill the chicken breasts for 5 to 6 minutes per side, or until done throughout.

GRILLED CHICKEN WITH PAPAYA, MANGO, AND CHIPOTLE CHILE RELISH

Many chicken breast recipes that call for grilling can be converted to broiling. Always preheat the broiler to high at least 10 minutes before cooking the chicken, and use a broiling pan that elevates the breasts above the drippings (or instead of broiling, the breasts will be boiled!)

4 to 6 servings

1 cup diced and peeled ripe mango
1 cup diced and peeled ripe papaya
1 cup peeled, seeded, and diced plum tomatoes
⅓ cup finely chopped red onion
¼ cup finely chopped scallion, green part only
1 tablespoon finely chopped fresh cilantro
1 tablespoon extra-virgin olive oil
¼ cup fresh lime juice
½ to 1 small jalapeño, to taste, seeded and finely minced
Pinch of salt

Marinade: Barbecue Sauce

1 can (8 ounces) crushed tomatoes
1 cup cubed and peeled ripe mango
2 tablespoons white wine vinegar
3 tablespoons honey
2 tablespoons smoky canned chipotle chiles in adobo*
Salt and freshly ground black pepper to taste
3 skinless, boneless chicken breasts (about 3 pounds), halved and flattened between plastic wrap to ½-inch thickness

***Available in Latin markets and some grocery stores**

1. To make the relish, combine the mango, papaya, tomato, red onion, scallion, cilantro, olive oil, lime juice, jalapeño, and salt in a glass or pottery bowl. Marinate for 1 hour before serving.

2. To prepare the chicken, combine the tomatoes, mango, vinegar, honey, and chiles in a blender or a food processor and process until smooth. Adjust the seasoning with salt and pepper.

3. Place the chicken in a shallow glass dish. Pour on the marinade and turn to coat all sides. Cover with plastic wrap and marinate in the refrigerator for 1 hour in the refrigerator. Let the chicken come to room temperature before cooking.

4. Meanwhile, fire up the grill or prepare the broiler. Lightly coat the grilling rack with cooking spray. Grill the chicken 3 to 4 minutes per side, basting several times with the marinade during cooking, or until done. Serve hot or at room temperature with the relish on the side.

BLACKENED CAJUN CHICKEN

This is the Cajun version of a simple, and quick, grilled chicken breast—sweet and spicy, with lots of rich, crusty barbecue color on the outside and with each delicious bite.

4 servings

2½ cups fresh orange juice
2 skinless, boneless chicken breasts (about 2 pounds), halved
2 to 3 tablespoons Louisiana or Cajun spice mix
2 teaspoons balsamic vinegar

1. In a small but heavy saucepan, boil 2 cups of the orange juice over high heat until reduced by half, about 5 to 6 minutes. Set aside in the saucepan.

2. Place the chicken breasts in a shallow glass dish along with the remaining ½ cup orange juice. Cover with plastic wrap and marinate for 30 minutes at room temperature or 1 hour in the refrigerator. Let chicken come to room temperature before cooking.

3. Meanwhile, fire up the grill or prepare the broiler. Lightly coat the grilling rack with cooking spray.

4. Remove the chicken from the marinade. Pat dry with paper towels. Rub the spice mix on to coat well.

5. Grill the chicken for 5 to 6 minutes per side, turning twice, or until the chicken is blackened on the outside and done throughout.

6. Add the balsamic vinegar to the reserved reduced orange juice and, over high heat, reduce to a syrupy sauce, about 3 to 4 minutes.

7. Drizzle the sauce over the blackened chicken breast while sizzling hot. Serve hot or at room temperature.

SMOKED CHICKEN SALAD WITH HORSERADISH SAUCE AND APPLE SLAW

If smoking your own chicken breasts is out of the question, but you like the sound of this salad, most specialty take-out delis carry smoked chicken breasts that are extremely moist and flavorful.

4 servings

2 skinless, boneless chicken breasts (about 2 pounds), or buy 4 smoked chicken breast halves from the deli or meat counter
Fruitwood charcoal and chips, including apple, cherry, or (see page 215 for preparing the wood for smoking)

Dressing

1 tablespoon finely grated fresh horseradish, or 1 tablespoon bottled, rinsed, and drained
⅓ cup plain yogurt, regular or low-fat
⅓ cup low-fat or nonfat sour cream
Pinch of salt
Pinch of freshly ground white pepper
1 to 2 teaspoons fresh lemon juice to taste

Apple Slaw

4 tart green apples, peeled, cored, and grated
¼ cup fresh lemon juice
2 stalks celery, very thinly sliced
½ cup finely chopped parsley leaves
2 small shallots, very finely sliced
1 teaspoon celery seed
½ cup plain yogurt, regular or low-fat
4 or more red leaf lettuce leaves

1. To smoke the chicken breasts, see page 215 for smoking instructions and tips, and finish the breasts in a 250°F oven for 10 minutes.

2. To make the dressing, whisk together the horseradish, yogurt, sour cream, salt, pepper, and lemon juice in a small bowl until well combined. Adjust the seasonings. Refrigerate until ready to use.

3. To make the apple slaw, combine the apples, lemon juice, celery, parsley, shallots, celery seed, and yogurt in a mixing bowl. Toss to mix well and refrigerate until chilled.

4. Cut the chicken breasts in thin slices on the diagonal.

5. Divide the lettuce among individual plates and top with apple slaw. Arrange the smoked chicken breast slices on the lettuce and drizzle on horseradish sauce. Top with a twist of the pepper mill filled with white peppercorns.

DALLAS-STYLE BARBECUED CHICKEN

This recipe for a delicate but very tasty version of Texas barbecue sauce makes enough for a whole lot of chicken breasts, so you may want to freeze half of the sauce for another night later on in the hot season.

6 to 8 servings

3 to 4 skinless, boneless chicken breasts (about 3 to 4 pounds), skinless and boneless if desired

Barbecue Sauce

2 to 4 cloves garlic, coarsely chopped
1 small dried red chile, seeded
1 tablespoon chopped fresh cilantro
¾ teaspoon ground cumin
½ teaspoon fennel seed
½ teaspoon salt
2 tablespoons dark brown sugar
1 tablespoon Worcestershire sauce
1 cup cider vinegar
2 cups ketchup
2 to 3 teaspoons Tabasco sauce

1. Combine the garlic, chile, cilantro, cumin, fennel seed, salt, brown sugar, and Worcestershire sauce in a blender or food processor and process until smooth.

2. Transfer the mixture to a small saucepan and add the vinegar and ketchup. Bring to a boil, reduce the heat to low, and simmer, uncovered, for 25 to 30 minutes. Add the Tabasco sauce. Set aside and cool to room temperature.

3. Place the chicken in a glass dish. Pour on the sauce and generously coat all sides. Marinate for 30 minutes at room temperature or up to 1 hour in the refrigerator.

4. Meanwhile, fire up the grill or prepare the broiler. Lightly coat the grilling rack with cooking spray. Grill the chicken breasts 8 inches or more from the heat source, basting once and turning several times, for 15 to 20 minutes, or until done throughout. Serve hot or at room temperature.

CARIBE-STYLE CHICKEN BREASTS

4 servings

2 skinless, boneless chicken breasts (about 2 pounds), flattened slightly between plastic wrap
Salt and freshly ground black pepper to taste
3 cloves garlic, minced

3 shallots, minced
1 cup fresh orange juice
⅓ cup dark Caribbean rum (best quality)
½ cup dry white wine
⅓ cup fresh lime juice
1 tablespoon soy sauce tamari
1 teaspoon ground ginger
2 tablespoons chopped fresh flat-leaf parsley

1. Place the chicken breasts in a shallow glass dish. Season with salt and pepper.

2. Combine the garlic, shallots, orange juice, rum, wine, lime juice, soy sauce, ginger, and parsley in a small bowl. Pour over the chicken, cover with plastic wrap, and marinate in the refrigerator for 1 to 3 hours. Let the chicken come to room temperature before cooking.

3. Drain the chicken and reserve marinade. Fire up the grill or prepare the broiler. Lightly coat the grill with cooking spray. Grill 5 to 6 minutes per side or until done throughout. Keep warm.

4. Meanwhile, boil the reserved marinade in a small heavy saucepan for about 5 minutes or until reduced by one third. Drizzle over the warm chicken breasts. Serve warm or at room temperature.

CHICKEN BREASTS WITH ROASTED ONION MARMALADE

Try smoking or grilling Maui onions for this marmalade.

4 servings

2 skinless, boneless chicken breasts (about 2 pounds), halved
¼ cup mixed chopped fresh herbs of choice (such as parsley, chervil, tarragon, and basil)
¼ cup apple juice
¼ cup chicken stock (see page 8)
2 large cloves garlic, thinly sliced
Salt and freshly ground white pepper

Onion Marmalade
1 large red onion, unpeeled and halved
1 large sweet onion (such as Vidalia, Maui, or Walla Walla), unpeeled and halved
1 teaspoon vegetable oil
2 cloves garlic, finely minced
½ cup port wine, or other sweet wine (best quality)
½ cup full-bodied red wine (such as merlot or cabernet)
3 tablespoons balsamic vinegar
¼ cup fresh orange juice
¼ cup honey

1 teaspoon orange zest
1 teaspoon lemon zest
Pinch of salt

1. Place the chicken in a glass dish. Sprinkle on the herbs. Combine the apple juice, chicken stock, garlic, and a scant amount of salt and pepper in a cup. Pour on the chicken, cover with plastic wrap, and marinate for 1 hour.

2. Meanwhile, to make the onion marmalade, preheat the oven to 450°F. Place the onion cut side down on a baking sheet lightly coated with cooking spray. Bake for 45 to 50 minutes, or until tender. Cool, peel, and coarsely chop the onions.

3. In a heavy sauté pan or skillet lightly coated with cooking spray, heat the oil over medium heat. Add the garlic and chopped onions and cook for 2 minutes, stirring constantly. Add the port, reduce the heat, and simmer for 5 minutes to reduce the liquid slightly.

4. Add the red wine, vinegar, orange juice, honey, both orange and lemon zest, and salt to the skillet and continue simmering about 8 to 10 minutes, or until the liquid is syrupy and the onions are tender. Transfer to a serving bowl. Cool to room temperature.

5. Drain the chicken breasts and reserve the marinade. Fire up the grill or prepare the broiler. Lightly coat the grilling rack with cooking spray. Grill the chicken for 6 to 7 minutes per side or until done throughout. Keep warm.

6. Meanwhile, simmer the reserved marinade for about 6 minutes in a saucepan over low heat or until reduced by half. Adjust the seasoning with salt and pepper to taste.

7. Place the chicken on a platter, pour on the sauce and serve, with onion marmalade on the side.

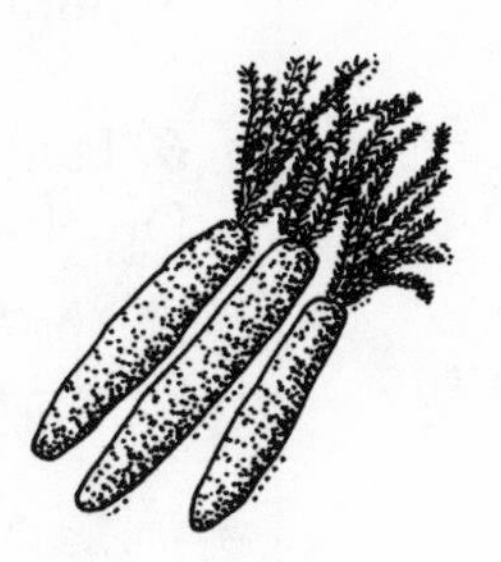

PLUM-BASTED CHICKEN BREASTS ON THYME COUSCOUS

4 to 6 servings

¼ cup Chinese plum sauce
¼ cup ketchup
Juice of 1 lime
1 tablespoon fresh grated horseradish or bottled horseradish, rinsed and drained
2 skinless, boneless chicken breasts (about 2 pounds), halved and pounded between plastic wrap to ½-inch thickness
1 tablespoon extra-virgin olive oil
Salt and freshly ground black pepper to taste
1 small tomato, peeled and diced for garnish
1 tablespoon finely chopped parsley for garnish

Couscous

2 cups filtered water
1 teaspoon fresh thyme leaves
1 medium carrot, peeled and finely diced
¼ onion, finely chopped
1 small tomato, peeled and diced
½ cup instant couscous
1 tablespoon extra-virgin olive oil
Salt and freshly ground black pepper to taste

1. Combine the plum sauce, ketchup, lime juice, and horseradish in a small mixing bowl.

2. Brush the chicken with the olive oil and season with salt and pepper. Brush on the plum sauce mixture and marinate for 30 minutes.

3. Meanwhile, to make the couscous, bring the water, thyme, carrot, onion, and tomato to a boil in a small saucepan.

4. Place the couscous in a mixing bowl. Pour on the boiling water and vegetables, cover with a tight lid, and let stand for 20 minutes, or until the water is completely absorbed.

5. Fire up the grill. Lightly coat the grilling rack with cooking spray. Grill the chicken for 5 to 6 minutes per side or until done throughout.

6. Fluff the couscous with a fork to mix. Drizzle on 1 tablespoon of olive oil and toss gently. Season lightly with salt and pepper and keep warm.

7. Place equal amounts of the couscous mixture in the center of warmed platter, make a well in the center, arrange the chicken breast pieces on the couscous. Sprinkle diced tomato and chopped parsley and serve hot or warm.

CRISPY BROILED CHICKEN CUTLETS ON GARLIC MASHED POTATOES

4 servings

5 cloves garlic, peeled
6 medium boiling potatoes (about 3 pounds), peeled and diced
4 cups nonfat milk
1 tablespoon unsalted butter
1 teaspoon salt
1 teaspoon freshly ground white pepper
2 skinless, boneless free-range chicken breasts (about 2½ pounds), halved and flattened between plastic wrap to ½ inch thickness
1 tablespoon dried bread crumbs
1 tablespoon finely grated Parmesan cheese
2 tablespoons finely chopped flat-leaf parsley

1. Prepare the broiler.

2. Bring the garlic, potatoes, and milk to a boil in a large saucepan or stockpot. Reduce the heat to a simmer and cook until tender, about 10 to 12 minutes. Drain, reserving the milk.

3. Mash the potatoes and garlic until smooth, adding the reserved milk as needed until fluffy. Season with salt and pepper to taste. Keep warm.

4. Meanwhile, broil the chicken about 3 to 4 minutes per side or just until done. Remove to a platter.

5. Toss the bread crumbs and the Parmesan together and press into the cutlets on one side. Return to the broiler for 1 to 2 minutes or just until the topping gets crispy. Transfer to a platter and keep warm, don't stack the pieces.

6. Make a bed of mashed potatoes on individual plates. Place a piece of chicken breast on the mashed potatoes and sprinkle with the parsley. Top with the turn of the pepper mill.

SWEET OR SAVORY BUTTER-BASTED CHICKEN BREASTS

A quick recipe doesn't have to be dull or boring. Here's a great example. The steps involved are few and uncomplicated. Simply pluck the herb butter from the garden or freezer, melt, and brush it on the chicken breast. Grill or broil for about 5 minutes on each side, starting with the bone side toward the fire. That's it! Make several fresh herb butters in advance and freeze so that when time is of the essence, they will be ready to help you make a memorable meal.

2 chicken breasts (about 2 pounds), skinned (optional) and halved
2 tablespoons or more herb-flavored butter (recipes to follow)

1. Preheat the oven broiler to very hot for about 15 minutes.

2. Remove the flavored butter from the freezer. Melt it in a saucepan or microwave over low heat.

3. Using a basting brush, coat the chicken breasts. Place under the broiler, starting with the bone side up, for 4 to 5 minutes, basting once more during cooking.

4. Turn the chicken breasts. Generously baste the skin (or skinless) side with the melted butter and continue broiling for 4 to 5 minutes more, or until done throughout. Baste once more. Serve hot or at room temperature.

Garlic Butter

8 tablespoons salted or unsalted butter
3 large cloves garlic, peeled
1 tablespoon extra-virgin olive oil
2 tablespoons grated Parmesan cheese (optional)
2 teaspoons fresh chives or ½ teaspoon dried)
Dash of salt and black pepper to taste

Green Herb Butter

Blanch the following fresh herbs, dry with paper towels, then chop:

3 tablespoons finely chopped parsley
2 tablespoons finely chopped spinach
1 tablespoon each: chopped fresh chervil, fresh shipped chives, tarragon
3 tablespoons chopped shallots

8 tablespoons salted or unsalted butter
Salt and black pepper to taste

Chutney Butter

8 tablespoons salted or unsalted butter
3 tablespoons vegetable or fruit chutney (such as tomato, onion, mango, peach, etc.)
1 teaspoon fresh lemon juice
Dash of cayenne pepper

Shallot Butter

4 shallots, blanched, dried with paper towels, and finely chopped
8 tablespoons salted or unsalted butter
Salt and black pepper to taste

Tarragon Butter

4 tablespoons fresh tarragon leaves, blanched and dried with paper towels, and chopped
1 small clove garlic, finely minced
8 tablespoons salted or unsalted butter
Salt and black pepper to taste

Lime or Lemon Butter

1 shallot, blanched, dried with paper towels, and minced
2 teaspoons grated lime or lemon zest
1 tablespoon finely chopped fresh parsley
Dash of salt
White pepper to taste

Orange Spice Butter

8 tablespoons unsalted butter
2 tablespoons orange marmalade
1 tablespoon ground cinnamon
Dash of allspice

Sweet Curry Butter

8 tablespoons unsalted butter
2 tablespoons honey
1 tablespoon curry powder

Mustard Butter

8 tablespoons salted or unsalted butter
3 tablespoons Dijon (or other French) mustard
½ teaspoon fresh lemon juice
Dash of salt

1. Put the ingredients for whichever flavor of butter you are making in a food processor or blender, or blend together with a mortar and pestle. Mix well.

2. Freeze in small quantities (2 to 4 tablespoons) shaped in cylinders, tightly wrapped in plastic sandwich bags or plastic wrap. Don't forget to mark the flavors on the packages.

Sauté

Sautéing is somewhere between searing and frying, but, it's a very specific classic French method of cooking in which the food literally jumps around in the pan. Traditionally, this method requires food to be cooked with a fairly high dose of heat and with a fairly large dose of butter and/or oil to keep it from sticking to the pan. But the new heavy-gauge cookware surfaces, including nonstick, have rescued the sauté. The secret of a sauté using less fat overall is to begin by lightly coating a pan (including nonstick surfaces) with vegetable oil cooking spray. This gives the pan a double nonstick coating and reduces to a minimum the amount of butter or oil required. Whether prepared in a regular sauté pan or on a nonstick surface, both offer the advantages of a delicious sauce. After the chicken breast is cooked according to any recipe in this chapter, the evaporated juices and browned flavor bits remaining in the pan can be transformed with just a splash of this and a dash of that! First, remove the chicken from the pan, turn up the heat, and add half a cup of stock or wine, scraping the bottom to loosen and incorporate the flavor bits and reduce the liquid until only a reduced and thickened sauce remains. Make it snappier with a splash of vermouth, stronger with shallots or garlic, more colorful with diced tomato, or richer with a dollop of cream or crème fraîche (see page 231 for more ideas). Season to taste, spoon over the chicken, and eat! That's all there is to creating the perfect sauté.

SAUTÉED BREASTS OF CHICKEN WITH FOIE GRAS AND TRUFFLE SAUCE

Chicken breasts no longer need be forgotten for the holidays. Make this wonderful dish especially during the winter months, when truffles are in season and foie gras is plentiful. This contemporary recipe uses an elegant and classic ingredient combination and offers an at-home experience equal to any of the great restaurants. **Note:** Fresh from Hudson Valley, New York, foie gras can be purchased online from D'Artagnan at www.dartagnan.com.

4 servings

½ ounce fresh black truffles (or jarred), finely diced
½ cup extra-virgin olive oil
¼ cup Madeira wine
1 cup rich chicken stock (see page 9)
¾ cup heavy cream
2 skinless, boneless chicken breasts (about 2 pound), halved
4 ounces fresh duck foie gras
2 large eggs, lightly beaten
½ cup fine fresh bread crumbs

1. Heat 2 tablespoons of the oil over medium heat in a small heavy sauté pan. Sauté the truffles briefly. Increase the heat to medium-high, add the Madeira, and deglaze the pan, reducing the liquid by half. Add ¾ cup of the stock and reduce by half again. Add the cream and reduce again, until the sauce is thickened. Set aside.

2. Make an incision in the thickest part of the breast on the underside. Insert even amounts of foie gras into the incisions. Press the meat closed. Dip each chicken breast into the egg, then coat with the bread crumbs.

3. Preheat the oven to 300°F.

4. Heat 2 tablespoons of the remaining oil in a large heavy sauté pan or skillet over medium-high heat. Add the chicken breast pieces and sauté 4 to 5 minutes or until brown on one side. Do not crowd the pan. Turn and brown on the other side, using a little more oil if necessary. The chicken should be crispy and brown, and bread crumbs forming a shell. Remove to an ovenproof dish and place the chicken in the oven for 5 minutes to finish cooking.

5. Reheat the sauce over low heat.

6. Place the chicken on individual heated plates. Pour the sauce around the sides of the chicken. Serve immediately.

CHICKEN CAKES WITH BALSAMIC-SHALLOT SAUCE

In addition to the crab-boiling spices, the Worcestershire and Tabasco, add Dijon mustard, cilantro, and scallions for a special taste sensation. These chicken cakes are versatile and can be served as a main dish or first course.

4 servings

8 medium shallots, unpeeled
1 to 2 teaspoon extra-virgin olive oil
1 cup dry white wine
1 cup chicken stock (page 8)
3 tablespoons balsamic vinegar
1 pound ground chicken breast
3 tablespoons finely chopped celery
2 tablespoons finely chopped onion
3 tablespoons finely diced red bell pepper
1 tablespoon finely chopped flat-leaf parsley
1 teaspoon grated lemon zest
1 small clove garlic, finely minced
1½ cups fresh bread crumbs (page 16)
1 large egg plus 1 large egg white, beaten
1 teaspoon salt
1 teaspoon ground crab-boiling spice mix (packaged)
1 teaspoon Worcestershire sauce
¼ teaspoon Tabasco
1 tablespoon unsalted butter
1 tablespoon canola oil

1. To make the sauce: preheat the oven to 350°F. Place a piece of aluminum foil on a baking sheet. Place the shallots on the foil and drizzle with the olive oil; toss to coat. Wrap the shallots tightly in the foil and roast for 30 to 40 minutes or until tender. Leave the oven on, set at 325°F. When the shallots are cool, peel and chop.

2. Meanwhile, bring the wine, stock, and balsamic vinegar to a boil in a nonreactive medium saucepan, and cook about 15 minutes or until reduced by half. Add the shallots and set the pan aside.

3. Combine the chicken, celery, onion, bell pepper, parsley, lemon zest, and garlic in a large bowl and mix well with your hands or a wooden spoon. Add 1 cup of the breadcrumbs, the egg, salt, crab boiling spice, Worcestershire, and Tabasco and stir until well combined.

4. Cover with plastic wrap and chill for 1 hour. Divide the mixture into 8 portions and form patties. Sprinkle the remaining breadcrumbs on all sides and pat into the cakes.

5. In a large nonstick sauté pan or in a skillet lightly coated with cooking spray, heat the butter and canola oil over medium heat. Sauté the chicken cakes about 3 minutes per side or until browned.

6. Place the chicken cakes in a single layer in a baking dish. Bake for 5 to 6 minutes, or until done.

7. Reheat the shallot sauce, spoon sauce onto four warmed plates, and nestle the chicken cakes into the sauce.

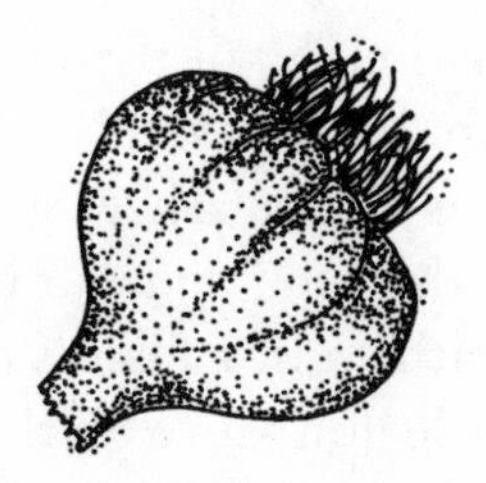

THE CLASSIC SAUTÉ

Heat a tablespoon or two of butter or oil, or combinations of the two, in a heavy skillet or sauté pan over medium-high heat. Adding oil allows the butter to cook over high heat without burning. Pat the chicken breasts dry and season with a scant amount of salt and pepper to taste. Place in the pan. Cook without moving the pieces until the underside is brown. Turn and sauté the other side. Don't crowd the pan or the pieces will steam instead of developing a golden crisp crust.

A companion technique to sautéing is deglazing the pan. This creates an instant, flavorful sauce. Start by removing the chicken breasts from the pan to a platter. Cover with a foil tent to keep the chicken warm. Pour off any excess oil from the pan. With the heat up high enough to boil the liquid, add a small amount of stock, wine or vermouth, lemon juice, or other flavorful liquid, about ½ cup, to the pan. At this point, minced garlic or shallots can be added, and you can scrape loose any browned particles stuck to the bottom of the pan during the reducing of the liquid. Continue boiling and stirring until the liquid is reduced to a sauce consistency. It will be fairly thin sauce since there is no thickener added. At this point, the flavorful pan sauce can be poured over the chicken and served. Or, continue reducing until the pan is almost dry. Then add cream, a splash of liqueur, such as brandy, port, Grand Marnier, or vermouth, as well as a few tablespoons of chopped fresh herbs, and cook down to a saucy consistency. At the very end for a velvety finish, stir in a tablespoon of butter. Taste and adjust the seasoning with salt and freshly ground pepper. Spoon the sauce over the chicken breasts and serve immediately.

CHICKEN PAILLARDS WITH MUSHROOMS AND PEPPERS

A paillard is a cutlet or flattened piece of meat, which, in this case, is chicken breast. It is a particularly elegant way of portioning this food and can be the basis for many variations. Paillards can be served with lemon sauce, with shiitake mushrooms, with a light, fresh Tomato-Herb Sauce (see page 126), with a ragout of fresh spring vegetables, or as the recipe suggests, with mushrooms and sweet red bell peppers.

4 servings

2 tablespoons seasoned dry bread-crumbs
2 teaspoon dried herbs of choice (such as oregano, thyme, basil, and rosemary)
Salt and freshly ground black pepper to taste
2 skinless, boneless chicken breasts (about 1½ pounds), flattened between plastic wrap to ¼-inch thickness
1 tablespoon extra-virgin olive oil
2 cloves garlic, minced
½ pound mushrooms, stems removed and caps sliced
⅔ cup chicken stock (page 8)
1 large red bell pepper, seeded and cut into strips
2 teaspoons fresh lemon juice
¼ teaspoon crushed red pepper
2 teaspoons cornstarch dissolved in 2 tablespoons chicken stock
2 tablespoons coarsely chopped flat-leaf parsley

1. Combine the breadcrumbs, 1 teaspoon of the dried herbs, and a pinch of salt and pepper in a small bowl. Place the paillards on a work surface and sprinkle with the bread crumb mixture on both sides.

2. In a large nonstick sauté pan or skillet lightly coated with cooking spray, heat the oil over medium-high heat. Add the chicken and sauté 1 minute per side or just until done. Do not overcook. Transfer on a platter and keep warm.

3. To the same skillet, add the garlic and cook over medium heat, stirring constantly, for 2 to 3 minutes. Add the mushrooms and cook until most of the liquid has evaporated, about 5 minutes. Add 1 tablespoon of the chicken stock and the bell pepper and cook over medium-high heat for about 3 minutes or until the moisture has evaporated.

4. Add the remaining stock, lemon juice, the remaining 1 teaspoon of dried herbs, and the crushed red pepper and reduce the heat to low. Stir in the cornstarch mixture and cook, partially covered, about 7 minutes or until the peppers are tender and the sauce is slightly thickened.

5. To assemble, place the paillards on four warmed plates, spoon the sauce over the chicken, and sprinkle with the chopped parsley.

PICKING HERBS AND AROMATICS FOR FLAVORFUL SAUTÉS

Chicken breasts, herbs, and spices can be partnered in many ways. Lots of shallots and garlic show up in the sauté pan, along with fresh basil, marjoram, flat-leaf parsley (with better character than curly parsley), sage, oregano, thyme, tarragon, cilantro, dill, rosemary, and chives. Fresh herbs should be selected over dried whenever possible in sautés since the cooking time is so short and the fresh garden flavors are more delicate. When dried herbs are substituted, use half the amount you would with fresh herbs.

CHICKEN BREASTS WITH TOMATO AND BASIL SAUCE ON LINGUINE

To vary the flavors of this dish, sauté a tablespoon of finely diced Italian panchetta, a minced onion, and some red pepper flakes in 1 to 2 teaspoons of garlic-infused olive oil and add it to this fresh, uncooked sauce. For another version, add a splash of white wine to 2 to 3 cups of the uncooked sauce, heat through, and serve over linguine with a shaving of fresh Parmesan.

4 servings

3 cups coarsely chopped, peeled, and seeded plum tomatoes
2½ tablespoons extra-virgin olive oil
¼ cup finely chopped fresh basil
2 tablespoons finely chopped flat-leaf parsley
3 tablespoons minced white onion
Salt and freshly ground black pepper to taste
¾ pound dried linguine
1 tablespoon unsalted butter
2 skinless, boneless chicken breasts (about 1½ pounds), halved and pounded between plastic wrap to ½-inch thickness
3 tablespoons dry white wine such as

sauvignon blanc or pinot grigio
2 teaspoons drained and rinsed capers, coarsely chopped
1 tablespoon chopped fresh parsley

1. To make the sauce, toss together the tomatoes, 1 tablespoon of the oil, basil, parsley, onion, and salt and pepper to taste in a small bowl. Set aside at room temperature.

2. Bring lightly salted water to a boil in a large stockpot. Cook the linguine to al dente. Rinse with hot water, drain well, toss with ½ tablespoon of the olive oil, and keep warm.

3. Meanwhile, in a large nonstick sauté pan or skillet lightly coated with cooking spray, heat the butter and the remaining ½ tablespoon olive oil over medium-high heat. Add the chicken breasts and sauté 3 to 4 minutes per side or until browned. Add the wine and capers and cook, partially covered, for 3 to 4 minutes more or until the chicken breasts are done. On a work surface, slice the chicken on the diagonal into ¼-inch-thick pieces.

4. To assemble, place the hot pasta in a large warmed pasta bowl, add the tomato sauce, chicken pieces, and parsley and toss.

SAUTÉING BASICS FOR LOW-FAT COOKING. JUST JUMP RIGHT IN!

First coat the bottom of a heavy sauté pan lightly with vegetable oil cooking spray. Just a touch will work fine! Then add a little butter or extra-virgin olive oil or a combination of both. Heat the pan over moderately high heat. Let the oil and butter come to a fairly high temperature before adding the chicken breasts. First pat the chicken breasts with a paper towel to remove excess moisture, including marinades, then place in the hot pan. Sauté the chicken breasts without moving the pieces around until the side sauteing is nicely browned according to the recipe instructions, or individual taste. Turn, brown the other side, and remove when cooked through or according to recipe instructions as some. If the breasts are to be returned to the pan later, they should be slightly undercooked at this stage. Now you're ready to make a wonderful pan sauce according the recipe of choice.

SAUTÉED CHICKEN WITH TARRAGON-TOMATO SAUCE

No need to strain this sauce. It looks very appealing with flecks of tomato and fresh tarragon.

4 servings

2 ripe plum tomatoes, peeled, seeded, and finely chopped
3 shallots, finely chopped
2 tablespoons chopped fresh tarragon, plus 1 tablespoon for garnish
½ teaspoon freshly ground black pepper
¼ cup tarragon wine vinegar
3 drops Worcestershire sauce
2 skinless boneless chicken breasts (about 2 pounds), halved
Salt and freshly ground black pepper to taste
1 tablespoon unsalted butter
⅔ cup dry white wine
1 cup sour cream, regular or light, at room temperature

1. To make the sauce, combine the tomatoes, shallots, 2 tablespoons of the tarragon, pepper, vinegar, and Worcestershire in a small saucepan. Over medium-high heat, cook for about 10 minutes or until only about 2 tablespoons of liquid remain. Set the pan aside.

2. Lightly season the chicken breasts with salt and pepper. In a large nonstick saucepan or skillet lightly coated with cooking spray, melt the butter over medium-high heat. Add the chicken breasts and sauté for about 2 to 3 minutes per side, or just until lightly browned. Do not overcook. Remove the chicken to a platter.

3. Add the wine to the pan and deglaze over high heat until the liquid is reduced by half. Reduce the heat to low, add the tomato mixture, return the chicken to the pan and cook, partially covered, 3 to 4 minutes, or just until the chicken is done.

4. Remove the pan from the heat and transfer the breasts to a serving platter and keep warm. Over very low heat, stir the sour cream into the tomato mixture just to re-warm the sauce. Spoon the sauce on the chicken and garnish with the remaining chopped tarragon.

SAUTÉED CHICKEN BREASTS WITH FRUIT AND COCONUT CURRY SAUCE

4 servings

Sauce

1 tablespoon unsalted butter
½ cup minced onion
1 peeled green apple, cored and grated
1 cup crushed fresh pineapple
2 tablespoons all-purpose flour
1 tablespoon curry powder or more to taste (Madras if possible)
1 teaspoon salt
1 teaspoon sugar
1 tablespoon fresh lemon juice
½ teaspoon finely minced peeled fresh ginger
3 tablespoons unsweetened shredded coconut
1 cup coconut milk
1 cup chicken stock (see page 8)

Chicken Breasts

2 tablespoon unsalted butter
1 medium onion, quartered
1 tablespoon dried herbs of choice (such as sage, savory, parsley, and basil)
2 skinless, boneless chicken breasts (about 2 pounds), halved and flattened slightly between plastic wrap
Salt and freshly ground black pepper to taste
¼ cup dry white wine or chicken stock
2 tablespoons Major Grey's chutney, chopped

1. To make the sauce, heat the butter over medium heat in a medium nonstick sauté pan lightly coated with cooking spray. Add the onion and cook 3 minutes or until tender. Add the apple and pineapple and cook for 2 minutes more. Sprinkle in the flour, curry powder, salt, sugar, lemon juice, ginger, coconut, coconut milk, and chicken stock, mix well, and cook over very low heat about 30 minutes or until the sauce thickens. Let cool slightly. Transfer to a blender and blend until smooth.

2. In a large nonstick sauté pan or skillet lightly coated with cooking spray, heat 1 tablespoon of the butter over medium-high heat. Add the onion and cook 3 to 4 minutes or until tender. Sprinkle on the dried herbs and cook for 1 minute more. Transfer to a bowl and set aside.

3. Season the chicken with salt and pepper. In the same pan, heat the remaining tablespoon of butter over medium-high heat. Add the chicken breasts and sauté about 3 to 4 minutes per side or until lightly browned. Transfer the chicken to a platter and keep warm.

4. Add the wine to the pan and deglaze over high heat, about 3 minutes or until the liquid is reduced by half. Stir in the onion and herbs, chutney, and the coconut curry sauce and return the chicken to the pan. Cook over medium heat, partially covered, about 3 minutes more or until the chicken is done. Serve immediately.

VEGETABLE OIL COOKING SPRAY HAS SURFACED . . . AGAIN!

It's been around for a long time. However, in the days of cooking with plenty of butter and oil, it was simply an ingredient that was pushed to the back of the cupboard or reserved for people with medical problems. Now, it's shelved front and center in the supermarket, available everywhere, and is more specifically designed for needs for those of us who are cooking lighter, low-fat fare. Oils under pressure now include canola, corn, and olive. If you spray just a touch on the grill top, the chicken breast doesn't stick. The aerosol spray container distributes the oil in a very fine and even spray over the cooking surface. It is even possible to create your own: buy a plastic spray bottle with a very fine spray (like the ones used to mist your plants) and fill it with the oil you use most frequently—extra-virgin olive oil, peanut oil, canola, or light sesame are good ones to have ready to spray.

FRENCH MEETS SOUTHWEST COOKING IN ONE CHEF'S KITCHEN

From the 1980s, California and its chefs have lead the pack with what's new in cooking. One of those chefs is John Sedlar, who was at the forefront of Southwest cuisine with his unique restaurant Saint Estephe, which was one of the country's most interesting and innovative eateries in its day. Chef/restaurateur John Sedlar applied his classical French training to the preparation of Southwestern dishes and came up with a cuisine that was as gorgeous to look at as it was to eat. Blue corn may now be ubiquitous as a chip, but it was Sedlar who first brought it from New Mexico to Southern California. While Sedlar does seek out the completely new (he is an avid gardener who experiments with purple beans and hot "inside-out" radishes), some of his "new" discoveries (all of which he incorporated into his dishes) go as far back as the ancient Mayans and Aztecs. In a couple of years we may all be eating black corn, which he rediscovered when studying Aztec food from a thousand years ago. These days, Sedlar is fondly known as the "tamale king," and he has taken the humble tamale to heights never before imagined.

GOAT CHEESE AND BASIL-STUFFED CHICKEN BREASTS

To change the personality of this dish from Provençal to Southwestern, substitute cilantro for the basil and add a little minced jalapeño to the tomatoes along with diced red onion.

4 servings

2 skinless, boneless chicken breasts (about 2 pounds), halved and flattened between plastic wrap to ⅓-inch thick
Salt and freshly ground black pepper to taste
4 tablespoons goat cheese (chevre)
3 teaspoons unsalted butter
1 teaspoon chopped fresh thyme leaves, or ½ teaspoon dried
12 large fresh basil leaves cut chiffonade, plus1 tablespoon chopped fresh basil for garnish
2 tablespoons chopped fresh chives
2 large ripe tomatoes, seeded and finely diced
¼ teaspoon dried thyme
2 tablespoons white wine vinegar, preferably thyme scented
2 tablespoons extra-virgin olive oil
2 cups torn salad greens (such as baby lettuce, curly endive, and radicchio)

1. Place the chicken breasts on a flat work surface. Lightly season with salt and pepper on both sides.

2. Combine the goat cheese, 2 teaspoons of the butter, thyme leaves, chiffonade cut basil leaves, 1 tablespoon of the chives, and a pinch of salt and pepper in a small bowl. Mix with a fork to form a paste. Place equal amounts of the stuffing mixture in the center of each chicken breast. Fold the ends in as if wrapping a package to cover the stuffing completely. Set on a plate lightly coated with cooking spray or oil, seam sides down.

3. Combine the tomatoes, the tablespoon of chopped basil, dried thyme, vinegar, and 1 tablespoon of the olive oil, in a medium bowl and gently toss. Season with salt and pepper. Set aside to marinate.

4. In a large nonstick sauté pan or skillet lightly coated with cooking spray, heat the remaining 1 teaspoon butter and the remaining 1 tablespoon of olive oil over medium-high heat. Add the chicken breasts seam sides down and sauté about 2 to 3 minutes per side or until browned. Reduce the heat, partially cover the pan, and cook seam sides down for 5 minutes more or until the chicken is done. Remove the pan from the heat. Gently transfer the chicken breasts to a work surface to cool slightly.

5. Meanwhile, arrange the salad greens around the edge of four plates. Drain the tomatoes, reserving the marinade, Drizzle the marinade over the lettuce leaves. With a very sharp knife, slice the chicken breasts on the diagonal and place overlapping chicken slices in the center of the plate. Sprinkle on the tomatoes and garnish with the remaining 1 tablespoon of chopped chives.

Q: IS COOKING WITH ALCOHOL THE SAME AS DRINKING IT?

A: No, not at all! The alcohol in any recipe is cooked off, leaving only the flavor essence. When the liquid has evaporated and the pan is dry, the alcohol is gone. Only the flavor of the liquid remains. Sauces must boil down for the same effect to occur. This is especially important to know for people who, for any of a multitude of reasons, do not consume alcohol. If you're looking for a substitute, try chicken stock, a few tablespoons of lemon juice, or fresh herbs boiled in ½ cup of water and reduced to 2 or 3 tablespoons for flavor boosters.

LEMON THYME CHICKEN BREASTS

This chicken is very lemony! Use the juice of all 5 lemons, but as few as 3 will produce a memorable citrus explosion on the taste buds as well.

4 servings

2 skinless, boneless chicken breasts (about 2 pounds), halved and flattened slightly between plastic wrap
Juice of 5 lemons, or less to taste
1 tablespoon grated lemon zest
Salt and freshly ground white pepper to taste
2 tablespoons vermouth
1 cup dry white wine
2 cloves garlic, finely minced
5 tablespoons chopped shallots
2 tablespoons minced fresh thyme or 3 teaspoons dried
1 ½ teaspoons extra-virgin olive oil
1 ½ teaspoons unsalted butter
1 teaspoon cornstarch dissolved in 1 tablespoon chicken stock

1. Place the chicken in a shallow dish large enough to hold the breasts in a single layer. Combine the lemon juice, zest, salt and pepper, vermouth, wine, garlic, 4 tablespoons of the shallots, and the thyme in a small bowl. Pour the mixture over the chicken, cover tightly with plastic wrap, and marinate in the refrigerator for 2 hours.

2. Drain off the marinade and reserve. Pat the chicken breasts dry with paper towels, scraping any shallots and garlic pieces back into the marinade. In a large nonstick sauté pan or skillet lightly coated with cooking spray, heat the oil and the butter over medium-high heat. Add the chicken and sauté 3 to 4 minutes or until lightly browned and done. Transfer to a platter and cover with foil to keep warm.

3. Combine the cornstarch mixture with ¼ cup of the reserved marinade. Set aside.

4. Add the remaining marinade to the sauté pan and deglaze over high heat about 6 minutes, scraping up any bits on the bottom of the pan or until reduced by half. Add the cornstarch and marinade mixture, stir to mix well, and cook for 5 minutes or until the sauce thickens. Place the chicken breasts on 4 individual plates and spoon on the sauce. Top with the reserved 1 tablespoon of chopped shallots.

A WORD ABOUT HERBS — FRESH OR DRIED, WHICH SHOULD WE USE?

Yes, there are a few recipes that call for dried herbs, but in most cases, fresh herbs are more desirable. Since the availability of fresh herbs in the market is now a fact, there's really no excuse to use dried herbs instead of fresh ones. If, sometimes, we must turn to little bottles, cans, and cellophane packages of the aromatic substances in order to enhance the flavor of the food we're cooking, the results will still be okay. Cooking with dried herbs is not as sinful a substitution as using a bouillon cube in place of homemade stock. Dried herbs can be successfully incorporated into certain recipes by following this simple suggestion: Unless the dried herbs are going to be cooked for at least 30 minutes with liquid ingredients, pour boiling water over dried herbs through a small strainer. Squeeze out the water before adding the herbs to other ingredients. This step refreshes the herbs and brings them back to life, to a state more closely resembling freshness. Here are a few helpful hints regarding herbs, spices, and flavorings: Never, never, never use dried parsley, which closely resembles sawdust in flavor and texture. The same goes for pre-ground black pepper—always use freshly ground from a pepper mill.

CHICKEN WITH GRAPEFRUIT, RED ONION, AND RADICCHIO

4 servings

2 skinless, boneless chicken breast halves (about 2 pounds), halved and flattened between plastic wrap to ⅓-inch thickness
Salt and freshly ground white pepper to taste
¾ cup dry white wine
1 tablespoon dry vermouth
¼ teaspoon dry mustard
2 tablespoons unsalted butter
3 medium red onions, halved and thinly sliced
1 cup fresh pink grapefruit juice
2 teaspoons honey
1 teaspoon dried thyme
1 medium head radicchio (about ½ pound), cut chiffonade
1 pink grapefruit, sectioned and membranes removed

1. Place the chicken breasts in a shallow glass dish and season with salt and pepper.

2. Mix together the grapefruit zest, ½ cup of the wine, vermouth, and dry mustard in a bowl. Drizzle over the chicken breasts, cover tightly with plastic wrap and marinate, refrigerated, for 1 hour.

2. In a large, nonstick sauté pan or skillet lightly coated with cooking spray, heat 1 tablespoon of the butter over medium heat. Add the red onions and cook until tender. Increase the heat, cover, and cook, stirring frequently, until the onions caramelize, about 6 to 8 minutes. Transfer to a bowl and set aside.

3. In the same skillet, melt the remaining tablespoon of butter over medium-high heat. Remove the chicken, pat dry, and discard the marinade. Add the chicken and sauté for about 3 to 4 minutes per side or until lightly browned and done. Remove and slice in ½-inch strips and keep warm.

4. Add the grapefruit juice to the pan and cook about 5 minutes or until reduced by half. Add the remaining ¼ cup wine, honey, and thyme to the pan and cook over high heat about 7 minutes or until reduced to just about 2 tablespoons of liquid. Lower the heat to medium, add the radicchio, and cook about 4 minutes or just until wilted. Remove from the pan with a slotted spoon and transfer to a plate. Add the grapefruit sections and gently heat through, about 2 minutes. Transfer to a dish and keep warm.

5. Make a bed of radicchio on individual plates, top with chicken strips, drizzle on some pan sauce, and top with the caramelized onions. Garnish with the grapefruit sections.

AN UPDATE ON SAUTÉ PANS

Investing in a heavy medium-size sauté pan is a good idea. One regular and one nonstick would be ideal. One larger pan, a 12-inch heavy-gauge skillet, will round off your collection and take you through this chapter with ease. Reducing the amount of butter and oil required to keep foods from sticking to the surface of the pan makes your cooking healthier. With a can of cooking spray, and the choice of the right recipe (or revision thereof), it is easily accomplished whether you're using a regular surface or nonstick surface for sautéing.

GLAZED CHICKEN BREASTS WITH WARM PEACH CHUTNEY

4 servings

3 large ripe peaches, peeled and chopped
1 medium yellow onion, finely chopped
Salt and freshly ground white pepper to taste
1 cinnamon stick, broken in 4 pieces
½ cup fresh orange juice
¼ cup fresh lemon juice
1 teaspoon grated orange zest
1 teaspoon grated lemon zest
½ teaspoon plus a pinch ground ginger
2 skinless, boneless chicken breasts (about 1½ pounds) halved
1½ teaspoons unsalted butter
1½ teaspoons extra-virgin olive oil
2 teaspoons honey
2 tablespoons red wine vinegar
2 tablespoons white wine

1. Combine the peaches, onion, a scant amount of salt and pepper, the cinnamon stick, orange and lemon juices, the orange and lemon zests, and the ½ teaspoon of ground ginger in a large bowl. Add the chicken breasts and cover well with the peach mixture. Cover with plastic wrap and marinate in the refrigerator for 2 hours.

2. Preheat the oven to 300°F.

3. Remove the chicken from the marinade, scrape any pieces of peach back into the bowl, and pat off any excess liquid. Reserve the marinade.

4. In a large nonstick sauté pan or skillet lightly coated with cooking spray, heat the butter and oil over medium-high heat. Sprinkle a pinch of ginger into the pan, add the chicken breasts, and sauté 2 to 3 minutes per side or until browned. Increase the heat to high and drizzle in the honey. Toss the chicken in the honey to coat and cook for about 1 minute more. Transfer the chicken to a baking pan and place in the oven and continue cooking until done throughout.

5. Over medium-high heat, add the vinegar and white wine to the pan and deglaze, scraping up the browned bits up from the bottom of the pan. Add the reserved peach marinade and over medium heat cook for about 6 to 8 minutes or until the peaches are tender and the liquid is almost evaporated. Remove and discard the cinnamon pieces. Serve the chicken with the hot peach chutney on the side.

CHICKEN WITH BASIL, ENDIVE, AND PEPPERS

1 tablespoon extra-virgin olive oil
4 large endives, trim the ends and slice into ½-inch thick pieces
2 cloves garlic, very thinly sliced
2 tablespoons chicken stock (see page 8)
Salt and freshly ground white pepper to taste
2 skinless, boneless chicken breasts (about 2 pounds), halved
¼ cup packed chiffonade cut fresh basil leaves
¼ cup fresh lemon juice
2 cups torn baby curly-leaf endive
1 red bell pepper, roasted, peeled, seeded, and cut julienne
1 yellow bell pepper, roasted, peeled, seeded, and cut julienne
1½ teaspoons white wine vinegar
1½ teaspoons balsamic vinegar

1. In a large nonstick sauté pan or skillet lightly coated with cooking spray, heat 1 teaspoon of the olive oil over medium heat. Cook the endive for 2 to 3 minutes, stirring occasionally. Stir in the garlic, stock, and a pinch of salt and pepper and continue cooking, partially covered,

1 to 2 minutes or until the endive is tender but still holds its shape. Transfer to a large bowl.

2. Add 1 teaspoon of the olive oil to the pan over medium heat. Lightly season the chicken breasts with salt and pepper. Sauté 4 to 5 minutes per side or until browned and done.

3. Transfer the chicken to a cutting board and slice thin on the diagonal. Add the chicken to the bowl with the endive. Add the basil, drizzle on the lemon juice, and toss to mix well. Adjust the seasoning with salt and pepper to taste. Set aside.

4. Combine the curly-leaf endive and the bell pepper strips in a large mixing bowl.

5. Combine the remaining 1 teaspoon of olive oil, white wine, and balsamic vinegars in a jar with a tight-fitting lid. Shake to mix well. Drizzle on the endive and peppers and toss to coat well.

6. Divide the curly endive and peppers among individual plates. Top with the chicken and endive. Pass the pepper mill.

CHICKEN BREASTS WITH BASIL WINE SAUCE

Simple and quick, you can whip this one up in a minute with ingredients from the fridge. It is sophisticated enough to serve at the most elegant celebrations, and as a bonus, the calorie count is low!

4 servings

2 tablespoons unsalted butter
2 skinless, boneless chicken breasts (about 2 pounds), halved and flattened slightly
2 shallots, minced
2 cloves garlic, minced
1 cup dry white wine
½ cup light cream
2 cups chopped fresh basil (not packed)
3 tablespoons chopped fresh flat-leaf parsley plus 2 teaspoons for garnish
Salt and freshly ground black pepper to taste

1. Preheat the oven to 275°F.

2. In a sauté pan, melt the butter over medium-high heat. Add the chicken breasts and sauté about 3 minutes per side or until golden brown. Transfer to an ovenproof platter and place in the oven.

3. Add the shallots and garlic to the pan. Cook over medium-low heat cook about 5 minutes or until soft but not brown.

4. Increase the heat, add the wine and cream, and deglaze the pan, scraping up any bits on the bottom of the pan. Cook about 3 minutes to reduce slightly. Add the basil, parsley, and salt and pepper, return the chicken breasts to the pan, and coat with the sauce. Pour the sauce on a platter and nestle the chicken pieces into the sauce; sprinkle on the remaining parsley.

CHICKEN PAILLARDS WITH WALNUTS AND PARSLEY SAUCE

4 servings

2 skinless, boneless chicken breasts (about 2 pounds) halved and flattened between plastic wrap to ¼-inch thickness
Salt and freshly ground white pepper to taste
½ cup toasted chopped walnuts
¼ cup all-purpose flour
3 tablespoons finely minced parsley, plus 1 teaspoon for garnish
½ teaspoon minced garlic
1 teaspoon unsalted butter
1 teaspoon extra-virgin olive oil
1 cup dry white wine

1. Preheat the oven to 200°F.

2. Season the chicken breasts with salt and pepper.

3. In a blender or food processor fitted with the metal blade, process three quarters of the walnuts to a powder. Mix with the flour and a pinch of salt and pepper. Spread evenly on a double sheet of wax paper on a plate.

4. Combine 2 tablespoons of the parsley, the remaining walnuts, and the garlic in a small bowl and set aside.

5. Dredge the chicken breasts in the flour mixture shaking off any excess.

6. In a large nonstick sauté pan or skillet lightly coated with cooking spray, heat half of the butter and half of the oil over medium-high heat. Add the chicken paillards two at a time and sauté about 1 to 2 minutes per side or until lightly browned. Do not overcook. Place on a baking sheet, cover with foil, and place in the over to keep warm. Repeat with the remaining butter, oil, and paillards.

7. Add the wine to the pan and deglaze, scraping up all the brown bits off the bottom of the pan until the liquid is slightly reduced. Add the walnut and parsley mixture and continue cooking about 3 minutes or until the liquid has reduced to about ½ cup. Transfer the chicken to a serving platter, drizzle on the sauce, and sprinkle with the remaining parsley.

SAUTÉED CHICKEN IN COINTREAU

Chicken breasts classically pair up with oranges and other citrus fruits. In this recipe, a splash of the intense French orange liqueur, Cointreau, deepens and enriches the orange flavor experience.

4 servings

2 skinless, boneless chicken breasts (about 2 pounds), halved and flattened to ½-inch thickness
Salt and freshly ground white pepper to taste
2 eggs, lightly beaten
All-purpose flour for dredging
7 tablespoons unsalted butter
2 tablespoons chopped shallots
¾ cup chardonnay or other good dry white wine
½ cup fresh orange juice reduced to ¼ cup
⅓ cup Cointreau
1 tablespoon Dijon mustard
1 teaspoon all-purpose flour
1 orange, peeled, trimmed and thinly sliced, for garnish

1. Preheat the oven to 275°F.

2. Sprinkle the chicken with salt and pepper. Put the eggs and flour in separate shallow bowls. Dip each breast in the eggs, then in the flour. Shake off any excess flour.

3. Melt 3 tablespoons of the butter in a sauté pan or skillet over medium-high heat. Add the chicken breasts and sauté about 3 to 4 minutes per side or until golden brown. Transfer to a heat-proof platter and keep warm in the oven.

4. Pour all but 1 tablespoon of fat from the sauté pan. Add the shallots and sauté until softened but not browned, about 1 minute. Set aside.

5. In a saucepan over high heat, reduce the wine, juice, and Cointreau by half. Whisk in the mustard, shallots, and the remaining butter. Continue whisking until the butter is melted. Add the flour and stir until the sauce comes to a boil. Place the chicken breasts on individual plates, spoon on the sauce, garnish with orange slices, and serve immediately.

CHICKEN WITH SOUR CHERRIES

If you would prefer a fruit other than cherries, substitute blackberries or raspberries in this recipe and choose a corresponding liqueur.

4 servings

2 tablespoons unsalted butter
1 tablespoon extra-virgin olive oil
2 skinless, boneless chicken breasts (about 2 pounds), halved and flattened between plastic wrap to ⅓-inch thickness
1 large shallot, finely minced
¼ cup fruit-scented vinegar
¼ cup chicken stock (see page 8)
¼ cup crème fraîche or heavy cream
1 tablespoon cherry liqueur or good-quality brandy
16 whole sour cherries, pitted (fresh if possible, otherwise in a jar)
Italian flat-leaf parsley for garnish

1. Heat the butter and olive oil in a large sauté pan over medium-high heat. Add the chicken breasts and sauté 2 to 3 minutes on each side or until lightly browned. Remove to a platter.

2. Lower the heat, add the shallot, and cook, stirring frequently, until tender.

3. Add the vinegar, increase the heat to high, and cook until reduced to about 2 tablespoons. Add the stock, crème fraîche or cream, and liqueur, reduce the heat to low, and simmer, stirring occasionally, for 2 minutes more.

4. Return the breasts and any juices collected on the plate to the pan and cook over medium-low heat for about 3 to 4 minutes or until done.

5. Transfer the chicken to a platter and keep warm. Turn the heat to medium and cook until the sauce reduces and thickens slightly. Add the cherries and cook 1 minute more. Spoon the sauce over the chicken and garnish with parsley.

COOKING WITH WINE

Here's the rule of thumb: If you'd put the wine in a glass and drink it, then it can be used for cooking. So-called "cooking wines" contain salt and sugar, which will upset the balance of a carefully prepared recipe. Stick with good wine and your chicken breasts will turn out great. Every time!

LEMON CHICKEN PAILLARDS

The thinly pounded chicken breast pieces called for in this recipe cook very quickly, so be ready to serve the dish before the cooking begins. Delicate and tender when properly cooked, it also makes a wonderful small meal or starter course.

6 servings

3 skinless, boneless chicken breasts (about 3 pounds), halved and flattened between plastic wrap to ¼-inch thickness
Salt and finely ground white pepper to taste
Zest of 3 lemons
Juice of 3 lemons
1 cup dry white wine (chardonnay)
2 cloves garlic, finely minced
½ cup finely chopped shallots
1 teaspoon finely chopped fresh rosemary, or ½ teaspoon dried rosemary
2 tablespoons chopped fresh oregano, or 1 teaspoon dried oregano
2 tablespoons extra-virgin olive oil
1 teaspoon arrowroot, mixed with 2 tablespoons cold stock or water

1. Place the chicken breasts in a shallow glass dish. Lightly sprinkle with salt and pepper.

2. Combine the lemon zest and juice, wine, garlic, shallots, rosemary, and oregano in a small bowl. Pour over the chicken breasts and coat well. Cover with plastic wrap and marinate in the refrigerator for 2 hours.

3. Drain the chicken, reserving the marinade, and pat dry with paper towels.

4. In a sauté pan or skillet, heat the oil over high heat. Add the chicken paillards and sauté for 1 to 2 minutes on each side or just until done. Do not overcook. Remove to a platter and keep warm.

5. Add the marinade to the pan and cook over high heat about 3 minutes or until reduced by half. Stir in the arrowroot mixture and stir constantly until the sauce thickens slightly.

6. Place the chicken breasts in the sauce and heat through. Serve immediately with the remaining sauce on the side.

SOUTHWESTERN SPICY SAUTÉED CHICKEN BREASTS

If you have a taste for garlic and spices, this is a good recipe to choose.

4 servings

2 tablespoons corn or other vegetable oil
8 cloves garlic, thinly sliced
1 to 1½ jalapeño or serrano chiles to taste, stemmed, deveined, and very finely minced
3 red bell peppers, stemmed, seeded, and finely chopped
2 skinless, boneless chicken breasts (about 2 pounds), halved and flattened between plastic wrap to ¾-inch thickness in plastic wrap
1 teaspoon paprika
2 teaspoons chile powder
1 tablespoon lime juice
2 cups dry white wine (chardonnay)
½ cup finely chopped fresh cilantro
Pinch of cayenne pepper
¼ teaspoon salt

1. In a sauté pan or heavy skillet, heat ½ tablespoon of the oil over medium heat. Add the garlic, chiles, and bell peppers and cook, stirring frequently, for 4 minutes. Remove to a bowl.

2. Add the remaining oil to the pan and heat over medium-high heat. Add the chicken and sauté about 2 minutes per side or until lightly golden. Sprinkle on the paprika and chile powder, add the lime juice, wine, and the peppers and increase the heat to high. Bring to a boil, then reduce the heat to low, and simmer, partially covered, 6 to 8 minutes or just until the chicken is done. Remove the chicken breasts to a platter and keep warm.

3. Over high heat, reduce the sauce by about half, stirring frequently. Add the cilantro, cayenne, and salt to taste. Place the chicken breasts on individual plates and spoon on the sauce. Serve immediately.

THE SUCCESSFUL SAUTÉ

It is wise to have all the ingredients you will be using measured, chopped, diced, sliced, minced, or melted and within arm's reach before the delicate chicken breasts are added into the heated pan. The extra minute or two it might take to chop parsley or slice a lemon while the chicken breasts are cooking (or overcooking) could mean the difference between moist, perfectly sautéed chicken breasts and something that turns out similar to the bottom of a well-worn shoe.

SAUTÉED CHICKEN BREASTS PAILLARDS WITH CITRUS BUTTER SAUCE

A light and airy sauce with the tang of lime or lemon is quick to fix once you know the method for making the delicate *beurre blanc* sauce. Simply, cold butter is whisked into a reduction of rich and flavorful ingredients in order to make a foamy, intense sauce that must be served immediately. Weight watchers or dieters, skip this one, please!

4 servings

2 skinless, boneless chicken breasts (about 2 pounds each), halved and flattened between plastic wrap to ¼-inch thickness
Salt and freshly ground black pepper to taste
2 tablespoons extra-virgin olive oil
8 tablespoons cold unsalted butter, cut into 16 pieces
8 shallots, peeled and finely diced
Juice of 1½ limes or lemons
¼ cup chicken stock (see page 8)
¼ cup dry white wine (chardonnay)
1 teaspoon chopped fresh parsley, plus 4 parsley sprigs for garnish

1. Sprinkle the chicken paillards with salt and black pepper.

2. In a sauté pan, heat the olive oil over high heat. Add the chicken pieces and sauté for about 1 to 2 minutes per side or just until done. Transfer to a platter and keep warm.

3. Melt 6 pieces of the butter in a medium sauté pan over medium-high heat. Add the shallot and cook about 2 minutes or until soft. Add the lemon or lime juice, stock, and wine and bring to a boil. Reduce the liquid by half. Reduce the heat to very low and whisk in the remaining butter one piece at a time until smooth and foamy. Remove from the heat, season with salt and pepper, and add the chopped parsley.

4. Place the chicken breast pieces on individual plates and spoon on the sauce. Sprinkle with chopped parsley and garnish with sprigs. Serve immediately.

SAUTÉED CHICKEN BREASTS WITH PARMESAN SAGE SAUCE

4 servings

2 skinned, boned chicken breasts (about 2 pound), halved and flattened between plastic wrap to ½-inch thickness
Salt and freshly ground black pepper to taste
2 tablespoons unsalted butter
8 whole fresh sage leaves
4 tablespoons unsalted butter, melted
3 tablespoons all-purpose flour
1 cup chicken stock (see page 8)
1 cup milk, regular or 2%
Pinch of cayenne pepper
¼ cup freshly grated Parmesan cheese

1. Season the chicken breasts with salt and pepper.

2. Melt the 2 tablespoons butter over medium-high heat in a sauté pan. Add the sage leaves and cook for about 30 seconds. Transfer to a plate.

3. Add the chicken breasts to the pan and sauté about 3 minutes per side or until lightly browned and done. Transfer to a platter and keep warm.

4. In a heavy saucepan over medium heat, whisk together the melted butter and flour to make a roux. Cook, whisking frequently, for 5 minutes.

5. Bring the stock and milk to a full boil in a saucepan. Slowly pour the boiling liquid into the roux, whisking vigorously until completely smooth. Reduce the heat and simmer for 5 minutes, stirring occasionally. (If not smooth, strain and return to the pan.)

6. Season with salt and pepper and cayenne. Stir in the cheese. Simmer 2 minutes more. Place some sauce on a serving platter. Arrange the chicken breasts in the sauce. Place the sage leaves on top the chicken pieces and pass the remaining sauce on the side.

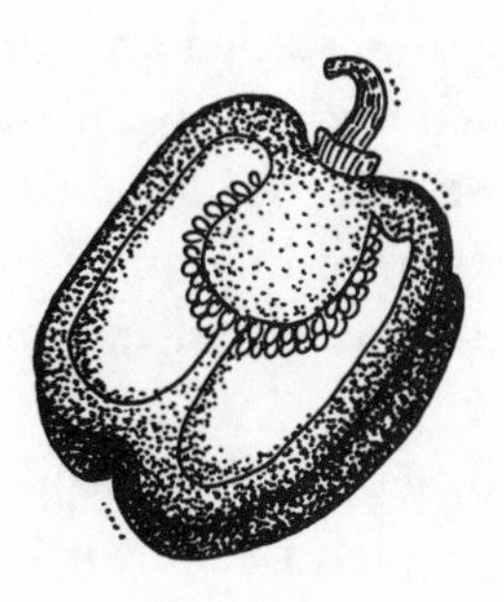

THAI CURRY CHICKEN

4 servings

Sauce

2 tablespoons canola oil
1 cup chopped onions
2½-ounces Thai green curry paste
2 tablespoons curry powder (Madras if available)
½ teaspoon ground cardamom
2 cloves garlic, minced
2 teaspoons minced peeled fresh ginger
1 teaspoon salt
1 pound ripe tomatoes, peeled, cored, seeded, and cut into ½-inch cubes (about 2½ cups)
Fresh ripe papaya, peeled and cut into ½-inch cubes (about 1½ cups)

2 tablespoons corn oil
1 skinless, boneless chicken breast (about 1 pound), cut across the grain into ½-inch wide strips
1 red bell pepper, seeded and cut into¼-inch-wide strips, blanched
1 cup broccoli florets, blanched
2 tablespoons fresh lime juice
¼ pound snow pea pods, trimmed and blanched
Salt and freshly ground black pepper to taste
1 cup plain yogurt, regular or low-fat
1 tablespoon finely chopped fresh mint

1. To make the sauce, heat the canola oil in a sauté pan over medium heat. Add the onion and cook 5 minutes or until soft. Stir in the curry paste, curry powder, cardamom, garlic, ginger, and a pinch of salt, and continue stirring to breaking up the curry paste, and cook for 2 to 3 minutes more. Turn the heat to high, add the tomatoes and papaya, and cook for 5 to 7 minutes or until sauce consistency forms. Set aside and keep warm.

2. Heat the 2 tablespoons of corn oil in a sauté pan over medium-high heat. Add the chicken and sauté for 5 minutes or until lightly browned. Add the red bell peppers and continue cooking for 2 minutes more. Set the pan aside, covered.

3. Add the broccoli, lime juice, and snow peas to the sauce and heat through.

4. Add the sauce to the chicken and heat through. Adjust the season with salt and pepper to taste. Transfer to a serving bowl.

5. Combine the yogurt and mint. Serve the yogurt sauce on the side.

NORTH AFRICAN STYLE SPICY CHICKEN BREASTS

Serve this dish with couscous or rice. Add currants or raisins to the mix along with a pinch of allspice and your average Moroccan meal is ready. Couscous is available in most markets and cooks almost instantly.

6 servings

3 skinless, boneless chicken breasts (about 3 pounds)
Salt and freshly ground black pepper to taste
3 tablespoons extra-virgin olive oil
1 large onion, chopped
2 teaspoons paprika
1 teaspoon ground ginger
¼ teaspoon turmeric
⅛ teaspoon ground cinnamon
2 tablespoons fresh lemon juice
1 cup chicken stock (see page 8)
1 pound carrots, peeled and cut on the diagonal into ½-inch slices
1 lemon, cut into 8 wedges and seeded

1. Season the chicken breasts with salt and pepper.

2. Heat the olive oil in a sauté pan over medium-high heat. Add the chicken breasts and sauté about 3 minutes on each side or until lightly browned. Transfer to a platter and set aside.

3. Add the onion to the pan, reduce the heat to medium low, and cook, stirring occasionally, about 8 minutes or until tender.

4. Add the paprika, ginger, turmeric, and cinnamon and cook, stirring constantly for 1 minute more.

5. Return the chicken to the sauté pan. Stir in the lemon juice and stock. Add the carrots, bring to a boil, reduce the heat to low, and simmer, covered, about 20 minutes or until the chicken is done.

6. Transfer to a platter. Arrange the lemon wedges around the edges of the platter and serve with couscous.

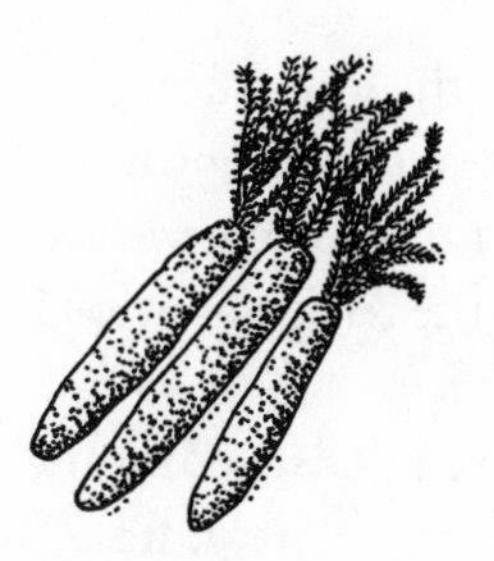

GINGER AND LIME CHICKEN BREASTS WITH MANGO SALSA

4 to 6 servings

⅓ cup fresh lime juice
2 teaspoons grated peeled fresh ginger
3 cloves garlic, peeled and flattened
½ teaspoon dried red pepper flakes
3 skinless, boneless chicken breasts (about 3 pounds), halved and cut into lengthwise strips ½-inch wide

Mango Salsa

1 ripe mango, peeled, seeded, and diced
1 small red onion, chopped
¼ cup chopped fresh cilantro
5 tablespoons lime juice
1 tablespoon chopped fresh mint
1 tablespoon extra-virgin olive oil
1 small serrano chile, seeded, deveined, and minced
⅛ teaspoon freshly ground black pepper
2 teaspoons extra-virgin olive oil
8 very thin lime slices for garnish
Fresh cilantro sprigs for garnish

1. Combine the lime juice, ginger, garlic and pepper flakes in a bowl. Add the chicken strips and toss to coat well. Cover and marinate in the refrigerator for 2 hours.

2. To make the salsa, combine the mango, onion, cilantro, lime juice, mint, 1 tablespoon olive oil, chile, and black pepper in a mixing bowl. Cover with plastic wrap and let set for 2 hours or more. Serve at room temperature.

3. Heat 2 teaspoons olive oil in a sauté pan over medium-high heat. Add the chicken and sauté about 2 to 3 minutes or until browned and done. Transfer to a platter and keep warm.

4. Add the lime slices to the pan and cook until brown on both sides. Place around a serving platter.

5. Arrange the chicken breast pieces over the lime slices. Garnish with cilantro sprigs. Serve with salsa on the side.

HOW HOT IS A HEATED PLATTER?

Serving plates and platters should be heated before placing cooked food on them. To heat a platter, turn the oven to the lowest setting. Set the platter or individual dinner plates on a rack in the center of the oven. If the platter becomes too hot to handle, allow it to cool on the counter before using. Otherwise, the food will continue to cook rather than just keep warm. Place a foil tent over the chicken breasts to retain the heat while you finish making the pan sauce.

CHICKEN BREASTS IN WATERCRESS SAUCE

6 servings

3 skinless, boneless chicken breasts (about 3 pounds), halved
Salt and freshly ground black pepper to taste
2 eggs, beaten well
All-purpose flour for dredging
¼ cup canola or other light vegetable oil
1 cup dry white wine (chardonnay)
1½ cups heavy cream
4 tablespoons cold unsalted butter, cut into small pieces
1 small clove garlic, minced
3 shallots, minced, or 1 small onion, minced
½ small bunch flat-leaf parsley, stemmed and blanched for 10 seconds
2 small bunches watercress, stemmed and blanched for 5 seconds
1 teaspoon all-purpose flour

1. Sprinkle the chicken breasts with salt and pepper. Place the eggs and flour in separate shallow bowls. Dip each piece of chicken in the eggs, then the flour, shaking off any excess back into the bowl.

2. Heat the oil in a sauté pan over medium-high heat. Add the chicken and sauté about 4 minutes on each side or until browned and done. Transfer to a platter and keep warm.

3. In a saucepan, bring the wine and cream to a boil and reduce by half.

4. Melt 1 tablespoon of the butter in a small sauté pan over medium heat. Add the garlic and shallots and cook until soft but not browned.

5. Combine the reduced cream, parsley, watercress, flour, and the garlic and shallot mixture in a blender or a food processor. Process until fairly smooth. Add to the sauté pan and cook over medium-low heat 2 to 3 minutes or until reduced to a thick sauce.

6. Lower the heat and whisk in the remaining butter one piece at a time. Adjust the seasoning with salt and freshly ground black pepper to taste.

7. Place the chicken breasts on individual plates, spoon on the sauce, and serve immediately.

CHICKEN BREASTS WITH SAGE AND RED WINE

2 to 4 servings

2 skinless, boneless chicken breasts (about 2 pounds), halved
Salt and freshly ground black pepper to taste
4 tablespoons clarified butter
4 fresh sage leaves
½ cup dry red wine (best quality)
¼ cup chicken stock (see page 8)

1. Sprinkle the chicken breasts with salt and pepper.

2. Melt the clarified butter in a sauté pan or heavy skillet over medium-high heat. Add the chicken breasts and sauté 2 to 3 minutes per side, or just until lightly browned.

3. Lower the heat to medium and add the sage. Stir in ¼ cup of the red wine and cook, covered, for 6 minutes. Uncover the pan and cook for 2 minutes more, or until the chicken is done. Transfer to a heated platter and keep warm.

4. Add the remaining ¼ cup of wine and the stock to the pan. Increase the heat to high and reduced by half. Pour over the chicken and serve.

Variation: Chicken Breasts with Tarragon and White Wine

In step 2, add 2 tablespoons olive oil to the pan and ½ cup chopped shallots; cook 5 minutes or until tender. Substitute 4 tablespoons chopped fresh tarragon for the sage and white wine for the red. Continue as directed.

MAKING PRETTY OF PLAIN

The chicken breast has been accused of adding little to the aesthetics of a dinner plate. However, an ounce of imagination can remedy this problem, if you consider it a problem at all. Interestingly arranged accompaniments, such as a medley of multicolored vegetables, can do much to enhance the look of a simple meal. Try bedding the chicken breast in a crunchy, buttery sautéed cabbage studded with caraway seeds, or crown a fan of cold chicken breast with halved green and red grapes. Try drizzling on pan juices, or napping the dinner plate with herb-flecked sauces that show off the delicately browned sauté of chicken breast. The old standards, parsley sprigs and lemon slices, are always acceptable, but there's more to life. There's orange zest, garlic-scented croutons, watercress purée, a sprinkling of freshly chopped herbs or nuts, toasted sesame seeds, and thinly sliced fruit. The produce department at your grocery store is full of interesting shapes, textures, and designs for garnishing. And they're edible! Many can even be used as accompaniments.

CHICKEN BREASTS WITH PERNOD

Pernod, a French semisweet anise-flavored liqueur, is usually drunk as an aperitif. Cooked with chicken breasts and the other ingredients in this recipe, it makes for a most interesting flavor combination.

4 to 6 servings

8 tablespoons unsalted butter
4 carrots, minced
½ tart green apple, peeled, cored, and minced
1 small onion, minced
½ celery stalk, minced
1½ cups chicken stock (see page 8)
1 classic bouquet garni, tied in a cheesecloth bag
Salt and freshly ground black pepper to taste
½ cup heavy cream
3 skinless, boneless chicken breasts (about 2½ pounds), halved
3 cloves garlic, finely minced
2 tablespoons Pernod
Chopped fresh chives for garnish

1. To prepare the sauce, melt 3 tablespoons of butter in a sauté pan over medium heat. Add the carrots, apple, onion, and celery and cook gently for about 5 minutes or until tender but not browned. Add ½ cup of chicken stock, the bouquet garni, salt, and pepper. Lower the heat and simmer for about 10 minutes or until the vegetables are very soft.

2. Squeeze the liquid from the cheesecloth bag back into the sauce and discard. Place the vegetables in a blender or food processor and process until smooth. Add the cream and process a few seconds more to combine well.

3. Melt 4 tablespoons of the butter in a sauté pan or heavy skillet over medium-high heat. Add the chicken breasts and sauté for 2 to 3 minutes on each side, or just until lightly browned. Add the garlic, cover, and cook over medium heat for about 5 minutes, or until done. Transfer to a platter and keep warm.

4. Remove any excess fat from the pan. With the heat at medium-high, add the Pernod and deglaze the pan, stirring and scraping up any brown bits from the pan.

5. Add the remaining stock and continue cooking until the liquid has reduced by half. With the heat low, add the vegetable purée and cook for about 5 minutes. Stir the remaining 1 tablespoon of butter into the sauce at the end. Place the chicken breast pieces on individual plates and spoon on the sauce.

NORMANDY-STYLE CHICKEN BREASTS

Fresh apple and Calvados apple brandy from Normandy, France, are the ingredients in this classic recipe.

3 to 4 servings

5 tablespoons clarified butter
2 skinless, boneless chicken breasts (about 2 pounds), halved
2 tablespoons minced shallots
1 tart green apple, peeled, cored, and finely chopped
¾ cup Calvados (apple brandy)
¼ cup chicken stock (see page 8)
½ cup heavy cream
2 tart green apples, peeled, cored, and cut into ¼-inch rounds
Salt and white pepper to taste

1. Melt the butter over high heat in a sauté pan or heavy skillet. Add the chicken breasts and sauté for 2 to 3 minutes on each side or until lightly browned. Remove the chicken breasts to a platter and keep warm.

2. Add the shallots and chopped apple to the pan and cook over medium-high heat until browned. Lower the heat, add the Calvados and ½ cup of the chicken stock, and simmer 2 minutes to reduce slightly. Return the chicken breasts to the pan and cook, covered, for 8 to 10 minutes or until done.

3. Remove the chicken breasts to a heated platter and keep warm, leaving the juices in the pan. Add the cream, the remaining ¼ cup chicken stock, and the apple rounds to the pan. Simmer for about 5 minutes, until the apples are tender and the sauce has thickened. Season with salt and pepper.

4. Arrange the chicken breasts and apple rounds on individual plates and spoon on the sauce.

THE MEANING OF SAUTÉ *EN FRANÇAISE*

The French verb *sauter* means "to jump" or "to leap." A grasshopper—the crooked-legged insect that seemingly propels itself with rocket force—is called *la sauterelle*. In cooking, *sauter* or *sauti*, means to cook over high heat with a small amount of fat, so that the food jumps with force in the pan as it cooks. If your chicken breasts aren't jumping slightly during the sauté methods of cooking, either there's too much fat in the pan or the fire isn't high enough. Never crowd the pan where a sauté is taking place because there won't be room to jump!

PAPRIKA CHICKEN BREASTS

2 to 4 servings

2 skinless, boneless chicken breasts (about 2 pounds), halved and flattened slightly
Salt and black pepper to taste
1½ tablespoons Hungarian paprika (sweet or mild to taste)
3 tablespoons unsalted butter
¼ cup finely chopped onion
½ cup dry white wine (chardonnay)
½ cup chicken stock (see page 8)
¾ cup sour cream, regular or low-fat
Finely chopped parsley for garnish

1. Sprinkle the chicken breasts with salt and pepper and paprika.

2. In a sauté pan or heavy skillet, melt the butter over medium-high heat. Sauté the chicken breasts for 2 to 3 minutes on each side or until lightly browned. Transfer to a platter and keep warm.

3. Add the onion to the pan and cook over medium heat until translucent. Add the wine and deglaze the pan over medium-high heat, stirring and scraping up any brown bits on the bottom of the pan. Continue cooking until the liquid has reduced by half. Lower the heat, return the chicken to the pan, add the stock, and simmer, covered, for 4 to 5 minutes or until the chicken breasts are tender.

4. Transfer the chicken breasts to a platter and keep warm. Over very low heat, stir in the sour cream and heat through, about 1 minute. Spoon the sauce over the chicken breasts and sprinkle with parsley.

CHICKEN SALTIMBOCCA

A twist on an Italian classic usually made with veal. Saltimbocca means "jumps in your mouth."

2 to 4 servings

4 fresh sage leaves
2 skinless, boneless chicken breasts (about 2 pounds), skinned, boned, flattened to ¼ inch and trimmed to squares about 5 to 6 inches
¼ pound thinly sliced prosciutto

3 tablespoons unsalted butter
Salt and black pepper to taste
¼ cup dry white wine

1. Divide the sage leaves among the pieces of chicken breast. Top each with a slice of prosciutto. Secure together with one or two large toothpicks which will be removed after sautéing. Season lightly with salt and pepper.

2. Melt the butter over medium-high heat in a large sauté pan or heavy skillet. Add the chicken breasts, starting with the prosciutto side down, and sauté for 2 to 3 minutes on each side. Do not overcook. Transfer the chicken pieces to a heated platter, prosciutto side up, and keep warm.

5. Add the white wine and deglaze the pan over high heat, scraping up any bits from the bottom of the pan. Reduce to a sauce consistency and drizzle over the chicken breasts.

BRANDY CHICKEN BREASTS

4 to 6 servings

8 tablespoons unsalted butter
3 skinless, boneless chicken breasts (about 2½ pounds), halved
1 medium onion, finely chopped
Salt and black pepper to taste
1 cup chicken stock (see page 8)
1 cup heavy cream
3 egg yolks, lightly beaten
¼ cup good-quality brandy

1. Melt the butter over medium-high heat in a sauté pan or heavy skillet. Add the chicken breasts and sauté for 2 to 3 minutes per side or just until lightly browned. Add the onion, salt and pepper, and stock. Lower the heat, cover, and simmer for 8 to 10 minutes, or until the chicken breasts are tender. Transfer to a platter and keep warm.

2. In a bowl, whisk together the cream into the egg yolks until well blended. Stir in the brandy.

3. With the pan off the heat, stir in the egg and cream mixture. Cook the sauce over a very low heat, stirring constantly, just until it begins to thicken.

4. Return the chicken breasts to the pan just to heat through.

CHICKEN BREASTS WITH FRESH CHIVES

2 skinless, boneless chicken breasts (about 2 pounds), halved
Salt and white pepper to taste
All-purpose flour for dredging
6 tablespoons unsalted butter
1 cup dry white wine or dry vermouth
1¼ cups heavy cream
Juice of ½ lemon
⅓ cup chopped fresh chives

1. Season the chicken breasts with salt and pepper. Dredge in the flour, shaking off the excess.

2. Melt 3 tablespoons of butter over medium-high heat in a sauté pan or heavy skillet. Add the chicken breasts and sauté for 3 to 5 minutes on each side or until done. Transfer to a heated platter.

3. Remove any excess fat remaining in the pan. Add the wine or vermouth and deglaze the pan over high heat, scraping up any bits on the bottom of the pan. Add the cream and cook until the liquid has reduced by half. Turn the heat to low and whisk in the cream and the remaining 3 tablespoons of butter, one at a time. Add the lemon juice and 5 tablespoons of chives and simmer, partially covered, for 15 minutes.

4. Return the chicken breasts to the pan to heat through. Transfer to a heated serving platter, spoon on the sauce and garnish with the remaining chives.

CHICKEN PICCATA

Chicken piccata is every bit as tasty as veal piccata, and about $10 cheaper per pound.

2 to 4 servings

2 skinless, boneless chicken breasts (about 2 pounds), flattened between plastic wrap to ¼-inch thickness
Salt and black pepper to taste
All-purpose flour for dredging
3 tablespoons unsalted butter
1 tablespoon extra-virgin olive oil
2 cloves garlic, peeled and minced
½ pound mushrooms, washed,

stemmed, and thinly sliced
2 teaspoons fresh lemon juice
½ cup dry white wine (chardonnay)
½ teaspoons capers, drained
3 tablespoons minced parsley
½ thinly sliced lemon

1. Season the chicken breasts with salt and pepper. Dredge in flour and shake off any excess.

2. Melt the butter with the olive oil in a sauté pan or heavy skillet over medium-high heat. Add the garlic and cook briefly. Add the chicken breasts and sauté for 1 to 2 minutes on each side, or just until lightly browned. Transfer to a platter.

3. Add the mushrooms to the pan and cook over medium heat for about 1 minute. Stir in the lemon juice and wine, and simmer for 10 minutes. Return the chicken to the pan and simmer until the chicken is done.

4. Transfer the chicken breasts to a platter and keep warm. Over high heat, reduce the pan juices to a few tablespoons. Lower the heat, add the capers, and heat through. Spoon the pan sauce over the chicken breasts and garnish with parsley and lemon slices.

CREOLE CURRY CHICKEN BREASTS

A fresh coconut is required for this recipe. Really, nothing else will do. Use an ordinary hammer from the tool chest to crack the coconut. Then, remove the milk and scoop out the coconut meat with a strong knife.

4 to 6 servings

4 tablespoons unsalted butter
1 clove garlic, crushed
1 large onion, sliced into thin rounds
3 skinless, boneless chicken breasts (about 3 pounds), halved
1 small serrano chile, seeded, deveined, and finely chopped (or ¼ teaspoon crushed red pepper flakes)
2 tablespoons curry powder (mild or hot to taste)
¼ teaspoon ground ginger
Pinch of powdered saffron (or 1 thread, chopped)
Salt to taste
4 tablespoons sugar
¼ cup chicken stock (see page 8)
1 fresh coconut (about 1 cup), white part only, grated
Milk from one coconut

1. Melt the butter over medium heat in a sauté pan or heavy skillet. Add the garlic and cook until brown. Add the onion and cook for 3 minutes more.

2. Increase the heat to medium-high, add the chicken breasts and sauté for 2 minutes per side or until lightly browned. Transfer the chicken breasts to a platter and set aside. To the sauté pan add the red pepper, curry powder, ginger, saffron, salt, and sugar. Lower the heat and simmer together for 1 minute.

3. Return the chicken breasts to the pan and add the stock and coconut. Cover and simmer for 20 minutes or until the chicken breasts are very tender. After the first 10 minutes, add the coconut milk.

4. Transfer the chicken breasts to a warmed platter. Turn up the heat to high and reduce the pan liquids to a saucy consistency. Spoon over the chicken.

CHICKEN BREASTS WITH PEACHES

Substitute tart Queen Anne cherries, winter pears, fresh figs, or other fruit for the peaches.

2 to 4 servings

2 cups fresh, ripe peaches (about 4 medium), peeled and sliced
6 tablespoons fresh lemon juice
1 tablespoon sugar
2 skinless, boneless chicken breasts (about 2 pounds), halved
Salt and black pepper to taste
½ teaspoon paprika
2 tablespoons canola or other light vegetable oil
1 cup chicken stock (see page 8)
4 tablespoons unsalted butter
1 cup finely chopped onion

1. Mix together the peaches, lemon juice, and sugar and set aside.

2. Season the chicken breasts with salt, pepper, and paprika. In a sauté pan or heavy skillet, heat the oil over medium-high heat. Add the chicken breasts and sauté for 2 to 3 minutes on each side or until lightly browned. Add the stock, lower the heat, cover, and simmer for 8 to 10 minutes or until done. Transfer the chicken to a platter.

3. Add 2 tablespoons of the butter to the pan and melt over medium heat. Add the onion and cook until golden brown. Transfer the onion to a bowl. Drain the juice from the peaches into the onion and set aside.

4. Melt the remaining 2 tablespoons of the butter in the pan over medium heat. Add the peaches and cook about 3 to 4 minutes or until tender.

5. Return the onion mixture and the juices from the chicken breasts to the pan. Cover and simmer for 10 minutes. Return the chicken breasts to the pan and simmer for 2 minutes more or just until heated through. Transfer to a platter.

CHICKEN BREASTS IN CHAMPAGNE

2 to 4 servings

2 skinless, boneless chicken breasts (about 2 pounds), flattened slightly
Salt and freshly ground black pepper to taste
5 tablespoons unsalted butter
1 cup chicken stock (see page 8)
1 cup dry champagne (Brut) at room temperature
¼ cup dry white wine (chardonnay)
2 tablespoons minced shallots
2 tablespoons Madeira
2 tablespoons minced fresh parsley
1 tablespoon minced fresh tarragon leaves (or ½ teaspoon dried)
2 tablespoons capers, drained

1. Season the chicken breasts with salt and pepper.

2. Melt the butter over medium-high heat in a sauté pan or heavy skillet. Add the chicken breasts and sauté for 3 to 4 minutes on each side or until browned and done. Transfer to a platter and keep warm.

3. Combine the stock, champagne, wine, and shallots in a saucepan. Bring to a boil and reduce the liquid by half.

4. Lower the heat to medium and stir in the Madeira, parsley, and tarragon. Whisk in the remaining 2 tablespoons of butter, one at a time.

5. Return the chicken breasts to the pan and heat through for about 2 minutes. Garnish with capers.

CHICKEN BREASTS WITH SPINACH CREAM SAUCE

This type of dish is also known as Florentine.

4 to 6 servings

6 tablespoons unsalted butter
2 bunches fresh spinach, stemmed, well washed, and dried
Salt and black pepper to taste
Juice of ½ lemon
2 tablespoons canola or other light vegetable oil
3 skinless, boneless chicken breasts (about 3 pounds), halved
1 cup port wine or golden sherry
½ cup chicken stock (see page 8)
½ cup heavy cream

1. Melt 1 tablespoon of the butter over medium heat in a sauté pan or heavy skillet. Add the spinach and cook just until wilted. Season with salt and pepper, add the lemon juice, and toss gently. Set the pan aside.

2. In another sauté pan or heavy skillet, melt 1 tablespoon of the butter and the oil together over medium-high heat. Add the chicken breasts and sauté for about 3 to 5 minutes on each side or just until lightly browned and done. Transfer to a platter and keep warm.

3. Remove any excess fat from the pan. Add the wine and stock and deglaze the pan over high heat, scraping up any bits on the bottom of the pan. Cook until reduced by half. Lower the heat, add the cream, and continue cooking until the sauce is slightly thickened. Remove the pan from the heat and whisk in the remaining 4 tablespoons of butter, one tablespoon at a time. Season with salt and pepper and heat through briefly.

4. Reheat the spinach for just a few seconds. Divide the spinach among individual plates, top with a chicken breast, and spoon on the sauce.

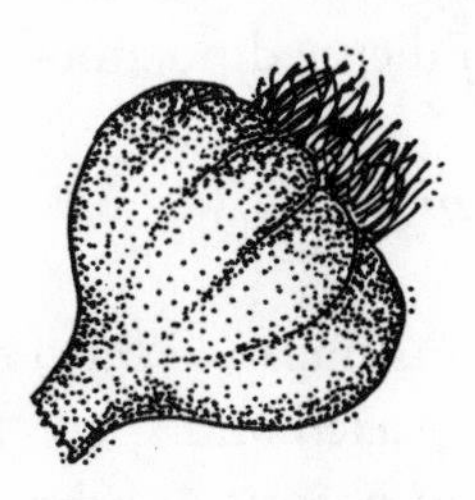

CHICKEN BREASTS IN PIQUANT CREAM

4 servings

2 skinless, boneless chicken breasts (about 2 pounds), halved
Salt and black pepper to taste
4 tablespoons unsalted butter
4 cloves garlic, peeled and halved
4 tablespoons white wine vinegar
⅓ cup dry white wine (chardonnay)
1 tablespoon Dijon mustard
4 tablespoons tomato purée
¼ cup heavy cream
1 teaspoon Worcestershire sauce

1. Season the chicken breasts with salt and pepper.

2. Melt the butter over medium heat in a sauté pan or heavy skillet. Add the chicken breasts and the garlic and sauté for about 2 minutes on each side or until lightly browned. Pour in the vinegar and wine and continue cooking for about 5 minutes more or until the liquid has almost evaporated. Transfer to a platter and keep warm. Discard the garlic.

3. Add the mustard and tomato purée to the pan and stir until smooth, adding a few drops of wine if necessary. Place the pan over very low heat, stir in the cream and Worcestershire sauce, and whisk until well blended. Heat through and pour over the chicken breasts.

BRAZILIAN CHICKEN BREASTS WITH SAUTÉED BANANAS

Traditionally, Brazilians serve this dish with fried julienned potatoes.

2 to 4 servings

5 tablespoons unsalted butter
2 bananas, peeled and sliced lengthwise
1 tablespoon peanut or other light vegetable oil
2 skinless, boneless chicken breasts (about 2 pounds), halved
¼ teaspoon ground ginger
Salt and black pepper to taste
3 tablespoons dark rum
⅓ cup dry white wine (chardonnay)

1. Melt 3 tablespoons of the butter over medium heat in a sauté pan or heavy skillet. Sauté the bananas for 4 to 5 minutes, until brown and crispy. Transfer to a platter and keep warm.

2. Melt the remaining 2 tablespoons of butter with the oil over medium-high heat in the same pan. Season the chicken breasts with ginger, salt, and pepper. Saute for 3 to 5 minutes per side or until browned and done. Transfer to a platter and keep warm.

3. Turn the heat to very low, add the rum, and heat through, about 30 seconds. Standing back, touch the side of the pan with a lighted kitchen match and allow the alcohol to burn off, stirring the sauce as the flame subsides. (Be careful to keep your head out the way, as alcohol flames can shoot up.)

4. Add the white wine and cook over medium heat for 3 minutes, or until the sauce has thickened. In the last minute, add the chicken breasts back to the pan to heat through.

5. Put the chicken breasts on the platter between the banana slices and spoon on the sauce.

CHICKEN BREASTS WITH RASPBERRIES

For a variation on this theme, substitute blueberry vinegar for raspberry and fresh blueberries for the raspberries.

2 to 4 servings

4 tablespoons unsalted butter
2 skinless, boneless chicken breasts (about 2 pounds), halved and flattened between plastic wrap to ⅓-inch thickness
Salt and freshly ground white pepper to taste
⅓ cup finely chopped onion
⅓ cup raspberry vinegar
⅓ cup chicken stock (see page 8)
¼ cup heavy cream
30 whole fresh raspberries (about ¾ pint)

1. Melt the butter over medium-high heat in a sauté pan or a heavy skillet. Season the chicken breasts with salt and pepper. Sauté for 2 to 3 minutes per side or until lightly browned. Transfer to a platter.

2. Add the onion to the pan and cook until tender over medium high heat. Add the vinegar and reduce the liquid by three quarters or to a syrupy consistency.

3. Reduce the heat to low and stir in the stock and cream. Simmer for 3 minutes. Add the chicken breasts and continue cooking for 5 minutes more. Transfer the chicken pieces to a heated platter. Immediately add the raspberries to the sauce and swirl the pan (don't stir) over very low heat for 1 minute just to heat through.

4. Pour the raspberry sauce over the chicken breasts.

MEDITERRANEAN CHICKEN BREASTS

Though this recipe calls for skinless, boneless breasts, leaving in the bone is okay, too. The choice is yours.

4 to 6 servings

3 skinless, boneless chicken breasts (3 pounds), halved
Salt and black pepper to taste
¼ cup extra-virgin olive oil
¼ cup dry white or red wine
2 medium tomatoes, peeled, seeded, and coarsely chopped
2 cloves garlic, finely chopped
⅛ teaspoon dried thyme
¼ teaspoon dried marjoram
¼ teaspoon finely crumbled dried bay leaf
3 sprigs of fresh basil (or 2 teaspoon dried)
15 pitted black or green olives (approximately ½ cup)
3 tablespoons minced flat-leaf parsley

1. Season the chicken breasts with salt and pepper.

2. Heat the olive oil over medium-high heat in a sauté pan or heavy skillet. Add the chicken breasts and sauté 2 to 3 minutes on each side or until browned. Transfer to a plate and keep warm.

3. Remove any excess oil from the pan. With the heat on high, add the wine and deglaze the pan, scraping up any bits on the bottom of the pan. Lower the heat and simmer for about 3 minutes or until the liquid has reduced by one third. Add the tomatoes, garlic, thyme, marjoram, bay leaf, and basil and continue to simmer for 5 minutes more.

4. Return the chicken breasts to the pan, cover, and simmer for 8 to 10 minutes more or until chicken is done. Add the olives and heat through. Transfer to a heated serving platter and sprinkle with parsley.

CHICKEN BREASTS VERONIQUE

Try this simple yet classic French recipe that uses seedless green grapes. If you want to go all out, peel the grapes!

4 servings

2 skinless, boneless chicken breasts (about 2 pounds), halved
Salt and black pepper to taste
2 tablespoons all-purpose flour
4 tablespoons unsalted butter
2 cups dry white wine
2 tablespoons fresh lemon juice
2 tablespoons slivered almonds
8 ounces (½ pound) seedless green grapes, washed and cut lengthwise

1. Rub the chicken breasts with a mixture of salt, pepper and flour.

2. Melt the butter over medium-high heat in a sauté pan or heavy skillet. Add the chicken breasts and sauté for 2 to 3 minutes on each side or until browned.

3. Add the wine, lemon juice and lower the heat, simmer for 7 to 8 minutes or until the breasts are done. Add the almonds and grapes for the last one minute.

4. Transfer the chicken to individual plates and spoon the sauce and grapes.

CHICKEN BREASTS WITH SWEET PEPPERS

Use a combination of sweet bell peppers for an especially colorful effect.

4 to 6 servings

2 green bell peppers
2 red bell peppers
2 yellow bell peppers
3 skinless, boneless chicken breasts (about 3 pounds), halved
Salt and black pepper to taste
3 tablespoons unsalted butter
3 tablespoons extra-virgin olive oil
3 cloves garlic, minced
¼ cup finely chopped onion
¼ cup chicken stock or wine
2 tablespoons chopped flat-leaf parsley

1. Broil the peppers under direct heat for about 5 minutes, turning frequently. When the skins have blackened, place the peppers in a paper bag. Allow to cool slightly, then peel off the loosened skin. Remove the seeds and cut into 1- to 1½-inch pieces. Set aside.

2. Season the chicken breasts with salt and pepper.

3. In a sauté pan or heavy skillet, melt 2 tablespoons of the butter and 2 tablespoons of the oil together over medium-high heat. Sauté the chicken breasts for 2 to 3 minutes on each side, or until browned. Transfer to a platter and keep warm.

4. Melt the remaining 1 tablespoon of butter and oil in the same pan over medium heat. Add the garlic and cook for 1 minute. Add the onion, reduce the heat, and cook until translucent.

5. Add the parsley, sweet peppers, stock, or wine and cook for 1 minute. Return the chicken breasts to the pan and simmer, covered, for 5 minutes more or until the chicken breasts are done.

CHICKEN BREASTS WITH WINE AND MUSTARD SAUCE

Experiment with any of the dozens of mustards available in the gourmet section of your market. Besides France, interesting mustards now pour in from all over the country, especially from the Napa Valley area. Look up the website for the Oakville Grocery and you'll find a surprising selection in the mustard department.

4 servings

2 skinless, boneless chicken breasts (about 2 pounds), quartered
Salt and black pepper to taste
6 tablespoons unsalted butter
3 shallots, minced
¾ cup dry white or red wine
¼ chicken stock (**see page 8**)
1 cup heavy cream
4 tablespoons grainy mustard of choice

1. Season the chicken breasts with salt and pepper.

2. Melt 4 tablespoons of the butter in a sauté pan or heavy skillet over medium-high heat. Add the chicken breasts and sauté for 3 to 5 minutes on each side, or until browned and done. Transfer to a platter and keep warm.

3. Remove any excess fat from the pan. Cook the shallots briefly over medium heat. Deglaze the pan over high heat with wine and stock, scraping up any bits on the bottom of the pan. Add the cream, lower the heat to medium, and cook until the sauce is reduced by half.

4. Lower the heat and whisk in the mustard and the remaining 2 tablespoons of butter, one at a time. Return the chicken to the sauce and heat through, about 2 minutes.

5. Place the chicken breasts on plates, spoon on the sauce and top with a twist of the pepper mill.

Variation

Substitute ½ cup of red port for the white or red wine. A large tomato, peeled, seeded, chopped, and lightly sautéed may be added to the sauce after the mustard in step 3.

CHICKEN BREASTS AND CANDIED ONIONS

2 to 4 servings

3 tablespoons fruit-scented vinegar (such as strawberry, blueberry, raspberry)
¼ cup currants
1¼ cups heavy cream
3 tablespoons unsalted butter
1 pound pearl onions, peeled
1 cup chicken stock (see page 8)
2 skinless, boneless chicken breasts (about 2 pounds), halved
Salt and black pepper to taste
Watercress for garnish

1. Combine the vinegar and currants in a bowl and marinate for 30 minutes.

2. Cook the cream in a saucepan over medium-high heat until reduced by half. Set aside to cool.

3. In a large sauté pan or heavy skillet, melt 1 tablespoon of the butter over medium heat. Add the onions and cook until golden brown. Add ¼ cup of the stock, lower the heat, and cook, covered, about 5 minutes or until the onions are tender.

4. Stir in the vinegar and currants continue cooking, uncovered, until the onions are glazed and the liquid has almost evaporated. Remove the onions to a dish and keep warm.

5. In the same pan, melt the remaining 2 tablespoons of butter over medium-high heat. Add the chicken breasts and sauté for 3 to 5 minutes on each side or until browned and done. Transfer to a heated platter and keep warm.

6. Add the remaining ¾ cup stock to the pan and cook over high heat until the liquid is reduced by half. Remove the pan from the fire and stir in the cream. Heat the sauce through. Adjust seasoning with salt and pepper.

7. Pour a small amount of sauce on the bottom of a heated serving platter. Arrange the chicken breasts on the sauce. Garnish the plate with watercress. Spoon the remaining sauce over the chicken breasts and scatter on the onions.

CHICKEN BREASTS WITH MUSHROOMS AND CREAM

This is a particularly elegant dish, great for company.

2 to 4 servings

6 tablespoons unsalted butter
2 skinless, boneless free-range chicken breasts (about 2½ pounds), halved
Salt and black pepper to taste
2 tablespoons finely minced shallots
1 small clove, finely minced
1 pound mushrooms, washed, stemmed, and thinly sliced (about 3 cups)
2 tablespoons fresh lemon juice
Freshly ground white pepper to taste
¼ cup dry white wine
¼ cup chicken stock (see page 8)
1 cup heavy cream

1. Melt 4 tablespoons butter over medium-high heat in a sauté pan or heavy skillet. Season the chicken breasts with salt and pepper. Add to the pan and sauté for 3 to 5 minutes on each side or until lightly browned and done. Transfer to a platter and keep warm.

2. Melt the remaining 3 tablespoons of butter over medium heat in the same pan. Add the shallots and garlic and cook about 2 to 3 minutes or until tender but not browned. Add the mushrooms, lemon juice, and white pepper. Continue cooking until the mushroom liquid has almost evaporated. Transfer the mushrooms to a bowl.

3. Add the wine and chicken stock to the pan and continue cooking until the liquid has almost evaporated. Reduce the heat to medium-low, stir in the cream, and cook for about 5 minutes, or until the sauce has thickened slightly. In the last minute of cooking, return the mushrooms to the pan.

4. Return the chicken breasts to the pan to heat through. Place on a serving platter and spoon on the sauce.

Variation: Chicken Breasts with Mushrooms and Cognac
Eliminate the lemon juice. In step 3, substitute ½ cup warmed cognac for the wine and increase the stock to 1 cup. Garnish with sprigs of fresh parsley.

SUPREMES DE VOLAILLE

Try this unexpected accompaniment with the recipe below: Julienned turnips, sautéed in a little butter, champagne vinegar, and a bit of brown sugar.

2 to 4 servings

½ cup currants
¼ cup Marsala wine
2 tablespoons clarified butter
2 skinless, boneless chicken breasts (about 2 pounds), halved
1 tablespoon Madeira wine
1 tablespoon cognac
2 tablespoons heavy cream
1 tablespoon orange blossom honey
1 teaspoon paprika
2 teaspoons water-packed green peppercorns, drained
2 tablespoons unsalted butter
1 large shallot, chopped
1 clove garlic, minced
½ pound fresh egg noodles, cooked and drained
Salt and black pepper to taste

1. Combine the currants, Marsala, and ¼ cup of filtered water in a saucepan. Over low heat, poach the currants until they are soft. Set aside.

2. In a sauté pan or heavy skillet, melt the clarified butter over medium-high heat. Add the chicken breasts and sauté for 2 to 3 minutes on each side, or until browned and done. Transfer the chicken breasts to a platter and keep warm.

3. Remove any excess fat from the pan. With medium heat, add the Madeira and cognac and deglaze, scraping up bits on the bottom of the pan. Stir in the cream, honey, and paprika and continue cooking until reduced by one quarter.

4. Strain the currants, discarding the marinating liquid. Stir in the currents and green peppercorns and set aside.

5. In another sauté pan, melt 2 tablespoons of butter over high heat. Quickly sauté the shallot and garlic. Add the cooked noodles and toss to heat through. Season with salt and pepper and keep warm.

6. Transfer the chicken breasts to a work surface. If any juice has collected on the plate, stir it into the noodles. Cut the chicken breasts lengthwise into half-inch strips.

7. Place the noodles on dinner plates, arrange chicken strips over the noodles, and spoon on the sauce.

> **Q: What does the word *volaille* have to do with chicken breasts?**
> **A:** That's what they call a chicken breast in France!

CHICKEN BREASTS IN TARRAGON SAUCE

4 servings

3 shallots, chopped
2 tablespoons chopped fresh tarragon leaves
Freshly ground black pepper to taste
1 cup dry white wine
¼ cup tarragon vinegar
3 drops Worcestershire sauce
2 skinless, boneless chicken breasts (about 2 pounds), halved
Salt and black pepper to taste
2 tablespoons unsalted butter
1½ cups heavy cream

1. In a small saucepan over low heat, combine the shallots, tarragon, pepper, ⅔ cup of the white wine, vinegar, and Worcestershire sauce and cook until the bottom of the saucepan is almost dry. Set the pan aside.

2. Season the chicken breasts with salt and pepper.

3. In a sauté pan or heavy skillet, melt the butter until hot and foamy over medium-high heat. Add the chicken breasts and sauté for 2 to 3 minutes or just until lightly browned. Remove the chicken breasts to a platter.

4. Add the remaining ⅓ cup of white wine to the pan over high heat and deglaze, scraping up any bits on the bottom of the pan. Add the reduced sauce mixture and continue cooking until most of the liquid has evaporated from the pan.

4. Lower the fire, add the cream and the chicken breasts and continue cooking for about 7 minutes or until the chicken breasts are done. Adjust seasoning in the sauce with salt and pepper. Place chicken pieces on heated plates and spoon on the sauce.

CHICKEN BREASTS WITH MORELS AND PECANS

Though expensive, morels are amazing little wild mushrooms. Until you taste them, your palate cannot understand the unique, earthy, woodsy flavor they impart to a dish. Buy morels in specialty food stores, fresh or dried.

4 servings

½ cup (½ ounce) dried morels, softened in hot water for 30 minutes. Drain and pat dry with paper towels, and clean well with a brush (dirt particles can be caught in the folds, so check before cooking the morels)
4 tablespoons unsalted clarified butter
2 skinless, boneless chicken breasts (about 2 pounds), halved
Salt and freshly ground black pepper to taste
1 tablespoon minced prosciutto
3 tablespoons cognac
2 tablespoons unsalted butter
⅓ cup coarsely chopped pecan halves
1 cup chicken stock (see page 8)
½ cup heavy cream

1. In a sauté pan or heavy skillet, melt the clarified butter over medium-high heat. Add the chicken breasts and sauté for 2 to 3 minutes per side, or until lightly browned. Season with salt and pepper.

2. Reduce heat to medium-low and add the prosciutto, 2 tablespoons of the cognac, and the morels to the pan. Cover and cook until the chicken breasts are done, about 5 minutes. Transfer the chicken breasts and morels to a platter and keep warm.

3. In a small heavy skillet, melt the butter over medium heat. Sauté the pecans until lightly browned and slightly crispy. Set aside.

4. Remove most of the fat from the pan. Over high heat, add the stock and deglaze the pan, scraping up any bits on the bottom of the pan. Cook until the liquid has reduced by half. Lower the heat to medium, stir in the cream and the remaining 1 tablespoon of cognac, and simmer until the sauce has thickened slightly. Spoon the sauce over the chicken breasts and morels. Sprinkle with the toasted pecans.

INDIAN-SPICE CHICKEN BREASTS

4 to 6 servings

1½ cups plain yogurt, regular or low-fat
1 small onion, minced
1 teaspoon finely ground cumin
1 teaspoon garam masala
1¼ teaspoons salt
¾ teaspoon finely ground turmeric
¼ teaspoon minced ginger
3 chicken breasts (about 3 pounds), halved
4 tablespoons clarified butter (or ghee)
2 large onions, thinly sliced
4 cloves garlic, minced
1 tablespoon tomato paste
1¼ teaspoon red pepper flakes
6 cups cooked white rice

1. Combine ½ cup of the yogurt, the onion, cumin, garam masala, salt, turmeric, and ginger in a large bowl and mix thoroughly. Add the chicken breasts and toss to coat well. Marinate for at least 1 hour at room temperature, turning to coat with the marinade several times.

2. Melt the clarified butter in a heavy skillet over medium-high heat. Add the sliced onions and cook until golden brown. Add the garlic and cook for 1 minute more. Stir in the tomato paste.

3. Add the chicken pieces and marinade and stir to combine well. Cook, covered, for 5 minutes. Lower the heat and simmer for 10 minutes more.

4. Stir in the remaining yogurt and sprinkle on the red pepper flakes. Simmer, covered, for another 10 minutes.

5. Mound the cooked rice in the center of a heated platter. Place the chicken breasts on top of the rice. Spoon the sauce and onions over the chicken breast pieces and rice.

NOTE:
Garam masala is a powdered mixture of cardamom seeds, cinnamon, cloves, pepper, and nutmeg. It is available at Indian groceries and specialty markets.

Stove Top

Variety is a key word in this collection of chicken breast recipes. This is undoubtedly the "every cooks" chapter; many recipes, you'll be pleased to know, are approved for low-fat and low-cal cooking and eating. A good example is the White Wine Coq au Vin (page 314), with a creamy finish of sour cream that can either be regular or light—the choice is yours, but the taste is never sacrificed. Other delicious recipes you'll discover in this section include a robust ragout of interesting mushrooms, and several that pair chicken breasts with fruit for a sweetly satisfying taste sensation. There's a recipe for the most popular Chinese restaurant appetizer ever, Pot Stickers, which are filled with delicious ginger-chicken breast filling and served with a traditional dipping sauce. If there's a brunch in your future, try the Southwestern Chicken Hash (page 308) with salsa on the side. A few Louisiana favorites, like Creole-style Chicken Gumbo (page 312), bring an extra-good and spicy balance to the chapter and to your cooking efforts. There's even a recipe for a hearty soup, Spicy Chicken and 3-Bean Chili (page 310). On a chilly night, rely on the recipe for Herbed Chicken Fricassee (page 315), which can be easily adjusted as seasonal ingredients change, as can any one of several risotto recipes herein. Obviously, this is also the "everyday" chapter because there are so many easy recipes that everyone loves. So, get a nice big skillet and plan on cooking your way from one end of this chapter to the other. Keep reminding yourself that, yes, even though the food tastes really, really rich and delicious, it's also lower in fat than many things you could be eating, because chicken breasts are naturally healthy and wholesome.

CHICKEN SCALLOPINI WITH PORCINI AND PEAS

Dried porcini mushrooms are always available. Add a mix of other mushrooms, dried or fresh, for an even more interesting dish. Always clean dried mushrooms well after they have been rehydrated. Bits of dirt or grit may be hiding in the crevices.

4 servings

1 cup chicken stock (see page 8)
2 ounces dried porcini mushrooms (or other dried mushrooms such as morels or chantarelles)
⅔ cup dry sherry (best quality)
2 skinless, boneless chicken breasts (about 2 pounds), halved and flattened to ¼-inch thickness between plastic wrap
½ teaspoon salt
½ teaspoon freshly ground black pepper
½ cup all-purpose flour
2 tablespoons unsalted butter
2 cups fresh peas or petite frozen, thawed at room temperature and drained
½ cup heavy cream
2 tablespoons chopped fresh flat-leaf parsley
2 tablespoons fresh chopped chives
2 teaspoons chopped fresh tarragon or 1 teaspoon dried

1. Bring the chicken stock and sherry to a boil in a small saucepan, add the dried porcine and remove from the heat. Cover and let stand for 30 minutes or until soft throughout. Drain in a strainer lined with several layers of cheesecloth and reserve the soaking liquid. Rinse the mushrooms well, drain, and set aside.

2. Dust the chicken pieces with salt and pepper. Place the flower on a plate and dredge the chicken through the flour. Shake off any excess.

3. In a large, heavy skillet, melt the butter over medium-high heat. Add the chicken pieces and cook 1 minute on each side or until well browned. Remove from the pan and keep warm.

4. Add the mushroom liquid to the pan and reduce to about ¼ cup. Add the chicken, peas, cream, parsley, chives, and tarragon, lower the heat, cover partially, and simmer about 5 minutes or until the sauce thickens and the peas are done. Serve immediately.

STOVE TOP BARBECUE CHICKEN BREASTS

This full-flavored interpretation is great on a big soft bun or over fluffy white rice.

4 servings

¼ cup light brown sugar
1 tablespoon chile powder
2 teaspoon ground cumin
½ teaspoon salt
½ teaspoon paprika
¼ teaspoon black pepper
2 skinless, boneless chicken breasts (about 1½ pounds), halved
1 tablespoon extra-virgin olive oil
1 cup chicken stock (see page 8)
¼ cup balsamic vinegar, reduced over low heat to 2 tablespoons

1. Combine the brown sugar, chile powder, ground cumin, salt, paprika, and pepper in a small bowl.

2. Place the chicken on plastic wrap and rub the mixture onto all sides; loosely cover with the plastic wrap and let stand for 15 minutes.

3. Heat the oil in a large heavy skillet over medium-high heat. Add the chicken pieces and cook 2 to 3 minutes on each side or until browned. Remove from the pan. Add the onion and cook 2 to 3 minutes, stirring constantly, until tender.

4. Return the chicken to the pan, add the broth, and bring to a boil. Cover the pan, reduce the heat to low, and simmer 20 to 25 minutes or until the chicken is done and very tender. Remove from the pan and shred, pulling crosswise with two forks. Return the chicken to the pan and bring the remaining liquid to a boil. Reduce the heat to low and simmer, uncovered, until the liquid is totally absorbed. Stir in the balsamic vinegar and simmer, covered, 5 minutes more. Serve hot.

PAN-FRIED ALMOND-CRUSTED CHICKEN BREASTS

4 servings

2 teaspoons extra-virgin olive oil
3 skinless, boneless chicken breasts (about 2 pounds), flattened between plastic wrap to ½-inch thickness
Salt and freshly ground black pepper to taste
½ cup all-purpose flour
½ cup buttermilk, regular or low-fat
¼ cup tablespoons Dijon mustard
1 tablespoon honey
1½ cups sliced almonds
1 cup dry bread crumbs (unseasoned)
2 tablespoons unsalted butter
1 tablespoon olive or peanut oil
2 tablespoons finely chopped chives or scallion tops

1. Preheat the oven to 450°F.

2. Place the chicken breasts on a work surface and dust with salt and pepper.

3. Add the flour to a plastic bag with a seal-tight top. Add the chicken one piece at a time and shake with the flour to coat well. Shake off any excess flour and return to the work surface. Repeat with all the chicken pieces.

4. Mix together the buttermilk, mustard, and honey in a small bowl until well combined. Pour into a shallow bowl.

5. Combine the bread crumbs and almonds and spread them out on a plate.

6. Dip each breast in the buttermilk then dredge in the almond mixture, pressing slightly. Repeat with all the breast pieces.

7. Melt half the butter and oil together in a large heavy skillet over high heat. Add half the chicken pieces and cook 2 minutes per side or until lightly browned and done. Transfer to a platter and keep warm. Add the remaining butter and oil to the pan and cook the remaining chicken pieces. Sprinkle with chives or scallions before serving.

ASIAN LEMONGRASS CHICKEN CAKES

Serve this with Mango or Pineapple Salsa. Use the recipes on page 130 and add a pinch of ground red pepper to turn up the heat!

2 to 4 servings

3 slices fresh white or egg bread
¼ cup finely chopped onion
¼ cup finely chopped scallion
¼ cup best quality mayonnaise, regular or low-fat
2 tablespoons chopped fresh cilantro
2 teaspoons chopped peeled fresh lemongrass*
2 tablespoons fresh lime juice
1 teaspoon fresh lime zest
1 tablespoon fish sauce*
1 large egg white, lightly beaten
2 cups coarsely chopped poached chicken breast (see page 352)
2 tablespoons peanut oil

***Available in Asian markets and some grocery stores**

1. Place the bread in the food processor and pulse to coarse crumbs. It should measure to 1½ cups.

2. Combine the bread crumbs, onion, scallions, mayonnaise, cilantro, lemongrass, lime zest and juice, fish sauce, egg white, and the chopped chicken in a bowl. Form into 8 to 10 patties about ½ inch thick.

3. In a heavy skillet, heat 1 tablespoon of the oil over high heat. Add half the patties to the pan and cook 3 minutes on each side, carefully turning, until golden brown and a crust has formed. Repeat with the remaining patties. Serve hot with chilled salsa.

PAN-SEARED CHICKEN PAILLARDS WITH SAVORY PARSLEY RELISH

Make this only with fresh herbs. Serve the chicken pieces on a bed or watercress with a dollop of the relish in the center.

4 servings

Relish
3 large finely chopped shallots
¼ cup chopped fresh flat-leaf parsley
1 teaspoon grated lemon zest
2 tablespoons fresh lemon juice

1 teaspoon chopped fresh thyme
1 tablespoon extra-virgin olive oil
Salt and freshly ground pepper to taste

Chicken
2 skinless boneless chicken breasts (about 2 pounds), flattened between plastic wrap to ¼-inch thickness
1 tablespoon extra-virgin olive oil
Salt and freshly ground black pepper

1. To make the relish, toss together the shallots, parsley, lemon zest and juice, thyme, olive oil, and salt and black pepper in a bowl. Set aside.

2. Sprinkle the chicken with salt and pepper. In a large skillet, heat half the oil over medium-high heat. Sear the chicken pieces for about 1 minute, turn and repeat, until golden brown. Do not overcook. Serve hot with the relish.

CHICKEN HERB ROULADE

This recipe is basically chicken breasts rolled around an herb filling mixture and pan braised on the stove top for the richest flavor. Use plump free-range breasts. Choose your favorite herb combinations as an alternative to sage.

4 servings

2 skinless, boneless free-range chicken breasts (at least 2½ pounds) flattened just to even the thickness, cut through widthwise to form four equal strips
Salt and freshly ground black pepper to taste
⅔ cup chopped fresh flat-leaf parsley
¼ cup chopped fresh sage (or herbs of choice)
2 tablespoons grated lemon zest
2 cloves garlic, minced
1 tablespoon extra-virgin olive oil
1 cup best-quality dry white wine (chardonnay or sauvignon blanc)
1 ½ cups chicken stock (see page 8)
1 teaspoon fresh lemon juice
4 or more lemon wedges

1. Place the chicken breast pieces on a work surface. Even the thickness of each piece to ½-inch by pounding slightly between plastic wrap. Season with a scant amount of salt and pepper.

2. Combine the parsley, sage, zest, and garlic in a bowl. Divide the mixture among the four breast pieces, spread evenly on the bone side, leaving a border of about ½ inch all around and rolled up. Secure with a toothpicks. Place seam side down on a plate. Sprinkle with salt and pepper, cover with plastic wrap, and place in the refrigerator for at least 1 hour.

3. Bring the stock to a boil in a small pan and reduce by half. Keep hot.

4. In a large skillet, heat the oil over medium-high heat. Add the chicken rolls and cook, gently turning, until browned on all sides or about 4 minutes. Add the wine, bring to a boil, and cook 2 minutes more. Add the hot stock, lower the heat, and cook 10 minutes more covered. Remove the rolls from the pan and keep warm.

5. Bring pan sauce to a boil and reduce by half. Stir in the lemon juice.

6. Slice into roulades about ¾-inch thick, arrange on plates, and drizzle on some sauce. Serve hot.

LEMON SHALLOT CHICKEN MEDALLIONS

Of all the aromatics (garlic, onions, shallots), the shallot is the most subtle and marries so well with the equally delicate chicken breast. This recipe turns the chicken breast into an elegant visual dish as well. Serve with orzo pasta or on salad greens for a luncheon course.

4 servings

1 tablespoon extra-virgin olive oil
2 skinless, boneless chicken breasts (about 2 pounds), flattened slightly to even the thickness, cut 1½ inch rounds out of the meat with a small biscuit cutter or glass
Salt and freshly ground black pepper to taste
2 tablespoon unsalted butter
⅔ cup minced shallots
1 minced clove garlic
½ cup dry white wine (chardonnay or sauvignon blanc)
1 tablespoon fresh lemon juice
2 tablespoons finely chopped flat-leaf parsley

1. Heat the oil over medium heat in a large skillet. Season the medallions with a scant amount of salt and pepper. Add the medallions and cook 3 minutes or until lightly browned on both sides and done. Transfer to a plate and keep warm.

2. In the same pan, melt the butter over medium heat. Add the shallots and garlic and cook for 2 minutes, stirring constantly. Add the wine and lemon juice and reduce the liquid slightly to make a sauce. Return the medallions to the pan and gently coat with the pan sauce.

Sprinkle on the parsley and top with a few turns of the pepper mill. Drizzle on the remaining sauce and serve hot.

CHICKEN PICADILLO

A Cuban-Latin dish usually made with beef or turkey, it's even lighter with chicken breast and can be rolled into a large flour tortilla as well as served with rice or roasted potatoes. Best of all, this variation of a full-flavored traditional dish all happens in one pan in about 10 minutes.

2 to 4 servings

1 pound coarsely chopped raw chicken breast meat
Salt and freshly ground pepper to taste
3 teaspoons extra-virgin olive oil or corn oil
¼ cup golden raisins
½ teaspoon ground cinnamon
⅛ teaspoon ground clove
¾ cup chicken stock (see page 8)
1 tablespoon white wine vinegar
1 tablespoon capers, drained
1 (6-ounce) jar prepared sofrito*
1 tablespoon tomato paste
1 tablespoon chopped fresh flat-leaf parsley
***A Caribbean combination, available in Latin markets and many supermarkets**

1. Add the chicken breast to the bowl of a food processor. Season with a scant amount of salt and pepper and pulse several times until ground.

2. In a skillet, heat 2 teaspoons of oil over medium-high heat. Add the ground chicken breast and cook, stirring constantly, just until the meat turns from pink to white and crumbles. Stir in the raisins, oregano, and cumin and continue cooking, stirring frequently, 3 minutes more. Add the stock, vinegar, capers, sofrito, and tomato sauce. Over low heat, cover and simmer for 5 minutes.

3. Stir in the chopped parsley and serve.

CRISPY CHICKEN BREAST CUTLETS WITH TOMATOES ARUGULA SALAD

The best in al fresco dining might include this dish. It's a wonderful potluck dish or at a buffet dinner.

6 servings

3 skinless boneless chicken breasts (about 3 pounds), halved and flattened between plastic wrap to ½-inch thickness
2 cups or more coarse yellow cornmeal
2 teaspoons salt
2 teaspoons freshly ground black pepper
½ teaspoon chile powder
3 eggs, beaten
3 tablespoons extra-virgin olive oil
2 small cloves garlic, finely minced
1 small red onion, sliced lengthwise very fine
2 tablespoons lemon juice
Extra-virgin olive oil for frying
Salt and freshly ground black pepper to taste
Pinch of sugar
Olive oil for frying
4 bunches arugula, rinsed, dried in a salad spinner, and chilled
4 cups diced, seeded, and juiced ripe tomato

1. Place the chicken breasts on a work surface. Combine the cornmeal, salt, black pepper, and chile powder in a bowl, then spread on a plate.

2. In a bowl, whisk together the beaten eggs with 1 tablespoon water, pour onto a shallow dish. Dredge a piece of chicken breast through the cornmeal, shaking the excess back into the plate. Then dip the piece into the egg and dredge again in the cornmeal, pressing slightly so the cornmeal sticks. Place on a baking sheet or platter. Continue with all the pieces. Place the pan in the refrigerator for 10 minutes.

2. Combine the olive oil, garlic, onion, lemon juice salt and pepper, and sugar in a jar with a tight-fitting cover. Shake to mix well.

3. Chiffonade cut the arugula just before cooking the chicken. Place in a bowl.

4. In a large heavy skillet, heat enough oil to coat the bottom of the pan over medium-high heat. Add several pieces of chicken breast and cook 2 minutes on each side or until crispy, browned, and done. Set aside and keep warm.

5. Toss the tomatoes with the arugula and the dressing in a large bowl. Serve the cutlets hot with the salad. Pass the pepper mill.

CHICKEN PAD THAI

This is a variation of the traditional noodle dish of Thailand which frequently include shrimp or other ingredients, depending on which Thai chef you favor. Everyone, from farmers to princes in their palaces to tourists in hotel restaurants, eats Pad Thai in Thailand. With so many Thai restaurants in the United States, Pad Thai is equally popular on this side of the Pacific. This version of the traditional dish features chicken breasts.

4 servings

1 8-ounce package wide rice stick noodles (Banh Pho)*
2 tablespoons ketchup
2 tablespoons tomato paste
1 tablespoon water
1 tablespoons sugar
3 tablespoons fish sauce*
1 tablespoon crushed red pepper or more to taste
2 tablespoons canola oil
2 cups coarsely chopped chicken breast (about 1⅓ pounds)
2 large eggs, lightly beaten
20 snow peapods, blanched, strings removed and sliced into very thin strips
¾ cup scallions, cut into 1-inch matchstick pieces
1 teaspoon minced garlic
1 cup bean sprouts
¼ cup chopped dry roasted unsalted peanuts, chopped
***Available at Asian markets or some grocery stores**

1. Place the noodles in a large bowl. Add boiling water and let stand 12 minutes or until the noodles are tender. Drain well.

2. Combine the ketchup or tomato paste, sugar, fish sauce, and pepper in a small bowl.

3. In a large skillet, heat half the oil over medium-high heat. Add the chicken and cook, stirring frequently, for 2 minutes or until the chicken has turned white. Transfer to a bowl and keep warm.

4. Heat the remaining oil over medium high heat and add the egg, stirring constantly to a moist scramble. Add the peapods, scallion, and garlic and continue cooking 1 minute more. Add the noodles, the ketchup, tomato paste, and the chicken, continue cooking 3 minutes more until heated throughout. In the last 1 minute of cooking, add the bean sprouts. Sprinkle on the peanuts and serve.

ASIAN COCONUT CURRY CHICKEN WITH VEGETABLES AND NOODLES

4 servings

1 8-ounce package thin rice stick noodles (Bahn Pao)* or any thin pasta such as vermicelli or angel hair
1 cup canned or fresh coconut milk
1 tablespoon honey
2 tablespoons soy sauce or tamari
1 ½ tablespoons minced peeled fresh ginger
2 cloves garlic, minced
1 teaspoon green curry paste or more to taste
1 teaspoon salt
1 tablespoon canola oil or other light vegetable oil
1 skinless, boneless chicken breast (about 1 pound), cut into bite-size chunks
1 cup coarsely chopped bell pepper
10 snow peapods, strings removed and cut into thin strips
1 cup chopped scallion
1 medium head shredded Napa cabbage
2 tablespoons chopped fresh cilantro

***Available in Asian markets or in some supermarkets**

1. Place the noodles in a large bowl. Add boiling water and let stand 6 minutes or until the noodles are tender. Drain.

2. Combine the coconut milk, honey, soy sauce, ginger, garlic, curry paste, and salt in a small bowl.

3. In a large skillet, heat the oil over medium-high heat. Add the chicken chunks and cook 6 minutes, stirring frequently, until browned and done. Transfer to a bowl and keep warm.

4. Add the bell pepper and snow peas to the pan and cook just until crisp-tender or about 2 minutes. Add the cabbage and cook 1 minute more. Stir in the noodles, coconut milk, scallions, and the chicken and cook 2 more minutes, or until the noodles are tender the heated through. Stir in the cilantro and serve hot.

CUBAN-STYLE LIME CHICKEN

A resurgence of interest in Cuba includes the county's unique architecture, music, and homey, unpretentious food. This is a perfect example of the ingredients frequently used in Cuban home cooking.

4 servings

2 skinless, boneless chicken breasts (about 2 pounds), halved
3 tablespoons bottled mojo marinade*
½ cup finely chopped onion
½ cup finely chopped parsley
1 tablespoon corn or canola oil
2 tablespoons fresh lime juice
2 limes, cut into wedges

***Available at Latin markets**

1. Place the chicken in a dish just large enough to hold all the breasts. Coat well with the mojo marinade, cover with plastic wrap, and marinate in the refrigerator for 1 hour.

2. Combine the onion and parsley in a small bowl.

3. In a large heavy skillet, heat the oil over medium-high heat. Add the chicken pieces and cook 4 minutes on each side or until done. Transfer to a plate, drizzle the breasts with lime juice, and top with the onion-parsley mixture. Serve with lime wedges.

TEQUILA CHICKEN

The traditional spice and lime flavors of Latin cooking come through in this recipe. Tender and spicy, this deliciously flavored chicken can be used to fill wraps, soft tacos or burritos, or serve as a side dish for a guacamole, chips, and margaritas for an instant fiesta!

4 servings

Seasoning
¼ teaspoon freshly ground black pepper
¼ teaspoon ground cumin
⅛ teaspoon ground red pepper
¼ chile powder
½ teaspoon salt

1 tablespoon extra-virgin olive oil
2 skinless, boneless chicken breasts (1½ pounds), cut into 1-inch cubes
1 clove garlic, minced
2 tablespoons minced fresh cilantro
1 tablespoons fresh lime juice
Lime wedges for garnish

1. Combine the black pepper, cumin, red pepper, chile powder, and salt in a small bowl.

2. Place the chicken breast pieces in a larger shallow bowl and sprinkle on the seasoning. Toss the coat the pieces well.

3. In a heavy large skillet, heat the oil over medium-high heat. Add the chicken pieces and cook 3 to 4 minutes or until the chicken is lightly browned. Add the garlic and cook 1 minute more. Add the tequila and the cilantro, cover, and cook 3 to 4 more minutes or until the chicken is done. Serve hot.

ITALIAN-STYLE CHICKEN AND ASPARAGUS PASTA

Choose a wide noodle for this dish, such as the nearly inch-wide pappardelle or slightly narrower fettuccine. If available in your neighborhood, use fresh pasta which is the tenderest. Pinot grigio or other dry white wine makes a great accompaniment to this flavorful and satisfying one-dish meal. Add Parmesan to this pasta dish at your own discretion.

4 servings

Sauce

3 tablespoons extra-virgin olive oil
1 pound medium asparagus, trimmed and cut into ½-inch pieces
1 teaspoon salt
1 teaspoon white pepper
2 large shallots, minced
2 cloves garlic, minced
2 skinless, boneless chicken breasts (about 2 pounds), halved, each piece cut into thirds
½ cup white wine
2 cup diced plum tomatoes
3 tablespoons chopped fresh flat-leaf parsley

1. In a large skillet, heat 2 tablespoons of the oil over medium-high heat. Add the asparagus and half the salt and pepper and stir. Cook, covered, for 2 minutes. Add the shallots and garlic and continue cooking, over medium heat, for 2 minutes more. Transfer the asparagus to a plate and keep warm.

2. Over high heat, add the remaining tablespoon of olive oil to the skillet. Add the chicken breast pieces. Season with the remaining salt and pepper and continue cooking 2 minutes, to lightly browned. Add the wine and tomatoes, lower the heat, and simmer for about 6 minutes or until the chicken breasts are done. Remove the pan from the heat, add the parsley and asparagus, and keep warm.

3. Meanwhile, bring lightly salted water to a boil and cook the pasta according to package instructions or until al dente. Wider pasta should be tender but firm enough to fold its shape when cooked. Drain, do not rinse.

4. Heat the chicken and asparagus over medium high heat for 1 minute, add the pappardelle to the pan, and toss. Serve hot.

SICILIAN-STYLE CHICKEN BREASTS CUTLETS WITH CAPERS

Here's one recipe that offers the unmistakable flavors of a region known for its distinctive cuisine, sort of Italian, sort of not.

4 to 6 servings

3 skinless, boneless chicken breasts (about 3 pounds), halved and flattened between plastic wrap to ½-inch thickness
½ teaspoon salt
¼ teaspoon freshly ground white pepper
½ cup all-purpose flour
¼ cup extra-virgin olive oil
⅓ cup white wine
2 tablespoons fresh lemon juice
2 tablespoons water
1 cup diced plum tomato
¼ cup pitted and chopped Italian black olives
2 tablespoons chopped flat-leaf parsley
1 tablespoon coarsely chopped capers
1 tablespoon chopped fresh oregano

1. On a work surface, season the chicken breast with salt and pepper.

2. Spread the flour on a large shallow glass dish or plate. Dredge each piece of chicken through the flour, coating it on both sides and shaking off any excess back onto the dish.

3. In a large skillet, heat half the oil over medium-high heat. Add half the chicken pieces and cook about 2 minutes per side or until golden brown. Set aside. Continue with the remaining chicken pieces.

4. Return all the chicken pieces to the pan and add the wine, lemon juice and water. Reduce the heat to medium and continue cooking, basting the chicken pieces with the liquid, for about 5 minutes or until the chicken is tender and done. Transfer the chicken pieces to a platter and keep warm.

5. To the skillet, add the tomato, olives, parsley, capers and oregano, simmer over medium heat for 2 to 3 minutes or until the tomatoes are softened and the sauce has reduced slightly. Pour the sauce over the chicken pieces. Serve hot.

CHICKEN, CORN, AND SWEET PEA RISOTTO

4 servings

¾ pound skinless boneless chicken breast meat, cut in ½-inch cubes
Salt and freshly ground black pepper to taste
2 cups rich chicken stock (see page 9)
3 cups chicken stock (see page 8)
2 tablespoons unsalted butter
1 tablespoon extra-virgin olive oil
3 tablespoons finely chopped onion
2 tablespoons minced garlic
2 cups Arborio rice (use only Arborio rice for this dish)
½ cup white wine
1 ½ cup fresh corn kernels
1 cup fresh sweet peas
⅓ cup grated Parmesan cheese
2 tablespoons chopped flat-leaf parsley

1. In a large saucepan, bring both stocks to a boil and turn off the heat.

2. In a large saucepan or deep skillet (about 12 inches across), melt 1 tablespoon of the butter and the olive oil over medium heat. Add the onion and cook until translucent. Add the garlic and cook 1 minute more. Add the rice and stir well to coat the grains with the butter and cook about 1 minute more. Add the wine and continue cooking, stirring constantly, until almost absorbed.

3. Turn the heat under the stock to very low. Begin adding the stock to the rice mixture ½ cup at a time, stirring until almost evaporated. Continue adding stock in ½ cups with the remaining broth. Make sure not to add more stock until the previous amount is absorbed into the rice. With the last ½ cup of stock, add the corn and peas and stir gently. Stir in the Parmesan, chicken pieces, butter, and parsley. Season with salt and pepper to taste.

4. Spoon the risotto into individual dishes. Serve immediately. Pass more Parmesan and the pepper mill.

TORTILLA SOUP

There are many variations of this soup from gourmet to soups made from recipes passed down for generations. Here's one in-between—easy to prepare and remarkably delicious.

4 to 6 servings

1 tablespoon corn oil or vegetable oil
1 cup finely chopped onion
2 cloves garlic, minced
1 tablespoon chile powder
1 teaspoon ground cumin
1 teaspoon dried oregano
2 cups chicken stock (see page 8)
1 14.5-ounce can chopped tomatoes with juice
1 16-ounce can refried beans
1 bay leaf
2 cups poached, shredded chicken breast (see page 352)
2 to 3 cups crushed tortilla chips
1 ripe avocado, peeled and diced
1 scallion, chopped

1. In a heavy large saucepan, heat the oil over medium heat. Add the onion and garlic and cook, stirring constantly, for 3 minutes. Add the chile powder, cumin, oregano, chicken, tomatoes, beans, and bay leaf. Bring to a boil, reduce the heat to low, and simmer, partially covered, 35 minutes.

2. Add the chicken meat and continue cooking 10 minutes more.

3. Remove the bay leaf, ladle soup into bowls, and serve topped with tortilla chips, avocado, and a sprinkle of scallion.

TOP TOOLS AND PERFECT PANS

The pans that enhance these recipes are heavy, well-balanced skillets, include at least one with a current, highly improved version of a nonstick surface. Nonstick surfaces eliminate the need for unnecessary fats and oils. In addition, a nonstick stove-top grill pan will allow you to cook cutlets and paillards in seconds without having to scrape this delicate cut of the chicken breast from the pan, which ruins the presentation completely. Keep a can of vegetable oil cooking spray around to coat surfaces before cooking with or without extra fats and oils.

VIETNAMESE PHO WITH CHICKEN

This staple in Vietnam is now widely made and consumed in the United States. Though usually made with beef, this fresh and delicious version requires only the delicate white meat of a chicken breast and the usual array of ingredients that go into Pho.

4 servings

2 cups sliced onion
4 slices peeled fresh ginger, cut to ⅛-inch each
5 cups chicken stock (see page 8)
2 tablespoons sugar
2 tablespoons fish sauce*
5 star anise
3 cloves
4 cups water
2 teaspoons canola oil
1 skinless, boneless chicken breast (about 1 pound), cut into ¼-inch slices across the grain
1 cup fresh bean sprouts
½ cup vertically sliced onion
½ cup chopped scallions
12 fresh basil leaves
4 lime wedges for garnish
1 small serrano or jalapeño chile, seeded, deveined, and chopped

***Available in Asian markets or some supermarkets**

1. In a heavy skillet over high heat, add the onion and ginger and cook, stirring frequently, 4 minutes or until charred. Remove from the heat.

2. Combine the stock, sugar, fish sauce, star anise, and cloves in a large saucepan. Bring to a boil, reduce the heat, cover, and simmer 30 minutes. Strain the broth and discard the remains. Return the soup broth to the pan and set aside.

3. Heat the oil in a large skillet over medium high heat. Add the chicken pieces and cook 2 minutes, stirring frequently, or just until done. Remove from the pan.

4. Bring the soup broth to a boil. Divide the sprouts, onion, scallions, basil, and the chicken pieces among large soup bowls. Ladle in the hot soup, squeeze the lime into each serving of soup and add the wedge to the bowl. Sprinkle on the chile. Serve hot.

CHINESE FIVE-SPICE CHICKEN & SCALLIONS

To this sweet and spicy flavor combination, add steamed white rice as a natural choice for the accompaniment, although Asian or pasta noodles are equally as delicious.

4 servings

½ cup hoisin sauce
¼ cup soy sauce or tamari
1 teaspoon prepared Chinese five-spice powder*
2 skinless, boneless chicken breast (about 2 pounds), cut into ¼-inch slices across the grain
1 tablespoon canola or vegetable oil
2 tablespoons minced scallions
2 teaspoons minced garlic
4 scallions, white and green parts, cut into 2-inch pieces
2 tablespoons chopped flat-leaf parsley
***Available in Asian markets or some grocery stores**

1. Combine the hoisin sauce, soy sauce, and five-spice powder in a bowl. Add the sliced chicken and toss to coat well.

2. In a large heavy skillet, heat the oil over medium-high heat. Add the minced scallions and garlic and cook 30 seconds. Add the chicken mixture and cook, stirring frequently, for 3 minutes. Add the scallion pieces and parsley and cook 2 minutes more, stirring occasionally, or until the chicken is done. Serve hot.

RECAPTURING THE COMFORT OF A CREAMY WHITE SAUCE—THE LOW-FAT WAY

Low-fat cooking doesn't have to mean removing all the good-tasting stuff from your diet. Really, the thought of never having a rich and creamy sauce again just isn't fair. Here's a rich and creamy sauce base to which you can add a pleasantly satisfying amount of finely grated Parmesan cheese, or keep it on the lighter side with a cup of sautéed shallots, tomato bits, and herbs of your choice. It's rich! So eat a little less.

1 tablespoon unsalted butter
1 clove garlic, minced
1 tablespoon flour
1½ cups nonfat milk
3 tablespoons nonfat cream cheese
2 tablespoons chopped fresh flat-leaf parsley
1 teaspoon freshly ground white pepper
Pinch of salt to taste

1. In a sauté pan, melt the butter over very low heat. Add the garlic and cook until tender.
2. Whisk in the flour and then slowly add the milk.
3. Cook 10 minutes over low heat, stirring frequently.
4. Add other flavorings and heat through.
5. Immediately pour over cooked food of choice.

Note: If the sauce is lumpy, strain it and put it back into the pan before serving.

CHICKEN AND RICE–STUFFED PABLANO CHILES

Naturally, green bell peppers are the most frequently stuffed in this manner, but the mildly hot pablano is a sophisticated alternative.

6 peppers or 3 to 6 servings

6 large fresh pablano peppers
¼ cup extra-virgin olive oil
½ medium onion, peeled and diced
1 clove garlic, minced
¼ pound ground pork
1 skinless, boneless chicken breast (about 1 pound), coarsely ground
Salt and freshly ground black pepper to taste
1 large tomato, peeled, seeded, and chopped
Pinch of ground nutmeg
1¼ cups cooked long-grain white rice
1 teaspoon chopped fresh marjoram
1 teaspoon chopped fresh thyme
1 teaspoon chopped fresh flat-leaf parsley
1¼ cup fresh bread crumbs

1. Char peppers over a gas flame or under a hot broiler, turning frequently until blackened all over. Place the peppers in a brown paper bag, close the bag tightly, and let steam for 15 minutes. Remove and cool slightly. Rub off the blackened skin carefully so the flesh does not tear. Cut a slit down the length of each pepper, stopping about ½ inch from the top and tip. Gently scrape out the veins and seeds and discard.

2. Heat 2 tablespoons of the olive oil in a skillet over medium heat. Add the onions and garlic and cook 12 minutes or until golden.

3. Increase the heat to medium-high, add the pork, and cook 5 minutes. Stir frequently to break up the pieces. Add the chicken breast and continue cooking, stirring frequently for 2 minutes. Reduce the heat to medium, season with salt and pepper, tomatoes and nutmeg. Stir to mix well and continue cooking 5 minutes more. Remove from the heat, stir in the rice, marjoram, thyme, parsley, and 1 tablespoon of oil.

4. Preheat the broiler.

5. Gently spoon equal amounts of hot filling into each pepper and place on a baking sheet with the stuffed side up. Sprinkle bread crumbs over the stuffing, drizzle on the remaining oil, and broil until the bread crumbs are golden. Serve hot or at room temperature.

PAN-SEARED CHICKEN ON A BED OF SHALLOT, MUSHROOM, & SPINACH

This is quick and with fresh spinach on the plate, it could also be called healthy. Use the pre-washed baby spinach in a bag and a package of presliced mushrooms for a wonderful 5 minute meal.

4 servings

1 tablespoon extra-virgin olive oil
2 skinless, boneless chicken breasts (about 2 pounds), halved
Salt and freshly ground black pepper to taste
1 tablespoon finely sliced shallots
1 clove garlic, minced
1½ cup sliced mushrooms
2 tightly packed cups baby spinach or regular-sized, stems removed
1 teaspoon grated lemon zest
1 teaspoon fresh lemon juice

1. In a large skillet, heat 2 teaspoons of the olive oil over medium-high heat. Sprinkle the chicken breasts with salt and pepper and add to the pan. Cook 5 minutes per side or until slightly browned and done throughout. Remove from the pan and keep warm.

2. Add the remaining olive oil to the pan. Add the shallots and garlic, cook over medium heat 1 minute or until translucent. Add the mushrooms and distribute over evenly throughout the pan, cover and continue cooking over for 2 minutes. Stir the mushrooms and cook, covered, for 2 minutes more. Add the spinach and cover, cooking about 30 seconds or just until wilted. Add the zest and juice and adjust the seasoning with salt and freshly ground pepper to taste.

3. Toss in the chicken pieces and serve hot.

WHEN WINE MEETS FOOD

For the right match, no formalities are necessary. The palate speaks. The synergy makes for an enhanced taste and the whole becomes greater than the sum of the parts. These days, there are plenty of new mixes and matches in the worlds of wine and food, and lots of highly personalized wine shops with truly dedicated wine merchants to help you through the maze of wine labels and regional wineries. Here are several hints that work every time: Lightly spiced and herbed chicken breast dishes go so well with chardonnay and sauvignon blanc. When the herbs and spices are rich and highly noticeable, such as with Creole, Caribbean, Latin, or Old Country European dishes, choose a pinot noir, French Beaujolais, dry Gamay Rose, or Italian dolcetto. But remember, when it comes to matching food with wine, it's really a matter of taste. Yours!

SPINACH PASTA WITH CHICKEN AND LENTILS

Tiny French puy lentils are widely available and really delicious. They look very delicate in this or any dish.

4 servings

4 cup dried tiny French green puy lentils
1½ cups filtered water
Pinch of salt
3 ripe plum tomatoes
3 teaspoons canola or extra-virgin olive oil
1 cup chicken stock (see page 8)
1 pound skinless, boneless chicken breast, cut into thin strips
2 cloves garlic, minced
½ cup finely chopped onion
1 cup packed baby spinach leaves, stemmed and coarsely chopped
Salt and freshly ground black pepper to taste
¾ pound fresh spinach pasta, or ½ pound dried pasta
2 teaspoons balsamic vinegar
1 teaspoon chopped dried oregano
2 tablespoons finely grated Parmesan cheese or more to taste

1. Combine the lentils, water, and salt in a large stockpot. Bring to a boil, reduce the heat to a simmer, and cook for 25 minutes or until tender.

2. Fill the same stockpot with water and bring to a boil. Have a large bowl of ice water available. Blanch the tomatoes for 1 minute, remove with a slotted spoon, and plunge into ice water. Peel, seed, dice, and set aside. Reserve the water in the stockpot.

3. In a large sauté pan or nonstick skillet, heat 1 teaspoon of oil and 2 tablespoons of the chicken stock over medium-high heat. Add the chicken strips and cook 3 to 4 minutes, tossing and stirring constantly, just until done. Remove with a slotted spoon and transfer to a bowl.

4. In the same skillet, heat 2 more tablespoons of the chicken stock over medium-high heat. Add the garlic and onion and cook, stirring frequently, 8 to 10 minutes or until caramelized. Drizzle in more stock as needed to keep the garlic and onion from sticking to the skillet.

5. Meanwhile, bring the stockpot of water to a boil. Blanch the spinach just until wilted, about 30 seconds. Remove with a slotted spoon and drain. Keep the water in the stockpot boiling.

6. Heat 1 teaspoon of oil in the skillet over medium heat. Add the lentils and the remaining chicken stock. Season with salt and pepper. Cover and simmer for 5 minutes. Lower the heat, add the chicken strips, and cook for 1 minute more, or until the chicken heats through.

7. Meanwhile, lightly salt the boiling water in the stockpot. Cook the pasta to al dente, according to package directions. Drain and transfer to a large mixing bowl. Drizzle on the remaining oil, the balsamic vinegar, oregano, and salt and pepper to taste. Toss gently to mix. Add the spinach, tomatoes, and chicken and lentil mixture, and toss again. Serve in a large warmed pasta bowl, sprinkle with Parmesan. Pass more Parmesan and the pepper mill.

CHICKEN IN RED WINE SAUCE WITH PAPPARDELLE PASTA

Pappardelle pasta makes a very special presentation, but other wide, fresh pastas may be substituted. If you have a pasta machine, this is the perfect recipe to use for homemade pasta. Only a few pappardelle are needed for each serving.

4 servings

2 tablespoons extra-virgin olive oil
2 skinless, boneless chicken breasts (about 2 pounds), cut into bite-size pieces
Salt and freshly ground black pepper to taste
1 tablespoon finely chopped onion
1 tablespoon finely chopped peeled carrot
1 tablespoon finely chopped celery
1 ½ teaspoons finely chopped fresh sage leaves, or ¾ teaspoon dried
½ teaspoon finely chopped fresh rosemary leaves, or ¼ teaspoon dried
¼ cup full-bodied red wine (such as cabernet sauvignon)
¼ cup rich chicken stock (see page 9)
2 ripe tomatoes, peeled, seeded, and diced
¾ pound fresh pappardelle pasta (2 to 3 pieces per serving)
2 tablespoons finely grated Parmesan
1 tablespoon finely chopped flat-leaf parsley

1. In a large sauté pan or nonstick skillet, heat the oil over medium-high heat. Season the chicken pieces with salt and pepper.

Add to the pan and cook, turning frequently, about 3 minutes or until browned.

2. To the same skillet, add the onion, carrot, celery, sage, and rosemary and cook over medium heat for 2 minutes. Pour in the wine and chicken stock, lower the heat, and simmer for 1 minute. Stir in the tomatoes, partially cover the pan, and simmer for 5 minutes more.

3. In a large stock pot of lightly salted boiling water, cook the fresh pasta about 4 minutes, or accordingly to package directions, until al dente. Drain and keep warm.

4. Meanwhile, add the chicken pieces and any juice that has collected in the bowl to the vegetables. Continue cooking, partially covered, for 3 to 5 minutes more, or just until the chicken is done. Season with salt and pepper to taste. Transfer the chicken to a bowl and keep hot.

5. Add the pasta to the pan and toss gently to coat. Divide among pasta bowls and top with pieces of chicken breast. Sprinkle on the Parmesan and parsley. Pass the pepper mill and more Parmesan.

TOMATO AND GARLIC CHICKEN WITH WILD RICE

4 servings

4 cups chicken stock (see page 8)
1 cup uncooked wild rice, soaked for 30 minutes in hot water and drained
Salt and freshly ground black pepper to taste
4 tablespoons seasoned bread crumbs
2 skinless, boneless chicken breast (about 2 pounds), halved
2 teaspoons extra-virgin olive oil
3 garlic cloves, minced
1 cup chopped onion
1 cup chopped celery
4 tablespoons rich chicken stock (see page 9)
2 cups canned tomatoes, well drained and chopped
1 teaspoon grated lemon zest
1 teaspoon chopped fresh rosemary, or ½ teaspoon dried rosemary

1. In a heavy saucepan, bring 4 cups of the stock and 1 cup of water to a boil. Add the wild rice, lightly salt the water and cook, covered, over very low heat for 45 minutes. Remove from the heat, let stand for 15 minutes, and drain thoroughly. Adjust the seasoning with salt and pepper.

2. Place the bread crumbs on a plate. Dredge the chicken breasts through the bread crumbs to coat well. Set aside.

3. In a large nonstick skillet or sauté pan coated with cooking spray, heat the oil over medium-high heat. Add the chicken and cook about 2 minutes per side or until brown. Remove to a platter and keep warm.

4. Add the garlic and onion to the skillet and cook over medium heat for 2 minutes. Add the celery and 4 tablespoons of chicken stock and cook for 5 minutes more. Add the tomatoes, lemon zest, and rosemary and continue cooking, stirring constantly, for 1 minute. Add the chicken breasts, cover, and simmer until done, about 10 minutes.

5. Reheat the wild rice.

6. Divide the hot wild rice among 4 warmed shallow bowls. Transfer the chicken breasts to a dish. Spoon the tomatoes and sauce over the rice. Arrange the chicken breasts on the rice and tomatoes. Pass the pepper mill.

POT STICKERS WITH CHINESE DIPPING SAUCE

Once prepared, these homemade pot stickers can be frozen on baking sheets, transferred to plastic bags, placed in the freezer, and cooked later for instant appetizers. To eliminate some of the calories in this already low-fat recipe, instead of pan-frying, bake the pot stickers in the oven at 450°F on a baking sheet sprinkled with a small amount of cornstarch, until nicely browned.

Makes 30 to 36 pieces or 6 servings

Dipping Sauce

¼ cup soy sauce or tamari
⅓ cup rice wine vinegar
2 tablespoons thinly sliced scallion, green part only
1 tablespoon grated peeled fresh ginger
2 tablespoons honey
2 tablespoons dry sherry

Pot Stickers

2 teaspoons peanut oil
1 teaspoon light sesame oil
1½ teaspoons grated peeled fresh ginger
1 garlic clove, finely minced
4 tablespoons finely chopped scallion
¼ cup drained, finely chopped water chestnuts
2 tablespoons finely chopped celery
3 tablespoons very finely grated peeled carrot

1 tablespoon dry sherry
1 tablespoon reduced-sodium soy sauce or tamari
2 large egg whites, whisked
¾ pound skinless, boneless ground chicken breast
3 teaspoons cornstarch, or more
30 to 36 wonton wrappers
2 tablespoons peanut, sesame, or other light vegetable oil
¼ cup filtered water, or more

1. To make the dipping sauce, combine the soy sauce, vinegar, scallion, ginger, honey, and sherry in a small bowl. Set aside.

2. In a large sauté pan or nonstick skillet, heat the peanut and sesame oils over medium heat. Add the ginger and garlic and cook for 1 minute. Do not brown. Add the scallion and cook about 3 minutes or until tender.

3. Add the ginger and garlic mixture, water chestnuts, celery, carrot, sherry, soy sauce, egg whites, and ground chicken to a medium mixing bowl. Mix by hand or with a wooden spoon until well combined.

4. Working quickly on a flat surface sprinkled with the cornstarch, take the wonton wrappers one at a time from the stack, keeping the rest covered so that they won't dry out. Place 1 rounded teaspoon of the chicken mixture in the center of the wrapper. Moisten the edges and join in the center to close, pinching the edges together to seal completely. The package will form a moon shape. Continue until all the wonton wrappers are filled.

5. In a large nonstick skillet lightly coated with cooking spray, heat 1 tablespoon of the canola oil over medium-high heat. Cover the bottom of the skillet with half the pot stick single layer. Cook for 2 to 3 minutes or until the bottoms are nicely browned. Add 2 tablespoons of the water and cook, partially covered, until the water has evaporated, the bottoms are crisp, and the wonton dough done, about 3 minutes more. Remove one pot sticker from the pan and cut to test for doneness. Repeat with remaining oil, pot stickers, and water.

6. Serve very hot with individual of dipping sauce.

DOWN FOR THE CALORIE COUNT

Weight Watchers says that 3 ounces of skinless, boneless chicken breast broiled or grilled plain has but 3 grams of fat. That's all! And it's under 100 calories. Here's an amazing fact: It's okay to grill the chicken breast with the skin on to keep it moist. Then remove the skin (because 50 of more fat calories are in the skin) and toss the chicken breast back on the grill for a minute or so to sear in some grill marks.

ESCALOPES OF CHICKEN ON SPINACH WITH LEMON SHALLOT SAUCE

An *escalope* is a slightly flattened piece of uncooked chicken breast.

4 servings

2 teaspoons canola or extra-virgin olive oil
4 cups chiffonnade-cut stemmed spinach
Salt and freshly ground white pepper to taste
2 skinless, boneless chicken breasts (about 2pounds), halved, thickly sliced across the grain at an angle, and pounded between plastic wrap to ¼-inch thickness
¼ cup all-purpose flour, for dusting
1 tablespoon unsalted butter, melted

Sauce
5 large shallots, finely diced
4 tablespoons fresh lemon juice
1 teaspoon grated lemon zest
¼ cup rich chicken stock (see page 9)
¼ cup dry white wine (chardonnay)
1 tablespoon very cold unsalted butter, cut into small pieces
1 tablespoon very finely chopped parsley

1. In a medium sauté pan or nonstick skillet lightly coated with cooking spray, heat the oil over medium-high heat. Sauté the spinach quickly for 2 minutes, shaking the pan back and forth to gently toss while cooking. Season with a scant amount of salt and white pepper and remove to a platter. Cover to keep warm. Reserve the pan aside.

2. Season the chicken breast slices with a scant amount of salt and pepper. Lightly dust with flour, shaking off any excess until just a trace of flour remains.

3. Brush another sauté pan or skillet with the melted butter and heat over medium-high heat. Add the chicken escalopes and briefly sauté just long enough to cook through, about 2 minutes per side. Test for doneness by cutting into 1 escalope. Do not overcook. Transfer to a plate and cover to keep warm.

4. To make the sauce, add the shallots to the reserved sauté pan over medium-high heat and cook for 2 minutes, or just until tender. Add the lemon juice, zest, chicken stock, and wine. Increase the heat to high and reduce by half, about 4 minutes. Remove the pan from the heat and add the cold bits of butter one at a time, whisking to incorporate each piece completely before adding the next. Stir in all but 1 tablespoon of the parsley. Adjust the seasoning with salt and pepper to taste. Do not reheat the sauce.

5. Make a bed of spinach on individual plates and top each with several escalopes. Drizzle the sauce over the chicken and dust with a small amount of parsley. Serve immediately.

HONEY-MUSTARD CHICKEN WITH MUSHROOM RAGOUT

4 servings

1½ tablespoons unsalted butter
4 shallots, thinly sliced
1½ pounds mixed mushrooms (white, oyster, chanterelle, cremini, morel, portobello), sliced
1 cup dry white wine
½ cup rich chicken stock (see page 9)
1 tablespoon chopped fresh tarragon leaves
Salt and freshly ground white pepper to taste

Chicken Breasts

¼ cup dried bread crumbs
2 skinless, boneless chicken breasts (about 1½ pounds), halved
1 tablespoon plus 1 teaspoon extra-virgin olive oil
1¼ cups dry white wine (chardonnay)
1 teaspoon dried savory, crushed, or 2 teaspoons minced parsley
1 teaspoon salt
1 teaspoon freshly ground black pepper
2 tablespoons fresh lemon juice
4 tablespoons mild honey mustard
1 tablespoon honey
½ cup low-fat or nonfat sour cream, at room temperature

1. To prepare the mushrooms, melt the butter over medium heat in a large sauté pan or nonstick skillet. Add the shallots and cook about 2 minutes or until tender. Add the mushrooms, increase the heat, and cook about 5 minutes or until the mushroom liquid has evaporated and the mushrooms are brown. Add the wine, chicken stock, and tarragon. Bring to a boil and cook about 15 minutes or until the liquid has almost evaporated. Season with salt and pepper. Set aside.

2. Place the bread crumbs on a plate. Dredge the chicken breasts in the crumbs to coat well.

3. In a heavy sauté pan or nonstick skillet lightly coated with cooking spray, heat 1 tablespoon of the oil over moderately high heat. Add the chicken and cook about 3 minutes per side or until brown. Add the wine, savory or parsley, and salt and pepper. Lower the heat and simmer, covered, about 15 minutes or until the chicken is tender and done.

4. Remove the chicken to a warmed platter and cover to keep warm. Reserve the juices in the skillet.

5. Add the lemon juice, mustard, honey, and the remaining 1 tablespoon of the oil to the skillet and mix well. Return the chicken to the pan and warm the chicken through over very low heat for about 2 minutes, basting the chicken with the sauce.

6. Meanwhile, heat the mushroom ragout. Remove from the heat and stir in the sour cream. Arrange the breasts on warmed plates and put mushroom ragout on the side.

CURRIED CHICKEN WITH CARROT AND ONION

A bowl of fluffy steamed rice is the natural accompaniment to this dish. It tends to balance the heat of the curry. If you like your curry "super hot" just increase the amount of curry powder and crushed red pepper.

4 servings

1 tablespoon honey
2 teaspoons medium to hot curry powder
1 teaspoon ground cumin
1½ teaspoons arrowroot or cornstarch, dissolved in 1 tablespoon stock
Pinch of salt
2 skinless, boneless chicken breasts (about 2 pounds), cut into bite-size pieces
6 medium carrots, peeled and cut in matchsticks
1 tablespoon canola or other vegetable oil
1 large onion, finely chopped
1 large garlic clove, finely minced
1½-inch piece peeled fresh ginger, finely minced
¼ teaspoon crushed red pepper
3 cups freshly cooked hot white or brown rice
Freshly ground black pepper to taste

1. Combine 2 tablespoons of the buttermilk, the honey, 1 teaspoon of the curry powder, the cumin, arrowroot mixture, and salt in a medium bowl and mix well. Add the chicken pieces and toss to coat well. Cover with plastic wrap and refrigerate for 2 hours.

2. Prepare a large bowl of ice water. In a stockpot of lightly salted boiling water, cook the carrots about 3 minutes, or until crisp-tender. Quickly plunge them into the bowl of ice water to stop cooking. Drain and set aside.

3. In a large sauté pan or nonstick skillet, heat the oil over medium-high heat. Add the onion, garlic, and ginger and cook for 30 seconds. Stir in the remaining 1 teaspoon of curry powder and the crushed red pepper. Add the carrots and continue cooking, about 4 to 5 minutes. Remove and set aside.

4. Meanwhile, drain the chicken pieces and discard the marinade. In the same skillet over medium-high heat, cook the chicken about 4 to 5 minutes per side, or until browned and done. Transfer the chicken with a slotted spoon to a serving plate and cover to keep warm.

5. Remove the skillet from the heat and immediately stir in the remaining butter, milk, and the carrot mixture. Adjust the seasoning with salt and pepper to taste and warm for 30 seconds. Spoon the sauce over the chicken and serve with the hot rice.

CHICKEN AND ROASTED ARTICHOKE RISOTTO

4 servings

6 cups chicken stock (see page 8)
¾ pound baby artichokes (about 8)
8 cloves garlic, peeled
2 teaspoons fresh thyme leaves
2 tablespoons plus 1 teaspoon extra-virgin olive oil
Salt and freshly ground black pepper to taste
1 skinless, boneless chicken breasts (about 1 pound)
3 tablespoons finely chopped prosciutto
1 teaspoon dried thyme
1 tablespoon unsalted butter
2 tablespoons finely minced shallots
1½ cups Arborio rice
1 cup dry white wine
3 tablespoons finely grated Parmesan

1. Preheat the oven to 375°F.

2. Simmer the chicken stock in a medium saucepan until reduced by one third, about 10 minutes. Set aside.

3. To prepare the artichokes, rinse well, trim off the tough part of the stem and the tops of the leaves. Snap off the tough outer leaves. Arrange the artichokes close together in a glass baking dish. Push the garlic cloves in between the artichokes. Sprinkle on the 2 teaspoons thyme leaves and drizzle on 1 tablespoon of the olive oil. Season lightly with salt and pepper. Cover tightly with foil and bake for 45 minutes. Remove the foil and return to the oven for 10 minutes more. Remove the garlic cloves and discard. Coarsely chop the artichokes. Set aside.

4. Meanwhile, heat 1 tablespoon of the oil in a large nonstick skillet over medium-high heat. Season the chicken breasts with salt and pepper and cook 3 minutes per side or until browned. Shred the chicken into strips and set aside.

5. Cook the prosciutto in a small nonstick saucepan over medium-high heat until crispy. Set on paper towels to drain.

6. In a medium saucepan, warm the reduced chicken stock and keep warm over very low heat. Add the 1 teaspoon dried thyme to the stock.

7. In a large heavy saucepan, heat the remaining 1 teaspoon of oil and the butter over medium heat. Add the shallots and cook for 3 minutes, or just until translucent. Add the rice and stir to coat with the oil, about 1 minute. Add 1 cup of warm chicken stock and cook over medium heat, stirring constantly until the moisture is almost absorbed into the rice. Continue adding all the stock, ½ cup at a time, stirring constantly, until the liquid is almost absorbed before adding more, and the mixture is creamy. In the last addition, add the wine with the stock, and stir in the chicken and chopped artichoke.

8. When the mixture is creamy, the liquid is absorbed, and the rice is done to al dente (after about 25 minutes), remove the pan from the heat. Stir in the Parmesan and divide among preheated shallow pasta bowls. Serve immediately with the pepper mill and additional Parmesan if desired.

CHICKEN, PEAS, AND PASTA

4 servings

1 cup frozen peas, thawed
1 cup chicken stock (see page 8)
1 cup fresh peas with shoots
1 tablespoon extra-virgin olive oil
1 garlic clove, finely minced
2 tablespoons very finely minced onion
1 pound skinless, boneless chicken breast halves, cut into ¾-inch strips
Salt and freshly ground black pepper to taste
3 cups uncooked pasta, such as ziti, penne, mostaccioli, or fusilli, cooked al dente according to package directions, rinsed, and drained
¼ cup grated Romano or Parmesan cheese, or more to taste

1. Combine the peas and the chicken stock in a blender or food processor and process until smooth. Pour through a fine mesh strainer and reserve in a bowl, discarding the residue.

2. In a medium saucepan, bring lightly salted water to a boil. Blanch the fresh peas with shoots for 1 minute. Run under cold water to stop the cooking process and drain well.

3. In a large sauté pan or nonstick skillet, heat the oil over medium-high heat. Add the garlic and cook, stirring constantly, for 30 seconds. Lower the heat, add the onion, and cook about 3 minutes or until tender. Add the chicken strips and cook over medium-high heat about 3 to 4 minutes or until done. Adjust the seasoning with salt and pepper to taste.

4. Add the pureed pea mixture to the skillet and bring to a boil. Add the pasta and blanched fresh peas and stir to mix well. Cook, stirring constantly, for 2 to 3 minutes, or until the sauce thickens and the pasta is heated through. Stir in the cheese and immediately divide among 4 pasta bowls. Pass the pepper mill.

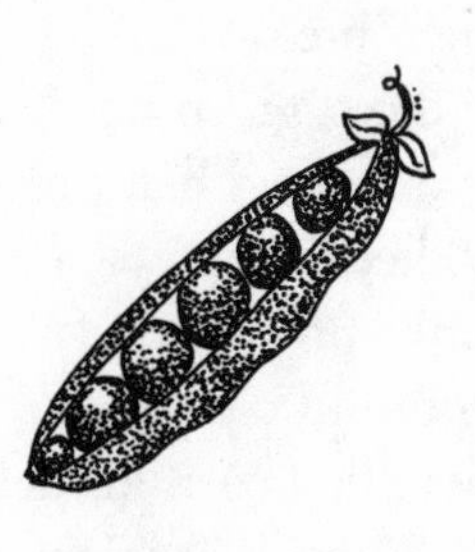

SOUTHWESTERN CHICKEN HASH WITH SPICY SALSA

Serve with a corn cake, corn bread, or soft, very fresh oven-warmed tortillas on the side.

4 servings

Spicy Salsa

1 small serrano or jalapeño chile, peeled, stemmed, and seeded
1 medium red onion, quartered
2 small cloves garlic
2 tomatoes, peeled, seeded, and chopped
2 to 3 tablespoons chopped cilantro
3 teaspoons red wine vinegar or fresh lemon juice
1 teaspoon salt

Chicken Breast Hash

2 teaspoons canola or corn oil
1 pound coarsely ground skinless, boneless chicken breast
½ cup finely diced green bell pepper
½ cup finely diced red bell pepper
⅓ cup finely diced onion
1 teaspoon chile powder
¼ teaspoon ground cumin
1 cup freshly grilled corn kernels (see page 205 for grilling instructions)

1. To make the salsa, process the chile, onion, and garlic in a food processor until finely minced. Transfer to a medium bowl. Add the tomatoes, cilantro, vinegar or lemon juice, and salt and mix well. Set aside at room temperature.

2. In a large sauté pan or nonstick skillet lightly coated with cooking spray, heat 1 teaspoon of the oil over medium heat. Add the ground chicken breast and cook, stirring constantly, for 3 minutes or just until white. Remove the partially cooked chicken from the skillet with a slotted spoon. Set aside in a strainer to drain.

3. In the same skillet, heat the remaining teaspoon of the oil over medium heat. Add the green and red bell peppers and the onion and cook, stirring constantly until soft. Stir in the chile powder and cumin and cook for 1 minute more.

4. Add the corn, chicken, and half the salsa and mix well. Continue cooking, partially covered, for 3 minutes more or until the chicken is done. Top with remaining salsa.

SMOKED CHICKEN WITH WATERCRESS SAUCE OVER PASTA

4 servings

3 large cloves garlic, peeled and halved
3 shallots, quartered
4 cups loosely packed watercress leaves
1 ½ teaspoons Dijon mustard
1 cup sour cream, regular or low-fat
2 teaspoons fresh lemon juice
Salt and freshly ground black pepper to taste
2 smoked skinless, boneless chicken breast halves (available in specialty markets or at the deli meat counter, or see the smoking instructions on page 215)
¾ pound dried bow-tie pasta or other shape
2 teaspoons unsalted butter, melted
2 tablespoons chopped watercress leaves for garnish

1. In a small saucepan, bring water to a boil. Blanch the garlic for 2 minutes. Drain.

2. In the bowl of a food processor, add the blanched garlic and shallots and process until finely minced. Add the watercress and continue pulsing. Add the mustard and sour cream and pulse to form a thick paste. Add the lemon juice, salt, and pepper. Pulse a few more times to mix well. Place in a medium saucepan and set aside.

3. Cut the smoked chicken into ¼-inch strips.

4. In a large stockpot, bring lightly salted water to a boil and cook the pasta to al dente. Drain, place in a large pasta bowl, and toss with teaspoon of the butter, and add salt and pepper to taste. Keep hot.

5. Meanwhile, add the remaining 1 teaspoon butter to a small nonstick skillet. Add the chicken breast strips and watercress sauce and warm over medium heat. Toss into the pasta, sprinkle with the chopped watercress, and serve.

SPICY CHICKEN & THREE-BEAN CHILI

Serve with your favorite toppings, such as sour cream (save calories and use "light"), chopped scallions, grated Cheddar cheese (consider fat-reduced), and chopped cilantro. This is a thick, chunky, and hearty approach to the usual one-bowl meal we know fondly as chili.

4 to 6 servings

2 tablespoons canola or other vegetable oil
1 large onion, chopped
3 garlic cloves, chopped
2 tablespoons chile powder
¼ teaspoon crushed red pepper, or more to taste
2 pounds ground skinless, boneless chicken breast
1 small eggplant, peeled and cut into small cubes
1 large can (16 ounces) black beans, rinsed, drained
1 large can (16 ounces) pinto or red kidney beans, rinsed and drained
1 large can (16 ounces) white great northern beans, rinsed and drained
1 large can (about 16 ounces) Mexican-style whole cooked tomatoes, drained and chopped
1 can (8 ounces) tomato sauce
2 stalks celery, sliced
1 medium green bell pepper, chopped
1 teaspoon ground cumin
Salt and freshly ground black pepper to taste

Toppings of choice
Sour cream, grated or crumbled cheese, chopped parsley, cilantro, or green onions

1. In a heavy large sauté pan or skillet, heat the oil over medium heat. Add the onion and garlic and cook about 2 minutes. Add the chile powder and red pepper and cook, stirring constantly, for 1 minute. Add the chicken breast and cook, stirring occasionally, for 3 minutes or until slightly browned. Add the eggplant and cook, stirring occasionally, about 5 minutes or until almost done.

2. Add all the beans, tomatoes, tomato sauce, celery, bell pepper, and cumin to the skillet. Lower the heat and bring to a simmer. Continue cooking, stirring frequently, for 25 to 30 minutes more. Adjust the seasoning with salt and pepper to taste.

3. Divide among large shallow bowls. Add toppings of choice.

COLD CHICKEN BREASTS WITH PINEAPPLE RELISH

Instead of pineapple, use several other fruits, such as cantaloupe, grapes, mangoes, and papayas. Why not make a "fruit salad" relish with a mix of fresh fruits?

4 servings

2 skinless, boneless chicken breasts (about 2 pounds), trimmed and flattened between plastic wrap to ⅓-inch thickness
Salt and freshly ground white pepper to taste
2 tablespoons vermouth or dry white wine
¼ cup rich chicken stock (see page 9)
2 teaspoons finely minced garlic
1½ tablespoons grated peeled fresh ginger
1 teaspoon dry mustard
3 tablespoons packed light brown sugar
3 cups chopped fresh pineapple with 3 tablespoons juice
3 tablespoons sherry vinegar

1. Place the chicken breasts in a large glass baking dish. Lightly season with salt and pepper. Combine the vermouth, chicken stock, and garlic in a cup. Drizzle over the chicken and marinate for 30 minutes covered with plastic wrap. Drain and reserve the marinade.

2. Coat a cast-iron stove-top grilling pan or large skillet with cooking spray. Heat to very hot, add the chicken breasts, and cook for 2 to 3 minutes per side, or until done. Do not overcook. Place the chicken on a platter, cover, and chill.

3. In a heavy skillet over medium-high heat, combine the reserved marinade, ginger, mustard seed, sugar, pineapple juice, vinegar and cook for about 5 minutes or until reduced by about two thirds. Add the pineapple and continue cooking for 10 minutes more, or until almost all the liquid is evaporated and just pineapple and syrup remain in the pan. Transfer to a bowl and chill. Serve the chicken with pineapple relish on the side.

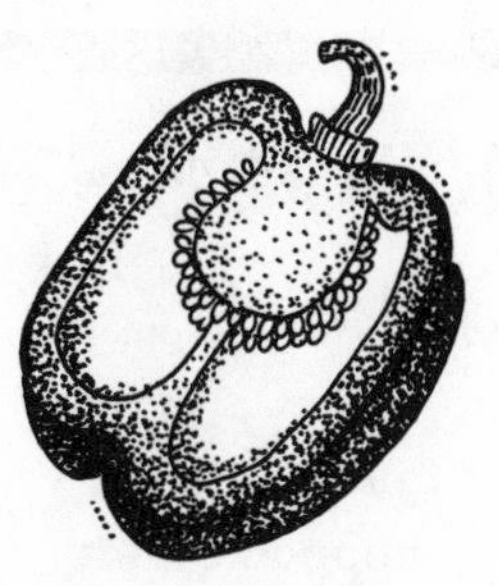

PAN-SEARED CHICKEN BREASTS WITH BASIL SAUCE

4 servings

1½ teaspoons unsalted butter
1½ teaspoons extra-virgin olive oil
2 skinless, boneless chicken breasts (about 2 pounds), halved and flattened between plastic wrap to ⅓-inch thick
½ cup chardonnay or other dry white wine
2 shallots, finely minced
1 medium clove garlic, finely minced
1 ¼ cups finely chopped fresh basil
4 tablespoons finely chopped flat-leaf parsley
¼ cup rich chicken stock (see page 9)
½ cup milk, regular or 2% milk
½ teaspoon fresh lemon juice
Salt and freshly ground white pepper to taste

1. In a large sauté pan or nonstick skillet lightly coated with cooking spray, heat the butter and oil over medium-high heat. When the pan is very hot, sear the chicken breasts for 2 to 3 minutes per side, or just until done. Transfer to a platter to keep warm.

2. Add ¼ cup wine to the pan over high heat and deglaze, scraping up the bits on the bottom of the pan. Add the shallots and garlic and cook for 1 minute more. Lower the heat to medium and add the basil, 3 tablespoons of the parsley, the remaining wine, chicken stock, milk, and lemon juice and cook, stirring constantly, until the mixture is reduced by half. Adjust the seasoning with salt and pepper.

3. Place sauce in the center of four preheated serving plates. Arrange a chicken breast on each plate into the sauce. Sprinkle with the remaining tablespoon of parsley and serve the remaining sauce on the side.

CREOLE-STYLE CHICKEN GUMBO

4 to 6 servings

1 tablespoon canola or other vegetable oil
1 cup finely chopped onion
1 cup finely chopped celery
2 large cloves garlic, finely minced
1 large green bell pepper, finely chopped

2 skinless, boneless chicken breasts (about 2 pounds), cut into quarters
4 ounces andouille (spicy Louisiana Creole) sausage, chopped
1 cup chicken stock (see page 8)
1 can (14 ounces) tomatoes in purée
1 teaspoon Tabasco sauce, or to taste
⅛ teaspoon cayenne
¼ cup chopped flat-leaf parsley
2 teaspoons chopped fresh thyme, or 1 teaspoon dried thyme
½ teaspoon freshly ground black pepper
2 teaspoons Louisiana gumbo seasoning
1 tablespoon tomato paste
4 cups or more freshly cooked, hot white rice

1. In a large sauté pan or nonstick skillet lightly coated with cooking spray, heat the oil over medium heat. Add the onion, celery, garlic, and bell pepper and cook, stirring, for about 5 minutes or until the onion is translucent.

2. Add the chicken pieces to the skillet and cook about 3 minutes over medium heat or until lightly browned. Add the sausage and cook for 3 minutes more.

3. Add the chicken stock, tomatoes in puree, Tabasco, cayenne, parsley, thyme, black pepper, gumbo seasoning, and tomato paste to the skillet and stir to mix well. Bring the sauce to a boil, reduce the heat to a simmer, and cook, stirring frequently, about 6 to 8 minutes, or until the chicken is done. Adjust the seasoning with salt and Tabasco. Serve over the hot rice.

CHICKEN SOUP WITH FARM STAND VEGETABLES

This fresh garden soup was inspired by Yvonne Doone, a private celebrity chef in Los Angeles.

4 to 6 servings

9½ cups rich chicken stock (see page 9)
1 clove garlic, peeled
1 large leek, quartered lengthwise and cut into matchsticks
2 parsnips, peeled and sliced
2 stalks celery, thinly sliced
4 small carrots, peeled and halved
4 new potatoes, scrubbed and quartered
4 small or baby turnips, peeled and halved
¼ cup dry white wine
2 skinless, boneless chicken breasts (about 2 pounds), halved and cut into thin strips
6 large mushrooms, stemmed and thinly sliced

2 tablespoons chopped flat-leaf parsley or fresh dill
1 cup cooked wide egg noodles, hot

1. Boil 8 cups of the chicken stock and garlic clove in a large stockpot; reduce by one quarter, about 10 minutes. Reduce the heat, add the leek, and simmer, partially covered, for 10 minutes.

2. In a vegetable steamer over simmering water, steam the parsnips, celery, carrots, potatoes, and turnips for 2 minutes. Do not overcook. Transfer to the stock. Cook for 20 minutes or until the vegetables are tender, skimming off any scum during cooking.

3. Meanwhile, heat the remaining stock and the wine to a simmer in a medium high-sided skillet. Poach the chicken strips about 5 minutes or just until done. Transfer to a strainer and rinse under cold running water. Set aside. Do not add this poaching liquid to the vegetables and soup or it will turn cloudy.

4. Remove the garlic from the stock. Add the mushrooms, chicken strips, and chopped parsley or dill. Over low heat, heat the chicken and ingredients through. Divide the noodles among 4 bowls, ladle on the hot soup (stock part only), and distribute the vegetables and chicken strips evenly. Serve hot.

WHITE WINE COQ AU VIN

4 to 6 servings

16 to 20 tiny white pearl onions
1 thick slice country bacon, chopped
1 teaspoon extra-virgin olive oil
2 skinless, boneless chicken breasts (about 2 pounds), halved and cut into 2-inch pieces
2 cups rich chicken stock (see page 9)
1 cup fruity white wine (such as chemin blanc)
2 teaspoons chopped fresh thyme, or 1 teaspoon dried thyme
5 tablespoons chopped flat-leaf parsley
3 bay leaves
1 tablespoon chopped fresh marjoram, or 1½ teaspoons dried marjoram
2 garlic cloves, minced
½ teaspoon freshly ground white pepper
½ pound mushrooms, trimmed and halved
1 ¼ cups nonfat sour cream
1 tablespoon cornstarch, dissolved in 2 tablespoons cold stock
3 cups cooked egg noodles; toss with 1 teaspoon melted butter and keep hot

1. In a medium saucepan, bring water

to a boil. Add the pearl onions and boil for 2 minutes. Cool, trim the root end, and peel, leaving the onion whole.

2. In a large sauté pan or nonstick skillet over high heat, cook the bacon until crispy. Drain on a paper towel and set aside. Pour the fat out but do not wipe the skillet.

3. In the same skillet, heat the oil over medium heat. Add the chicken breast pieces and cook 3 to 5 minutes or just until lightly browned. Transfer to a bowl with a slotted spoon.

4. Add the stock, wine, thyme, 4 tablespoons of the parsley, the bay leaves, marjoram, garlic, and pepper to the skillet and bring to a boil. Reduce the heat to low and simmer for 10 minutes, or until reduced by one third.

5. Add the onions and mushrooms to the pan and simmer for 5 minutes. Increase the heat to medium and reduce the sauce by half about 8 to 10 minutes. Reduce the heat to low and stir in the sour cream.

6. Stir in the cornstarch mixture and cook 1 to 2 minutes or until the sauce thickens. Remove the bay leaves. Add the reserved chicken and bacon and continue cooking over low heat until the chicken is done, about 4 minutes.

7. Place noodles in shallow pasta bowls, top with the chicken mixture and sprinkle on the chopped parsley

HERBED CHICKEN FRICASSEE

Lots of garlic and fresh herbs recall a hearty stew, cooked Dutch-oven style. Serve with a light red wine, such as dolcetto or pinot noir. You'll appreciate the taste of free-range chicken in this case, even though these breasts are a bit more expensive than other chicken breasts.

4 to 6 servings

3 large cloves garlic
⅔ cup chopped fresh herbs of choice (such as marjoram, thyme, sage, rosemary, and savory)
3 tablespoons red wine vinegar
2 tablespoons extra-virgin olive oil
2 skinless, boneless chicken breasts (about 2 pounds), halved and cut into 1½-inch pieces
Salt and freshly ground black pepper to taste
1 small red onion, thinly sliced
1 small white onion, thinly sliced
2 tablespoons all-purpose flour

2 cups dry white wine
2 cups rich chicken stock (see page 9)
16 baby carrots, peeled and trimmed
16 baby zucchini, trimmed
16 baby turnips, scrubbed and trimmed
16 tiny red potatoes (or other tiny potatoes)
¼ cup finely chopped parsley

1. In the bowl of a food processor fitted with the metal blade, combine the garlic and fresh herbs and process to a paste. With the motor running, add the vinegar and 1 tablespoon of the oil in a thin stream, and process until smooth.

2. Place the chicken in a shallow glass baking dish. Coat with the herb mixture, cover tightly with plastic wrap, and marinate for 1 to 3 hours in the refrigerator.

3. Scrape the herb marinade off the chicken and reserve. Season the chicken with salt and pepper. In a large nonstick high-sided skillet or Dutch oven, heat the remaining 1 tablespoon oil over medium-high heat. Add the chicken and cook about 5 to 7 minutes until browned and done. Remove from the skillet and keep warm.

4. To the same pan, add both onions and cook over medium heat, partially covered, until tender, about 5 minutes. Remove from the skillet and set aside. Put the flour in a small bowl. Add enough wine just to make a thin paste. Add the remaining wine to the same skillet and stir in the flour paste over medium heat. Cook, stirring constantly, about 8 to 10 minutes or until reduced by half. Scrape the sides and bottom of the pan frequently to loosen any brown bits.

5. Add the reserved herb marinade. Pour the chicken stock into the skillet and cook over high heat until the sauce is reduced by one third, about 8 minutes. Strain and reserve, discarding the cooked herbs. The sauce should equal about 2 cups.

6. In a vegetable steamer over simmering water, steam all the vegetables just until crisp-tender, about 2 minutes. Steam the potatoes until tender, about 5 to 7 minutes. Do not overcook. Set aside.

7. Melt the butter in a large skillet. Add all the steamed vegetables and heat through. Season with salt and pepper to taste. Transfer to a bowl and cover with foil to keep warm. Add the reserved onions, chicken, and sauce to the same skillet. Warm thoroughly over low heat.

8. Place the chicken in the center of a platter. Arrange the vegetables around it, drizzle 1 cup of the sauce over the chicken, and sprinkle with the parsley. Pass the remaining sauce on the side.

CHICKEN AND SUMMER VEGETABLES WITH PAN-FRIED POLENTA

To save time, look for pre-prepared polenta in the supermarket, which can be sliced and quickly pan-fried.

4 1½- by l-inch polenta cakes (pre-mixed, uncooked polenta)
2 skinless, boneless chicken breasts (about 2 pounds), quartered
Salt and freshly ground black pepper to taste
1 tablespoon canola or other vegetable oil
1 medium onion, coarsely chopped
2 stalks celery, cut on the diagonal
1 green bell pepper, seeded and sliced
1 large zucchini, cut on the diagonal
3 cups rich chicken stock (see page 9)
2 cups peeled, seeded, and coarsely chopped plum tomatoes
2 tablespoons tomato paste
1 garlic clove, finely minced
1 teaspoon crushed red pepper
1 tablespoon fresh lemon juice
2 tablespoons red wine vinegar
4 tablespoons chopped flat-leaf parsley

1. In a large sauté pan or skillet generously coated with cooking spray over medium-high heat, brown the polenta cakes. Keep warm in the oven set on low.

2. Season the chicken pieces with salt and pepper. In a large sauté pan or non-stick skillet, heat the oil over medium-high heat. Add the chicken and cook 3 to 4 minutes or until lightly browned. Transfer the chicken to a plate.

3. Add the onion, celery, bell pepper, and zucchini to the skillet and cook, stirring constantly, 5 minutes or until the onion is translucent. Add ¼ cup of the chicken stock, partially cover, and continue cooking about 5 minutes or until the vegetables are tender. Transfer to a bowl. Set aside.

4. Add the tomatoes, tomato paste, the remaining 2¾ cups stock, the garlic, red pepper, lemon juice, and vinegar to the skillet. Bring to a boil and reduce by half. Add the chicken pieces, reduce the heat to low, and simmer, stirring occasionally, about 5 minutes or until the chicken pieces are done and the liquid is reduced to a thickened sauce. Serve hot.

CHICKEN BRAISED IN APPLE JUICE AND FRESH SAGE

Serve this with a nutty-flavored mix of white, brown, and wild rice to perfectly complement this strong sage-flavored sauce. Make sure fresh sage is available before beginning this recipe.

4 servings

2 skinless, boneless chicken breasts halves (about 2 pounds), halved
Salt and freshly ground black pepper to taste
1 teaspoon unsalted butter
1 teaspoon extra-virgin olive oil
1 large clove garlic, minced
1 medium onion, halved and sliced
1 cup dry white wine
1 Bosc pear, peeled, cored, and diced
1½ tablespoons chopped fresh sage
2 ripe plum tomatoes, peeled, seeded, and finely diced
½ cup sour cream, regular or light
4 sage leaves for garnish

1. In a saucepan over medium-high heat, reduce the apple juice by one third, about 5 minutes.

2. Season the chicken breasts with salt and pepper.

3. In a medium high-sided skillet lightly coated with cooking spray, heat the butter and olive oil over medium heat. Add the garlic and onion and cook, stirring constantly, for 2 minutes. Add the chicken breasts and cook about 3 minutes or just until slightly browned.

4. Pour in the reduced apple juice and the wine and bring to a boil. Add the pear and sage, reduce the heat, and simmer, partially covered, about 10 to 12 minutes or until the chicken is done. Remove the chicken breasts to a platter and keep warm.

5. Increase the heat and reduce the sauce to about ⅔ cup. Remove the pan from the heat and stir in the tomatoes and sour cream. Return to low heat, just to heat the sauce through. Adjust the seasoning with salt and pepper to taste. Place the chicken breasts on a platter, garnish with the sage leaves, and spoon on the sauce.

CHICKEN BREASTS WITH BLACK WALNUTS

4 servings

2 skinless, boneless chicken breasts (about 2 pounds), cut into 1 × 1-inch pieces
1 teaspoon salt
1 tablespoon cornstarch
1 egg white
1 tablespoon Chinese rice wine or dry sherry
2 cups (or more) plus 2 tablespoons vegetable oil for deep frying
1½ cups black walnuts, blanched, drained, and skinned
1 green bell pepper, peeled, seeded, and julienned
1 red bell pepper, peeled, seeded, and julienned
2 tablespoons bean paste (canned)*
1 teaspoon sugar
2 tablespoons dry white wine
¼ cup chicken stock (see page 8)

***Available in Asian markets**

1. Combine the chicken pieces, salt, cornstarch, egg white, and sherry in a bowl. Toss gently to coat completely.

2. Heat 2 cups of the oil in a wok at medium-high heat until very hot. Put the walnuts in a strainer and immerse in the hot oil. Gently deep-fry the walnuts, moving the strainer up and down so the hot fat cooks the walnuts evenly without splashing out of the wok. Cook for 2 minutes, or until golden brown, remove and drain well. Reserve the oil for cooking the chicken.

3. In a sauté pan or heavy skillet, heat 2 tablespoons of the oil over medium-high heat. Add the green and red peppers and cook for 3 minutes or until tender. Add the bean paste and cook, stirring constantly, for 1 minute more. Stir in the sugar and cook for 1 minute. Set aside.

4. Return the wok to the fire and heat the oil to very hot. Deep-fry the chicken pieces for 1 to 1½ minutes, or until golden brown. Drain on paper towel briefly, and add to the peppers.

5. Add the chicken and the wine to the peppers. Cook over medium high heat for 1 minute or until the sauce thickens. Add the stock and cook for 1 minute more to reduce the stock. Stir in the walnuts and toss to heat through. Serve immediately so the walnuts remain crispy.

SPICY COUNTRY-FRIED CHICKEN BREASTS

Truly old-fashioned, Southern-style fried chicken.

4 to 6 servings

2 eggs, lightly beaten
½ cup buttermilk
½ teaspoon Tabasco or chile oil
1½ cups all-purpose flour
1 tablespoon salt
1 teaspoon black pepper
½ teaspoon Hungarian hot paprika
3 boned chicken breasts (about 3 pounds), halved
3 tablespoons fat rendered from 3 to 4 large pieces of bacon
Vegetable oil for deep frying (3 cups or more)

1. Thoroughly mix the eggs, buttermilk, and hot sauce in a bowl. Pour into a shallow dish.

2. Put the flour, salt, pepper, and paprika in a large plastic freezer bag a zipper top. Close the top of the bag tightly and shake to combine the ingredients.

3. One at a time, first dip the chicken breast pieces in the egg mixture allowing the excess to drip back into the dish. Place the pieces in the bag and gently shake the chicken around in the flour, allowing the excess flour to stay in the bag. Set the chicken on a plate.

4. In a large, high-sided cast iron skillet, heat the bacon fat and oil for frying over medium-high heat, or at 375°F. Text for readiness with a cube of bread which should deep-fry and begin to turn brown. Use long-handled tongs to gently lower the chicken breasts into the fat, starting skin side down. Fry for about 10 minutes on each side, or until golden brown. Drain on brown paper or several layers of paper towel before serving. Serve hot or cold.

Bread Crumb Coating

In place of flour, use 2 cups dried bread crumbs to coat the chicken. Substitute lemon juice for hot sauce, and increase the paprika to 1 teaspoon.

Deep-Fried Chicken Breast with Pan Gravy

When the chicken is done, remove all but 2 tablespoons of fat from the skillet. Over medium heat, add 2 tablespoons of all-purpose flour to the fat. Cook, stirring constantly, for 2 to 3 minutes to form a roux (roux cooked longer will add a brown color to the gravy). Lower the heat and slowly add a mixture of 1 cup milk and 1 cup half-and-half or heavy cream to the flour and stir until smooth. Cook until reduced by one third and the sauce is a gravy consistency, Adjust seasoning with salt and pepper. Pour some of the sauce on a heated serving platter and arrange the chicken over it. Serve with the remaining sauce on the side.

CRISPY HAZELNUT CHICKEN

4 servings

2 skinless, boneless chicken breasts (about 2 pounds), halved
1 cup buttermilk
2 eggs, well beaten
1 cup very finely chopped blanched hazelnuts
1 cup dry bread crumbs
½ teaspoon salt
Black pepper to taste
1 teaspoon Hungarian paprika
Vegetable oil for deep frying (2 cups or more)

1. Combine the chicken breasts and the buttermilk in a shallow bowl; marinate for at least 1 hour. Drain and pat dry with paper towels. Reserve ½ cup of the buttermilk.

2. Beat together the eggs and the reserved buttermilk until thoroughly combined. Pour into a shallow dish.

3. Combine the nuts, bread crumbs, salt, pepper, and paprika. Dip the chicken breasts in the egg mixture, allowing any excess to drain back into the dish. Then coat well with the nut-crumb mixture. Refrigerate the chicken breasts for 1 hour.

4. Preheat the oven to 300°F.

5. In a deep-frying pot, heat the oil to about 375°F. (Test for readiness with a small chunk of bread which should deep fry and turn brown.) Gently immerse the chicken breasts in the hot oil and deep fry until a golden-brown crust forms. Do this in several batches, as necessary, so the pan isn't crowded during cooking. Place on paper towels to drain. When all the chicken breast pieces are fried, place in an oven-proof dish and bake for 5 minutes or until done and very crispy.

HEARTY CORN, CHICKEN, & CHILE SOUP

If you're expecting guests, double this recipe to make a big pot of wonderfully flavored, yet amazingly low-fat, soup for a chilly evening.

4 servings

2 ears husked corn
2 teaspoons extra-virgin olive oil
2 teaspoons canola or other vegetable oil
2 skinless, boneless chicken breasts (about 1½ pounds), cut into strips
1 tablespoon cornmeal
¼ teaspoon salt
¼ teaspoon freshly ground white pepper
1 teaspoon ground cumin
1 cup chopped green bell pepper
¼ cup chopped red bell pepper
1 cup chopped scallion, white and green parts
2 cups chicken stock (see page 8)
¼ cup drained and chopped canned green chiles
1 cup buttermilk, regular or fat reduced
2 tablespoons chopped fresh cilantro

1. Fire up the grill. Rub each ear of corn with 1 teaspoon of olive oil. Grill 4 to 6 inches from the hot coals, turning frequently, for 5 to 6 minutes on each side or until done. Cut the kernels from cob. Set aside.

2. In a large sauté pan or nonstick skillet, heat the oil over medium-high heat. Add the chicken breast strips and cook for about 2 minutes or just until browned. Remove and set aside.

3. Sprinkle the cornmeal, salt, pepper, and cumin into the skillet and stir. Add the red and green bell peppers and cook over medium-high heat, stirring constantly, about 2 minutes or until the bell peppers are partially cooked. Add the corn and scallion and stir constantly for 1 minute more.

4. Add 1 cup of the chicken stock to the skillet and cook over medium heat, stirring constantly, for about 4 minutes or until the liquid reduces slightly. Add the green chiles, chicken strips, the remaining 1 cup stock, and the buttermilk. Reduce the heat to very low and cook, partially covered, for 5 minutes more until the chicken is done throughout. Divide among 4 bowls and sprinkle with the chopped cilantro.

CARIBBEAN COCONUT CHICKEN

Truly old-fashioned, tasty fried chicken with a flavorful twist. Great to accompany sundown drinks as appetizers, or you can make a meal out of it.

4 servings

2 skinless, boneless chicken breasts (about 2 pounds), halved and flattened to ¼-inch thickness
4 thin slices prosciutto
1 ripe mango, peeled and cut into 8 1-inch-wide strips
1 cup all-purpose flour
½ teaspoon salt
⅛ teaspoon black pepper
½ teaspoon curry powder
⅛ teaspoon finely crumbled dried thyme
2 eggs, well beaten
2 cups grated fresh coconut (or unsweetened shredded coconut)
2 cups (or more) vegetable oil for deep frying
Juice of 1 lime
1 to 2 limes, cut into wedges

1. Inside the edge of each pounded chicken breast, place a slice of prosciutto trimmed to ½-inch. Place a slice of mango in the center. Roll lengthwise to completely enclose the mango and prosciutto. Tuck in and pinch the ends of the chicken breasts to seal tightly. Arrange the rolls on a baking sheet and refrigerate for about 30 minutes or until very cold and firm.

2. Combine the flour, salt, pepper, curry powder, and thyme in a bowl and mix well. Spread the mixture on a plate. Pour the beaten eggs onto into a shallow dish. Loosely sprinkle the coconut onto a third plate.

3. Roll each chicken breast cylinder in the flour mixture and shaking off the excess. Then roll in the beaten eggs until completely covered, allowing any excess to drip back into the dish. Finally, roll in the coconut until completely covered.

4. Arrange the chicken rolls on a plate in a single layer. Cover and refrigerate for 30 minutes.

5. Preheat the oven to 325°F.

6. In a heavy high-sided skillet, heat the oil over high heat. The oil should be deep enough to cover the chicken rolls completely. When the oil is hot enough to deep-fry, test for readiness with a cube of bread which should immediately deep-fry and begin to turn brown. Gently place half the chicken rolls to the skillet and deep-fry about 4 minutes or until golden brown. Remove with a slotted spoon and drain on several layers of paper towel. Repeat with the remaining chicken rolls.

7. Put the chicken rolls on a baking sheet and bake for about 10 minutes or until done and very crispy and brown. Splash with lime juice and serve with lime wedges.

JAPANESE-STYLE CHICKEN CROQUETTES

4 to 6 servings

2 skinless, boneless chicken breasts (about 2 pounds), minced
6 Japanese dried mushrooms, softened in cold water for 15 minutes, drained, dried with paper towels, and minced
4 scallions, minced
1 egg
2 tablespoons sake (Japanese rice wine)
1 tablespoon tamari or soy sauce
1 teaspoon sugar
1½ teaspoon salt
¼ cup dried bread crumbs
2 cups (or more) vegetable oil for deep frying
1 cup chopped fresh parsley

1. Combine the chicken, mushrooms, scallions, egg, sake, soy sauce, sugar, salt, and bread crumbs in a bowl and mix well with your hands or the back of a wooden spoon.

2. With an oiled spoon, scoop out 1-inch balls. Roll in the palms of your hands. Place on a lightly oiled plate. Repeat with all the mixture.

3. In a heavy, high-sided skillet or deep-frying pan, heat enough oil to deep-fry to very hot, or 375°F. Test for readiness with one croquette. The oil should be deep enough to cover the croquettes. Gently place croquettes in the pan so that they are not touching and can bob freely in the hot oil and begin to brown immediately. Fry in two batches and do not crowd the croquettes while deep-frying.

4. Remove the croquettes from the oil with a slotted spoon and place on several layers of paper towel to drain for a minute. Roll the croquettes in chopped parsley. Arrange on a platter and serve hot.

Stir-Fry

When you hear the word "wok," do you think of Chinese food? Well, in this, the era of fast food, the wok has become a multicultural cooking tool, stirring up Mexican and Mediterranean as easily as a beloved Mandarin feast. When it comes to reorienting our traditional cooking methods to new taste trends, the wok and its stir-frying method of cooking offers a couple of very specific advantages: a short cooking time, which allows food to retain much of its natural flavor and moisture, and the limited need for oil, since the food is literally tossed to and fro on the already-slippery surface of the wok which keeps it from sticking. Stir-fry cooking was invented in a time when little firewood was available so the food needed to cook fast. In order to intensify the taste of wok-cooked foods, instant flavorings and seasonings were used, such as soy sauce, hoisin, chile-garlic paste, and ginger. When cooking with this high-heat quick method, seek out ingredients that add an intrinsic kick to the ingredients when splashed into the wok: balsamic vinegar, infused oils, reduced and concentrated stocks or liquids, intensely flavored wines like sherry, fresh herbs, chopped garlic, and citrus zest that explode with flavor, as well as vegetables like scallions and bell peppers, for their quick cooking qualities. Another thing to consider: Always set the table before you begin tossing the food around in the wok, since when your stir-fry is ready, you'd better be ready, too!

JAPANESE STIR-FRY WITH PEA SHOOTS

Pea shoots (sugar snap peas) include the leaves and tendrils. These tasty fresh seasonal vegetables are also interesting visually. Available during the summer growing season, look for pea shoots at an open-air farmers' market.

4 servings

2 skinless, boneless chicken breasts (about 1½ pounds), halved and flattened slightly between plastic wrap and cut into ½-inch strips
1 tablespoon dark sesame oil
2 large cloves garlic, minced
1 tablespoon minced peeled fresh ginger
¼ teaspoon crushed red pepper
3 tablespoons soy sauce or tamari
2 teaspoons cornstarch dissolved in 2 tablespoons chicken stock
½ cup chicken stock (see page 8)
¼ cup rice wine vinegar
1 tablespoon honey
1 tablespoon light sesame oil
6 scallions, white and green parts, cut into 1-inch pieces
½ red bell pepper, seeded and julienned
1 pound sugar snap peas, including tendrils and leaves
¼ pound buckwheat soba noodles, cooked in lightly salted water according to directions, tossed with 1 tablespoon dark sesame oil, kept warm

1. Combine the chicken strips, dark sesame oil, garlic, ginger, pepper, and 1 tablespoon of the soy sauce in a mixing bowl. Toss to coat the pieces well. Marinate for 15 minutes.

2. Whisk together the cornstarch mixture, chicken stock, the remaining 2 tablespoons soy sauce, vinegar, and honey in a small bowl.

3. Heat the light sesame oil in a wok over medium-high heat. Add the chicken strips, reserving the marinade, and stir-fry 2 to 3 minutes or until lightly browned. Add the scallions, bell pepper, and a little of the marinade and stir-fry 1 minute more. Add the remaining marinade and the stock mixture and bring to a boil, cooking 2 to 3 minutes or until the chicken strips are done and the sauce thickens. In the last 1 minute of cooking time, add the sugar snap peas and cook until just wilted.

4. Place the hot noodles in a large serving bowl, top with the chicken, peas, and sauce, toss to mix. Serve hot.

THAI CHICKEN BREAST STIR-FRY

4 servings

½ cup chicken stock (see page 8)
1 tablespoon fresh lime juice
2 teaspoons cornstarch, dissolved in 1½ tablespoons soy sauce
2 teaspoons light brown sugar
½ teaspoon crushed red pepper
1½ teaspoons canola or other vegetable oil
2 skinless, boneless chicken breasts (about 2 pounds), halved and cut into 1½-inch cubes
¾ pound fresh spinach, stemmed and washed
1 cup bean sprouts
½ teaspoon grated lime zest
3 tablespoons grated unsweetened coconut

1. Whisk together all but 2 tablespoons of the chicken stock, the lime juice, cornstarch mixture, brown sugar, and red pepper in a small bowl. Set aside.

2. Heat the oil in a wok over high heat. Add the chicken cubes and stir-fry about 4 minutes or until done throughout. Remove with a slotted spoon to a bowl and keep warm.

3. Add the reserved 2 tablespoons of stock to the wok over medium heat. Add the spinach and stir-fry 30 seconds or just until wilted. Transfer to a platter, make a bed of spinach, and keep warm.

4. Increase the heat to medium-high, add the bean sprouts, and stir-fry 30 seconds. Add the chicken stock mixture and the chicken cubes and stir-fry 1 minute more or until heated through. Remove the chicken and bean sprouts with a slotted spoon and arrange over the spinach.

5. Add the lime zest and coconut to the wok, bring to a boil, and cook until the sauce thickens. Pour over the chicken and spinach. Serve hot.

OIL: THE NUMBER ONE INGREDIENT IN A STIR-FRY

If you have been wondering what type of oil is best to use when stir frying, here is the final word on oiling up the wok. Use only oils that can withstand the high temperatures required for stir-fry, such as canola, safflower, corn, and peanut. Butter and olive oil begin to burn well before reaching the high temperatures needed for a successful stir-fry. Oils used as flavorings, such as dark sesame oil, are added after the entire cooking process is completed and the dish is ready to be turned out onto a serving platter and immediately served.

CHICKEN VEGETABLE & RICE STIR-FRY

2 to 4 servings

2 tablespoons soy sauce or tamari
2 tablespoons dry sherry
1 tablespoon rice wine vinegar
2 teaspoons sugar
2 teaspoons cornstarch, dissolved in 1 tablespoon chicken stock
1 tablespoon fresh lemon juice
1 skinless, boneless chicken breast (about 1 pound), cut into ½-inch strips
2 cups broccoli florets
2 medium carrots, peeled and sliced on the diagonal
1 green bell pepper, trimmed, seeded, chopped into 1-inch pieces
2 tablespoons light sesame oil
1 tablespoon minced garlic
1 tablespoon finely minced, peeled fresh ginger
1 cup thinly sliced scallion, white and green parts
1 teaspoon dark sesame oil
2 cups cooked white rice

1. Whisk together the soy sauce, sherry, vinegar, and sugar in a small bowl.

2. Whisk together the cornstarch mixture and lemon juice in a medium mixing bowl. Add the chicken strips, toss to coat, and marinate for 15 minutes.

3. Fill a large bowl with ice water and keep near the stove. In a large pot of lightly salted boiling water, blanch the broccoli florets for 1 minute. Remove the broccoli with a slotted spoon and plunge into the ice water to stop the cooking process. Remove with a slotted spoon and set aside to drain. Repeat with the carrot slices and bell pepper pieces, blanching separately, for 1 minute each.

4. Heat 1 tablespoon of the light sesame oil in a wok over medium-high heat. Add the garlic and ginger and stir-fry 30 seconds.

5. Add the scallion and stir-fry 1 minute more. Add the dark sesame oil and heat. Add the rice and stir-fry 2 minutes, just to heat the rice through and combine the ingredients. Transfer to a bowl and keep warm.

6. Drain the chicken pieces, reserving the marinade.

7. Heat the remaining 1 tablespoon light sesame oil in the wok. Add the chicken strips and stir-fry 4 minutes, or until the chicken turns white. Add the reserved marinade, broccoli, carrots, and bell pepper and stir-fry 2 to 3 minutes, or until the vegetables are crisp-tender, the chicken breast pieces are done, and the sauce is thickened. Serve in a bowl with the rice on the side.

STIR-FRIED CHICKEN WITH CABBAGE AND WATER CHESTNUTS

4 servings

⅓ cup light teriyaki sauce
1 teaspoon cornstarch, dissolved in 1 tablespoon soy sauce or tamari
2 skinless, boneless chicken breast (about 2 pounds), cut into 1-inch strips or chunks
1 teaspoon dark sesame oil
2 teaspoons light sesame oil
1 clove garlic, minced
¾ cup thinly sliced water chestnuts
1 to 2 tablespoons chicken stock (see page 8)
1½ cups shredded napa cabbage

1. Whisk together 1 tablespoon of the teriyaki sauce and the cornstarch mixture in a small bowl. Add the chicken breast pieces and toss to coat well. Marinate 20 minutes.

2. Heat both sesame oils in a wok over medium-high heat. Add the chicken and marinade, stir-fry 3 to 4 minutes, or until done. Remove the chicken with a slotted spoon and set aside.

3. Add the garlic to the hot wok and stir-fry 30 seconds. Add the water chestnuts and stir-fry 1 minute more. Add the remaining teriyaki sauce and 1 or 2 tablespoons of chicken stock as needed. Add the cabbage and stir-fry 1 minute, or until it begins to wilt.

4. Return the chicken pieces to the wok and stir-fry for 1 minute more, or until the sauce is thickened.

STIR-FRY — A DEFINITION

Stir-fry is the cooking method most often used in Chinese kitchens all over the world. It is the most sophisticated cooking method used in perhaps the oldest cuisine on earth. Essentially, it is cooking in a very small amount of oil over very high heat, stirring constantly so that food is never in contact with the cooking surface longer than a few seconds, or long enough to burn. Simple! With stir-frying, vegetables retain their natural color and texture, chicken breasts come out tender, juicy, and never overcooked, and the flavoring possibilities are limitless.

SWEET AND SOUR CHICKEN STIR-FRY

2 to 4 servings

1 tablespoon light sesame oil
2 skinless, boneless chicken breasts (about 2 pounds), halved, cut into1-inch strips
1 clove garlic, minced
2 tablespoons dark brown sugar
1½ cups crushed fresh pineapple with 2 tablespoons fresh pineapple juice
3 tablespoons white wine vinegar
2 tablespoons sherry
½ teaspoon grated peeled fresh ginger
½ cup chopped green bell pepper
½ cup chopped red bell pepper
½ cup thinly sliced celery
½ cup carrots, peeled and thinly sliced on the diagonal
¼ cup chopped scallion, white and green parts
1 tablespoon soy sauce or tamari
2 teaspoons cornstarch, dissolved in 2 tablespoons soy sauce

1. Heat the oil in a wok over medium-high heat. Add the chicken and garlic and stir-fry about 4 minutes or until the chicken is brown. Remove from the wok and set aside.

2. Combine the sugar, pineapple juice, vinegar, sherry, and ginger in a small bowl and stir until the sugar is dissolved. Set aside.

3. Add both bell peppers, celery, carrots, and scallion to the wok and stir-fry for 1 minute. Add the soy sauce and continue stir-frying 1 minute more.

4. Add the chicken pieces to the wok and stir in the cornstarch mixture and pineapple. Bring to a boil, stirring constantly, and cook for 2 minutes more, or until the sauce thickens and the chicken is done. Serve immediately.

GET READY, GET SET, STIR-FRY!

Start your stir-fry by lining up all the ingredients in order of use, including marinated chicken breast pieces, uniformly chopped vegetables, and chopped fresh herbs as well as the sauce ingredients that go in last. Keep proper utensils at arm's length, cooking tools for stir-frying as well as for removing the food from the wok. It's also a good idea to have the table set and ready to go. Ask your family or friends to gather around the table when the ingredients start to sizzle in the hot wok. Remember, don't over fill the wok; if you do, there won't be enough surface to cook the foods evenly. Divide the total amount of ingredients into serving batches if necessary, keeping the already-cooked ingredients warm under foil until all is ready to be served.

ORANGE CHICKEN AND PEPPERS WITH CURLY NOODLES

The noodles in this dish come packaged in water. They are usually found in Japanese markets or specialty food sections of the supermarket, and there are many brands to choose from, all delicious.

4 servings

3 tablespoons soy sauce or tamari
½ cup orange juice
1 skinless, boneless chicken breast (about 1 pound), halved and cut into 1-inch pieces
2 tablespoons rice wine vinegar
1 tablespoon honey
2 teaspoons cornstarch, dissolved in 1 tablespoon chicken stock
Salt to taste
2 teaspoons freshly ground black pepper
2 teaspoons light sesame oil
2 to 3 cups 1-inch pieces red and yellow bell peppers
1 navel orange, peeled, white pith removed, and sections removed from the membranes
1 package (8 ounces) fresh Oriental curly noodles, cooked according to package directions, drained, and rinsed

1. Combine 2 tablespoons of the soy sauce and 1 tablespoon of the orange juice in a medium mixing bowl. Add the chicken and toss to coat well. Marinate 10 minutes.

2. Combine the remaining soy sauce and orange juice, the vinegar, honey, cornstarch mixture, and salt and pepper in a jar with a tight-fitting lid. Shake to mix well.

3. Heat the oil in a wok over high heat. Add the chicken pieces and stir-fry 3 to 4 minutes or until browned. Transfer to a bowl and set aside.

4. Over medium-high heat, add the bell peppers to the wok and stir-fry 2 minutes or until partially cooked.

5. Return the chicken pieces and marinade to the wok along with the reserved soy and orange juice mixture. Bring to a simmer and cook 2 to 3 minutes or until the chicken pieces are done throughout. In the last 30 seconds of cooking, add the orange sections and noodles and heat through. Divide among large pasta bowls and serve hot.

CHICKEN AND ASPARAGUS STIR-FRY

4 servings

2 teaspoons cornstarch, dissolved in 1 tablespoon chicken stock
1 teaspoon salt
2 skinless, boneless chicken breasts (about 1½ pounds), halved and cut into 1½-inch cubes
2 tablespoons light sesame oil
2 tablespoons minced onion
2 cloves garlic, minced
2 tablespoons minced parsley
¼ teaspoon crushed red pepper
2 cups 1-inch pieces asparagus tips
½ teaspoon salt
1 tablespoon fresh orange juice
1 teaspoon grated orange zest
Freshly ground black pepper

1. Combine the cornstarch mixture, salt, and chicken cubes in a medium bowl and toss to mix well. Marinate in the refrigerator for 1 hour. Drain well just before cooking.

2. Heat 1 tablespoon of the oil in a wok over medium-high heat. Add the chicken and stir-fry 4 to 5 minutes or until browned and done. Remove to a bowl and keep warm.

3. Heat the remaining 1 tablespoon oil in the wok. Add the onion and garlic and stir-fry 15 seconds. Add 1 tablespoon of the parsley and the red pepper and stir-fry 10 seconds more. Add the asparagus tips, the ½ teaspoon salt, orange juice, and zest and cook about 2 minutes or to crisp-tender.

4. Return the chicken pieces to the wok and stir-fry 1 minute or just to heat through. Adjust the season with salt and pepper to taste. Toss with the remaining 1 tablespoon parsley, and serve. Serve hot.

PERFECT BROWN RICE

Boiling brown rice with seasonings is yet another chance to create the perfect accompaniment for many stir-fry dishes.

For each cup of brown rice, bring approximately 4 cups water and ¼ teaspoon salt to a full boil. Add dried herbs and fresh parsley, or some salt-free vegetable seasoning (such as Spike or Mrs. Dash). Test the rice after 10 to 12 minutes. Do not overcook, but do not undercook. Keep testing every few minutes until done to al dente or softer as desired. Drain the rice in a colander. Since much of the starch stays in the water, immediately rinse the cooked rice with hot tap water, then drain for 2 or 3 minutes. Rice cooked this way is always fluffy and tender.

HOW TO MAKE PERFECT WHITE RICE

Rice cookery and its many methods could fill a book—albeit a thin one. The first recipe is a typical Chinese rice-cooking technique, used for generations. In other words, it's tried and trustworthy. The second method is equally as good but requires tending, especially in the last minutes when the rice can easily overcook. Try both and use them appropriately.

Steamed Rice: For 3 cups of cooked rice, put 1 cup of long-grain or short-grain white rice in a saucepan. Rinse the rice by covering it with water. Pour off the rinse water and add 1¾ cups of water to the rice, along with ½ teaspoon salt. Bring the water to a boil, cook for 2 minutes, reduce the heat to very low, cover the pan tightly, and cook for 20 minutes. Remove the rice from the heat and allow to set, covered, for 10 minutes. Stir to fluff and separate the rice grains before serving.

Boiled Rice: Fill a large saucepan or stockpot with 6 cups of hot water from the tap. For 3 cups of rice, add 1 cup of long- or short-grain white rice along with 1 teaspoon salt. Bring the water to a boil. Continue boiling until the rice is almost done al dente. Add more hot water during the cooking period if necessary. (Boil water on the stove in a pan. Don't add cold water to the boiling rice.) In the last few minutes of cooking time, test the rice frequently. When done, quickly drain in a strainer, rinse with hot tap water, and drain.

A WOK IS A WOK IS A WOK?

It's not! If you intend to develop a repertoire of stir-fry dishes, the best wok you can buy is a hand-pounded low-carbon steel wok made in China. These woks are available in Asian markets. Though they are much more expensive than the American machine-made steel woks, any skilled Chinese chef will tell you it is the thickness of these woks—usually twice as thick as the machine-made—that keeps the food from burning on the amazingly hard carbon surface. Stainless-steel woks are available but require too much oil to keep the food from sticking. Electric woks turn everything into mush and seldom stay hot enough for successful stir-frying. Wok cooking on electric stoves is possible if the smallest burner is used at the highest heat. But for the best results, use a hand-pounded low-carbon steel wok over a high gas flame. Since cooking in a wok is done only in the bottom of the pan, a "chan," or spatula that is rounded across the bottom, and a long-handled ladle are essential tools for tossing and pushing the stir-frying food against the sides of the pan to prevent overcooking. A lid is also useful for longer cooking ingredients, or for quick-steaming vegetables that are arranged around the sides of the wok, with only a little water boiling in the center.

CHICKEN AND MELON STIR-FRY

4 servings

1 teaspoon dark sesame oil
2 teaspoons soy sauce or tamari
1 tablespoon dry white wine
1 teaspoon oyster sauce
½ teaspoon ground ginger
2 teaspoons cornstarch, dissolved in 1 tablespoon stock
½ teaspoon sugar
Pinch of salt and black pepper
1 skinless, boneless chicken breast (about 1 pound), halved and cut into 1-inch thick slices
1 tablespoon peanut oil
2 teaspoons minced garlic
½ cup snow pea pods, trimmed and cut in half on the diagonal
4 scallions, cut into ¼-inch pieces, white and green parts, separated
½ medium cantaloupe, cut into balls
½ medium-firm honeydew melon, cut into balls using a melon baller
2 tablespoons toasted sesame seeds for garnish

1. Combine the dark sesame oil, soy sauce, white wine, oyster sauce, ginger, cornstarch mixture, sugar, salt, pepper, and chicken slices in a small bowl; toss to mix well. Marinate in the refrigerator for 1 hour.

2. Heat half of the peanut oil in a wok over medium-high heat. Add the garlic and stir-fry about 30 seconds. Add the snow peas and the scallions and stir-fry 30 seconds more. Add the cantaloupe and honeydew melon balls and gently stir-fry about 1 minute or just until heated through. Remove all the ingredients to a bowl with a slotted spoon. Set aside.

3. Drain the chicken, reserving the marinade. Add the remaining peanut oil to the wok and heat over medium-high heat. Add the chicken and stir-fry about 4 minutes or until the chicken is done throughout, about 4 minutes. Return the melon balls and snow peas to the wok and stir to combine. Drizzle in the marinade along the side of the wok and stir-fry about 1 minute more or until the sauce has thickened. Turn onto a serving platter and garnish with the sesame seeds.

Q: When is the oil hot enough for stir frying?
A: When it's very hot, but not smoking. The ingredients will usually sizzle when they are placed in the wok and begin to cook immediately. The hot oil covering the surface of the wok also distributes the oil throughout all the pieces in the wok.

CHICKEN, SNOW PEA, & RICE SALAD

This chicken breast and fresh snow pea stir-fry is prepared and cooled before serving over lettuce leaves. It makes a wonderful appetizer.

4 to 6 servings

2 skinless, boneless chicken breasts (about 2 pounds), halved and cut into ¼-inch strips
1 teaspoon cornstarch, dissolved in 1 tablespoon dry sherry
1 teaspoon soy sauce or tamari
½ teaspoon crushed red pepper
1 tablespoon light sesame oil
½ large onion, sliced into paper thin rounds
1 teaspoon minced peeled fresh ginger
2 cloves garlic, minced
1½ pounds snow peas, trimmed
¾ cup chopped scallion, white and green parts, plus 2 tablespoons finely chopped for garnish
2 tablespoons rice wine vinegar
3 tablespoons fresh lemon juice
2 teaspoons sherry
1 teaspoon honey
Salt and freshly ground white pepper
3 cups freshly cooked white rice
2 tablespoons toasted sesame seeds
3 tablespoons chopped flat-leaf parsley
4 cups mixed salad greens of choice, washed and dried in a salad spinner, chilled

1. Combine the chicken strips, cornstarch mixture, soy sauce, and red pepper in a small bowl and toss to mix well. Marinate for 10 minutes.

2. Heat half the oil in a wok over medium-high heat. Add the onion and stir-fry 1 minute. Add the ginger and garlic and stir-fry 30 seconds more. Add the chicken strips and the marinade and stir-fry 2 to 3 minutes more, or until the strips are done throughout. Transfer to a bowl and set aside.

3. Heat the remaining oil in the wok over medium heat. Add the pea pods and ¾ cup of scallion and stir-fry 1 minute. Add the vinegar, 1 tablespoon of the lemon juice, the sherry, and honey and stir-fry for 1 minute more. Add the chicken mixture to the wok, season with salt and pepper, and stir-fry about 1 minute more, or just until the chicken strips are warmed through. Transfer the mixture to a bowl and cool the salad to room temperature.

4. Toss together the chicken, peas, rice, the remaining 2 tablespoons of lemon juice, sesame seeds, and parsley in a large mixing bowl. Serve on the salad greens and sprinkle with the remaining scallion.

CHICKEN WITH CHINESE VEGETABLES

This recipe calls for oil-fried diced chicken pieces. It is possible to reduce the frying oil to 1 tablespoon and simply stir-fry the pieces until browned or about 4 minutes. Remember to drain the chicken on a paper towel before continuing with the recipe.

2 to 4 servings

2 skinless, boneless chicken breast (about 1½ pounds), diced
1 egg white
½ teaspoon soy sauce
½ teaspoon salt
1 tablespoon cornstarch
½ cup vegetable oil
2 tablespoons unsalted butter
¾ cup whole blanched almonds
½ cup mild rice wine vinegar
3 tablespoons sugar
⅛ teaspoon salt
1 cup finely chopped celery
1 cup chopped bok choy, blanched, drained and dried
½ cup fresh peas, shelled, blanched, drained, and dried
½ cup julienned green bell pepper
1 tablespoon cornstarch dissolved in 2 tablespoons chicken stock

1. Combine the chicken, egg white, soy sauce, and salt in a bowl. Sprinkle on the cornstarch and marinate for 15 minutes.

2. Heat the oil in a wok over medium heat. Add the chicken breast and marinade, stir-fry 1 minute or until lightly browned. Remove the chicken with a slotted spoon and set on a plate lined with paper towels to drain.

3. Melt the butter in a small skillet over medium heat. Sauté the almonds until brown. Transfer to a bowl and set aside.

4. Combine the vinegar, sugar, and salt in a bowl. Remove all but 1 tablespoon of oil from the wok and heat over medium-high heat. Add the celery, bok choy, peas, and bell pepper and stir-fry 1 minute. Add the vinegar mixture and stir-fry 30 seconds more. Add the cornstarch paste and stir until the sauce is thickened. Add the chicken and almonds and toss to heat through. Serve hot.

CANTONESE LEMON CHICKEN

4 servings

2 skinless, boneless chicken breast (about 2 pounds), cut into to 1-inch thick pieces
1 tablespoon dry sherry
1½ tablespoons soy sauce
1 tablespoon cornstarch
1 egg white
2 tablespoons canola or other vegetable oil
1 teaspoon peeled and minced fresh ginger
½ cup chicken stock
2 tablespoons lemon juice
½ tablespoon sugar
¼ teaspoon salt
1 teaspoon cornstarch, dissolved in 2 tablespoons chicken stock
½ tablespoon lemon zest
1 lemon, thinly sliced

1. Combine the chicken, sherry, 1 tablespoon soy sauce, cornstarch, and egg white in a bowl and marinate for 15 minutes.

2. Heat the oil in a wok over medium-high heat. Add the chicken and marinade.

3. Stir-fry about 2 minutes or until the chicken turns white. Remove with a slotted spoon and drain.

4. Remove all but 1 tablespoon of oil from the wok. Over medium-high heat, add the ginger and stir-fry about 30 seconds.

5. Add the stock, lemon juice, sugar, salt, and remaining ½ teaspoon soy sauce and bring to a boil. Stir in the cornstarch mixture and continue stirring until the sauce thickens. Add the lemon zest and return the chicken breast pieces to the sauce. Stir-fry about 30 seconds or just to heat through. Turn onto a serving platter and garnish with lemon slices.

THE WELL-SEASONED WOK

A low-carbon-steel woks must first be seasoned before it can be used. This is a good project for an afternoon. First, add ½ cup oil to the wok and spread it around to coat the surface evenly. Cook over medium-low heat for 15 minutes, recoating the surface thoroughly during cooking. Discard the oil, wipe the wok clean, and wash it with soap and water. Dry the wok over medium heat. This will keep the wok from rusting. Air-dry the wok. After at least the first twenty uses, the sealing process will continue. After that, the wok may be wiped dry without fear of rust.

KUNG POW CHICKEN

4 servings

Sauce

4 tablespoons soy sauce
1½ tablespoons cornstarch
2 tablespoons sugar
2 tablespoons light sesame oil
4 tablespoons chicken stock
1 teaspoon Chinese red pepper sauce (*sambal oeleck*)*

2 skinless, boneless chicken breasts (about 2 pounds), cut into 1-inch cubes
1 egg white
1 tablespoon sherry
1 tablespoon cornstarch
3 tablespoons vegetable oil
16 scallions, white part only, cut into ½-inch pieces
16 paper-thin slices peeled fresh ginger, quartered
1 cup roasted unsalted peanuts
*Available in Asian Markets or some grocery stores

1. To make the sauce, combine the soy sauce, cornstarch, sugar, sesame oil, chicken stock, and red pepper sauce. Set aside.

2. Combine the chicken, egg white, and sherry in a bowl and sprinkle on the tablespoon of cornstarch. Marinate for 15 minutes.

3. Heat the oil in a wok over medium-high heat. Add the chicken and marinade, stir-fry about 3 minutes or until done. Remove the chicken with a slotted spoon and drain.

4. Add the scallions and ginger and stir-fry 30 seconds more. Add the sauce and heat through. Return the chicken to the wok and continue cooking until the sauce thickens.

5. In the last few seconds of cooking, add the peanuts and toss to coat with the sauce. Turn onto a platter and serve hot.

Q: Why should you always wear rubber gloves when handling hot chiles?

A: The chiles naturally contain oils. This is where the heat comes from. When chiles are handled, these oils will quickly be absorbed by the skin. Once they penetrate, no amount of water will cool the burn. It can take many hours for the burning sensation to subside. What's more, any other part of the body, especially the eyes, can be seriously affected by the oil of a chile. So, be very careful when handling these flavorful but potentially treacherous little things.

WALNUT CHICKEN STIR-FRY

4 servings

2 skinless, boneless chicken breasts (about 2 pounds), cut into ½-inch cubes
2 tablespoons cornstarch
2 tablespoons dry sherry
1 egg white
2 tablespoons soy sauce
1 teaspoon sugar
½ teaspoon salt
4 teaspoons sesame oil
½ cup walnuts, quartered
1 teaspoon minced, peeled fresh ginger
1 tablespoon chopped scallion, white part only

1. Combine the chicken, cornstarch, sherry, and egg white in a bowl and marinate for 15 minutes.

2. Combine the soy sauce, sugar, and salt in another bowl.

3. Heat the oil in a wok over medium-high heat. Add the walnuts and stir-fry about 1 minute. Remove the walnuts with a slotted spoon and drain.

4. Add the chicken and marinade and stir-fry about 2 minutes. Add the ginger and scallions and continue stir-frying about 30 seconds more.

5. Add the soy sauce mixture and stir-fry 30 seconds more. Stir in the walnuts and cook just to heat through. Serve hot.

ADVANCE PREPARATION – THE SECRET OF A SUCCESSFUL STIR-FRY

Several of the Chinese recipes in this chapter were contributed by Bert Gader (whose Chinese cooking classes were legendary in Los Angeles). Bert, boasting some 2,500 Chinese recipes in his card file, has gone so far as to make a science of cooking and serving this cuisine. Because of his extraordinary emphasis on advance planning and preparation (herein lies the secret), he has developed a method of turning out an impressive five- or six-course Cantonese or Szechwan meal for ten from stove to table in ten minutes. Sporting a spotless white linen suit, this 100-percent Irish "artist of the wok and steamer" seats his guests at the long lacquered dining table. By the time each crystal wineglass is filled, he bursts forth from the kitchen with dish after platter after bowl of Kung Pao Chicken, Spicy Eggplant, Steamed Custard, and more. Many of his standard recipes revolve around chicken breasts—an indispensable ingredient in Chinese cuisine.

STIR-FRIED RICE WITH CHICKEN CHUNKS

4 servings

2 tablespoons canola or other light vegetable oil
1 cup minced onions
2 skinless, boneless chicken breast (about 2 pounds), cut into 1-inch cubes
1 cup cooked white rice, at room temperature
½ cup fresh peas, blanched
½ teaspoon salt
3 eggs, lightly beaten
6 scallions, white and some green part, chopped
3 to 4 tablespoons soy sauce

1. Heat the oil in a wok over medium-high heat. Add the onions and stir-fry 2 to 3 minutes, or until lightly browned. Add the chicken and stir-fry about 2 minutes more or until the chicken turns white.

2. Add the rice, peas, and salt and stir-fry just to heat through. Push the mixture to the sides of the wok. Pour the eggs into the center. Cook the eggs, stirring constantly, about 30 seconds. Toss the rice and eggs together. Add the scallions, sprinkle on 2 tablespoons of the soy sauce, mix, and heat through. Serve hot with more soy sauce on the side.

HOW TO MAKE ORIENTAL CHICKEN STOCK

3 pounds raw chicken carcasses, necks, legs, gizzards, hearts, and trimmings
1 tablespoon rice wine or dry sherry
4 slices peeled fresh ginger root, about 1 inch in diameter and ½ inch thick
4 large scallions chopped
8 cups spring or filtered water
Pinch of salt

1. Place the chicken pieces in a large saucepan or stockpot. Add wine or sherry, ginger, scallions, water, and a pinch of salt and bring to a rapid boil over high heat. Skim off the scum that floats to the top.
2. Reduce the heat to very low and simmer, covered, for 3 hours, skimming the stock often. Strain the stock, using a fine strainer lined with several piece of cheesecloth, and let cool to room temperature.
3. If you're not planning to use the stock right away, freeze it in small plastic containers or in ice cube trays and store the frozen cubes a plastic bag in the freezer (see page 8 for further instructions). A stock cube is a perfect amount to use in wok cooking; it can be placed along the side of a sizzling hot wok; it quickly melts at high-heat cooking temperatures.

CHICKEN AND BROCCOLI

4 servings

2 skinless, boneless chicken breast (about 1½ pounds), cut into 1 × 2-inch pieces
½ tablespoon rice wine or sherry
½ teaspoon salt
1 tablespoon soy sauce
Pinch of white pepper
½ tablespoon cornstarch
2 tablespoons canola or other light vegetable oil
3 cups broccoli, cut into small pieces
½ cup chicken stock
1 teaspoon cornstarch, dissolved in 1 tablespoon chicken stock

1. Combine the chicken, wine, half the salt, soy sauce, white pepper, and cornstarch in a small bowl. Marinate for 15 minutes.

2. Heat 1 tablespoon of the oil in a wok over medium-high heat. Add the chicken and marinade, stir-fry 1 minute or until the chicken turns white. Remove with a slotted spoon and drain.

3. Add the remaining 1 tablespoon of oil from the wok and heat over medium-high heat. Add the broccoli and the remaining salt and stir-fry 30 seconds. Add the stock, cover, and cook 2 minutes more.

4. Uncover, stir in the cornstarch paste, and stir-fry until the sauce is thickened. Return the chicken breast pieces to the wok and stir-fry for 30 seconds to heat through.

NONSTICK WOK VS. TRADITIONAL

Both are good for the stir-fry cooking method. Both have thair own advantages. If you're using a nonstick surface, remember to keep the heat to medium and to add the fat before heating; never add fat to a heated nonstick pan. Traditional wok surfaces cook the food faster since they can be heated to higher temperatures. However, they require a little oil to prevent sticking. Plan to have a variety of wok and/or metal cooking utensils available as required for the various cooking surfaces.

Note: The stir-fry recipes in this chapter are written for traditional wok surfaces using high temperatures to stir-fry ingredients. For non-stick wok (or skillet) surfaces, adjust the temperature to medium and increase the cooking time appropriately.

PLUM CHICKEN

4 servings

1 tablespoon sugar
3 tablespoons cornstarch
2 tablespoons dry sherry
¼ teaspoon ground ginger
⅛ teaspoon black pepper
¾ cup chicken stock
2 tablespoons soy sauce
1 tablespoon lemon juice
1 tablespoon white wine vinegar
3 tablespoons canola or peanut oil
2 skinless, boneless chicken breast (about 2 pounds), julienned
1 cup thinly sliced red onion
1 cup thinly sliced celery (cut on the diagonal)
½ teaspoon minced garlic
6 large firm but ripe plums, halved and seed removed

1. In a small saucepan, combine the sugar, cornstarch, sherry, ginger, black pepper, stock, soy sauce, lemon juice, and vinegar. Over medium-high heat, cook about 2 minutes or until the sauce. Set aside.

2. Heat the oil in a wok over medium-high heat. Add the chicken and stir-fry 2 minutes or until it turns white. Remove with a slotted spoon and drain.

3. Add the onion, celery, and garlic to the wok and stir-fry about 1 minute, or until the vegetables are slightly translucent.

4. Add the plums, toss the ingredients together gently, lower the heat and cook, partially covered, about 3 minutes or until the plums are soft. Return the chicken and sauce to the wok; heat through. Serve hot

MOO GOO GAI PAN

Serve this dish with perfectly cooked white rice (see page 333), sprinkled generously with toasted sliced almonds.

4 servings

2 skinless, boneless chicken breast (about 2 pounds), cut into 1-inch cubes
2 tablespoons cornstarch
1 egg white
1 tablespoon dry sherry
¼ teaspoon salt
¼ teaspoon black pepper

⅓ cup chicken stock (see page 8)
2 tablespoons canola or peanut oil
½ tablespoon minced and peeled fresh ginger
1 clove garlic, minced
½ pound small mushrooms, washed and stems removed
5 water chestnuts, thinly sliced

1. Combine the chicken, 1 tablespoon of the cornstarch, the egg white, sherry, salt, and pepper in a bowl. Marinate for 15 minutes.

2. Combine the stock and the remaining 1 tablespoon of cornstarch. Set aside.

3. Heat the oil in a wok over medium-high heat. Add the ginger and garlic and stir-fry for 1 minute. Add the chicken and marinade and stir-fry 3 minutes more or just until the chicken begins to brown. Add the mushrooms and stir-fry 1 minute more.

4. Stir the stock and cornstarch mixture into the wok; cook for about 30 seconds or until the sauce thickens. Toss in the water chestnuts and heat through. Serve hot.

SZECHUAN ORANGE CHICKEN

A hot and spicy combination of flavors! To cool down the "Szechuan" in this recipe reduce the amounts of red chile and roasted peppercorns considerably, or turn to the next recipe!

4 servings

2 skinless, boneless chicken breasts (about 2 pounds), cut into 1-inch cubes
1 teaspoon cornstarch
¾ cup chopped onion
4 scallions, green and white parts, cut into 1-inch pieces
3 small serrano chile peppers, seeded, deveined, and minced
2 teaspoons finely crushed, oven-roasted Szechuan peppercorns
2 teaspoons minced, peeled fresh ginger
2 tablespoons orange juice
2 tablespoons soy sauce
1 tablespoon hoisin sauce
½ teaspoon sugar
½ teaspoon Szechuan chile paste with garlic
3 tablespoons canola or other light vegetable oil
2 tablespoons fresh orange rind cut into very fine threads
1 teaspoon white wine vinegar
1 teaspoon dark sesame oil

1. Combine the chicken and cornstarch in a bowl and toss to coat the pieces.

2. Combine the onion and the scallions in another bowl.

3. Combine the chiles, Szechuan peppercorns, and ginger in another bowl.

4. Stir together the orange juice, soy sauce, hoisin sauce, sugar, and chile paste in another bowl; mix well.

5. Heat the oil in a wok over medium-high heat. Add the chicken and stir-fry about 2 minute or just until it turns white; remove with a slotted spoon and drain.

6. Remove all but 1 tablespoon of oil from the wok. Turn the heat up to high. Add the chile pepper mixture and stir-fry 15 seconds. Add the orange rind and onions and stir-fry another 30 seconds.

7. Add the cooked chicken and the orange juice mixture and stir-fry another 30 seconds. Add the vinegar and stir-fry about 15 seconds more. Drizzle on the dark sesame oil, toss, and serve.

CHICKEN WITH SHIITAKE MUSHROOMS

The flavor of this Szechuan-style dish is hot and sour. Shiitake mushrooms add an interesting subtle flavor and texture to the dish. Shiitakes may be used fresh or dried, in which case they should be rehydrated in warm water for 15 minutes before using. Brush the mushrooms on the underside to loosen any particles, rinse, and drain.

4 servings

2 skinless, boneless chicken breasts (about 2 pounds), cut into 1½-inch pieces
1½ teaspoons finely crushed, oven-roasted Szechuan peppercorns
6 tablespoons rice wine vinegar
1 tablespoon soy sauce
½ teaspoon sugar
3 tablespoons canola or peanut oil
6 large shiitake mushrooms (or about 1 ounce dried, softened in hot water for 30 minutes, rinsed, drained, squeezed dry, and chopped), cleaned, stems removed, and sliced into ¼-inch thick pieces
2 scallions, white and some green part, chopped
1 large clove garlic, minced

1 teaspoon peeled, minced fresh ginger
1 cup chicken stock (see pgae 8)
1 teaspoon dark sesame oil
1 tablespoon chopped cilantro for garnish

1. Combine the chicken, ½ teaspoon of the crushed peppercorns, 2 tablespoons of rice wine vinegar, soy sauce, and sugar in a bowl. Marinate for 30 minutes. Drain the chicken, reserving the marinade, before using.

2. Heat the oil in a wok over medium-high heat. Add the chicken and stir-fry about 3 minutes or until lightly browned. Remove with a slotted spoon and drain.

3. Remove all but 1 tablespoon of oil from the wok. Over medium-high heat, add the scallion, garlic, and ginger and stir-fry about 30 seconds or until the onions lightly brown. Return the chicken to the wok, add the mushrooms, reduce the heat to low, and cook about 5 minutes, or until the chicken pieces are done. Transfer to a serving platter and keep warm.

4. Over medium-high heat, add the chicken stock to the wok along with the remaining 1 teaspoon of Szechwan peppercorns and remaining 4 tablespoons of rice wine vinegar. Bring to a boil and cook about 5 minutes, or until reduced to ¼ cup. Stir in the sesame oil, pour the sauce over the chicken and sprinkle with sesame oil and cilantro. Serve hot.

> **Q: What type of pan can be substituted for a wok?**
> **A:** In a pinch, a large heavy cast-iron skillet or stainless-steel frying pan can be used. The principle is the same—use high heat and oil that withstands high temperatures. Keep the food sliding over the entire surface of the pan, and don't crowd the food in the pan while stir-frying. Don't overcook the ingredients.

CHICKEN BREAST AND SWEET PEPPER STIR-FRY

4 servings

1 tablespoon soy sauce
1 tablespoon oyster sauce*
2 tablespoons dry sherry
Freshly ground black pepper to taste
3 tablespoons peanut oil
1 medium onion, very thinly sliced
2 cloves garlic, chopped
2 skinless, boneless chicken breast (about 2 pounds), cut into 1-inch strips

1 red bell pepper, cored, seeded, and cut into thin strips
1 green bell pepper, cored, seeded, and cut into thin strips
⅓ cup chopped toasted cashews
*** Available at Asian markets or some grocery stores**

1. Combine the soy sauce, oyster sauce, sherry, and black pepper in a small bowl.

2. Heat the oil in a wok over medium-high heat. Add the onion and garlic and stir-fry about 3 minutes. Add the chicken and stir-fry 3 minutes more or until it turns white.

3. Add the peppers, cashews, and the soy sauce mixture. Stir-fry 2 minutes or until the peppers are tender and the chicken is cooked through. Serve hot.

HOISIN CHICKEN

This recipe works well as a hot main course or serve it cold as a very interesting small appetizer or lunch serving. The slices of papaya splashed with lemon juice make a delightful flavor accent.

4 servings

2 skinless, boneless chicken breasts (about 2 pounds), pounded to ¼-inch thick and cut into ½-inch wide strips
Juice of 1 lemon
Juice of 1 small lime
2 tablespoons hoisin sauce
2 tablespoons black bean sauce*
⅛ teaspoon ground ginger
1 garlic clove, pressed
Pinch nutmeg
Pinch cinnamon
2 tablespoons soy sauce
4 tablespoons toasted sesame seeds
3 tablespoons canola or peanut oil
½ pound fresh asparagus, trimmed and sliced very thin on the diagonal
6 whole water chestnuts, very thinly sliced
½ pound snow pea pods, strings removed, blanched, and drained
4 tablespoons cornstarch
1 ripe papaya, peeled, seeded, and sliced

***Available in Asian Markets or some grocery stores**

1. Combine the chicken, lemon and lime juice, hoisin sauce, black bean sauce, ginger, pressed garlic, nutmeg, cinnamon, and soy sauce in a bowl. Toss to coat well, cover and marinate in the refrigerator for 2 hours.

2. Drain the chicken and reserve the marinade.

3. Heat the oil in a wok over medium-high heat. Add the chicken and 1 tablespoon of the sesame seeds and stir-fry for about 2 minutes or just until the chicken turns white. Remove and set aside.

4. Add the asparagus and water chestnuts and cook 1 minute. Add the snow peas and cook 1 more minute, stirring occasionally.

5. Combine the reserved marinade with the cornstarch and add to the wok, stirring until the sauce is slightly thickened. Return the chicken to the wok and heat through, tossing and stirring until the sauce has completely thickened.

6. Arrange papaya slices around the edge of a serving platter. Spoon the chicken mixture into the center of the platter and sprinkle on the remaining sesame seeds. Serve hot or cool to room temperature.

STIR-FRIED GINGER CHICKEN

6 servings

1 pound trimmed broccoli (about 2 cups)
2 cups snow pea pods, trimmed
1 tablespoon peanut oil
3 skinless, boneless chicken breasts (about 3 pounds), cut into 1-inch strips
2 cups chicken stock (see page 8)
1 2-inch slice of peeled fresh ginger, grated
2 cloves garlic, quartered
1 tablespoon cornstarch, mixed with 3 tablespoons chicken stock
4 tablespoons soy sauce
⅓ cup dry sherry
1 teaspoon dark sesame oil

1. Blanch the broccoli florets in boiling water for 3 minutes. Run under cold water to stop the cooking process. Repeat with the snow peas for 1 minute. Drain and set aside.

2. Heat the peanut oil in a wok over high heat. Add the chicken and stir-fry just until done. Remove the chicken and keep warm.

3. Combine the stock, ginger, and garlic in the wok. Bring to a boil, cook for 5 minutes or until reduced by half, let cool slightly, strain, and return to the wok. Stir in the cornstarch mixture and cook until the sauce thickens. Add the soy sauce, sherry, and sesame oil. Add the chicken and vegetables and heat through. Serve immediately.

CHICKEN BREAST AND OYSTER MUSHROOM SAUCE

4 servings

½ cup dry sherry
3 tablespoons soy sauce
3 tablespoons freshly squeezed lime juice
2 teaspoons sugar
1 tablespoon dark sesame oil
1 tablespoon canola or peanut oil
1 tablespoon chopped fresh ginger
¼ teaspoon ground Szechuan peppercorns
2 cloves garlic, chopped
2 skinned, boned chicken breast (about 2 pound), cut into 1-inch pieces
4 scallions, cut into 1-inch pieces
2 celery stalks, sliced
1 pound snow pea pods, trimmed
1 red bell pepper, stemmed, seeded, and julienned
12 dried oyster mushrooms (or other dried mushrooms, like shiitake), rehydrated in 1 cup boiling water for 15 minutes, well cleaned, stemmed and coarsely chopped
¼ pound fresh mushrooms (white or shiitake), washed, stemmed, and cut into thin slices
2 teaspoons cornstarch, dissolved in 2 tablespoons chicken stock

1. Combine the sherry, soy sauce, lime juice, and sugar in a small bowl.

2. Heat both oils in a wok over high heat. Add the ginger, garlic, and pepper and stir-fry 30 seconds. Add the chicken and stir-fry 2 to 3 minutes or just until the chicken pieces turn white. Remove from the wok and set aside.

3. Add the scallions, celery, snow peas, red pepper, and mushrooms and stir-fry 2 minutes. Return the chicken pieces to the wok and add the sherry mixture and, with the heat on high, partially cover the wok and cook for 2 minutes to reduce slightly. Add the cornstarch mixture and stir until slightly thickened or about 1 minute more. Serve hot.

CHICKEN WITH CHINESE LONG BEANS AND WALNUTS STIR-FRY

4 servings

2 skinned, boned chicken breast (about 2 pounds), cut into 1-inch strips
¾ teaspoon salt
¾ teaspoon sugar
1 teaspoon soy sauce
1 teaspoon cornstarch
Dash of black pepper
1 pound Chinese long beans* (or string beans), stringed and tips removed, and cut into quarters on the diagonal
¼ cup canola or other light vegetable oil
1 tablespoon Chinese hot bean sauce*
2 cloves garlic, finely chopped
½ cup chicken stock (see page 8)
2 teaspoons cornstarch, mixed with 2 tablespoons chicken stock
½ cup walnuts, quartered and toasted until crisp

* Available in Asian markets

1. Combine the chicken, ½ teaspoon of the salt, ½ teaspoon of the sugar, soy sauce, cornstarch, and pepper in a bowl and toss to coat well.

2. Add 1 tablespoon of the oil to a sauce pan of lightly salted boiling water. Add the beans and cook 7 minutes, or until crisp-tender. Rinse under cool water to stop the cooking process. Drain.

3. Mash the hot bean sauce and garlic to a paste.

4. Heat 2 tablespoons of the oil in a wok over high heat. Add the chicken and stir-fry for 2 minutes. Add half of the stock, cover, and cook for 2 minutes. Remove from the wok and set aside.

4. Add the remaining oil to the wok. Add the bean sauce paste and the beans. Stir-fry for 2 minutes. Add the remaining salt, sugar, and stock and bring to a boil. Return the chicken to the wok, stir in the cornstarch mixture, and stir until slightly thickened, or about a minute more. Remove from the heat, toss in the walnuts, heat through, and serve.

CHICKEN, CHILE, & SCALLION STIR-FRY

This is a Thai-style dish, so certain ingredients (like bai gaprow, fresh holy basil leaves) are available at Thai and some Asian markets. Another unusual ingredient is the famous Thai sauce naam pla. Check to make sure you have these ingredients before starting this recipe. It just wouldn't be the same without them. Serve with steamed or boiled rice.

4 servings

⅓ cup canola or peanut oil
3 cloves garlic, minced
2 skinless, boneless chicken breasts (about 2 pounds), cut into bite-size pieces
2 serrano chiles, stemmed, seeded, and sliced very thinly crosswise
¾ cup coarsely chopped scallion, white and green parts
½ cup naam pla*
1 tablespoon sugar
¼ cup chopped fresh bai gaprow*
***Available in Thai and some Asian markets**

1. Heat the oil in a wok over medium-high heat. Add the garlic and stir-fry until lightly browned. Add the chicken and stir-fry for 2 to 3 minutes more.

2. Add the chiles, scallions, naam pla, and sugar. Stir fry for about 5 minutes, or until the chicken is done.

3. Add the bai gaprow, toss to mix well, and serve immediately.

CASHEW CHICKEN BREAST STIR-FRY

4 servings

2 skinless, boneless chicken breast (about 2 pounds), skinned, boned, and cut into ½-inch strips
¾ teaspoon salt
¾ teaspoon sugar
1 teaspoon soy sauce
1 teaspoon oyster sauce*
1 tablespoon cornstarch
2 tablespoons canola or peanut oil
1 celery stalk, strings removed, cut into 1½-inch pieces lengthwise, and julienned
½ onion, cut into 8 wedges
1 carrot, peeled and thinly sliced

½ cup thinly sliced mushrooms
1 cup chicken stock (see page 8)
¾ cup canned sliced bamboo shoots
1 tablespoon cornstarch, mixed with 3 tablespoons chicken stock
2 teaspoons dark sesame oil
½ cup unsalted roasted cashews

*** Available in Asian markets and some grocery stores**

1. Combine the chicken, ½ teaspoon of the salt, ½ teaspoon of the sugar, soy sauce, oyster sauce, 1 tablespoon of the cornstarch in a bowl and toss to coat well.

2. Heat 1 tablespoon of the oil in a wok over high heat. Add the celery, onion, carrot, and mushrooms and stir-fry for 2 minutes. Add the remaining salt and sugar and stir-fry for 30 seconds more. Remove the vegetables from the wok and keep warm.

3. Add the remaining oil to the wok over high heat. Add the chicken and marinade and stir-fry 2 minutes. Add the stock, reserving 1 tablespoon, and the bamboo shoots and stir-fry 3 minutes until the chicken is done.

4. Add the cornstarch mixture. Stir until slightly thickened or about 1 minute more. Remove from the heat, toss in the sesame oil and cashews, and serve.

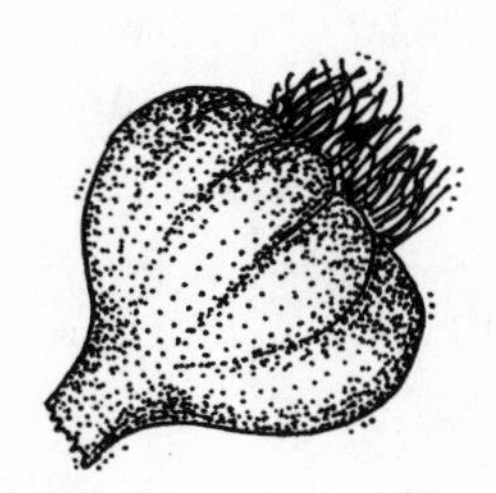

Poach

For the naturally lean chicken breast, poaching is one of the most favorable of all the cooking methods. Do not, however, confuse it with boiling. Once the chicken breasts are placed, always in a single layer, within the simmering poaching liquid, the meat slowly and gently cooks to a tender and flavorful finish in just about 8 to 10 minutes. This is also a great flavor opportunity, so avoid using just plain water in the poaching pan. A successful poach requires a flavored liquid which can be made up of a variety of stocks (see pages 7–11 for several suggestions), including chicken or vegetables, as well as wines or juices. Next comes the poaching bouquet. Fresh herbs and spices, citrus rind, and aromatics (onion, shallot, garlic) should be used abundantly to enhance this liquid since the chicken breasts will absorb all their flavors during cooking (see page 354 for instructions on how to make interesting and ethnic bouquets). Once done, the delicate white poached breast meat lends itself to a wide variety of dishes, from ethnic flavored salads and appetizers fit for any party, to simple slices served with a fruit- or herb-laced sauce drizzled on top. See the Sauces and Purées section on pages for a lineup of quick, fresh sauces that all pair with poached chicken breasts. Instructions for the perfect poach can be found on page 353. One issue with poaching the delicate chicken breast is how to tell when it's done? Simple! Just press slightly on it with the back of a fork. The meat will feel firm but not hard or squishy! Take it out of the liquid and proceed with the recipe. Poaching renders the chicken breast extraordinarily tender and filled with the essences absorbed during cooking. This is just the beginning of what is destined to be an interesting dish.

THE PERFECT "QUICK POACH"

Once poached, the chicken breast is so incredibly versatile, it's like the plain canvas of an artist—ready to be decorated with flavors of your choice.

Poaching Liquid

2 to 4 cups chicken stock depending on the size of your poaching pan (see page 8 for recipes for stocks, including defatted, herb & wine and other poaching liquid ingredients on pages 7–11) or vegetable stock, wine, or juice
1 parsley sprig
1 celery leaf
Pinch of salt
Several peppercorns

Chicken

2 skinless boneless chicken breasts, halved (You may choose to leave the bone in and skin on during cooking. Remove and discard when the chicken is cool enough to handle.)

1. Bring all the ingredients except the chicken to a simmer in a high-sided skillet. Add the chicken breasts, arrange them in a single layer covered completely by the poaching liquid, reduce the heat to very low, and gently simmer for 8 to 10 minutes, or just until cooked throughout. The chicken will feel firm when pressed with the back of a fork. Remember, the delicate meat is easily overcooked, so be sure to keep the heat low, never boil, and remove from the poaching liquid immediately when done. Place on a plate to cool. Continue with one of the many recipes for deliciously sauced or tossed (into salad) chicken breast meat.

2. Cut or shred the cooked chicken into bite-size pieces, or make thin or thick slices; always slice on the diagonal, across the grain, and use a very sharp knife. Wrap tightly in plastic wrap if not using immediately and refrigerate in a plastic bag or airtight container for up to 2 days.

Variation:

Instead of the herbs listed, use a poaching bouquet (see page 354) containing the fresh herbs and spices of your choice.

Note: Other ingredients may be added to the poaching liquid, such as 2 tablespoons lemon juice, 1 tablespoon lemon zest strips, 1 tablespoon dried herbs, or whole cloves or allspice berries. See the examples on the following page for Poaching Bouquets.

FLAVORFUL POACHES START WITH POACHING BOUQUETS

Place the ingredients for a poaching bouquet together on a piece of cheesecloth, fold over two opposite ends to cover the ingredients, then tie the bag with the two free ends. If using small ingredients, tie all the ends together on top. The bouquet will impart flavor to the liquid and is easy to retrieve when the cooking is finished. Discard the bag after cooking the chicken breasts. A freshly assembled bouquet each time is a must. The following poaching bouquets will impart different types of ethnic flavors to the poaching liquid and the breast meat.

Asian: 1 piece fresh peeled ginger, 12 star anise, scallions, garlic cloves

Provençal: Garlic cloves, chervil, tarragon, basil, chives, parsley

American: Parsley, garlic, onion, peppercorns, celery leaf, carrot

Mexican: Red bell peppers, cumin, cinnamon, parsley or cilantro, lime rind

Southwestern: Red dried chile peppers, cilantro, citrus, ginger

Thai: Lemongrass, mint, coriander, lime rind, ginger, chiles

Caribbean: Chiles, allspice, curry, mint, cilantro, lime, ginger, coconut

Classic French bouquet garni: Bay leaf, fresh parsley sprigs, thyme, black peppercorns

NO-FRILL, NO-FAT, SUPER-FAST POACHING LIQUID

Although some poaching liquids in this chapter may call for additional ingredients, you can safely follow this recipe for a perfect poaching liquid. No need to make a poaching bouquet here, just toss all the ingredients together in the poaching pan.

4 plump chicken breast halves (about 2 pounds)

Poaching Liquid

1 cup dry white wine
1 cup defatted or 2 cups regular chicken stock (see pages 8–10) or more to cover the chicken pieces
2 to 3 shallots, or 1 onion, peeled and quartered
½ carrot, peeled and thinly sliced
1 celery leaf, chopped
1 leek, white part only, cleaned and coarsely chopped
4 to 6 black peppercorns
Pinch of salt

1. Combine all the ingredients in a poacher, stockpot, or high-sided skillet, bring to a boil, and cook 5 minutes. Reduce the heat to low and add chicken breasts. Simmer gently until done throughout. The breasts will be firm when pressed with the back of a fork. Immediately remove to a plate to cool.
2. Proceed as directed in the individual recipes in this and other chapters.

BREAST OF CHICKEN WITH BLACK OLIVE MOUSSE AND TOMATO CREAM SAUCE

6 to 8 servings

½ pound finely chopped skinless, boneless chicken breast meat (chop in a food processor)
1 egg
1 egg white
¼ cup heavy cream
5 heaping teaspoons chopped pitted Niçoise olives
½ teaspoon salt
½ teaspoon freshly ground white pepper
4 skinless, boneless, free-range chicken breasts (about 4½ pounds) halved
4 cups chicken stock
½ teaspoon salt

Tomato Cream Sauce

2 tablespoons extra-virgin olive oil
4 very ripe pear tomatoes, peeled, seeded, and cut into large chunks
1 shallot, finely chopped
1 small garlic clove, finely chopped
½ cup dry white wine
2 cups heavy cream

1. Mix together the chopped chicken, egg, and egg white in a mixing bowl. Add the olives and mix again. Add the cream in a slow but steady stream. Mix in the salt and pepper. Cover with plastic wrap and chill.

2. Make an incision through the thickest ends of the breasts with a sharp pointed knife to make a pocket for filling.

3. Fill a pastry bag with the mousse and fill the pockets in the chicken breasts with the chicken mixture. Roll each breast in plastic wrap to form sausage shapes. Chill slightly, then remove the plastic wrap.

4. Meanwhile, to make the sauce, heat the oil in a saucepan until hot over medium heat. Add the tomatoes and cook until most of the liquid has evaporated. Add the shallot and garlic. Cook for about 1 minute more. Add the wine and cook until it has evaporated.

5. Add the cream and cook over medium heat until the sauce is thick and coats the back of a metal spoon. Keep warm over a pan of hot water.

6. Bring the stock and salt to a boil in a 2-quart saucepan over medium heat. Reduce the heat to low, add the chicken breasts, and gently simmer just until done. They will be firm when pressed with the pack of a fork. Remove to a plate and drain.

7. Slice the breasts thinly on an angle. Pour the hot sauce around the sides of the rounds. Serve immediately.

CHILLED POACHED CHICKEN SKEWERS WITH HERB AND RAISIN COUSCOUS

Once prepared, this dish is beautiful when placed on a serving platter, a nest of couscous in the center and the skewers placed on top. Couscous and chicken breast are a prefect pair, served hot or at room temperature. Note several variations on making couscous at the end of this recipe.

6 servings

3 skinless, boneless chicken breasts (about 3 pounds), trimmed and cut into quarters
12 cherry tomatoes
1 green bell pepper, seeded and cut lengthwise into 8 pieces
1 red bell pepper, seeded and cut lengthwise into 8 pieces
12 medium mushrooms, washed
8 pearl onions, peeled
2 cups dry white wine
2 cups chicken stock (see page 8)
1 bouquet garni (see page 354), including at least 2 sprigs parsley
5 8-inch long wooden skewers

Couscous

2 tablespoons unsalted butter
3 medium shallots or 2 large shallots, peeled and minced
¼ teaspoon ground cumin
1 teaspoon fennel seeds
1¼ cup couscous (instant if desired)
2 cups chicken stock (see page 8)
2 teaspoons salt
3 tablespoons finely chopped fresh flat-leaf parsley
1 tablespoon finely chopped fresh sage leaves or 1½ teaspoons dried sage
2 teaspoons finely chopped fresh marjoram or 1 teaspoon dried marjoram
½ cup golden raisins, soaked in 2 tablespoons dry sherry for 30 minutes

l. To assemble the skewers, divide the chicken and vegetables into equal amounts. Thread onto the skewers, alternating chicken breast pieces and vegetables.

2. Bring the wine, stock, and the bouquet garni to a boil in a large high-sided skillet or stockpot. Add the skewers in a single layer, lower the heat, and simmer for 6 to 8 minutes, or until the chicken pieces are firm to the touch. Remove the chicken skewers to a platter, cool slightly, cover with plastic wrap, and cool to room temperature or refrigerate to chill.

3. To prepare the couscous, melt the butter in a saucepan over medium heat. Add the shallots and cook until translucent. Add the cumin and fennel seeds and continue cooking for 2 minutes. Add the couscous, chicken stock, and salt. Stir to mix well. Cover tightly, reduce the heat to very low, and simmer until the liquid is completely absorbed, about 5 minutes. Remove the cover, remove the pan from the heat, and toss the couscous so any large pieces will break up. Stir in the parsley, sage, marjoram, and the raisins. Cool to room temperature.

4. Place the couscous in the center of a platter. Place the chicken breast skewers in over the rice. Serve hot or at room temperature. Pass the pepper mill on the side.

POACHED CHILLED CHICKEN BREASTS WITH CUCUMBER-DILL SAUCE

The cucumber-dill sauce should be served the same day it's made or it will turn watery.

4 lunch servings

2 large cucumbers, peeled, seeded, halved, and very thinly sliced
1 teaspoon kosher salt
2 cups chicken stock (see page 8)
¼ cup fresh lemon juice
Poaching bouquet (see page 354) containing: 1 stalk celery with leaf, ½ leek sliced lengthwise, parsley sprigs, 6 black peppercorns, 1 large piece lemon zest, ½ bay leaf
2 skinless, boneless chicken breast (about 2 pounds), halved
Salt to taste
2 tablespoons white wine
2 tablespoons finely chopped fresh dill
1 cup sour cream, low-fat or regular
Freshly ground white pepper
Fresh dill sprigs for garnish

1. Place the cucumber slices around the inside of a colander, sprinkle on the kosher salt and drain for 30 minutes. Rinse, pat dry, and chop very fine. Set aside in the refrigerator.

2. Bring the chicken stock, lemon juice, and poaching bouquet to a boil in a medium high-sided skillet or stockpot. Reduce the heat to low, add the chicken breasts, lightly salt the liquid, and simmer 8 to 10 minutes or until done throughout. The breasts will be firm when pressed with the back of a fork. Remove the breasts and cool to room temperature. Cover with plastic wrap and refrigerate to chill.

3. Combine the vinegar, dill, chopped cucumber, and sour cream in a medium bowl; stir to mix well. Season with salt and pepper to taste. Cover with plastic wrap and refrigerate to chill.

4. Slice the chicken and arrange on plates. Spoon the cucumber sauce beside and through the center of the slices. Garnish with dill sprigs.

POACHED CHICKEN BREASTS WITH PARSLEY-BASIL PESTO SAUCE

Serve with steaming angel hair pasta or grilled French or Italian bread. Check out the pesto variations at the end of this recipe for another day.

4 servings

1 cup dry white wine
1 cup chicken stock (see page 8)
Juice of 1 lemon
Poaching bouquet (see page 354) containing: ½ juiced lemon cut into pieces, 4 whole black peppercorns, and 1 bunch flat-leaf parsley
2 skinless, boneless chicken breasts (about 2 pounds), halved
Salt to taste

Pesto
1 cup fresh flat-leaf parsley leaves
1 cup fresh basil leaves
3 garlic cloves
1 tablespoon toasted pine nuts
1¾ tablespoons extra-virgin olive oil
1 cup poaching liquid (reserved form the poaching)
Freshly ground white pepper
¼ cup finely grated fresh Parmesan cheese

1. Bring the wine, chicken stock, half of the lemon juice, and the poaching bouquet to a boil in a medium high-sided skillet or stockpot. Lower the heat and simmer for 5 minutes. Add the chicken breasts, lightly salt the liquid, and gently simmer 8 to 10 minutes or until done throughout. The chicken breasts will be firm when pressed with the back of a fork. Transfer the chicken to a plate and keep warm. Strain the liquid, reserving 1 cup.

2. To make the pesto, combine the parsley, basil, remaining lemon juice, garlic, and pine nuts in a blender or processor. Blend to a paste. With the motor running, add the olive oil in a thin but steady stream until a smooth paste forms.

3. Heat the reserved poaching liquid in a skillet over moderate heat. Stir in the pesto and bring to a simmer over medium heat. Return the chicken breasts to the pan to heat through, about 2 to 3 minutes.

4. Transfer the breasts to a platter with a slotted spoon and cover to keep warm. Increase the heat to high and continue cooking to reduce the liquid until a sauce forms, about 2 or 3 minutes. Season with salt and pepper to taste and spoon over the chicken. Sprinkle with the Parmesan cheese.

Pesto Variations:

Walnut Arugula Pesto: Use 2 cups basil leaves, 2 cups arugula leaves, ½ cup flat-leaf parsley leaves, ¼ cup chpoped walnuts, 4 cloves garlic. Blend or process to a smooth paste. Add 3 tablespoons extra-virgin olive oil in a thin stream. Add ¾ cup grated Parmesan (Parmigiano-Reggiano cheese if available), and ⅓ cup chicken stock. Blend to a smooth paste. Adjust seasoning with salt and freshly ground black pepper to taste.

Sage Pesto: Use 1 cup fresh flat-leaf parsley leaves, ⅓ cup fresh sage leaves, 3 tablespoons finely chopped fresh rosemary. 3 cloves garlic. Blend or process to a paste, and add ¾ cup extra-virgin olive oil, ⅓ cup toasted pine nuts, ¾ cup Parmesan cheese. Blend to a smooth paste. Adjust seasoning with salt and freshly ground black pepper to taste.

Genovese-Style Pesto: Use 3 cups fresh basil leaves, ¼ cup chopped toasted walnuts, ¼ cup pinenuts, 3 cloves garlic, 4 tablespoons unsalted butter. Blend or process to a paste. With the motor running add ¾ cup extra-virgin olive oil in a thin but steady stream to form a smooth paste. Add ¾ cup freshly grated Parmesan cheese, ⅓ cup grated pecorino cheese and blend to mix well. Adjust seasoning with salt and freshly ground black pepper to taste.

Seasonal Mixed Herb Pesto: Use spinach, flat-leaf parsley, arugula leaves, fresh oregano, fresh thyme, basil, chives in any proportion with oil, pine nuts or walnuts and Parmesan.

Note: Pesto can be stored in the freezer in small amounts, or in the coldest part of the refrigerator up to 10 days.

POACHED CHICKEN BREASTS WITH BEAN RAGOUT

This recipe was influenced by a dish created at Pinot Bistro in Los Angeles by Octavio Becerra, the restaurant's outstanding executive chef. This is one of the most time-consuming recipe in this book, but certainly one of the most rewarding and perfect for special occasions. (For information about the French-style Herb and Wine Stock see page 10.)

4 servings

Herb and Wine Stock

1½ teaspoons canola or other vegetable oil
1 large yellow onion, chopped
1 large leek, washed and chopped
½ stalk celery, chopped
1 whole head garlic, loose outside papery skin removed, cut in half crosswise
1 large fennel bulb, diced
½ bunch fresh thyme
3 bay leaves
½ bunch fresh flat-leaf parsley
1 bottle (750 ml) dry white wine, preferably chardonnay (best quality)

Chicken Breasts and Bean Ragout

16 cloves garlic, unpeeled
3 tablespoons extra-virgin olive oil
1 tablespoon canola or other vegetable oil
¾ pound mixed fresh mushrooms (such as chantarelle, porcine, shiitake, portobello, and oyster) diced
1 cup dry white wine
4 cups Herb and Wine Stock
1 cup uncooked beans (such as chestnut, cranberry, or great northern), soaked overnight and drained, reserving ¾ cup soaking liquid
2 sprigs fresh thyme
2 bay leaves
½ onion, quartered
½ medium carrot, peeled and halved
4 sage leaves
2 skinless, boneless chicken breasts (about 2 pounds), halved
Salt and freshly ground white pepper
1 tablespoon finely chopped fresh chives

1. To make the stock, heat the oil in a large saucepan over medium heat. Add the onion, leek, celery, garlic, and fennel and cook until the vegetables are translucent but not browned, or about 4 minutes. Add the thyme, bay leaves, parsley, wine, and water. Bring to a boil, reduce the heat, and simmer for 1 hour. Strain through a fine mesh strainer and chill, covered.

2. To prepare the garlic, preheat the oven to 300°F.

3. Combine the garlic and 2 teaspoons of the olive oil in a small baking dish and stir to coat well. Cover tightly with foil and bake for 45 minutes, or until the garlic is soft. Cool slightly, then squeeze the pulp of 12 cloves into a small bowl. Peel the remaining 4 and reserve for garnish.

4. Heat the remaining oil in a large skillet over medium-high heat. Add the mushrooms and cook until the mushroom liquid evaporates or about 8 minutes. Add ½ cup of the wine and cook until the liquid is almost evaporated. Add 1 cup of the stock, bring to a boil, reduce the heat, and simmer until the mushrooms are tender, about 7 minutes. Set aside.

5. Combine the soaked beans, the reserved soaking liquid, 1 cup of the stock, thyme, bay leaves, onion, carrot, and sage in a medium saucepan. Bring to a boil, reduce the heat, and simmer until the beans are tender, about 45 minutes. Strain the beans, reserving the liquid. Combine the beans and mushrooms and set aside.

6. In a medium high-sided skillet, bring the reserved bean liquid, 1 cup of the stock and the remaining wine to a simmer. Add the chicken breasts and gently poach 8 to 10 minutes or until done throughout. The breasts will be firm when pressed with the back of a fork. Remove to a platter and keep warm.

7. To make the sauce, warm the remaining 1 cup of stock and pour into a blender. Add the roasted garlic puree and the remaining 1 teaspoon olive oil and blend until smooth. Season with salt and pepper to taste. Return to the pan.

8. To assemble the dish, heat the beans and mushrooms. Heat the sauce. Place equal amounts of bean and mushroom ragout in the bottom of 4 shallow soup or pasta bowls. Place the chicken breasts on top of the beans, and spoon on the sauce. Garnish with the roasted garlic cloves and chives.

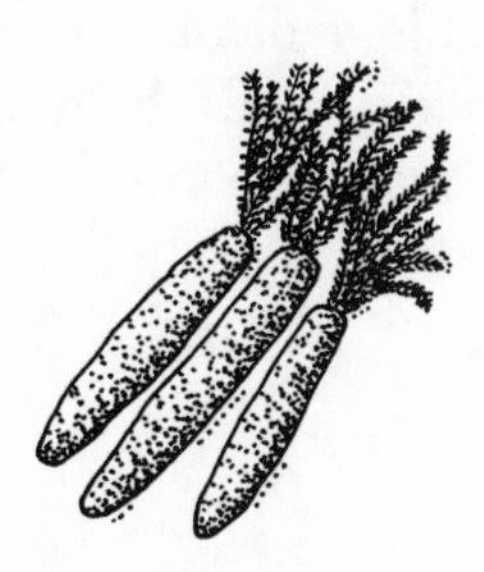

CHILLED LIME & BASIL MARINATED CHICKEN BREASTS

From an extraordinary cook, Jack Leutze.

4 servings

2 poached skinless, boneless chicken breasts (about 2 pounds), halved and chilled (see instructions on page 353 for poaching instructions)
Marinade
½ cup fresh lime juice
2 large cloves garlic, crushed
2 tablespoons packed fresh basil or 1 tablespoon crushed, dried basil
2 large shallots, minced
½ cup extra-virgin olive oil
⅓ cup canola or other light vegetable oil
¾ teaspoon sugar
½ teaspoon salt
1 teaspoon or more freshly ground black pepper
Assorted salad ingredients including torn lettuce, arugula, baby spinach leaves, or a combination of the above

1. Combine the lime juice, garlic, basil, shallots, olive and vegetable oils, sugar, salt, and pepper in a small bowl.

2. Slice the chicken breasts into ½-inch wide strips. Place in a shallow, non-reactive glass or pottery dish and pour in the marinade. Cover tightly with plastic wrap and marinate in the refrigerator for 24 hours.

3. Drain off the marinade. Place the salad greens on a serving platter, making a bed in the center. Arrange the chicken in the center and serve chilled.

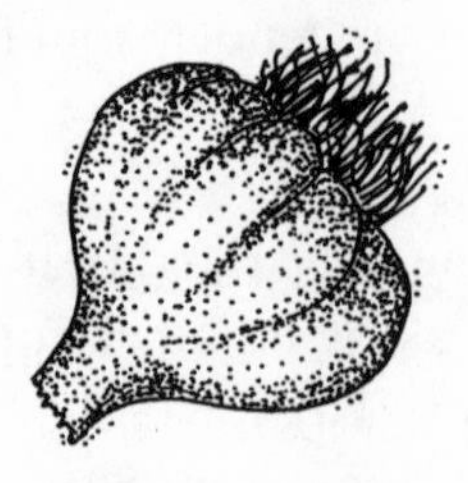

Steam

It's the fresh, hot, and healthy cooking method for chicken breasts! It's also an appropriate description for any food cooked in a steamer. The finished food keeps its shape and color more readily than food cooked with other processes. But when you consider the facts, steaming is no more than a delicate, though super-hot, vapor that cooks foods very quickly. It's also totally fat-free! The first step in creating a successful "steamed" chicken breast recipe is giving the vapor some character. Before placing the steamer basket over the hot water in the wok, stockpot, or fitted steaming pans, consider adding some of these flavorful ingredients: whole and toasted spices, citrus peel, stock, wine or sake, fresh herbs, and aromatics. (See page 369 for complete steaming instructions.) First boil these ingredients for 5 minutes to allow the flavors to infuse the water. During this easy and healthful cooking process, a transfer of subtle flavors will naturally occur between the chicken and the vapor. Each of the following steaming recipes calls for a customized steaming broth. For entertaining, try the delicate Stuffed Chicken Rolls and Yellow Pepper Sauce (page 368) or Steamed Lemon Chicken Breast Bundles (page 366), in which lettuce leaves are used as natural wrappings. For the basis of a light shredded salad, use Soy Lime Chicken Breasts Steamed in Sake. It's also possible to cook several dishes at once in a two- or three-tiered Oriental bamboo steamer. Just consider all the vegetables you've steamed in the past as practice for the recipes ahead of you in this chapter.

STEAMED CHICKEN BREAST AND ZUCCHINI BUNDLES

Vapor, infused with the essence of fresh rosemary and white wine, cooks these bundles while adding subtle flavors that complement and enhance the delicate low-fat filling. Experiment by creating a steaming broth that reflects your own favorite flavors. Almost any strong ingredients will add a subtle essence.

Serves 4 or for appetizers

Steaming Broth

1 cup white wine
2 cups filtered water, or more
1 lemon, cut in thin round slices
3 branches fresh rosemary
1 teaspoon black peppercorns

Chicken Breasts

1 pound small zucchini
1 tablespoon coarse salt
½ cup minced flat-leaf parsley
1 teaspoon minced garlic
1½ teaspoons grated lemon zest
Salt and freshly ground white pepper to taste
1 skinless, boneless chicken breast (about 1 pound), cut into small pieces
1 large egg white
2 tablespoons minced shallot
12 large romaine lettuce leaves
12 long strips of scallion, green part only
Lemon wedges for garnish

1. Place the wine, water, lemon slices, rosemary branches, and peppercorns in a wok. Bring to a boil, cover, lower the heat, and simmer for 20 minutes. Reserve the broth in the wok.

2. Meanwhile, soak the zucchini in a bowl of cold water with the coarse salt for 30 minutes to remove the bitterness. Rinse and then pat dry with paper towels. Coarsely grate the zucchini with a hand grater. Set in a strainer to continue draining for a few minutes more.

3. Combine the parsley, garlic, lemon zest, and zucchini in a medium bowl. Season lightly with salt and pepper and set aside.

4. Process the chicken for about 20 seconds in the bowl of a food processor. Add the egg white and process to a smooth consistency. Add the shallots and pulse just to mix.

5. Transfer the chicken mixture to the bowl with the zucchini mixture. Season lightly with salt and pepper. Set aside.

6. Heat the broth in a wok over low heat to a simmer. Place the lettuce leaves and scallion strips in the top tier of a steamer and cover tightly. Place the steamer over the simmering broth and steam just until wilted or about 30 seconds. Turn the heat off. Transfer the vegetables to a work surface. Reserve the broth in the wok.

7. Lay the lettuce leaves flat. Trim down the tough ends and the heavy center stems.

8. Divide the chicken mixture into 12 equal mounds placed in the center of each lettuce leaf. Fold the sides in toward the center and then fold the bottoms up and over the filling. Finally, fold down the top portion of each leaf to cover the filling completely. Tie each bundle with one of the scallion strips. Repeat until all the bundles are filled and tied.

9. Position the bundles in the steamer so that they are just touching. Do not crowd or press together.

10. Bring the broth in the wok to a boil over high heat, reduce to a simmer, and place the steamer on top. Steam the bundles for 15 to 17 minutes or until done. The bundles should be moist, tender, and cooked through. Arrange the bundles on a platter or in a clean bamboo steamer basket lined with fresh lettuce leaves, and garnish with lemon wedges.

WHERE TO GET A STEAMER IF YOUR LOCAL GOURMET COOKWARE STORE IS STILL WAITING FOR A SHIPMENT OF HAND-MADE STEAMERS FROM RURAL CHINA

Try trusty sources like Williams-Sonoma. Or, if you're lucky enough to have an area in your city designated as "Chinatown," such as in San Francisco, New York City, and Los Angeles, then you'll only need to visit the Asian market to find an amazing array of bamboo steamers sized from 9 inches to gigantic 36-inch steamers used in dim sum restaurants. Some even have carved cedar-wood bottoms, so that the vapor picks up the flavor of the wood and transports it to the ingredients above. Steamers are priced as low as $15. While you're there, have lunch at a local restaurant and ask for steamed chicken breasts, just to try the real thing before your experiment begins. If you want a metal pot with a fitted steaming basket—typically used for vegetables—try the cookware section of any department store.

STEAMED LEMON CHICKEN BREAST BUNDLES

An Oriental two-tiered bamboo steamer works well for in this recipe. See page 369 for steaming details.

4 servings

Steaming Broth

6 to 8 garlic cloves, smashed
2 lemons, cut into thin, round slices
1 fresh thyme sprig
1 teaspoon black peppercorns
4 cups filtered water, or more
½ cup white wine

Lemon Chicken Breast

12 large romaine lettuce leaves
12 long strips scallion, green part only
1 skinless, boneless chicken breast (about 1 pound), halved
2 teaspoons grated lemon zest
1 cup cooked white rice
1 medium yellow bell pepper, seeded and finely diced
2 tablespoons finely chopped scallions, white and green parts
¼ cup chopped flat-leaf parsley
2 garlic cloves, minced
2 teaspoons fresh lemon juice
2 teaspoons coarse salt
½ teaspoon freshly ground white pepper

1. Place the smashed garlic, lemon slices, thyme sprig, peppercorns, spring water, and wine in a wok. Bring to a boil, cover, lower the heat, and simmer for 20 minutes.

2. Meanwhile, place the lettuce leaves and scallion strips in the top tier of a steamer and cover tightly. Place the steamer over the top of the simmering broth and steam until the lettuce leaves are wilted, about 30 seconds. Turn the heat off. Transfer the vegetables from the steamer to a work surface. Reserve the broth in the wok.

3. Reserve the scallion strips. Lay the lettuce leaves flat. Trim down the tough ends and the heavy center stems.

4. In the bowl of a food processor fitted with a metal blade, process the chicken until a spread-like consistency forms. Add the lemon zest and pulse.

5. Transfer to a medium mixing bowl and stir in the rice, bell pepper, chopped scallion, parsley, minced garlic, lemon juice, salt, and pepper.

6. Divide the chicken mixture into 12 equal mounds. Place a mound in the center of each lettuce leaf. Working delicately, fold the sides in toward the center and then the bottom up and over the filling. Finally, fold down the top portion each leaf to cover the filling completely. Tie each bundle with one of the scallion strips. Repeat until all bundles are filled and tied.

7. Position the bundles in the steam so that they are just touching. Do not crowd or press together.

8. Bring the broth into the wok over high heat, reduce to a simmer, and place the steamer on top. Steam the bundles for 15 to 17 minutes or until done. The bundles should be moist, tender, and cooked throughout.

CHICKEN BREASTS WITH CHINESE BLACK BEAN PURÉE

This dish brings with it a full-flavored combination of ingredients often found in Chinese dishes, namely, ginger, soy, oyster sauce, and fermented black beans.

4 servings

2 teaspoons cornstarch, dissolved in 2 tablespoons medium-dry sherry
1 tablespoon peanut oil
¼ cup minced fermented black beans*
1 tablespoon minced peeled fresh ginger
1 tablespoon minced garlic
⅓ cup Asian flavor chicken stock (see page 354)
1 tablespoon oyster sauce*
1 tablespoon soy sauce or tamari
2 skinless, boneless chicken breast (about 2 pounds), halved
1 tablespoon medium-dry sherry
1 tablespoon dark sesame oil
¼ cup chopped scallion, plus 2 tablespoons for garnish

***Available in Asian grocery stores or some supermarkets**

1. Place the cornstarch mixture in a small saucepan. Set aside.

2. Heat the peanut oil in a wok over medium-high heat. Add the black beans, ginger, and garlic and stir-fry for 15 seconds. Add the chicken stock, oyster sauce, soy sauce, and bring to a boil. Cook for 2 minutes. Transfer to bowl of a blender or mini food processor and process until smooth. Place in the saucepan with the cornstarch mixture and cook, stirring constantly, for about 1 minute or over medium heat until the sauce thickens. Remove from the heat and set the pan aside.

3. Wipe the wok clean and bring water to a boil for steaming. Position a bamboo steamer on top of the wok.

4. Place the chicken breasts in a heatproof dish that fits loosely inside the bamboo steamer. Sprinkle with the sherry, sesame oil, and ¼ cup of the chopped scallion. Place the dish in the steamer, the second tier up from the water. Steam for 12 to 17 minutes until done throughout. Do not overcook.

5. Meanwhile, reheat the black bean sauce. Place the breasts in 4 individual shallow bowls. Stir any juices remaining in the steaming dish into the sauce and heat through. Pour the sauce over the chicken breasts and sprinkle on the remaining 2 tablespoons of scallion.

CHICKEN BREAST SAUSAGE AND YELLOW PEPPER SAUCE

This is basically chicken breast stuffed with a light mousse-like chicken breast mixture. It is a very delicate dish. This sauce recipe can also be used to make zucchini, onion, or other vegetable purées.

4 servings

Chicken Rolls

2 skinless, boneless, free-range chicken breasts (about 2 pounds), pounded between plastic wrap to ¼ inch thick
Salt and freshly ground white pepper to taste
¾ pound ground skinless, boneless chicken breast meat
1 large egg white
1 garlic clove, minced
2 shallots, minced
2 tablespoons mixed fresh chopped herbs (such as oregano, chervil, sage, tarragon, and basil)
3 tablespoons chopped fresh chives
1 cup finely chopped spinach

Sauce

2 teaspoons unsalted butter
2 large yellow bell peppers, seeded and cut into pieces
1 garlic clove, crushed
1 tablespoon chopped shallots
2 sprigs fresh thyme
3 cups rich chicken stock (see page 9)

Salt and freshly ground white pepper to taste

1. On a flat work surface, place each whole chicken breast on a large double layer of plastic wrap. Season with a scant amount of salt and pepper.

2. Stir together the ground chicken, egg white, garlic, shallots, herbs, chives, and spinach in a medium mixing bowl.

3. Spread half the chicken mixture over each whole chicken breast, leaving a 1-inch border free of the mixture. Starting with the long end, roll up the chicken breasts like a jelly roll. Wrap the chicken rolls tightly in the plastic wrap, seam side down. Place in a heatproof dish that fits loosely in a bamboo steamer.

4. Bring water to a simmer in a wok. Position a steamer on top of the wok. Place the dish in the steamer in the second tier up from the water. Cover tightly and steam the chicken sausage for about 12 to 17 minutes or until done throughout. Remove the dish from the steamer, transfer the chicken rolls to a work surface, and let cool at least 10 minutes. Slice in rounds.

5. Meanwhile, make the sauce while the chicken is cooking. In a medium heavy sauté pan or skillet, melt the butter over medium heat. Add the bell peppers, garlic, shallots and thyme. Cook the vegetables for about 2 minutes. Add the chicken stock and simmer, uncovered, for about 20 minutes or until the liquid is reduced to 1 cup and the vegetables are tender. Remove the thyme sprigs, transfer the mixture to a blender, and blend until smooth. Season with salt and pepper.

6. Place chicken sausage rounds on individual plates and spoon on the sauce. Serve the remaining sauce on the side. For appetizers, serve the sauce as a dipping sauce on the side.

STEAMER TIMINGS VARY FROM BAMBOO TO METAL, AND EVEN FROM SHAPE TO SHAPE

This means a little more testing will be necessary to perfect your steamer cooking times for perfectly cooked chicken breasts every time. If the seal is not absolutely tight, which is often the case with bamboo, the cooking time can be as much as 50 percent more than with the top-of-the-line, precision, heavy-gauge stainless steel steamers. Use the steamer guide to follow as a starting point; prepare one chicken breast in your steamer and then adjust the timings that work best for you by adding or subtracting time in one-minute segments. Leaky steamers should be replaced, as they tend to take too long to cook and produce rubbery, dense meat instead of a moist and tender chicken breast.

STEAMED CHICKEN BREASTS WITH FRUIT SALSA

4 servings

2 skinless, boneless chicken breasts (about 2 pounds), halved
Salt and freshly ground black pepper to taste
Juice of 1 lemon
2 scallions, coarsely chopped

Salsa
2 cups peeled and diced peaches
2 cups diced banana
½ cup finely chopped red onion
2 tablespoons finely chopped fresh cilantro, plus1 tablespoon for garnish
1 small jalapeño pepper, stemmed, seeded, and minced
1 small clove garlic, minced
2 tablespoons champagne or white wine vinegar
2 tablespoons fresh lime juice

1. Place the chicken in a heatproof dish that loosely fits in a bamboo steamer. Season the chicken with salt and pepper.

2. Add just enough water to reach nearly to the bottom of the steamer, the lemon juice, and scallions to a wok and bring to a simmer.

3. Position the steamer on top of the wok. Put the dish in the steamer in the second tier up from the liquid. Cover tightly and steam the chicken until done throughout, about 12 to 17 minutes. Cool to room temperature.

4. Meanwhile, combine the peaches, banana, onion, 2 tablespoons of the cilantro, the jalapeño, garlic, vinegar, and lime juice in a bowl. Toss to mix and marinate for 30 minutes before serving.

5. Thinly slice the chicken on the diagonal and arrange on 4 individual plates. Sprinkle with the remaining cilantro and serve with the fruit salsa.

DON'T TAKE THE LID OFF, PLEASE. . . !

. . . Until you think the chicken is completely done. Hot steam will burn you and interfere with the steaming process when all the heat is let out of the steamer. Always turn the heat off first. Lift the lid of the steamer away from you, so that the steam escapes out the back. Remember, if you let the steam out while cooking and then replace the lid, the results will either be chicken that's not fully done or chicken that is rubbery and overcooked.

SOY LIME CHICKEN BREASTS STEAMED IN SAKE

4 servings

2 skinless, boneless chicken breasts (about 2 pounds), halved
2¼ cups sake (Japanese rice wine)
⅓ cup soy sauce or tamari
2 teaspoons grated lime zest
¼ cup fresh lime juice
2 garlic cloves, minced
1 tablespoon hot Oriental mustard
1 tablespoon peanut oil
¼ cup finely chopped scallion, white and green parts
½ teaspoon freshly ground white pepper
Lime zest, cut into thin strips for garnish

1. Place the chicken in a heatproof dish that fits loosely inside a bamboo steamer.

2. To a wok, add 2 cups of the sake and enough water to fill just below the bottom of the steamer. Bring to a simmer.

3. Position the steamer on the wok and place the dish in the steamer in the second tier up from the water. Cover tightly and steam the chicken until done throughout, about 12 to 17 minutes.

4. Meanwhile, in a small bowl, whisk together the soy sauce, grated lime zest, lime juice, garlic, and mustard. In a thin but steady stream, add the oil, whisking constantly until well combined. Stir in the scallion and pepper.

5. In a small saucepan, boil the remaining ¼ cup sake over medium-high heat and reduce to 1 tablespoon, about 5 minutes. Stir in the soy-and-lime mixture and heat through. Drizzle over the chicken, turning to coat well. Garnish with the strips of lime zest.

MORE STEAMED CHICKEN BREAST RECIPES ARE HIDING IN THIS BOOK

Quite a few of the recipes in this book can be converted easily into steaming recipes. When using the recipes listed below for steaming (instead of the cooking method called for in each recipe), wrap the chicken breasts and other ingredients in aluminum foil, parchment paper, or heavy-duty cooking plastic wrap before placing in the steaming basket or pot.

- Baked Chicken-Stuffed Zucchini, page 138
- Chicken, Rice and Spinach Filled Cabbage Rolls, page 137
- Glazed Chicken Loaf,, page 142
- Balsamic Chicken Breasts with Vegetables en Papillote, page 146
- Tarragon Chicken Breasts with Artichokes, page 152

Microwave

To microwave or not to microwave chicken breasts? This is no longer the question! With over 90 percent of the homes across the country including one of these devices among their most frequently used pieces of kitchen equipment, microwave cooking as well as heating is here to stay. But let's take a vote. What do you think of microwave cooking? In a pinch, is it an alternative to takeout, or the perfect method for people who like their water boiled fast? Yes, to all those thoughts, though there's more, especially when it involves chicken breasts. A microwave oven can cook up a wonderfully succulent chicken breast along with a tasty sauce in just a few minutes when you have the recipe. The variety of microwave chicken breast recipes is rather limited in this book; they stick to the basics and offer several great-tasting approaches for the day when your stove doesn't light. Note the variety, for instance, in the recipe for Microwave Veloute Sauce for Quick Poached Chicken Breasts (page 374), where you'll discover 4 delicious sauces that can be adapted from the basic Veloute (white sauce). Pick one, then turn over to page 376 for the microwave recipe for Quick Micro Chicken Breasts to round off the meal. These quick-cooked breasts can also be used for chicken salad of any kind when the idea of poaching is the last thing on your mind. Check out the salad section for dozens of recipes and ideas for the next step. However, chicken breasts should never be defrosted in the microwave. Put them in a dish and let them defrost naturally in the lowest part ot the refrigerator which takes about 10 hours or overnight.

MICROWAVE SALSA CHICKEN STRIPS

This is a recipe that translates into a single serving, or a prepare-in-advance meal easily stored in the refrigerator—tightly covered with plastic wrap—and popped directly into the microwave. Particularly low in calories, it makes a perfectly tasty dieter's meal as well.

4 servings

1 cup diced seeded ripe tomato
⅓ cup diced green bell pepper
⅓ cup diced red bell pepper
3 tablespoons chopped flat-leaf parsley or cilantro
¾ cup petit white corn kernels, refreshed in boiling water for 2 minutes and drained
2 tablespoons red wine vinegar
2 tablespoons extra-virgin olive oil
1 clove garlic, minced
½ teaspoon salt
½ teaspoon cumin
Freshly ground black pepper to taste
2 boneless, skinless chicken breasts (about 2 pounds), halved
Salt and freshly ground black pepper to taste

1. Combine the tomato, both bell peppers, parsley or cilantro, vinegar, olive oil, garlic, cumin, and pepper in a glass or pottery bowl. Set aside.

2. Place the chicken breasts on a work surface. With a very sharp knife, cut each breast into 4 to 5 slices cutting lengthwise.

3. Brush or rub 4 plates (that fit in your microwave) with olive oil or coat lightly with cooking spray. Place the chicken strips at the outer edge of the plates. Divide the salsa among the plates, spooning it over the chicken pieces. Cook 3 to 5 minutes on "high" or full power or until the chicken is done. Serve hot or at room temperature.

Q: How should chicken breasts be arranged in order to cook evenly in the microwave oven?

A: The food closest to the outside of the dish cooks fastest. If you have uneven pieces of chicken, place the thickest ends at the edges of the plate. A carousel usually offers even cooking throughout.

MICROWAVE CHICKEN STOCK

Makes 3 cups

3 pounds chicken parts, including backs, necks, and bones
1 carrot, peeled and coarsely chopped
1 small onion, quartered
2 celery stalks, coarsely chopped
¼ cup minced flat-leaf parsley
1 bay leaf
4 peppercorns
¼ teaspoon dried thyme
4 cups filtered water

1. Combine all the ingredients in a 3-quart microwave-proof bowl.

2. Cover and cook on full power for 20 minutes. Skim off any scum that collects on top of the stock several times during cooking.

3. Reduce the power to medium and cook 1 hour more.

4. Strain through a sieve or colander lined with dampened cheesecloth. Use as needed or store as stock cubes in the freezer.

CREAMY VELOUTE SAUCE FOR MICRO-POACHED CHICKEN BREAST

Here's a sauce which starts out as ordinary white sauce. The variations listed below show off its versatility with a quartet of tasty and useful variations. Who says microwave cooking has to be plain?

4 servings

2½ tablespoons unsalted butter
3 tablespoons all-purpose flour
1½ cups rich chicken stock (see page 9)
½ cup heavy cream
1 tablespoon lemon juice or a splash of sweet or dry vermouth
Salt and freshly ground white pepper to taste

1. In a microwave-proof 1-quart dish, melt the butter for 30 seconds on medium power.

2. Whisk in the flour. Slowly add the chicken stock and cream, whisking continuously until completely combined. Cook for 5 minutes on "high" or full power stirring every 2 minutes.

3. The sauce is done when it coats the back of a spoon. Whisk in the lemon juice, salt and pepper.

Variations on Basic Veloute:

Fresh Herb: Add ½ cup fresh chopped herbs of choice in step 2.

Curry: Add 1 to 2 teaspoons curry powder, or to taste, with the flour.

Sauce Supreme: Increase the butter to 6 tablespoons and add 3 tablespoons each of very finely minced carrot, onion, and celery. Reduce the stock to 1 cup. Increase the cream to 1 cup and add 2 tablespoons dry white wine.

Roasted Garlic: Add 1 whole head of garlic. (Trim to expose the top of each clove. Put the garlic and 2 tablespoons of chicken stock in a 4-cup glass dish. Drizzle 1½ tablespoons extra-virgin olive oil over the garlic. Cover tightly with microwave plastic wrap. Cook on "high" or full power for 6 to 8 minutes, cooking longer if the cloves are very large. Remove from the microwave and let stand 10 minutes.) Scoop or squeeze out the soft garlic and whisk it into the finished veloute.

MICROWAVE POACHED CHICKEN BREASTS

This is one of the microwave basics for the chicken breast. With just this one recipe, an endless array of chicken dinner combinations can be achieved.

4 servings

2 skinless, boneless chicken breasts (about 2 pounds), halved
4 cup chicken stock (see page 8)
¼ cup dry white wine
1 tablespoon chopped fresh tarragon
Salt and freshly ground white pepper to taste

1. Arrange the chicken breasts in a microwave-proof dish, with the smaller thinner ends together in the center. Pour on the stock and wine and sprinkle with tarragon, salt, and pepper.

2. Cover the dish tightly with microwave plastic wrap. Cook on high for 8 minutes.

3. Serve with the pan juices or a sauce of your choice. To use at another time, chill, tightly wrapped in plastic wrap.

FOR STOCK, HOLD THE SALT!

The stock can be refrigerated, covered, for up to 3 days. Remove the layer of fat from the surface before using. Remember, never add salt, pepper, or strong seasonings to stock. Most seasonings are added according to a specific recipe of which the stock is a part.

Q: Does reheating chicken breasts in the microwave make the meat tough?

A: Not really. To reheat, add a few drops of water to the dish containing the chicken breasts and cover with microwave plastic wrap. Reheat no longer than absolutely necessary, usually about 20 seconds on "high" or full power.

QUICK MICROWAVE CHICKEN BREASTS

Chill the cooked chicken and combine with salad ingredients or a pasta of your choice, and it's moist and perfect to slice for sandwiches.

4 servings

2 skinless, boneless chicken breasts (about 2 pounds), cut into 1-inch cubes
2 tablespoons fresh lemon juice
1 teaspoon paprika
Salt and freshly ground black pepper to taste

1. Place the chicken breasts in a shallow microwave-proof casserole dish. Sprinkle with the lemon juice, paprika, salt, and pepper, coating well.

2. Cover and microwave on "high" or full power for 6 minutes, stirring every 2 minutes to baste, or until the chicken is done throughout. Halfway through the cooking time, turn the lesser-cooked portions toward the edges of the casserole.

3. Remove the chicken breasts with a slotted spoon. Serve combined with a sauce or other ingredients.

CHICKEN BREASTS WITH LIME AND CILANTRO

4 servings

2 skinless, boneless chicken breasts (about 2 pounds), halved
1 tablespoon fresh lime juice
Salt and freshly ground black pepper to taste
1 tablespoon chopped fresh cilantro

1. Place the chicken breasts in a shallow microwave-proof casserole dish. Sprinkle with lime juice, salt, and pepper.

2. Cover and microwave on high for 6 minutes, or until the chicken breasts are done throughout. Halfway through the cooking time, turn the lesser-cooked portions toward the edges of the casserole.

3. Sprinkle with cilantro and serve.

CHICKEN, PROSCIUTTO, AND PARMESAN RISOTTO

When risotto is done, it's done. So be ready, forks in hand, to eat it as soon as it's come out of the microwave. If prepared the conventional way, risotto takes about 30 minutes from start to finish, with someone attending the pot for the entire time. Risotto in the microwave requires no arm-aching antics and comes out great in half that time or less. Test your imagination when it comes to variations. Almost anything from mushrooms to fresh peas can be added to this Italian delight.

4 servings

1 skinless, boneless chicken breast (about 1 pound), trimmed
1 tablespoon extra-virgin olive oil
2 shallots, minced
1 cup finely chopped leeks, white and some green part
1 cup Arborio rice (do not substitute other types of rice)
3 cups rich chicken stock (see page 9)
⅔ cup dry white wine (chardonnay)
½ teaspoon salt
¼ teaspoon freshly ground white pepper

4 tablespoons chopped prosciutto, sautéed for 3 minutes in a scant amount of extra-virgin olive oil
2 teaspoons unsalted butter
¾ cup grated Parmesan cheese
2 tablespoons chopped fresh chives
Freshly ground black pepper to taste

1. Shred the chicken breast across the grain into thin pieces (it should equal at least 1 ½ cups). Set aside.

2. In a microwave-proof 2-quart casserole dish, heat the olive oil for 30 seconds on full power.

3. Add the shallots and leeks. Cook 3 minutes on "high" or full power.

4. Add the rice and stir to mix well. Cook 1 minute more on "high" or full power.

5. Add ½ cup of the stock, the wine, salt, and pepper and cook for 12 minutes on "high" or full power, uncovered.

6. Stir in the remaining stock, the chicken, and prosciutto. Cook 4 minutes on "high" or full power. Stir in the butter and continue cooking 1 minute.

7. Add the cheese and stir to combine well. Serve the risotto in the center of shallow soup plates and sprinkle on the chives. Pass the pepper mill and more Parmesan cheese on the side.

Variations:

Bacon, Olive, Mushroom, or Truffle Risotto: Use Italian black and green chopped, pitted olives, or dried wild mushrooms that have been rehydrated in your favorite red or white wine (then add the wine to the cooking liquid), Canadian bacon, or white or black truffles for special risotto dinners. In this case, use a dash of truffle oil at the end for a nice smooth finish and the added perfume of the truffle.

CHICKEN AND DIJON MUSTARD SAUCE

Try this over your favorite pasta.

2 to 4 servings

1 cup milk, whole or low-fat
½ cup heavy cream
3 to 4 tablespoons Dijon mustard
2 teaspoons fresh lemon juice
Salt and freshly ground white pepper to taste
3 cups poached chicken breast chunks (see page 375)

1 tablespoon chopped flat-leaf parsley

1. Combine the milk, cream, mustard, and lemon juice in an 8-cup microwave-proof measuring cup.

2. Cook, uncovered, for 11 minutes at full power.

3. Combine the chicken with the sauce and heat through for 1 minute on "high" or full power. Stir in the parsley for the last few seconds of cooking.

CHICKEN BREASTS WITH TARRAGON BUTTER

4 servings

4 tablespoon unsalted butter
2 tablespoons chopped fresh tarragon, or 2 teaspoons dried tarragon
2 skinless, boneless chicken breasts (about 2 pounds), flattened to 1-inch thickness
3 tablespoons fresh lemon juice
Salt and freshly ground black pepper to taste

1. Place the butter on a sheet of waxed paper in a microwave-proof dish. Cook on low or defrost for 15 seconds or just until soft. Roll the butter in tarragon and form a stick or cylinder. Wrap and chill until ready to use.

2. Place the chicken breasts in a microwave-proof, shallow, 10-inch round dish, with the thickest portions toward the edges; keep the center of the dish open. Sprinkle the chicken breasts with lemon juice. Cover loosely with microwave plastic wrap that has been pierced with a fork.

3. Cook on "medium" power for 7 minutes. Turn over and place the less cooked portions toward the edges of the baking dish. Cook 7 minutes longer or until done throughout. For the last minute of cooking time, place pats of tarragon butter on each breast.

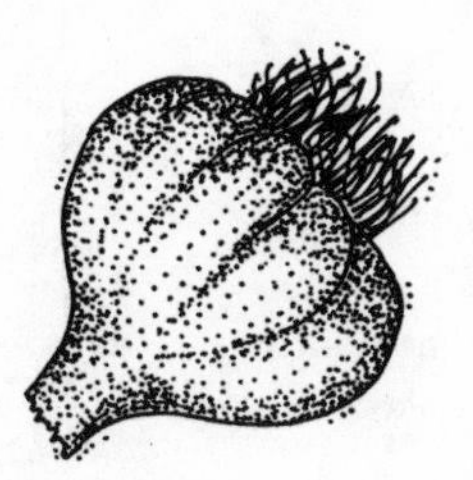

Index